PRINCIPLES
OF
ECONOMICS

T0266691

PRINCIPLES
OF
ECONOMICS

ALFRED
MARSHALL

GREAT MINDS SERIES

 Prometheus Books

59 John Glenn Drive
Amherst, New York 14228-2119

Published 1997 by Prometheus Books

Inquiries should be addressed to
Prometheus Books
59 John Glenn Drive
Amherst, New York 14228–2119

VOICE: 716–691–0133, EXT. 210; FAX: 716–691–0137.
WWW.PROMETHEUSBOOKS.COM

Library of Congress Cataloging-in-Publication Data

Marshall, Alfred, 1842–1924.
    Principles of economics / Alfred Marshall.
        p. cm.—(Great minds series)
    Reprint. Originally published: 8th ed. London : Macmillan, 1920.
    ISBN 978–1–57392–140–4 (pbk.: alk. paper)
    1. Evolution. I. Title. II. Series.

HB171.5.M289 1997
330—dc21

                              97–3368

Printed in the United States of America on acid-free paper

Great Minds Paperback Series
(Economics)

See the back of this volume for a complete list of titles in
Prometheus's Great Books in Philosophy and Great Minds series.

ALFRED MARSHALL, distinguished British economist, was born in London on July 26, 1842. His interest in economics arose out of his earlier studies of philosophy and mathematics. Following his tenure as first principal of University College, Bristol (1877–1881), Marshall taught at Cambridge University from 1885 to 1908, and lived in Cambridge for the remainder of his life.

Marshall's chief work is the *Principles of Economics* (1890; eighth edition 1920). One of the founders of the so-called neoclassical school, Marshall argued that the economy would run best if left on its own, and that the normal functioning of a market economy leads to full employment. Though influenced by the ideas of John Stuart Mill, Marshall substantially altered Mill's frame of reference: instead of analyzing how the production of goods and the distribution of income among different social classes affected, often dramatically, economic well-being, he studied price setting in a static context, focusing on small, gradual changes and the complex interrelations by which market balance, or "equilibrium," is achieved. And while the earlier political economists Adam Smith and David Ricardo had identified labor as the force determining the exchange value of goods, Marshall identified it as satisfaction of consumers' desires, or utility.

Marshall's orderly Victorian picture of supply, demand, and price, particularly at a time when contemporary socialists and trade unions were challenging the status quo, came under attack by later economists, including John Maynard Keynes, who demonstrated that market forces can be ineffective in promoting full employment and who advocated enlightened government intervention over laissez-faire policies. Nonetheless, Marshall's work continues to influence orthodox economics. Alfred Marshall died in Cambridge on July 13, 1924.

Marshall's other published works include *Industry and Trade* (1919) and *Money, Credit, and Commerce* (1923).

This is an abridgement of the eighth edition (1920),
which excludes Books 4 and 6 and the appendices.

Contents

ix

BOOK V. GENERAL RELATIONS OF DEMAND, SUPPLY AND VALUE

PREFACE TO THE FIRST EDITION.

ECONOMIC conditions are constantly changing, and each generation looks at its own problems in its own way. In England, as well as on the Continent and in America, Economic studies are being more vigorously pursued now than ever before; but all this activity has only shown the more clearly that Economic science is, and must be, one of slow and continuous growth. Some of the best work of the present generation has indeed appeared at first sight to be antagonistic to that of earlier writers; but when it has had time to settle down into its proper place, and its rough edges have been worn away, it has been found to involve no real breach of continuity in the development of the science. The new doctrines have supplemented the older, have extended, developed, and sometimes corrected them, and often have given them a different tone by a new distribution of emphasis; but very seldom have subverted them.

The present treatise is an attempt to present a modern version of old doctrines with the aid of the new work, and with reference to the new problems, of our own age. Its general scope and purpose are indicated in Book I.; at the end of which a short account is given of what are taken to be the chief subjects of economic inquiry, and the chief practical issues on which that inquiry has a bearing. In accordance with English traditions, it is held that the function of the science is to collect, arrange and analyse economic facts, and to apply the knowledge, gained by observation and experience, in determining what are likely to be the immediate and ultimate effects of various groups of causes; and it is held that the Laws of

Economics are statements of tendencies expressed in the indicative mood, and not ethical precepts in the imperative. Economic laws and reasonings in fact are merely a part of the material which Conscience and Common-sense have to turn to account in solving practical problems, and in laying down rules which may be a guide in life.

But ethical forces are among those of which the economist has to take account. Attempts have indeed been made to construct an abstract science with regard to the actions of an "economic man," who is under no ethical influences and who pursues pecuniary gain warily and energetically, but mechanically and selfishly. But they have not been successful, nor even thoroughly carried out. For they have never really treated the economic man as perfectly selfish: no one could be relied on better to endure toil and sacrifice with the unselfish desire to make provision for his family; and his normal motives have always been tacitly assumed to include the family affections. But if they include these, why should they not include all other altruistic motives the action of which is so far uniform in any class at any time and place, that it can be reduced to general rule? There seems to be no reason; and in the present book normal action is taken to be that which may be expected, under certain conditions, from the members of an industrial group; and no attempt is made to exclude the influence of any motives, the action of which is regular, merely because they are altruistic. If the book has any special character of its own, that may perhaps be said to lie in the prominence which it gives to this and other applications of the Principle of Continuity.

This principle is applied not only to the ethical quality of the motives by which a man may be influenced in choosing his ends, but also to the sagacity, the energy and the enterprise with which he pursues those ends. Thus stress is laid on the fact that there is a continuous gradation from the actions of "city men," which are based on deliberate and far-reaching calculations, and are executed with vigour and ability, to those of ordinary people who have neither the power nor the will to conduct their affairs in a business-like way. The normal willingness to save, the normal willingness to undergo a certain exertion for a certain pecuniary reward, or the normal alertness to seek the best markets in which to buy and sell, or to search out the most advantageous occupation for oneself or for one's children—all these and similar phrases must be relative to the members of a particular class at a given place and time: but, when that is once understood, the theory of normal value is applicable to the actions of the unbusiness-like classes in the same way, though not with the same precision of detail, as to those of the merchant or banker.

And as there is no sharp line of division between conduct which is normal, and that which has to be provisionally neglected as abnormal, so there is none between normal values and "current" or "market" or "occasional" values. The latter are those values in which the accidents of the moment exert a preponderating influence; while normal values are those which would be ultimately attained, if the economic conditions under view had time to work out undisturbed their full effect. But there is no impassable gulf between these two; they shade into one another by continuous gradations. The values which we may regard as normal if we are thinking of the changes from hour to hour on a Produce Exchange, do but indicate current variations with regard to the year's history: and the normal values with reference to the year's history are but current values with reference to the history of the century. For the element of Time, which is the centre of the chief difficulty of almost every economic problem, is itself absolutely continuous: Nature knows no absolute partition of time into long periods and short; but the two shade into one another by imperceptible gradations, and what is a short period for one problem, is a long period for another.

Thus for instance the greater part, though not the whole, of the distinction between Rent and Interest on capital turns on the length of the period which we have in view. That which is rightly regarded as interest on "free" or "floating" capital, or on new investments of capital, is more properly treated as a sort of rent—a *Quasi-rent* it is called below—on old investments of capital. And there is no sharp line of division between floating capital and that which has been "sunk" for a special branch of production, nor between new and old investments of capital; each group shades into the other gradually. And thus even the rent of land is seen, not as a thing by itself, but as the leading species of a large genus; though indeed it has peculiarities of its own which are of vital importance from the point of view of theory as well as of practice.

Again, though there is a sharp line of division between man himself and the appliances which he uses; and though the supply of, and the demand for, human efforts and sacrifices have peculiarities of their own, which do not attach to the supply of, and the demand for, material goods; yet, after all, these material goods are themselves generally the result of human efforts and sacrifices. The theories of the values of labour, and of the things made by it, cannot be separated: they are parts of one great whole; and what differences there are between them even in matters of detail, turn out on inquiry to be, for the most part, differences of degree rather than of kind. As, in spite of the great differences in form between birds and quadrupeds, there is one Fundamental Idea running through all their frames, so the general theory of the equilibrium of demand and supply is a Fundamental Idea running through the frames of all the various parts of the central problem of Distribution and Exchange[1].

[1] In the *Economics of Industry* published by my wife and myself in 1879 an endeavour was made to show the nature of this fundamental unity. A short provisional account of the relations of demand and supply was given before the theory of Distribution; and then this one scheme of general reasoning was applied in

Another application of the Principle of Continuity is to the use of terms. There has always been a temptation to classify economic goods in clearly defined groups, about which a number of short and sharp propositions could be made, to gratify at once the student's desire for logical precision, and the popular liking for dogmas that have the air of being profound and are yet easily handled. But great mischief seems to have been done by yielding to this temptation, and drawing broad artificial lines of division where Nature has made none. The more simple and absolute an economic doctrine is, the greater will be the confusion which it brings into attempts to apply economic doctrines to practice, if the dividing lines to which it refers cannot be found in real life. There is not in real life a clear line of division between things that are and are not Capital, or that are and are not Necessaries, or again between labour that is and is not Productive.

The notion of continuity with regard to development is common to all modern schools of economic thought, whether the chief influences acting on them are those of biology, as represented by the writings of Herbert Spencer; or of history and philosophy, as represented by Hegel's *Philosophy of History*, and by more recent ethico-historical studies on the Continent and elsewhere. These two kinds of influences have affected, more than any other, the substance of the views expressed in the present book; but their form has been most affected by mathematical conceptions of continuity, as represented in Cournot's *Principes Mathématiques de la Théorie des Richesses*. He taught that it is necessary to face the difficulty of regarding the various elements of an economic problem,— not as determining one another in a chain of causation, A determining B, B determining C, and so on—but as all mutually

succession to the earnings of labour, the interest on capital and the Earnings of Management. But the drift of this arrangement was not made sufficiently clear; and on Professor Nicholson's suggestion, more prominence has been given to it in the present volume.

determining one another. Nature's action is complex: and nothing is gained in the long run by pretending that it is simple, and trying to describe it in a series of elementary propositions.

Under the guidance of Cournot, and in a less degree of von Thünen, I was led to attach great importance to the fact that our observations of nature, in the moral as in the physical world, relate not so much to aggregate quantities, as to increments of quantities, and that in particular the demand for a thing is a continuous function, of which the "marginal[1]" increment is, in stable equilibrium, balanced against the corresponding increment of its cost of production. It is not easy to get a clear full view of continuity in this aspect without the aid either of mathematical symbols or of diagrams. The use of the latter requires no special knowledge, and they often express the conditions of economic life more accurately, as well as more easily, than do mathematical symbols; and therefore they have been applied as supplementary illustrations in the footnotes of the present volume. The argument in the text is never dependent on them; and they may be omitted; but experience seems to show that they give a firmer grasp of many important principles than can be got without their aid; and that there are many problems of pure theory, which no one who has once learnt to use diagrams will willingly handle in any other way.

The chief use of pure mathematics in economic questions seems to be in helping a person to write down quickly, shortly and exactly, some of his thoughts for his own use: and to make sure that he has enough, and only enough, premises for his conclusions (i.e. that his equations are neither more nor less in number than his unknowns). But when a great many symbols have to be used, they become very laborious to any

---

[1] The term "marginal" increment I borrowed from von Thünen's *Der isolirte Staat*, 1826—63, and it is now commonly used by German economists. When Jevons' Theory appeared, I adopted his word "final"; but I have been gradually convinced that "marginal" is the better.

one but the writer himself. And though Cournot's genius must give a new mental activity to everyone who passes through his hands, and mathematicians of calibre similar to his may use their favourite weapons in clearing a way for themselves to the centre of some of those difficult problems of economic theory, of which only the outer fringe has yet been touched; yet it seems doubtful whether any one spends his time well in reading lengthy translations of economic doctrines into mathematics, that have not been made by himself. A few specimens of those applications of mathematical language which have proved most useful for my own purposes have, however, been added in an Appendix.

September, 1890.

PREFACE TO THE EIGHTH EDITION.

THIS edition is a reprint of the seventh, which was almost a reprint of the sixth, the only changes being in small matters of detail: the Preface is almost the same as in the seventh edition.

It is now thirty years since the first edition of this volume implied a promise that a second volume, completing the treatise, would appear within a reasonable time. But I had laid my plan on too large a scale; and its scope widened, especially on the realistic side, with every pulse of that Industrial Revolution of the present generation, which has far outdone the changes of a century ago, in both rapidity and breadth of movement. So ere long I was compelled to abandon my hope of completing the work in two volumes. My subsequent plans were changed more than once; partly by the course of events, partly by my other engagements, and the decline of my strength.

Industry and Trade, published in 1919, is in effect a continuation of the present volume. A third (on Trade, Finance and the Industrial Future) is far advanced. The three volumes are designed to deal with all the chief problems of economics, so far as the writer's power extends.

The present volume therefore remains as a general introduction to the study of economic science; similar in some respects, though not in all, to that of volumes on *Foundations* (*Grundlagen*), which Roscher and some other economists have put in the forefront of groups of semi-independent volumes on economics. It avoids such special topics as currency and the organization of markets: and, in regard to such matters as the structure of industry, employment, and the problem of wages, it deals mainly with normal conditions.

Economic evolution is gradual. Its progress is sometimes arrested or reversed by political catastrophes: but its forward movements are never sudden; for even in the Western world and in Japan it is based on habit, partly conscious, partly unconscious. And though an inventor, or an organizer, or a financier of genius may seem to have modified the economic structure of a people almost at a stroke; yet that part of his influence, which has not been merely superficial and transitory, is found on inquiry to have done little more than bring to a head a broad constructive movement which had long been in preparation. Those manifestations of nature which occur most frequently, and are so orderly that they can be closely watched and narrowly studied, are the basis of economic as of most other scientific work; while those which are spasmodic, infrequent, and difficult of observation, are commonly reserved for special examination at a later stage: and the motto *Natura non facit saltum* is specially appropriate to a volume on Economic Foundations.

An illustration of this contrast may be taken from the distribution of the study of large businesses between the present volume and that on *Industry and Trade*. When any branch of industry offers an open field for new firms which rise to the first rank, and perhaps after a time decay, the normal cost of production in it can be estimated with reference to "a representative firm," which enjoys a fair share both of those internal economies which belong to a well-organized individual business, and of those general or external economies which arise out of the collective organization of the district as a whole. A study of such a firm belongs properly to a volume on Foundations. So also does a study of the principles on which a firmly established monopoly, in the hands of a Government department or a large railway, regulates its prices with main reference indeed to its own revenue; but also with more or less consideration for the wellbeing of its customers.

But normal action falls into the background, when Trusts are striving for the mastery of a large market; when communities of interest are being made and unmade; and, above all, when the policy of any particular establishment is likely to be governed, not with a single eye to its own business success, but in subordination to some large stock-exchange manœuvre, or some campaign for the control of markets. Such matters cannot be fitly discussed in a volume on Foundations: they belong to a volume dealing with some part of the Superstructure.

The Mecca of the economist lies in economic biology rather than in economic dynamics. But biological conceptions are more complex than those of mechanics; a volume on Foundations must therefore give a relatively large place to mechanical analogies; and frequent use is made of the term "equilibrium," which suggests something of statical analogy. This fact, combined with the predominant attention paid in the present volume to the normal conditions of life in the modern age, has suggested the notion that its central idea is "statical," rather than "dynamical." But in fact it is concerned throughout with the forces that cause movement: and its key-note is that of dynamics, rather than statics.

The forces to be dealt with are however so numerous, that it is best to take a few at a time; and to work out a number of partial solutions as auxiliaries to our main study. Thus we begin by isolating the primary relations of supply, demand and price in regard to a particular commodity. We reduce to inaction all other forces by the phrase "other things being equal": we do not suppose that they are inert, but for the time we ignore their activity. This scientific device is a great deal older than science: it is the method by which, consciously or unconsciously, sensible men have dealt from time immemorial with every difficult problem of ordinary life.

In the second stage more forces are released from the hypothetical slumber that had been imposed on them: changes in the conditions of demand for and supply of particular groups of commodities come into play; and their complex mutual interactions begin to be observed. Gradually the area of the dynamical problem becomes larger; the area covered by provisional statical assumptions becomes smaller; and at last is reached the great central problem of the Distribution of the National Dividend among a vast number of different agents of production. Meanwhile the dynamical principle of "Substitution" is seen ever at work, causing the demand for, and the supply of, any one set of agents of production to be influenced through indirect channels by the movements of demand and supply in relation to other agents, even though situated in far remote fields of industry.

The main concern of economics is thus with human beings who are impelled, for good and evil, to change and progress. Fragmentary statical hypotheses are used as temporary auxiliaries to dynamical—or rather biological—conceptions: but the central idea of economics, even when its Foundations alone are under discussion, must be that of living force and movement.

There have been stages in social history in which the special features of the income yielded by the ownership of land have dominated human relations: and perhaps they may again assert a pre-eminence. But in the present age, the opening out of new countries, aided by low transport charges on land and sea, has almost suspended the tendency to Diminishing Return, in that sense in which the term was used by Malthus and Ricardo, when the English labourers' weekly wages were often less than the price of half a bushel of good wheat. And yet, if the growth of population should continue for very long even at a quarter of its present rate, the aggregate rental values of land for all its uses (assumed to be as free as now from restraint by public authority) may again exceed the aggregate of incomes derived from all other forms of material property; even though that may then embody twenty times as much labour as now.

Increasing stress has been laid in successive editions up to the present on these facts; and also on the correlated fact that in every branch of production and trade there is a margin, up to which an increased application of any agent will be profitable under given conditions; but beyond which its further application will yield a diminishing return unless there be some increase of demand accompanied by an appropriate increase of other agents of production needed to co-operate with it. And a similar increasing stress has been laid on the complementary fact that this notion of a margin is not uniform and absolute: it varies with the conditions of the problem in hand, and in particular with the period of time to which reference is being made. The rules are universal that, (1) marginal costs do not govern price; (2) it is only at the margin that the action of those forces which do govern price can be made to stand out in clear light; and (3) the margin, which must be studied in reference to long periods and enduring results, differs in character as well as in extent from that which must be studied in reference to short periods and to passing fluctuations.

Variations in the nature of marginal costs are indeed largely responsible for the well-known fact that those effects of an economic cause, which are not easily traced, are frequently more important than, and in the opposite direction to, those which lie on the surface and attract the eye of the casual observer. This is one of those fundamental difficulties which have underlain and troubled the economic analysis of past times; its full significance is perhaps not yet generally recognized, and much more work may need to be done before it is fully mastered.

The new analysis is endeavouring gradually and tentatively to bring over into economics, as far as the widely different nature of the material will allow, those methods of the science of small increments (commonly called the differential calculus) to which man owes directly or indirectly the greater part of the control that he has obtained in recent times over physical nature. It is still in its infancy; it has no dogmas, and no standard of orthodoxy. It has not yet had time to obtain a perfectly settled terminology; and some differences as to the best use of terms and other subordinate matters are but a sign of healthy life. In fact however there is a remarkable harmony and agreement on essentials among those who are working constructively by the new method; and especially among such of them as have served an apprenticeship in the simpler and more definite, and therefore more advanced, problems of physics. Ere another generation has passed, its dominion over that limited but important field of economic inquiry to which it is appropriate will probably be no longer in dispute.

My wife has aided and advised me at every stage of successive editions of this volume. Each one of them owes a great deal to her suggestions, her care, and her judgment. Dr Keynes and Mr L. L. Price read through the proofs of the first edition and helped me greatly; and Mr A. W. Flux also has done much for me. Among the many who have helped me on special points, in some cases in regard to more than one edition, I would specially mention Professors Ashley, Cannan, Edgeworth, Haverfield, Pigou and Taussig; Dr Berry, Mr C. R. Fay, and the late Professor Sidgwick.

BALLIOL CROFT,
  6, MADINGLEY ROAD, CAMBRIDGE.
  October 1920.

BOOK I.

PRELIMINARY SURVEY.

CHAPTER I.

INTRODUCTION.

§ 1. POLITICAL ECONOMY or ECONOMICS is a study of I, I, 1. mankind in the ordinary business of life; it examines that part of individual and social action which is most closely connected with the attainment and with the use of the material requisites of wellbeing.

Thus it is on the one side a study of wealth; and on the Economics is a study of wealth and a part of the study of man. other, and more important side, a part of the study of man. For man's character has been moulded by his every-day work, and the material resources which he thereby procures, more than by any other influence unless it be that of his religious ideals; and the two great forming agencies of the world's history have been the religious and the economic. Here and there the ardour of the military or the artistic spirit has been for a while predominant: but religious and economic influences have nowhere been displaced from the front rank even for a time; and they have nearly always been more important than all others put together. Religious motives are more intense than economic, but their direct action seldom extends over so large a part of life. For the Man's character formed by his daily work. business by which a person earns his livelihood generally fills his thoughts during by far the greater part of those hours in which his mind is at its best; during them his character is

I, i, 1.　　being formed by the way in which he uses his faculties in
his work, by the thoughts and the feelings which it suggests,
and by his relations to his associates in work, his employers
or his employees.

Poverty
causes de-
gradation.
And very often the influence exerted on a person's
character by the amount of his income is hardly less, if it
is less, than that exerted by the way in which it is earned.
It may make little difference to the fulness of life of a family
whether its yearly income is £1000 or £5000; but it makes
a very great difference whether the income is £30 or £150:
for with £150 the family has, with £30 it has not, the material
conditions of a complete life. It is true that in religion, in
the family affections and in friendship, even the poor may
find scope for many of those faculties which are the source of
the highest happiness. But the conditions which surround
extreme poverty, especially in densely crowded places, tend
to deaden the higher faculties. Those who have been called
the Residuum of our large towns have little opportunity for
friendship; they know nothing of the decencies and the quiet,
and very little even of the unity of family life; and religion
often fails to reach them. No doubt their physical, mental,
and moral ill-health is partly due to other causes than poverty:
but this is the chief cause.

And, in addition to the Residuum, there are vast numbers
of people both in town and country who are brought up with
insufficient food, clothing, and house-room; whose education
is broken off early in order that they may go to work for
wages; who thenceforth are engaged during long hours in
exhausting toil with imperfectly nourished bodies, and have
therefore no chance of developing their higher mental faculties.
Their life is not necessarily unhealthy or unhappy. Rejoicing
in their affections towards God and man, and perhaps even
possessing some natural refinement of feeling, they may lead
lives that are far less incomplete than those of many, who
have more material wealth. But, for all that, their poverty
is a great and almost unmixed evil to them. Even when they
are well, their weariness often amounts to pain, while their
pleasures are few; and when sickness comes, the suffering
caused by poverty increases tenfold. And, though a contented

spirit may go far towards reconciling them to these evils, I, 1, 2.
there are others to which it ought not to reconcile them.
Overworked and undertaught, weary and careworn, without
quiet and without leisure, they have no chance of making
the best of their mental faculties.

Although then some of the evils which commonly go with May we not
poverty are not its necessary consequences; yet, broadly the belief
speaking, "the destruction of the poor is their poverty," and that
the study of the causes of poverty is the study of the causes necessary?
of the degradation of a large part of mankind.

§ 2. Slavery was regarded by Aristotle as an ordinance
of nature, and so probably was it by the slaves themselves in
olden time. The dignity of man was proclaimed by the
Christian religion: it has been asserted with increasing
vehemence during the last hundred years: but, only through
the spread of education during quite recent times, are we
beginning to feel the full import of the phrase. Now at last
we are setting ourselves seriously to inquire whether it is
necessary that there should be any so-called "lower classes"
at all: that is, whether there need be large numbers of people
doomed from their birth to hard work in order to provide for
others the requisites of a refined and cultured life; while they
themselves are prevented by their poverty and toil from
having any share or part in that life.

The hope that poverty and ignorance may gradually be
extinguished, derives indeed much support from the steady
progress of the working classes during the nineteenth century.
The steam-engine has relieved them of much exhausting
and degrading toil; wages have risen; education has been
improved and become more general; the railway and the
printing-press have enabled members of the same trade in
different parts of the country to communicate easily with
one another, and to undertake and carry out broad and
far-seeing lines of policy; while the growing demand for
intelligent work has caused the artisan classes to increase
so rapidly that they now outnumber those whose labour is
entirely unskilled. A great part of the artisans have ceased
to belong to the "lower classes" in the sense in which the
term was originally used; and some of them already lead a

　more refined and noble life than did the majority of the
upper classes even a century ago.

This progress has done more than anything else to give
practical interest to the question whether it is really impossible that all should start in the world with a fair chance
of leading a cultured life, free from the pains of poverty and
the stagnating influences of excessive mechanical toil; and
this question is being pressed to the front by the growing
earnestness of the age.

The question cannot be fully answered by economic
science. For the answer depends partly on the moral and
political capabilities of human nature, and on these matters
the economist has no special means of information: he must
do as others do, and guess as best he can. But the answer
depends in a great measure upon facts and inferences, which
are within the province of economics; and this it is which
gives to economic studies their chief and their highest
interest.

Causes of
the tardy
growth of
economic
science.
§ 3. It might have been expected that a science, which
deals with questions so vital for the wellbeing of mankind,
would have engaged the attention of many of the ablest
thinkers of every age, and be now well advanced towards
maturity. But the fact is that the number of scientific
economists has always been small relatively to the difficulty
of the work to be done; so that the science is still almost
in its infancy. One cause of this is that the bearing of
economics on the higher wellbeing of man has been overlooked. Indeed, a science which has wealth for its subject-
matter, is often repugnant at first sight to many students;
for those who do most to advance the boundaries of knowledge, seldom care much about the possession of wealth for
its own sake.

Changeful-
ness of
economic
conditions.
But a more important cause is that many of those conditions of industrial life, and of those methods of production,
distribution and consumption, with which modern economic
science is concerned, are themselves only of recent date. It
is indeed true that the change in substance is in some respects
not so great as the change in outward form; and much more
of modern economic theory, than at first appears, can be

I, I, 4.

adapted to the conditions of backward races. But unity in substance, underlying many varieties of form, is not easy to detect; and changes in form have had the effect of making writers in all ages profit less than they otherwise might have done by the work of their predecessors.

The economic conditions of modern life, though more complex, are in many ways more definite than those of earlier times. Business is more clearly marked off from other concerns; the rights of individuals as against others and as against the community are more sharply defined; and above all the emancipation from custom, and the growth of free activity, of constant forethought and restless enterprise, have given a new precision and a new prominence to the causes that govern the relative values of different things and different kinds of labour.

§ 4. It is often said that the modern forms of industrial life are distinguished from the earlier by being more competitive. But this account is not quite satisfactory. The strict meaning of competition seems to be the racing of one person against another, with special reference to bidding for the sale or purchase of anything. This kind of racing is no doubt both more intense and more widely extended than it used to be: but it is only a secondary, and one might almost say, an accidental consequence from the fundamental characteristics of modern industrial life.

The funda-
mental cha-
racteristic
of modern
industrial
life is
not com-
petition,

There is no one term that will express these characteristics adequately. They are, as we shall presently see, a certain independence and habit of choosing one's own course for oneself, a self-reliance; a deliberation and yet a promptness of choice and judgment, and a habit of forecasting the future and of shaping one's course with reference to distant aims. They may and often do cause people to compete with one another; but on the other hand they may tend, and just now indeed they are tending, in the direction of co-operation and combination of all kinds good and evil. But these tendencies towards collective ownership and collective action are quite different from those of earlier times, because they are the result not of custom, not of any passive drifting into association with one's neighbours, but of free choice by

but se
reliance,
inde-
pendence,
deliberate
choice and
fore-
thought.

each individual of that line of conduct which after careful
deliberation seems to him the best suited for attaining his
ends, whether they are selfish or unselfish.

"Com
petition"
implies too
much as
well as
too little.
Man is not
more
selfish than
he was.
The term "competition" has gathered about it evil
savour, and has come to imply a certain selfishness and
indifference to the wellbeing of others. Now it is true that
there is less deliberate selfishness in early than in modern
forms of industry; but there is also less deliberate unselfishness. It is deliberateness, and not selfishness, that is the
characteristic of the modern age.

For instance, while custom in a primitive society extends
the limits of the family, and prescribes certain duties to
one's neighbours which fall into disuse in a later civilization,
it also prescribes an attitude of hostility to strangers. In
a modern society the obligations of family kindness become
more intense, though they are concentrated on a narrower
area; and neighbours are put more nearly on the same
footing with strangers. In ordinary dealings with both of
them the standard of fairness and honesty is lower than in
some of the dealings of a primitive people with their
neighbours: but it is much higher than in their dealings
with strangers. Thus it is the ties of neighbourhood alone
that have been relaxed: the ties of family are in many ways
stronger than before, family affection leads to much more
self-sacrifice and devotion than it used to do; and sympathy
with those who are strangers to us is a growing source of
a kind of deliberate unselfishness, that never existed before
the modern age. That country which is the birthplace of
modern competition devotes a larger part of its income than
any other to charitable uses, and spent twenty millions on
purchasing the freedom of the slaves in the West Indies.

In every age poets and social reformers have tried to
stimulate the people of their own time to a nobler life by
enchanting stories of the virtues of the heroes of old. But
neither the records of history nor the contemporary observation of backward races, when carefully studied, give any
support to the doctrine that man is on the whole harder and
harsher than he was; or that he was ever more willing than
he is now to sacrifice his own happiness for the benefit of

others in cases where custom and law have left him free to choose his own course. Among races, whose intellectual capacity seems not to have developed in any other direction, and who have none of the originating power of the modern business man, there will be found many who show an evil sagacity in driving a hard bargain in a market even with their neighbours. No traders are more unscrupulous in taking advantage of the necessities of the unfortunate than are the corn-dealers and money-lenders of the East.

I, I, 4.

Again, the modern era has undoubtedly given new openings for dishonesty in trade. The advance of knowledge has discovered new ways of making things appear other than they are, and has rendered possible many new forms of adulteration. The producer is now far removed from the ultimate consumer; and his wrong-doings are not visited with the prompt and sharp punishment which falls on the head of a person who, being bound to live and die in his native village, plays a dishonest trick on one of his neighbours. The opportunities for knavery are certainly more numerous than they were; but there is no reason for thinking that people avail themselves of a larger proportion of such opportunities than they used to do. On the contrary, modern methods of trade imply habits of trustfulness on the one side and a power of resisting temptation to dishonesty on the other, which do not exist among a backward people. Instances of simple truth and personal fidelity are met with under all social conditions: but those who have tried to establish a business of modern type in a backward country find that they can scarcely ever depend on the native population for filling posts of trust. It is even more difficult to dispense with imported assistance for work, which calls for a strong moral character, than for that which requires great skill and mental ability. Adulteration and fraud in trade were rampant in the middle ages to an extent that is very astonishing, when we consider the difficulties of wrong-doing without detection at that time.

Man is not more dishonest than he was.

In every stage of civilization, in which the power of money has been prominent, poets in verse and prose have delighted to depict a past truly "Golden Age," before the pressure of

Dreams of a past Golden Age are beautiful but misleading.

mere material gold had been felt. Their idyllic pictures have been beautiful, and have stimulated noble imaginations and resolves; but they have had very little historical truth. Small communities with simple wants for which the bounty of nature has made abundant provision, have indeed sometimes been nearly free from care about their material needs, and have not been tempted to sordid ambitions. But whenever we can penetrate to the inner life of a crowded population under primitive conditions in our own time, we find more want, more narrowness, and more hardness than was manifest at a distance: and we never find a more widely diffused comfort alloyed by less suffering than exists in the western world to-day. We ought therefore not to brand the forces, which have made modern civilization, by a name which suggests evil.

Modern competition is of two kinds,

It is perhaps not reasonable that such a suggestion should attach to the term "competition"; but in fact it does. In fact, when competition is arraigned, its anti-social forms are made prominent; and care is seldom taken to inquire whether there are not other forms of it, which are so essential to the maintenance of energy and spontaneity, that their cessation might probably be injurious on the balance to

constructive and destructive.

social wellbeing. The traders or producers, who find that a rival is offering goods at a lower price than will yield them a good profit, are angered at his intrusion, and complain of being wronged; even though it may be true that those who buy the cheaper goods are in greater need than themselves, and that the energy and resourcefulness of their rival is a social gain. In many cases the "regulation of competition" is a misleading term, that veils the formation of a privileged class of producers, who often use their combined force to frustrate the attempts of an able man to rise from a lower class than their own. Under the pretext of repressing anti-social competition, they deprive him of the liberty of carving out for himself a new career, where the services rendered by him to the consumers of the commodity would be greater than the injuries, that he inflicts on the relatively small group which objects to his competition.

If competition is contrasted with energetic co-operation

in unselfish work for the public good, then even the best
forms of competition are relatively evil; while its harsher
and meaner forms are hateful. And in a world in which all
men were perfectly virtuous, competition would be out of
place; but so also would be private property and every form
of private right. Men would think only of their duties; and
no one would desire to have a larger share of the comforts
and luxuries of life than his neighbours. Strong producers
could easily bear a touch of hardship; so they would wish
that their weaker neighbours, while producing less should
consume more. Happy in this thought, they would work
for the general good with all the energy, the inventiveness,
and the eager initiative that belonged to them; and mankind
would be victorious in contests with nature at every turn.
Such is the Golden Age to which poets and dreamers may
look forward. But in the responsible conduct of affairs, it is
worse than folly to ignore the imperfections which still cling
to human nature.

History in general, and especially the history of socialistic
ventures, shows that ordinary men are seldom capable of
pure ideal altruism for any considerable time together; and
that the exceptions are to be found only when the masterful
fervour of a small band of religious enthusiasts makes
material concerns to count for nothing in comparison with
the higher faith.

No doubt men, even now, are capable of much more
unselfish service than they generally render: and the
supreme aim of the economist is to discover how this latent
social asset can be developed most quickly, and turned to
account most wisely. But he must not decry competition
in general, without analysis: he is bound to retain a neutral
attitude towards any particular manifestation of it until he
is sure that, human nature being what it is, the restraint of
competition would not be more anti-social in its working
than the competition itself.

We may conclude then that the term "competition" is
not well suited to describe the special characteristics of
industrial life in the modern age. We need a term that
does not imply any moral qualities, whether good or evil, but

I, i, 4.

Even con-
structive
competi-
tion is less
beneficent
than ideal
altruistic
co-opera-
tion.

I, I, 5.   which indicates the undisputed fact that modern business
            and industry are characterized by more self-reliant habits,
Economic   more forethought, more deliberate and free choice. There
Freedom.   is not any one term adequate for this purpose: but *Freedom
            of Industry and Enterprise*, or more shortly, *Economic
            Freedom*, points in the right direction; and it may be used in
            the absence of a better. Of course this deliberate and free
            choice may lead to a certain departure from individual
            freedom when co-operation or combination seems to offer the
            best route to the desired end. The questions how far these
            deliberate forms of association are likely to destroy the
            freedom in which they had their origin and how far they
            are likely to be conducive to the public weal, lie beyond
            the scope of the present volume[1].

Rough   § 5. This introductory chapter was followed in earlier
sketches
of the   editions by two short sketches: the one related to the growth
growth of   of free enterprise and generally of economic freedom, and the
economic
freedom   other to the growth of economic science. They have no claim
and of   to be systematic histories, however compressed; they aim
economic
science are only at indicating some landmarks on the routes by which
transferred economic structure and economic thought have travelled to
from this
Book to Ap- their present position. They are now transferred to Appen-
pendices   dices A and B at the end of this volume, partly because their
A and B.
            full drift can best be seen after some acquaintance has been
            made with the subject-matter of economics; and partly
            because in the twenty years, which have elapsed since they
            were first written, public opinion as to the position which the
            study of economic and social science should hold in a liberal
            education has greatly developed. There is less need now
            than formerly to insist that the economic problems of the
            present generation derive much of their subject-matter from
            technical and social changes that are of recent date, and that
            their form as well as their urgency assume throughout the
            effective economic freedom of the mass of the people.

The   The relations of many ancient Greeks and Romans with
growth of
economic   the slaves of their households were genial and humane. But
freedom.   even in Attica the physical and moral wellbeing of the great

---

[1] They occupy a considerable place in the forthcoming volumes on *Industry
and Trade*.

body of the inhabitants was not accepted as a chief aim of the citizen. Ideals of life were high, but they concerned only a few: and the doctrine of value, which is full of complexities in the modern age, could then have been worked out on a plan; such as could be conceived to-day, only if nearly all manual work were superseded by automatic machines which required merely a definite allowance of steam-power and materials, and had no concern with the requirements of a full citizen's life. Much of modern economics might indeed have been anticipated in the towns of the Middle Ages, in which an intelligent and daring spirit was for the first time combined with patient industry. But they were not left to work out their career in peace; and the world had to wait for the dawn of the new economic era till a whole nation was ready for the ordeal of economic freedom.

England especially was gradually prepared for the task; but towards the end of the eighteenth century, the changes, which had so far been slow and gradual, suddenly became rapid and violent. Mechanical inventions, the concentration of industries, and a system of manufacturing on a large scale for distant markets broke up the old traditions of industry, and left everyone to bargain for himself as best he might; and at the same time they stimulated an increase of population for which no provision had been made beyond standing-room in factories and workshops. Thus free competition, or rather, freedom of industry and enterprise, was set loose to run, like a huge untrained monster, its wayward course. The abuse of their new power by able but uncultured business men led to evils on every side; it unfitted mothers for their duties, it weighed down children with overwork and disease; and in many places it degraded the race. Meanwhile the kindly meant recklessness of the poor law did even more to lower the moral and physical energy of Englishmen than the hard-hearted recklessness of the manufacturing discipline: for by depriving the people of those qualities which would fit them for the new order of things, it increased the evil and diminished the good caused by the advent of free enterprise.

And yet the time at which free enterprise was showing itself in an unnaturally harsh form, was the very time in

I, 1, 5.

The early roughness of economic freedom in England.

The growth of economic science.

I, i, 5. which economists were most lavish in their praises of it.
This was partly because they saw clearly, what we of this
generation have in a great measure forgotten, the cruelty of
the yoke of custom and rigid ordinance which it had displaced; and partly because the general tendency of Englishmen at the time was to hold that freedom in all matters,
political and social, was worth having at every cost except
the loss of security. But partly also it was that the productive forces which free enterprise was giving to the nation,
were the only means by which it could offer a successful
resistance to Napoleon. Economists therefore treated free
enterprise not indeed as an unmixed good, but as a less evil
than such regulation as was practicable at the time.

Adhering to the lines of thought that had been started
chiefly by mediæval traders, and continued by French and
English philosophers in the latter half of the eighteenth
century, Ricardo and his followers developed a theory of the
action of free enterprise (or, as they said, free competition),
which contained many truths, that will be probably important so long as the world exists. Their work was wonderfully
complete within the narrow area which it covered. But
much of the best of it consists of problems relating to rent
and the value of corn:—problems on the solution of which
the fate of England just then seemed to depend; but many
of which, in the particular form in which they were worked
out by Ricardo, have very little direct bearing on the
present state of things.

A good deal of the rest of their work was narrowed
by its regarding too exclusively the peculiar condition of
England at that time; and this narrowness has caused a
reaction. So that now, when more experience, more leisure,
and greater material resources have enabled us to bring free
enterprise somewhat under control, to diminish its power
of doing evil and increase its power of doing good, there is
growing up among many economists a sort of spite against
it. Some even incline to exaggerate its evils, and attribute
to it the ignorance and suffering, which are the results either
of tyranny and oppression in past ages, or of the misunderstanding and mismanagement of economic freedom.

Intermediate between these two extremes are the great I, I, 5.
body of economists who, working on parallel lines in many
different countries, are bringing to their studies an un-
biassed desire to ascertain the truth, and a willingness to
go through with the long and heavy work by which alone
scientific results of any value can be obtained. Varieties
of mind, of temper, of training and of opportunities lead
them to work in different ways, and to give their chief
attention to different parts of the problem. All are bound
more or less to collect and arrange facts and statistics relating
to past and present times; and all are bound to occupy
themselves more or less with analysis and reasoning on
the basis of those facts which are ready at hand: but some
find the former task the more attractive and absorbing, and
others the latter. This division of labour, however, implies
not opposition, but harmony of purpose. The work of all
adds something or other to that knowledge, which enables us
to understand the influences exerted on the quality and tone
of man's life by the manner in which he earns his livelihood,
and by the character of that livelihood.

CHAPTER II.

THE SUBSTANCE OF ECONOMICS.

I, ii, 1.
———
The chief
motives of
business
life can be
measured
indirectly
in money.

§ 1. ECONOMICS is a study of men as they live and move and think in the ordinary business of life. But it concerns itself chiefly with those motives which affect, most powerfully and most steadily, man's conduct in the business part of his life. Everyone who is worth anything carries his higher nature with him into business; and, there as elsewhere, he is influenced by his personal affections, by his conceptions of duty and his reverence for high ideals. And it is true that the best energies of the ablest inventors and organizers of improved methods and appliances are stimulated by a noble emulation more than by any love of wealth for its own sake. But, for all that, the steadiest motive to ordinary business work is the desire for the pay which is the material reward of work. The pay may be on its way to be spent selfishly or unselfishly, for noble or base ends; and here the variety of human nature comes into play. But the motive is supplied by a definite amount of money: and it is this definite and exact money measurement of the steadiest motives in business life, which has enabled economics far to outrun every other branch of the study of man. Just as the chemist's fine balance has made chemistry more exact than most other physical sciences; so this economist's balance, rough and imperfect as it is, has made economics more exact than any other branch of social science. But of course economics cannot be compared with the exact physical sciences: for it deals with the ever changing and subtle forces of human nature.

The advantage which economics has over other branches of social science appears then to arise from the fact that its special field of work gives rather larger opportunities for exact methods than any other branch. It concerns itself chiefly with those desires, aspirations and other affections of human nature, the outward manifestations of which appear as incentives to action in such a form that the force or quantity of the incentives can be estimated and measured with some approach to accuracy; and which therefore are in some degree amenable to treatment by scientific machinery. An opening is made for the methods and the tests of science as soon as the force of a person's motives—*not* the motives themselves—can be approximately measured by the sum of money, which he will just give up in order to secure a desired satisfaction; or again by the sum which is just required to induce him to undergo a certain fatigue.

I, II, 1.

It is essential to note that the economist does not claim to measure any affection of the mind in itself, or directly; but only indirectly through its effect. No one can compare and measure accurately against one another even his own mental states at different times: and no one can measure the mental states of another at all except indirectly and conjecturally by their effects. Of course various affections belong to man's higher nature and others to his lower, and are thus different in kind. But, even if we confine our attention to mere physical pleasures and pains of the same kind, we find that they can only be compared indirectly by their effects. In fact, even this comparison is necessarily to some extent conjectural, unless they occur to the same person at the same time.

Even common pleasures and pains can be compared only through the incentives which they supply to action,

For instance the pleasures which two persons derive from smoking cannot be directly compared: nor can even those which the same person derives from it at different times. But if we find a man in doubt whether to spend a few pence on a cigar, or a cup of tea, or on riding home instead of walking home, then we may follow ordinary usage, and say that he expects from them equal pleasures.

If then we wish to compare even physical gratifications, we must do it not directly, but indirectly by the incentives

I, II, 1.   which they afford to action. If the desires to secure either of two pleasures will induce people in similar circumstances each to do just an hour's extra work, or will induce men in the same rank of life and with the same means each to pay a shilling for it; we then may say that those pleasures are equal for our purposes, because the desires for them are equally strong incentives to action for persons under similar conditions.

and this indirect comparison can be applied to all classes of desire.   Thus measuring a mental state, as men do in ordinary life, by its motor-force or the incentive which it affords to action, no new difficulty is introduced by the fact that some of the motives of which we have to take account belong to man's higher nature, and others to his lower.

For suppose that the person, whom we saw doubting between several little gratifications for himself, had thought after a while of a poor invalid whom he would pass on his way home; and had spent some time in making up his mind whether he would choose a physical gratification for himself, or would do a kindly act and rejoice in another's joy. As his desires turned now towards the one, now the other, there would be change in the quality of his mental states; and the philosopher is bound to study the nature of the change.

Economics follows the practice of ordinary discourse.   But the economist studies mental states rather through their manifestations than in themselves; and if he finds they afford evenly balanced incentives to action, he treats them *primâ facie* as for his purpose equal. He follows indeed in a more patient and thoughtful way, and with greater precautions, what everybody is always doing every day in ordinary life. He does not attempt to weigh the real value of the higher affections of our nature against those of our lower: he does not balance the love for virtue against the desire for agreeable food. He estimates the incentives to action by their effects just in the same way as people do in common life. He follows the course of ordinary conversation, differing from it only in taking more precautions to make clear the limits of his knowledge as he goes. He reaches his provisional conclusions by observations of men in general under given conditions without attempting to fathom the mental and spiritual characteristics of individuals. But he

does not ignore the mental and spiritual side of life. On the I, II, 2.
contrary, even for the narrower uses of economic studies, it
is important to know whether the desires which prevail are
such as will help to build up a strong and righteous
character. And in the broader uses of those studies, when
they are being applied to practical problems, the economist,
like every one else, must concern himself with the ultimate
aims of man, and take account of differences in real value
between gratifications that are equally powerful incentives to
action and have therefore equal economic measures. A study
of these measures is only the starting-point of economics:
but it is the starting-point[1].

§ 2. There are several other limitations of the measurement of motive by money to be discussed. The first of
these arises from the necessity of taking account of the

---

[1] The objections raised by some philosophers to speaking of two pleasures as
equal, under any circumstances, seem to apply only to uses of the phrase other
than those with which the economist is concerned. It has however unfortunately
happened that the customary uses of economic terms have sometimes suggested
the belief that economists are adherents of the philosophical system of Hedonism
or of Utilitarianism. For, while they have generally taken for granted that the
greatest pleasures are those which come with the endeavour to do one's duty, they
have spoken of "pleasures" and "pains" as supplying the motives to all action;
and they have thus brought themselves under the censure of those philosophers,
with whom it is a matter of principle to insist that the desire to do one's duty is
a different thing from a desire for the pleasure which, if one happens to think of
the matter at all, one may expect from doing it; though perhaps it may be not
incorrectly described as a desire for "self-satisfaction" or "the satisfaction
of the permanent self." (See for instance T. H. Green, *Prolegomena to Ethics*,
pp. 165—6.)

It is clearly not the part of economics to appear to take a side in ethical
controversy: and since there is a general agreement that all incentives to action,
in so far as they are conscious desires at all, may without impropriety be spoken
of shortly as desires for "satisfaction," it may perhaps be well to use this word
instead of "pleasure," when occasion arises for referring to the aims of all
desires, whether appertaining to man's higher or lower nature. The simple
antithesis to satisfaction is "dissatisfaction": but perhaps it may be well to use
the shorter and equally colourless word "detriment" in its place.

It may however be noted that some followers of Bentham (though perhaps not
Bentham himself) made this large use of "pain and pleasure" serve as a bridge
by which to pass from individualistic Hedonism to a complete ethical creed, without
recognizing the necessity for the introduction of an independent major premiss;
and for such a premiss the necessity would appear to be absolute, although
opinions will perhaps always differ as to its form. Some will regard it as the
Categorical Imperative; while others will regard it as a simple belief that,
whatever be the origin of our moral instincts, their indications are borne out by a
verdict of the experience of mankind to the effect that true happiness is not to be
had without self-respect, and that self-respect is to be had only on the condition
of endeavouring so to live as to promote the progress of the human race.

I, II, 2.

variations in the amount of pleasure, or other satisfaction, represented by the same sum of money to different persons and under different circumstances.

The same price measures different satisfactions even to persons with equal incomes;

A shilling may measure a greater pleasure (or other satisfaction) at one time than at another even for the same person; because money may be more plentiful with him, or because his sensibility may vary[1]. And persons whose antecedents are similar, and who are outwardly like one another, are often affected in very different ways by similar events. When, for instance, a band of city school children are sent out for a day's holiday in the country, it is probable that no two of them derive from it enjoyment exactly the same in kind, or equal in intensity. The same surgical operation causes different amounts of pain to different people. Of two parents who are, so far as we can tell, equally affectionate, one will suffer much more than the other from the loss of a favourite son. Some who are not very sensitive generally are yet specially susceptible to particular kinds of pleasure and pain; while differences in nature and education make one man's total capacity for pleasure or pain much greater than another's.

It would therefore not be safe to say that any two men with the same income derive equal benefit from its use; or that they would suffer equal pain from the same diminution of it. Although when a tax of £1 is taken from each of two persons having an income of £300 a-year, each will give up that £1 worth of pleasure (or other satisfaction) which he can most easily part with, i.e. each will give up what is measured to him by just £1; yet the intensities of the satisfaction given up may not be nearly equal.

but these differences may generally be neglected when we consider the average of large numbers of people.

Nevertheless, if we take averages sufficiently broad to cause the personal peculiarities of individuals to counterbalance one another, the money which people of equal incomes will give to obtain a benefit or avoid an injury is a good measure of the benefit or injury. If there are a thousand persons living in Sheffield, and another thousand in Leeds, each with about £100 a-year, and a tax of £1 is levied on all of them; we may be sure that the loss of pleasure or other

---

[1] Compare Edgeworth's *Mathematical Psychics*.

injury which the tax will cause in Sheffield is of about equal I, II, 2. importance with that which it will cause in Leeds: and anything that increased all the incomes by £1 would give command over equivalent pleasures and other benefits in the two towns. This probability becomes greater still if all of them are adult males engaged in the same trade; and therefore presumably somewhat similar in sensibility and temperament, in taste and education. Nor is the probability much diminished, if we take the family as our unit, and compare the loss of pleasure that results from diminishing by £1 the income of each of a thousand families with incomes of £100 a-year in the two places.

Next we must take account of the fact that a stronger *The significance of a given price is greater for the poor than the rich.* incentive will be required to induce a person to pay a given price for anything if he is poor than if he is rich. A shilling is the measure of less pleasure, or satisfaction of any kind, to a rich man than to a poor one. A rich man in doubt whether to spend a shilling on a single cigar, is weighing against one another smaller pleasures than a poor man, who is doubting whether to spend a shilling on a supply of tobacco that will last him for a month. The clerk with £100 a-year will walk to business in a much heavier rain than the clerk with £300 a-year; for the cost of a ride by tram or omnibus measures a greater benefit to the poorer man than to the richer. If the poorer man spends the money, he will suffer more from the want of it afterwards than the richer would. The benefit that is measured in the poorer man's mind by the cost is greater than that measured by it in the richer man's mind.

But this source of error also is lessened when we are able *But this is not important in comparing two groups composed of rich and poor in like proportions.* to consider the actions and the motives of large groups of people. If we know, for instance, that a bank failure has taken £200,000 from the people of Leeds and £100,000 from those of Sheffield, we may fairly assume that the suffering caused in Leeds has been about twice as great as in Sheffield; unless indeed we have some special reason for believing that the shareholders of the bank in the one town were a richer class than those in the other; or that the

loss of employment caused by it pressed in uneven proportions on the working classes in the two towns.

Increase of
material
means
sometimes
a fair
measure
of real
progress.

By far the greater number of the events with which
economics deals affect in about equal proportions all the
different classes of society; so that if the money measures
of the happiness caused by two events are equal, it is reasonable and in accordance with common usage to regard the
amounts of the happiness in the two cases as equivalent.
And, further, as money is likely to be turned to the higher
uses of life in about equal proportions, by any two large
groups of people taken without special bias from any two
parts of the western world, there is even some *primâ facie*
probability that equal additions to their material resources
will make about equal additions to the fulness of life, and
the true progress of the human race.

Action is
largely
ruled by
habit,

§ 3. To pass to another point. When we speak of the
measurement of desire by the action to which it forms the
incentive, it is not to be supposed that we assume every
action to be deliberate, and the outcome of calculation. For
in this, as in every other respect, economics takes man just
as he is in ordinary life: and in ordinary life people do
not weigh beforehand the results of every action, whether
the impulses to it come from their higher nature or their
lower[1].

especially
as regards
business
conduct.

Now the side of life with which economics is specially
concerned is that in which man's conduct is most deliberate,
and in which he most often reckons up the advantages and

---

[1] This is specially true of that group of gratifications, which is sometimes
named "the pleasures of the chase." They include not only the light-hearted
emulation of games and pastimes, of hunts and steeplechases, but the more serious
contests of professional and business life: and they will occupy a good deal of our
attention in discussions of the causes that govern wages and profits, and forms of
industrial organization.

Some people are of wayward temperament, and could give no good account
even to themselves of the motives of their action. But if a man is steadfast and
thoughtful, even his impulses are the products of habits which he has adopted
more or less deliberately. And, whether these impulses are an expression of his
higher nature or not; whether they spring from mandates of his conscience, the
pressure of social connection, or the claims of his bodily wants, he yields a certain
relative precedence to them without reflection now, because on previous occasions
he has decided deliberately to yield that relative precedence. The predominant
attractiveness of one course of action over others, even when not the result of
calculation at the time, is the product of more or less deliberate decisions made by
him before in somewhat similar cases.

disadvantages of any particular action before he enters on it. I, II, 3.
And further it is that side of his life in which, when he
does follow habit and custom, and proceeds for the moment
without calculation, the habits and customs themselves are
most nearly sure to have arisen from a close and careful
watching the advantages and disadvantages of different
courses of conduct. There will not in general have been any
formal reckoning up of two sides of a balance-sheet: but
men going home from their day's work, or in their social
meetings, will have said to one another, "It did not answer
to do this, it would have been better to do that," and so on.
What makes one course answer better than another, will not
necessarily be a selfish gain, nor any material gain; and it
will often have been argued that "though this or that plan
saved a little trouble or a little money, yet it was not fair
to others," and "it made one look mean," or "it made one
feel mean."

It is true that when a habit or a custom, which has
grown up under one set of conditions, influences action under
other conditions, there is so far no exact relation between the
effort and the end which is attained by it. In backward
countries there are still many habits and customs similar to
those that lead a beaver in confinement to build himself
a dam; they are full of suggestiveness to the historian, and
must be reckoned with by the legislator. But in business
matters in the modern world such habits quickly die
away.

Thus then the most systematic part of people's lives is
generally that by which they earn their living. The work
of all those engaged in any one occupation can be carefully
observed; general statements can be made about it, and
tested by comparison with the results of other observations;
and numerical estimates can be framed as to the amount
of money or general purchasing power that is required to
supply a sufficient motive for them.

The unwillingness to postpone enjoyment, and thus
to save for future use, is measured by the interest on
accumulated wealth which just affords a sufficient incentive to save for the future. This measurement presents

however some special difficulties, the study of which must be postponed.

The motives that lead to the pursuit of money may themselves be noble.

§ 4. Here, as elsewhere, we must bear in mind that the desire to make money does not itself necessarily proceed from motives of a low order, even when it is to be spent on oneself. Money is a means towards ends, and if the ends are noble, the desire for the means is not ignoble. The lad who works hard and saves all he can, in order to be able to pay his way afterwards at a University, is eager for money; but his eagerness is not ignoble. In short, money is general purchasing power, and is sought as a means to all kinds of ends, high as well as low, spiritual as well as material[1].

And there is no truth in the common opinion that economics regards man as absorbed in a selfish pursuit of wealth.

Thus though it is true that "money" or "general purchasing power" or "command over material wealth," is the centre around which economic science clusters; this is so, not because money or material wealth is regarded as the main aim of human effort, nor even as affording the main subject-matter for the study of the economist, but because in this world of ours it is the one convenient means of measuring human motive on a large scale. If the older economists had made this clear, they would have escaped many grievous misrepresentations; and the splendid teachings of Carlyle and Ruskin as to the right aims of human endeavour and the right uses of wealth, would not then have been marred by bitter attacks on economics, based on the mistaken belief that that science had no concern with any motive except the selfish desire for wealth, or even that it inculcated a policy of sordid selfishness[2].

The desire for money does not exclude other influences;

Again, when the motive to a man's action is spoken of as supplied by the money which he will earn, it is not meant that his mind is closed to all other considerations save those

1 See an admirable essay by Cliffe Leslie on *The Love of Money.* We do indeed hear of people who pursue money for its own sake without caring for what it will purchase, especially at the end of a long life spent in business: but in this as in other cases the habit of doing a thing is kept up after the purpose for which it was originally done has ceased to exist. The possession of wealth gives such people a feeling of power over their fellow-creatures, and insures them a sort of envious respect in which they find a bitter but strong pleasure.

2 In fact a world can be conceived in which there is a science of economics very much like our own, but in it there is no money of any sort. . . .

of gain. For even the most purely business relations of life I, II, 5.
assume honesty and good faith; while many of them take
for granted, if not generosity, yet at least the absence of
meanness, and the pride which every honest man takes in
acquitting himself well. Again, much of the work by which
people earn their living is pleasurable in itself; and there is
truth in the contention of socialists that more of it might be
made so. Indeed even business work, that seems at first
sight unattractive, often yields a great pleasure by offering
scope for the exercise of men's faculties, and for their
instincts of emulation and of power. For just as a racehorse
or an athlete strains every nerve to get in advance of his
competitors, and delights in the strain; so a manufacturer
or a trader is often stimulated much more by the hope of
victory over his rivals than by the desire to add something
to his fortune.

such as the pleasure afforded by the work itself and the instinct of power.

§ 5. It has indeed always been the practice of economists to take careful account of all the advantages which
attract people generally towards an occupation, whether
they appear in a money form or not. Other things being
equal, people will prefer an occupation in which they do
not need to soil their hands, in which they enjoy a good
social position, and so on; and since these advantages
affect, not indeed every one exactly in the same way, but
most people in nearly the same way, their attractive force
can be estimated and measured by the money wages to
which they are regarded as equivalent.

Economists have always reckoned for advantages of an occupation other than material gain;

Again, the desire to earn the approval, to avoid the
contempt of those around one is a stimulus to action which
often works with some sort of uniformity in any class of
persons at a given time and place; though local and temporary conditions influence greatly not only the intensity
of the desire for approval, but also the range of persons
whose approval is desired. A professional man, for
instance, or an artisan will be very sensitive to the approval
or disapproval of those in the same occupation, and care
little for that of other people; and there are many economic

and they have allowed for class sympathies,

I, II, 5. problems, the discussion of which would be altogether unreal, if care were not taken to watch the direction and to estimate pretty closely the force of motives such as these.

and family affections. As there may be a taint of selfishness in a man's desire to do what seems likely to benefit his fellow-workers, so there may be an element of personal pride in his desire that his family should prosper during his life and after it. But still the family affections generally are so pure a form of altruism, that their action might have shown little semblance of regularity, had it not been for the uniformity in the family relations themselves. As it is, their action is fairly regular; and it has always been fully reckoned with by economists, especially in relation to the distribution of the family income between its various members, the expenses of preparing children for their future career, and the accumulation of wealth to be enjoyed after the death of him by whom it has been earned.

It is then not the want of will but the want of power, that prevents economists from reckoning in the action of motives such as these; and they welcome the fact that some kinds of philanthropic action can be described in statistical returns, and can to a certain extent be reduced to law, if sufficiently broad averages are taken. For indeed there is scarcely any motive so fitful and irregular, but that some law with regard to it can be detected by the aid of wide and patient observation. It would perhaps be possible even now to predict with tolerable closeness the subscriptions that a population of a hundred thousand Englishmen of average wealth will give to support hospitals and chapels and missions; and, in so far as this can be done, there is a basis for an economic discussion of supply and demand with reference to the services of hospital nurses, missionaries and other religious ministers. It will however probably be always true that the greater part of those actions, which are due to a feeling of duty and love of one's neighbour, cannot be classed, reduced to law and measured; and it is for this reason, and not because they are not based on self-interest, that the machinery of economics cannot be brought to bear on them.

§ 6. Perhaps the earlier English economists confined their attention too much to the motives of individual action. But in fact economists, like all other students of social science, are concerned with individuals chiefly as members of the social organism. As a cathedral is something more than the stones of which it is made, as a person is something more than a series of thoughts and feelings, so the life of society is something more than the sum of the lives of its individual members. It is true that the action of the whole is made up of that of its constituent parts; and that in most economic problems the best starting-point is to be found in the motives that affect the individual, regarded not indeed as an isolated atom, but as a member of some particular trade or industrial group; but it is also true, as German writers have well urged, that economics has a great and an increasing concern in motives connected with the collective ownership of property, and the collective pursuit of important aims. The growing earnestness of the age, the growing intelligence of the mass of the people, and the growing power of the telegraph, the press, and other means of communication are ever widening the scope of collective action for the public good; and these changes, together with the spread of the co-operative movement, and other kinds of voluntary association are growing up under the influence of various motives besides that of pecuniary gain: they are ever opening to the economist new opportunities of measuring motives whose action it had seemed impossible to reduce to any sort of law.

I, II, 6, 7.

The motives to collective action are of great and growing importance.

But in fact the variety of motives, the difficulties of measuring them, and the manner of overcoming those difficulties are among the chief subjects with which we shall be occupied in this treatise. Almost every point touched in the present chapter will need to be discussed in fuller detail with reference to some one or more of the leading problems of economics.

§ 7. To conclude provisionally: economists study the actions of individuals, but study them in relation to social rather than individual life; and therefore concern themselves but little with personal peculiarities of temper and character.

Economists study the individual as a member of an

I, II, 7.
industrial
group;

They watch carefully the conduct of a whole class of people, sometimes the whole of a nation, sometimes only those living in a certain district, more often those engaged in some particular trade at some time and place: and by the aid of statistics, or in other ways, they ascertain how much money on the average the members of the particular group, they are watching, are just willing to pay as the price of a certain thing which they desire, or how much must be offered to them to induce them to undergo a certain effort or abstinence that they dislike. The measurement of motive thus obtained is not indeed perfectly accurate; for if it were, economics would rank with the most advanced of the physical sciences; and not, as it actually does, with the least advanced.

and measure the play of motives in demand and supply at first in simple cases,

But yet the measurement is accurate enough to enable experienced persons to forecast fairly well the extent of the results that will follow from changes in which motives of this kind are chiefly concerned. Thus, for instance, they can estimate very closely the payment that will be required to produce an adequate supply of labour of any grade, from the lowest to the highest, for a new trade which it is proposed to start in any place. When they visit a factory of a kind that they have never seen before, they can tell within a shilling or two a week what any particular worker is earning, by merely observing how far his is a skilled occupation and what strain it involves on his physical, mental and moral faculties. And they can predict with tolerable certainty what rise of price will result from a given diminution of the supply of a certain thing, and how that increased price will react on the supply.

and afterwards in more complex cases.

And, starting from simple considerations of this kind, economists go on to analyse the causes which govern the local distribution of different kinds of industry, the terms on which people living in distant places exchange their goods with one another, and so on: and they can explain and predict the ways in which fluctuations of credit will affect foreign trade; or again the extent to which the burden of a tax will be shifted from those on whom it is levied, on to those for whose wants they cater; and so on.

In all this they deal with man as he is: not with an

abstract or "economic" man; but a man of flesh and blood. I, II, 7.
They deal with a man who is largely influenced by egoistic They deal
motives in his business life to a great extent with reference mainly
to them; but who is also neither above vanity and reckless- side of
ness, nor below delight in doing his work well for its own but it is
sake, or in sacrificing himself for the good of his family, his life of a
neighbours, or his country; a man who is not below the love real man
of a virtuous life for its own sake. They deal with man as he fictitious
is: but being concerned chiefly with those aspects of life in being.
which the action of motive is so regular that it can be predicted, and the estimate of the motor-forces can be verified
by results, they have established their work on a scientific
basis.

For in the first place, they deal with facts which can The
be observed, and quantities which can be measured and claims of
recorded; so that when differences of opinion arise with to be a
regard to them, the differences can be brought to the test are its
of public and well-established records; and thus science appeal to
obtains a solid basis on which to work. In the second external
place, the problems, which are grouped as economic, because tests, and
they relate specially to man's conduct under the influence of homo-
motives that are measurable by a money price, are found to geneity.
make a fairly homogeneous group. Of course they have a
great deal of subject-matter in common: that is obvious
from the nature of the case. But, though not so obvious
à priori, it will also be found to be true that there is a
fundamental unity of form underlying all the chief of them;
and that in consequence, by studying them together, the
same kind of economy is gained, as by sending a single
postman to deliver all the letters in a certain street, instead
of each one entrusting his letters to a separate messenger.
For the analyses and organized processes of reasoning that
are wanted for any one group of them, will be found generally
useful for other groups.

The less then we trouble ourselves with scholastic inquiries as to whether a certain consideration comes within
the scope of economics, the better. If the matter is important
let us take account of it as far as we can. If it is one as
to which there exist divergent opinions, such as cannot be

I, II, 7.　brought to the test of exact and well-ascertained knowledge; if it is one on which the general machinery of economic analysis and reasoning cannot get any grip, then let us leave it aside in our purely economic studies. But let us do so simply because the attempt to include it would lessen the certainty and the exactness of our economic knowledge without any commensurate gain; and remembering always that some sort of account of it must be taken by our ethical instincts and our common sense, when they as ultimate arbiters come to apply to practical issues the knowledge obtained and arranged by economics and other sciences.

CHAPTER III.

ECONOMIC GENERALIZATIONS OR LAWS.

§ 1. It is the business of economics, as of almost every I, iii, 1. other science, to collect facts, to arrange and interpret them, Economics and to draw inferences from them. "Observation and de- uses both induction scription, definition and classification are the preparatory and deduction. activities. But what we desire to reach thereby is a knowledge of the interdependence of economic phenomena....Induction and deduction are both needed for scientific thought as the right and left foot are both needed for walking[1]." The methods required for this twofold work are not peculiar to economics; they are the common property of all sciences. All the devices for the discovery of the relations between cause and effect, which are described in treatises on scientific method, have to be used in their turn by the economist: there is not any one method of investigation which can properly be called the method of economics; but every method must be made serviceable in its proper place, either singly or in combination with others. And as the number of combinations that can be made on the chess-board, is so great that probably no two games exactly alike were ever played; so no two games which the student plays with nature to wrest from her her hidden truths, which were worth playing at all, ever made use of quite the same methods in quite the same way.

But in some branches of economic inquiry and for some but in different purposes, it is more urgent to ascertain new facts, than to proportrouble ourselves with the mutual relations and explanations tions for different of those which we already have. While in other branches purposes.

---

[1] Schmoller in the article on *Volkswirtschaft* in Conrad's *Handwörterbuch*.

I, III, 2. there is still so much uncertainty as to whether those causes
of any event which lie on the surface and suggest themselves
at first are both *true* causes of it and the *only* causes of it,
that it is even more urgently needed to scrutinize our
reasoning about facts which we already know, than to seek
for more facts.

Analytical
and
historical
schools
are both
needed and
supplement
each other.

For this and other reasons, there always has been and
there probably always will be a need for the existence side
by side of workers with different aptitudes and different
aims, some of whom give their chief attention to the ascer-
tainment of facts, while others give their chief attention to
scientific analysis; that is taking to pieces complex facts,
and studying the relations of the several parts to one another
and to cognate facts. It is to be hoped that these two
schools will always exist; each doing its own work thoroughly,
and each making use of the work of the other. Thus best
may we obtain sound generalizations as to the past and
trustworthy guidance from it for the future.

Imagina-
tion acting
on organ-
ized study
of facts
frames
general
state-
ments;
and some
of these
are selected
for the title
of "laws."

§ 2. Those physical sciences, which have progressed
most beyond the points to which they were brought by the
brilliant genius of the Greeks, are not all of them strictly
speaking "exact sciences." But they all aim at exactness.
That is they all aim at precipitating the result of a multitude of observations into provisional statements, which are
sufficiently definite to be brought under test by other
observations of nature. These statements, when first put
forth, seldom claim a high authority. But after they have
been tested by many independent observations, and especially
after they have been applied successfully in the prediction
of coming events, or of the results of new experiments,
they graduate as *laws*. A science progresses by increasing
the number and exactness of its laws; by submitting them
to tests of ever increasing severity; and by enlarging their
scope till a single broad law contains and supersedes a
number of narrower laws, which have been shown to be
special instances of it.

In so far as this is done by any science, a student of it
can in certain cases say with authority greater than his own
(greater perhaps than that of any thinker, however able, who

relies on his own resources and neglects the results obtained I, III, 3.
by previous workers), what results are to be expected from
certain conditions, or what are the true causes of a certain
known event.

Although the subject-matter of some progressive physical
sciences is not, at present at least, capable of perfectly exact
measurement; yet their progress depends on the multi-
tudinous co-operation of armies of workers. They measure
their facts and define their statements as closely as they
can: so that each investigator may start as nearly as possible
where those before him left off. Economics aspires to a place
in this group of sciences: because though its measurements
are seldom exact, and are never final; yet it is ever working
to make them more exact, and thus to enlarge the range of
matters on which the individual student may speak with the
authority of his science.

§ **3.** Let us then consider more closely the nature of Nearly all
economic laws, and their limitations. Every cause has a ${}^{\text{laws of}}_{\text{science are}}$
tendency to produce some definite result if nothing occurs to ${}^{\text{statements}}_{\text{of ten-}}$
hinder it. Thus gravitation tends to make things fall to the dencies.
ground: but when a balloon is full of gas lighter than air,
the pressure of the air will make it rise in spite of the
tendency of gravitation to make it fall. The law of gravitation states how any two things attract one another; how
they tend to move towards one another, and will move
towards one another if nothing interferes to prevent them.
The law of gravitation is therefore a statement of tendencies.

It is a very exact statement—so exact that mathe- The exact
maticians can calculate a Nautical Almanac, which will show ${}^{\text{laws of}}_{\text{simple}}$
the moments at which each satellite of Jupiter will hide sciences.
itself behind Jupiter. They make this calculation for
many years beforehand; and navigators take it to sea, and
use it in finding out where they are. Now there are no
economic tendencies which act as steadily and can be
measured as exactly as gravitation can: and consequently
there are no laws of economics which can be compared for
precision with the law of gravitation.

But let us look at a science less exact than astronomy. The
The science of the tides explains how the tide rises and falls ${}^{\text{inexact}}$

twice a day under the action of the sun and the moon: how
there are strong tides at new and full moon, and weak tides
at the moon's first and third quarter; and how the tide
running up into a closed channel, like that of the Severn,
will be very high; and so on. Thus, having studied the lie
of the land and the water all round the British isles, people
can calculate beforehand when the tide will *probably* be at
its highest on any day at London Bridge or at Gloucester;
and how high it will be there. They have to use the word
probably, which the astronomers do not need to use when
talking about the eclipses of Jupiter's satellites. For, though
many forces act upon Jupiter and his satellites, each one of
them acts in a definite manner which can be predicted
beforehand: but no one knows enough about the weather to
be able to say beforehand how it will act. A heavy down-
pour of rain in the upper Thames valley, or a strong
north-east wind in the German Ocean, may make the tides
at London Bridge differ a good deal from what had been
expected.

The
science of
man is
complex
and its
laws are
inexact.

The laws of economics are to be compared with the laws
of the tides, rather than with the simple and exact law of
gravitation. For the actions of men are so various and
uncertain, that the best statement of tendencies, which we can
make in a science of human conduct, must needs be inexact
and faulty. This might be urged as a reason against making
any statements at all on the subject; but that would be
almost to abandon life. Life is human conduct, and the
thoughts and emotions that grow up around it. By the
fundamental impulses of our nature we all—high and low,
learned and unlearned—are in our several degrees constantly
striving to understand the courses of human action, and to
shape them for our purposes, whether selfish or unselfish,
whether noble or ignoble. And since we *must* form to
ourselves some notions of the tendencies of human action,
our choice is between forming those notions carelessly and
forming them carefully. The harder the task, the greater
the need for steady patient inquiry; for turning to account
the experience, that has been reaped by the more advanced
physical sciences; and for framing as best we can well

thought-out estimates, or provisional laws, of the tendencies
of human action.

§ 4. The term "law" means then nothing more than
a general proposition or statement of tendencies, more or
less certain, more or less definite. Many such statements
are made in every science: but we do not, indeed we can
not, give to all of them a formal character and name them
as laws. We must select; and the selection is directed
less by purely scientific considerations than by practical
convenience. If there is any general statement which we
want to bring to bear so often, that the trouble of quoting
it at length, when needed, is greater than that of burdening
the discussion with an additional formal statement and an
additional technical name, then it receives a special name,
otherwise not[1].

Thus a law of social science, or a *Social Law*, is a state- Definition
ment of social tendencies; that is, a statement that a certain of law social, course of action may be expected under certain conditions
from the members of a social group.

Economic laws, or statements of economic tendencies, are and
those social laws which relate to branches of conduct in economic.
which the strength of the motives chiefly concerned can be
measured by a money price.

There is thus no hard and sharp line of division between
those social laws which are, and those which are not, to be
regarded also as economic laws. For there is a continuous
gradation from social laws concerned almost exclusively with
motives that can be measured by price, to social laws in
which such motives have little place; and which are therefore
generally as much less precise and exact than economic
laws, as those are than the laws of the more exact physical
sciences.

Corresponding to the substantive "law" is the adjective
"legal." But this term is used only in connection with
"law" in the sense of an ordinance of government; not in

---

[1] The relation of "natural and economic laws," is exhaustively discussed
by Neumann (*Zeitschrift für die gesamte Staatswissenschaft*, 1892) who concludes
(p. 464) that there is no other word than Law (*Gesetz*) to express those statements
of tendency, which play so important a part in natural as well as economic science.
See also Wagner (*Grundlegung*, §§ 86—91).

connection with "law" the sense of a statement of relation between cause and effect. The adjective used for this purpose is derived from "norma," a term which is nearly equivalent to "law," and might perhaps with advantage be substituted for it in scientific discussions. And following our definition of an economic law, we may say that the course of action which may be expected *under certain conditions* from the members of an industrial group is the *normal action* of the members of that group relatively to those conditions.

Definition of normal economic action.

This use of the term Normal has been misunderstood; and it may be well to say something as to the unity in difference which underlies various uses of the term. When we talk of a Good man or a Strong man, we refer to excellence or strength of those particular physical mental or moral qualities which are indicated in the context. A strong judge has seldom the same qualities as a strong rower; a good jockey is not always of exceptional virtue. In the same way every use of the term normal implies the predominance of certain tendencies which appear likely to be more or less steadfast and persistent in their action over those which are relatively exceptional and intermittent. Illness is an abnormal condition of man: but a long life passed without any illness is abnormal. During the melting of the snows, the Rhine rises above its normal level: but in a cold dry spring when it is less than usual above that normal level, it may be said to be abnormally low (for that time of year). In all these cases normal results are those which may be expected as the outcome of those tendencies which the context suggests; or, in other words, which are in accordance with those "statements of tendency," those Laws or Norms, which are appropriate to the context.

The term Normal implies harmony with whatever conditions happen to be under discussion.

This is the point of view from which it is said that normal economic action is that which may be expected in the long run under certain conditions (provided those conditions are persistent) from the members of an industrial group. It is normal that bricklayers in most parts of England are willing to work for 10d. an hour, but refuse to work for 7d. In Johannesburg it may be normal that a bricklayer should refuse work at much less than £1 a day. The

Thus normal conditions may imply high wages or low wages;

normal price of *bona fide* fresh laid eggs may be taken to be I, III, 4. a penny when nothing is said as to the time of the year: and yet threepence may be the normal price in town during January; and twopence may be an abnormally low price then, caused by "unseasonable" warmth.

Another misunderstanding to be guarded against arises they may from the notion that only those economic results are normal, imply the which are due to the undisturbed action of free competition. or the But the term has often to be applied to conditions in which of eager perfectly free competition does not exist, and can hardly even tition. be supposed to exist; and even where free competition is most dominant, the normal conditions of every fact and tendency will include vital elements that are not a part of competition nor even akin to it. Thus, for instance, the normal arrangement of many transactions in retail and wholesale trade, and on Stock and Cotton Exchanges, rests on the assumption that verbal contracts, made without witnesses, will be honourably discharged; and in countries in which this assumption cannot legitimately be made, some parts of the Western doctrine of normal value are inapplicable. Again, the prices of various Stock Exchange securities are affected "normally" by the patriotic feelings not only of the ordinary purchasers, but of the brokers themselves: and so on.

Lastly it is sometimes erroneously supposed that normal action in economics is that which is right morally. But that is to be understood only when the context implies that the action is being judged from the ethical point of view. When we are considering the facts of the world, as they are, and not as they ought to be, we shall have to regard as "normal" to the circumstances in view, much action which Normal we should use our utmost efforts to stop. For instance, the action is normal condition of many of the very poorest inhabitants of right a large town is to be devoid of enterprise, and unwilling to action. avail themselves of the opportunities that may offer for a healthier and less squalid life elsewhere; they have not the strength, physical, mental and moral, required for working their way out of their miserable surroundings. The existence of a considerable supply of labour ready to make match-boxes at a very low rate is normal in the same way that a contortion

I, III, 5. of the limbs is a normal result of taking strychnine. It is one result, a deplorable result, of those tendencies the laws of which we have to study. This illustrates one peculiarity which economics shares with a few other sciences, the nature of the material of which can be modified by human effort. Science may suggest a moral or practical precept to modify that nature and thus modify the action of laws of nature. For instance, economics may suggest practical means of substituting capable workers for those who can only do such work as match-box making; as physiology may suggest measures for so modifying the breeds of cattle that they mature early, and carry much flesh on light frames. The laws of the fluctuation of credit and prices have been much altered by increased powers of prediction.

Again when "normal" prices are contrasted with temporary or market prices, the term refers to the dominance in the long run of certain tendencies under given conditions. But this raises some difficult questions which may be postponed[1].

All scientific doctrines tacitly or implicitly assume certain conditions and are in this sense hypothetical.

§ 5. It is sometimes said that the laws of economics are "hypothetical." Of course, like every other science, it undertakes to study the effects which will be produced by certain causes, not absolutely, but subject to the condition that *other things are equal*, and that the causes are able to work out their effects undisturbed. Almost every scientific doctrine, when carefully and formally stated, will be found to contain some proviso to the effect that other things are equal: the action of the causes in question is supposed to be isolated; certain effects are attributed to them, but only *on the hypothesis* that no cause is permitted to enter except those distinctly allowed for. It is true however that the condition that time must be allowed for causes to produce their effects is a source of great difficulty in economics. For meanwhile the material on which they work, and perhaps even the causes themselves, may have changed; and the tendencies which are being described will not have a sufficiently "long run" in which to work themselves out fully. This difficulty will occupy our attention later on.

[1] They are discussed in Book V, especially chapters III and V.

The conditioning clauses implied in a law are not con- I, III, 5.
tinually repeated, but the common sense of the reader But in
supplies them for himself. In economics it is necessary to economics the implied
repeat them oftener than elsewhere, because its doctrines are conditions must be
more apt than those of any other science to be quoted by empha-
persons who have had no scientific training, and who perhaps sized.
have heard them only at second hand, and without their
context. One reason why ordinary conversation is simpler
in form than a scientific treatise, is that in conversation we
can safely omit conditioning clauses; because, if the hearer
does not supply them for himself, we quickly detect the
misunderstanding, and set it right. Adam Smith and many
of the earlier writers on economics attained seeming simplicity by following the usages of conversation, and omitting
conditioning clauses. But this has caused them to be
constantly misunderstood, and has led to much waste of
time and trouble in profitless controversy; they purchased
apparent ease at too great a cost even for that gain[1].

Though economic analysis and general reasoning are of
wide application, yet every age and every country has its own
problems; and every change in social conditions is likely to
require a new development of economic doctrines[2].

[1] Compare Book II, chapter I.

[2] Some parts of economics are relatively abstract or *pure*, because they are
concerned mainly with broad general propositions: for, in order that a proposition
may be of broad application it must necessarily contain few details: it cannot
adapt itself to particular cases; and if it points to any prediction, that must be
governed by a strong conditioning clause in which a very large meaning is given
to the phrase "other things being equal."

Other parts are relatively *applied*, because they deal with narrower questions
more in detail: they take more account of local and temporary elements; and they
consider economic conditions in fuller and closer relation to other conditions of
life. Thus there is but a short step from the applied science of banking in its more
general sense, to broad rules or precepts of the general Art of banking: while the
step from a particular local problem of the applied science of banking to the
corresponding rule of practice or precept of Art may be shorter still.

CHAPTER IV.

THE ORDER AND AIMS OF ECONOMIC STUDIES.

§ 1. WE have seen that the economist must be greedy of facts; but that facts by themselves teach nothing. History tells of sequences and coincidences; but reason alone can interpret and draw lessons from them. The work to be done is so various that much of it must be left to be dealt with by trained common sense, which is the ultimate arbiter in every practical problem. Economic science is but the working of common sense aided by appliances of organized analysis and general reasoning, which facilitate the task of collecting, arranging, and drawing inferences from particular facts. Though its scope is always limited, though its work without the aid of common sense is vain, yet it enables common sense to go further in difficult problems than would otherwise be possible.

Economic laws are statements with regard to the tendencies of man's action under certain conditions. They are hypothetical only in the same sense as are the laws of the physical sciences: for those laws also contain or imply conditions. But there is more difficulty in making the conditions clear, and more danger in any failure to do so, in economics than in physics. The laws of human action are not indeed as simple, as definite or as clearly ascertainable as the law of gravitation; but many of them may rank with the laws of those natural sciences which deal with complex subject-matter.

The *raison d'être* of economics as a separate science is that it deals chiefly with that part of man's action which is most under the control of measurable motives; and which

therefore lends itself better than any other to systematic I, IV, 2.
reasoning and analysis. We cannot indeed measure motives
of any kind, whether high or low, as they are in themselves:
we can measure only their moving force. Money is never a
perfect measure of that force; and it is not even a tolerably
good measure unless careful account is taken of the general
conditions under which it works, and especially of the riches
or poverty of those whose action is under discussion. But
with careful precautions money affords a fairly good measure
of the moving force of a great part of the motives by which
men's lives are fashioned.

The study of theory must go hand in hand with that
of facts: and for dealing with most modern problems it is
modern facts that are of the greatest use. For the economic
records of the distant past are in some respects slight and
untrustworthy; and the economic conditions of early times
are wholly unlike those of the modern age of free enterprise,
of general education, of true democracy, of steam, of the
cheap press and the telegraph.

§ 2. Economics has then as its purpose firstly to acquire Scientific
knowledge for its own sake, and secondly to throw light on inquiries
practical issues. But though we are bound, before entering are to be
arranged
on any study, to consider carefully what are its uses, we with reference
should not plan out our work with direct reference to them. not to the
For by so doing we are tempted to break off each line of practical
aims which
thought as soon as it ceases to have an immediate bearing they sub-
serve, but
on that particular aim which we have in view at the time: to the
the direct pursuit of practical aims leads us to group nature
of the
together bits of all sorts of knowledge, which have no subjects
with which
connection with one another except for the immediate they are
concerned.
purposes of the moment; and which throw but little light
on one another. Our mental energy is spent in going from
one to another; nothing is thoroughly thought out; no real
progress is made.

The best grouping, therefore, for the purposes of science
is that which collects together all those facts and reasonings
which are similar to one another in nature: so that the
study of each may throw light on its neighbour. By
working thus for a long time at one set of considerations,

we get gradually nearer to those fundamental unities which are called nature's laws: we trace their action first singly, and then in combination; and thus make progress slowly but surely. The practical uses of economic studies should never be out of the mind of the economist, but his special business is to study and interpret facts and to find out what are the effects of different causes acting singly and in combination.

Questions investigated by the economist. § 3. This may be illustrated by enumerating some of the chief questions to which the economist addresses himself. He inquires:—

What are the causes which, especially in the modern world, affect the consumption and production, the distribution and exchange of wealth; the organization of industry and trade; the money market; wholesale and retail dealing; foreign trade, and the relations between employers and employed? How do all these movements act and react upon one another? How do their ultimate differ from their immediate tendencies?

Subject to what limitations is the price of anything a measure of its desirability? What increase of wellbeing is *primâ facie* likely to result from a given increase in the wealth of any class of society? How far is the industrial efficiency of any class impaired by the insufficiency of its income? How far would an increase of the income of any class, if once effected, be likely to sustain itself through its effects in increasing their efficiency and earning power?

How far does, as a matter of fact, the influence of economic freedom reach (or how far has it reached at any particular time) in any place, in any rank of society, or in any particular branch of industry? What other influences are most powerful there; and how is the action of all these influences combined? In particular, how far does economic freedom tend of its own action to build up combinations and monopolies, and what are their effects? How are the various classes of society likely to be affected by its action in the long run; what will be the intermediate effects while its ultimate results are being worked out; and, account being taken of the time over which they will spread, what is the relative importance of these two classes of ultimate and intermediate effects? What will be the incidence of any system of taxes? What burdens will it impose on the community, and what revenue will it afford to the State?

§ 4. The above are the main questions with which economic science has to deal directly, and with reference to which its main work of collecting facts, of analysing them and reasoning about them should be arranged. The practical issues which, though lying for the greater part outside the range of economic science, yet supply a chief motive in the background to the work of the economist, vary from time to time, and from place to place, even more than do the economic facts and conditions which form the material of his studies. The following problems seem to be of special urgency now in our own country:—

I, IV, 4.

Practical issues which stimulate the inquiries of the English economist at the present time, though they do not lie wholly within the range of his science.

How should we act so as to increase the good and diminish the evil influences of economic freedom, both in its ultimate results and in the course of its progress? If the first are good and the latter evil, but those who suffer the evil, do not reap the good; how far is it right that they should suffer for the benefit of others?

Taking it for granted that a more equal distribution of wealth is to be desired, how far would this justify changes in the institutions of property, or limitations of free enterprise even when they would be likely to diminish the aggregate of wealth? In other words, how far should an increase in the income of the poorer classes and a diminution of their work be aimed at, even if it involved some lessening of national material wealth? How far could this be done without injustice, and without slackening the energies of the leaders of progress? How ought the burdens of taxation to be distributed among the different classes of society?

Ought we to rest content with the existing forms of division of labour? Is it necessary that large numbers of the people should be exclusively occupied with work that has no elevating character? Is it possible to educate gradually among the great mass of workers a new capacity for the higher kinds of work; and in particular for undertaking co-operatively the management of the business in which they are themselves employed?

What are the proper relations of individual and collective
action in a stage of civilization such as ours? How far ought
voluntary association in its various forms, old and new, to
be left to supply collective action for those purposes for
which such action has special advantages? What business
affairs should be undertaken by society itself acting through
its government, imperial or local? Have we, for instance,
carried as far as we should the plan of collective ownership
and use of open spaces, of works of art, of the means of
instruction and amusement, as well as of those material
requisites of a civilized life, the supply of which requires
united action, such as gas and water, and railways?

When government does not itself directly intervene, how
far should it allow individuals and corporations to conduct
their own affairs as they please? How far should it regulate
the management of railways and other concerns which are
to some extent in a position of monopoly, and again of land
and other things the quantity of which cannot be increased
by man? Is it necessary to retain in their full force all the
existing rights of property; or have the original necessities
for which they were meant to provide, in some measure
passed away?

Are the prevailing methods of using wealth entirely
justifiable? What scope is there for the moral pressure of
social opinion in constraining and directing individual action
in those economic relations in which the rigidity and violence
of government interference would be likely to do more harm
than good? In what respect do the duties of one nation to
another in economic matters differ from those of members of
the same nation to one another?

The dominant aim of economics in the present generation is to contribute to a solution of social problems.

Economics is thus taken to mean a study of the economic
aspects and conditions of man's political, social and private
life; but more especially of his social life. The aims of the
study are to gain knowledge for its own sake, and to obtain
guidance in the practical conduct of life, and especially of
social life. The need for such guidance was never so urgent
as now; a later generation may have more abundant leisure
than we for researches that throw light on obscure points in

abstract speculation, or in the history of past times, but do I, IV, 5.
not afford immediate aid in present difficulties.

But though thus largely directed by practical needs,
economics avoids as far as possible the discussion of those
exigencies of party organization, and those diplomacies of
home and foreign politics of which the statesman is bound
to take account in deciding what measures that he can
propose will bring him nearest to the end that he desires to
secure for his country. It aims indeed at helping him to
determine not only what that end should be, but also what
are the best methods of a broad policy devoted to that end.
But it shuns many political issues, which the practical man
cannot ignore: and it is therefore a science, pure and applied,
rather than a science and an art. And it is better described
by the broad term "Economics" than by the narrower
term "Political Economy."

§ 5. The economist needs the three great intellectual The functions
faculties, perception, imagination and reason: and most of of percep-
all he needs imagination, to put him on the track of those tion, imagi-
causes of visible events which are remote or lie below the reason in economics.
surface, and of those effects of visible causes which are remote
or lie below the surface.

The natural sciences and especially the physical group
of them have this great advantage as a discipline over all
studies of man's action, that in them the investigator is
called on for exact conclusions which can be verified by
subsequent observation or experiment. His fault is soon
detected if he contents himself with such causes and such
effects as lie on the surface; or again if he ignores the
mutual interaction of the forces of nature, wherein every
movement modifies and is modified by all that surround it.
Nor does the thorough student of physics rest satisfied with
a mere general analysis; he is ever striving to make it
quantitative; and to assign its proper proportion to each
element in his problem.

In sciences that relate to man exactness is less attainable. An external
The path of least resistance is sometimes the only one open: standard of
it is always alluring; and though it is also always treacherous, measure-ment to
the temptation is great to follow it even when a more steady the

I, IV, 5. thorough way can be fought out by resolute work. The

judgment is in some measure attainable by the economist.

scientific student of history is hampered by his inability to experiment and even more by the absence of any objective standard to which his estimates of relative proportion can be referred. Such estimates are latent in almost every stage of his argument: he cannot conclude that one cause or group of causes has been overridden by another without making some implicit estimate of their relative weights. And yet it is only by a great effort that he perceives how dependent he is on his own subjective impressions. The economist also is hampered by this difficulty, but in a less degree than other students of man's action; for indeed he has some share in those advantages which give precision and objectivity to the work of the physicist. So long, at all events, as he is concerned with current and recent events, many of his facts group themselves under classes as to which statements can be made that are definite, and often were approximately accurate numerically: and thus he is at some advantage in seeking for causes and for results which lie below the surface, and are not easily seen; and in analyzing complex conditions into their elements and in reconstructing a whole out of many elements.

But his main reliance must be on disciplined imagination;

In smaller matters, indeed, simple experience will suggest the unseen. It will, for instance, put people in the way of looking for the harm to strength of character and to family life that comes from ill-considered aid to the thriftless; even though what is seen on the surface is almost sheer gain. But greater effort, a larger range of view, a more powerful exercise of the imagination are needed in tracking the true results of, for instance, many plausible schemes for increasing steadiness of employment. For that purpose it is necessary to have learnt how closely connected are changes in credit, in domestic trade, in foreign trade competition, in harvests, in prices; and how all of these affect steadiness of employment for good and for evil. It is necessary to watch how almost every considerable economic event in any part of the Western world affects employment in some trades at least in almost every other part. If we deal only with those causes of unemployment which are near at hand, we are likely to make no good cure of the evils we see; and we are likely I, IV, 5. to cause evils, that we do not see. And if we are to look for those which are far off and weigh them in the balance, then the work before us is a high discipline for the mind.

Again, when by a "standard rule" or any other device wages are kept specially high in any trade, imagination set agoing will try to track the lives of those who are prevented by the standard rule from doing work, of which they are capable, at a price that people are willing to pay for it. Are they pushed up, or are they pushed down? If some are pushed up and some pushed down, as commonly happens, is it the many that are pushed up and the few that are pushed down, or the other way about? If we look at surface results, we may suppose that it is the many who are pushed up. But if, by the scientific use of the imagination, we think out all the ways in which prohibitions, whether on Trade Union authority or any other, prevent people from doing their best and earning their best, we shall often conclude that it is the many who have been pushed down, and the few who have been pushed up. Partly under English influence, some Australasian colonies are making bold ventures, which hold out specious promise of greater immediate comfort and ease to the workers. Australasia has indeed a great reserve of borrowing power in her vast landed property: and should the proposed short cuts issue in some industrial decadence, the fall may be slight and temporary. But it is already being urged that England should move on similar lines: and a fall for her would be more serious. What is needed, and what we may hope is coming in the near future, is a larger study of such schemes of the same kind and by the same order of minds as are applied to judging a new design for a battleship with reference to her stability in bad weather.

In such problems as this it is the purely intellectual, and and he needs sometimes even the critical faculties, which are most in active demand. But economic studies call for and develop the sympathy. faculty of sympathy, and especially that rare sympathy which enables people to put themselves in the place, not only of their comrades, but also of other classes. This class sympathy

I, ɪv, 6.

is, for instance, strongly developed by inquiries, which are becoming every day more urgent, of the reciprocal influences which character and earnings, methods of employment and habits of expenditure exert on one another; of the ways in which the efficiency of a nation is strengthened by and strengthens the confidences and affections which hold together the members of each economic group—the family, employers and employees in the same business, citizens of the same country; of the good and evil that are mingled in the individual unselfishness and the class selfishness of professional etiquette and of trade union customs; and of movements by which our growing wealth and opportunities may best be turned to account for the wellbeing of the present and coming generations[1].

Caution is demanded by an increasing recognition of the limitation of our knowledge and the uncertain permanence of our present social ideals.

§ 6. The economist needs imagination especially in order that he may develop his ideals. But most of all he needs caution and reserve in order that his advocacy of ideals may not outrun his grasp of the future.

After many more generations have passed, our present ideals and methods may seem to belong to the infancy, rather than to the maturity of man. One definite advance has already been made. We have learnt that every one until proved to be hopelessly weak or base is worthy of full economic freedom: but we are not in a position to guess confidently to what goal the advance thus begun will ultimately lead. In the later Middle Ages a rough beginning was made of the study of the industrial organism, regarded as embracing all humanity. Each successive generation has seen further growths of that organism; but none has seen so large a growth as our own. The eagerness with which it has been studied has grown with its growth; and no parallel can be found in earlier times to the breadth and variety of the efforts that have been made to comprehend it. But the chief outcome of recent studies is to make us recognize more fully, than could be done by any previous generation, how little we know of the causes by which

---

[1] This Section is reproduced from a *Plea for the creation of a curriculum in economics and associated branches of political science* addressed to the University of Cambridge in 1902, and conceded in the following year.

progress is being fashioned, and how little we can forecast I, IV, 6.
the ultimate destiny of the industrial organism.

Some harsh employers and politicians, defending exclusive Popular
class privileges early in last century, found it convenient to misconcep-
claim the authority of political economy on their side; and tions of the character
they often spoke of themselves as "economists." And even in of the founders of
our own time, that title has been assumed by opponents of modern economics.
generous expenditure on the education of the masses of the
people, in spite of the fact that living economists with one
consent maintain that such expenditure is a true economy,
and that to refuse it is both wrong and bad business
from a national point of view. But Carlyle and Ruskin,
followed by many other writers who had no part in their
brilliant and ennobling poetical visions, have without
examination held the great economists responsible for sayings and deeds to which they were really averse; and in
consequence there has grown up a popular misconception of
their thoughts and character.

The fact is that nearly all the founders of modern
economics were men of gentle and sympathetic temper,
touched with the enthusiasm of humanity. They cared little
for wealth for themselves; they cared much for its wide
diffusion among the masses of the people. They opposed
antisocial monopolies however powerful. In their several
generations they supported the movement against the class
legislation which denied to trade unions privileges that were
open to associations of employers; or they worked for a
remedy against the poison which the old Poor Law was
instilling into the hearts and homes of the agricultural
and other labourers; or they supported the factory acts,
in spite of the strenuous opposition of some politicians
and employers who claimed to speak in their name. They
were without exception devoted to the doctrine that the
wellbeing of the whole people should be the ultimate goal
of all private effort and all public policy. But they were
strong in courage and caution; they appeared cold, because
they would not assume the responsibility of advocating rapid
advances on untried paths, for the safety of which the only
guarantees offered were the confident hopes of men whose

I, IV, 6. imaginations were eager, but not steadied by knowledge nor disciplined by hard thought.

Biology has given new hopes as to the future of the human race.

Their caution was perhaps a little greater than necessary: for the range of vision even of the great seers of that age was in some respects narrower than is that of most educated men in the present time; when, partly through the suggestions of biological study, the influence of circumstances in fashioning character is generally recognized as the dominant fact in social science. Economists have accordingly now learnt to take a larger and more hopeful view of the possibilities of human progress. They have learnt to trust that the human will, guided by careful thought, can so modify circumstances as largely to modify character; and thus to bring about new conditions of life still more favourable to character; and therefore to the economic, as well as the moral, wellbeing of the masses of the people. Now as ever it is their duty to oppose all plausible short cuts to that great end, which would sap the springs of energy and initiative.

But it is still true that short cuts are dangerous: progress must be cautious and tentative.

The rights of property, as such, have not been venerated by those master minds who have built up economic science; but the authority of the science has been wrongly assumed by some who have pushed the claims of vested rights to extreme and antisocial uses. It may be well therefore to note that the tendency of careful economic study is to base the rights of private property not on any abstract principle, but on the observation that in the past they have been inseparable from solid progress; and that therefore it is the part of responsible men to proceed cautiously and tentatively in abrogating or modifying even such rights as may seem to be inappropriate to the ideal conditions of social life.

BOOK II.

SOME FUNDAMENTAL NOTIONS.

CHAPTER I.

INTRODUCTORY.

§ 1. We have seen that economics is, on the one side, a II, i, 1. Science of Wealth; and, on the other, that part of the Social Science of man's action in society, which deals with his Efforts to satisfy his Wants, in so far as the efforts and wants are capable of being measured in terms of wealth, or its general representative, *i.e.* money. We shall be occupied during the greater part of this volume with these wants and efforts; and with the causes by which the prices that measure the wants are brought into equilibrium with those that measure the efforts. For this purpose we shall have to study in Book III. wealth in relation to the diversity of man's wants, which it has to satisfy. . . .

Economics regards wealth as satisfying Wants and as the result of Efforts.

But in the present Book, we have to inquire which of all the things that are the result of man's efforts, and are capable of satisfying man's wants, are to be counted as Wealth; and into what groups or classes these are to be divided. For there is a compact group of terms connected with Wealth itself, and with Capital, the study of each of which throws light on the others; while the study of the whole together is a direct continuation, and in some respects a completion, of that inquiry as to the scope and methods of economics on which we have just been engaged. And, therefore, instead of taking what may seem the more natural

II, I, 2. course of starting with an analysis of wants, and of wealth in
direct relation to them, it seems on the whole best to deal
with this group of terms at once.

In doing this we shall of course have to take some
account of the variety of wants and efforts; but we shall not
want to assume anything that is not obvious and a matter of
common knowledge. The real difficulty of our task lies in
another direction; being the result of the need under which
economics, alone among sciences, lies of making shift with a
few terms in common use to express a great number of
subtle distinctions.

Principles
of classifi-
cation.

§ 2. As Mill says[1]:—"The ends of scientific classification
are best answered when the objects are formed into groups
respecting which a greater number of general propositions
can be made, and those propositions more important, than
those which could be made respecting any other groups into
which the same things could be distributed." But we meet
at starting with the difficulty that those propositions which
are the most important in one stage of economic development, are not unlikely to be among the least important in
another, if indeed they apply at all.

The diffi-
culties of
classifying
things
which are
changing
their
characters
and their
uses.

In this matter economists have much to learn from the
recent experiences of biology: and Darwin's profound discussion of the question[2] throws a strong light on the difficulties
before us. He points out that those parts of the structure
which determine the habits of life and the general place of
each being in the economy of nature, are as a rule not those
which throw most light on its origin, but those which throw
least. The qualities which a breeder or a gardener notices
as eminently adapted to enable an animal or a plant to
thrive in its environment, are for that very reason likely to
have been developed in comparatively recent times. And in
like manner those properties of an economic institution
which play the most important part in fitting it for the
work which it has to do now, are for that very reason likely
to be in a great measure of recent growth.

Instances are found in many of the relations between

---

[1] *Logic*, Bk. IV. ch. VII. Par. 2.
[2] *Origin of Species*, ch. XIV.

employer and employed, between middleman and producer, II, I, 3.
between bankers and their two classes of clients, those from
whom they borrow and those to whom they lend. The
substitution of the term "interest" for "usury" corresponds
to a general change in the character of loans, which has
given an entirely new key-note to our analysis and classification of the different elements into which the cost of production
of a commodity may be resolved. Again, the general scheme
of division of labour into skilled and unskilled is undergoing
a gradual change; the scope of the term "rent" is being
broadened in some directions and narrowed in others; and
so on.

But on the other hand we must keep constantly in mind
the history of the terms which we use. For, to begin with,
this history is important for its own sake; and because it
throws side lights on the history of the economic development of society. And further, even if the sole purpose of our
study of economics were to obtain knowledge that would
guide us in the attainment of immediate practical ends, we
should yet be bound to keep our use of terms as much as
possible in harmony with the traditions of the past; in order
that we might be quick to perceive the indirect hints and
the subtle and subdued warnings, which the experiences of
our ancestors offer for our instruction.

§ 3. Our task is difficult. In physical sciences indeed, In its use
whenever it is seen that a group of things have a certain set of terms
economics
of qualities in common, and will often be spoken of together, must
follow as
they are formed into a class with a special name; and as soon closely as
possible
as a new notion emerges, a new technical term is invented the practice
to represent it. But economics cannot venture to follow this of every-
day life.
example. Its reasonings must be expressed in language
that is intelligible to the general public; it must therefore
endeavour to conform itself to the familiar terms of every-
day life, and so far as possible must use them as they are
commonly used.

In common use almost every word has many shades of But that is
meaning, and therefore needs to be interpreted by the con- not always
consistent,
text. And, as Bagehot has pointed out, even the most
formal writers on economic science are compelled to follow

II, 1, 3. this course; for otherwise they would not have enough words
at their disposal. But unfortunately they do not always
avow that they are taking this freedom; sometimes perhaps
they are scarcely even aware of the fact themselves. The
bold and rigid definitions, with which their expositions of
the science begin, lull the reader into a false security. Not
being warned that he must often look to the context for a
special interpretation clause, he ascribes to what he reads
a meaning different from that which the writers had in
their own minds; and perhaps misrepresents them and
accuses them of folly of which they had not been guilty[1].

definite. Again, most of the chief distinctions marked by economic
terms are differences not of kind but of degree. At first
sight they appear to be differences of kind, and to have
sharp outlines which can be clearly marked out; but a more
careful study has shown that there is no real breach of
continuity. It is a remarkable fact that the progress of
economics has discovered hardly any new real differences in
kind, while it is continually resolving apparent differences in
kind into differences in degree. We shall meet with many
instances of the evil that may be done by attempting to
draw broad, hard and fast lines of division, and to formulate
definite propositions with regard to differences between things
which nature has not separated by any such lines.

---

[1] We ought "to write more as we do in common life, where the context is a
sort of unexpressed 'interpretation clause'; only as in Political Economy we have
more difficult things to speak of than in ordinary conversation, we must take
more care, give more warning of any change; and at times write out 'the interpretation clause' for that page or discussion lest there should be any mistake.
I know that this is difficult and delicate work; and all that I have to say in
defence of it is that in practice it is safer than the competing plan of inflexible
definitions. Any one who tries to express various meanings on complex things
with a scanty vocabulary of fastened senses, will find that his style grows cumbrous without being accurate, that he has to use long periphrases for common
thoughts, and that after all he does not come out right, for he is half the time
falling back into the senses which fit the case in hand best, and these are sometimes one, sometimes another, and almost always different from his 'hard and
fast' sense. In such discussions we should learn to vary our definitions as we
want, just as we say 'let x, y, z, mean' now this, and now that, in different problems; and this, though they do not always avow it, is really the practice of the
clearest and most effective writers." (Bagehot's *Postulates of English Political
Economy*, pp. 78, 9.) Cairnes also (*Logical Method of Political Economy*, Lect. VI.)
combats "the assumption that the attribute on which a definition turns ought to
be one which does not admit of degrees"; and argues that "to admit of degrees is
the character of all natural facts."

§ 4. We must then analyze carefully the real character- **II, i, 4.**
istics of the various things with which we have to deal; and **It is neces-**
we shall thus generally find that there is some use of each **sary that notions**
term which has distinctly greater claims than any other to **should be clearly**
be called its leading use, on the ground that it represents a **defined, but not**
distinction that is more important for the purposes of modern **that the**
science than any other that is in harmony with ordinary **use of terms**
usage. This may be laid down as the meaning to be given **should be rigid.**
to the term whenever nothing to the contrary is stated or
implied by the context. When the term is wanted to be
used in any other sense, whether broader or narrower, the
change must be indicated.

Even among the most careful thinkers there will always
remain differences of opinion as to the exact places in which
some at least of the lines of definition should be drawn. The
questions at issue must in general be solved by judgments as
to the practical convenience of different courses; and such
judgments cannot always be established or overthrown by
scientific reasoning: there must remain a margin of debatable
ground. But there is no such margin in the analysis itself:
if two people differ with regard to that, they cannot both be
right. And the progress of the science may be expected
gradually to establish this analysis on an impregnable basis[1].

---

[1] When it is wanted to narrow the meaning of a term (that is, in logical language, to diminish its extension by increasing its intension), a qualifying adjective will generally suffice, but a change in the opposite direction cannot as a rule be so simply made. Contests as to definitions are often of this kind: *A* and *B* are qualities common to a great number of things, many of these things have in addition the quality *C*, and again many the quality *D*, whilst some have both *C* and *D*. It may then be argued that on the whole it will be best to define a term so as to include all things which have the qualities *A* and *B*, or only those which have the qualities *A*, *B*, *C*, or only those which have the qualities *A*, *B*, *D*; or only those which have *A*, *B*, *C*, *D*. The decision between these various courses must rest on considerations of practical convenience, and is a matter of far less importance than a careful study of the qualities *A*, *B*, *C*, *D*, and of their mutual relations. But unfortunately this study has occupied a much smaller space in English economics than controversies as to definitions; which have indeed occasionally led indirectly to the discovery of scientific truth, but always by roundabout routes, and with much waste of time and labour.

CHAPTER II.

WEALTH.

Wealth consists of desirable things or Goods.

§ **1.** ALL wealth consists of desirable things; that is, things which satisfy human wants directly or indirectly: but not all desirable things are reckoned as wealth. The affection of friends, for instance, is an important element of wellbeing, but it is not reckoned as wealth, except by a poetic licence. Let us then begin by classifying desirable things, and then consider which of them should be accounted as elements of wealth.

In the absence of any short term in common use to represent all desirable things, or things that satisfy human wants, we may use the term *Goods* for that purpose.

Material goods.

Desirable things or goods are Material, or Personal and Immaterial. *Material goods* consist of useful material things, and of all rights to hold, or use, or derive benefits from material things, or to receive them at a future time. Thus they include the physical gifts of nature, land and water, air and climate; the products of agriculture, mining, fishing, and manufacture; buildings, machinery, and implements; mortgages and other bonds; shares in public and private companies, all kinds of monopolies, patent-rights, copyrights; also rights of way and other rights of usage. Lastly, opportunities of travel, access to good scenery, museums, etc. are the embodiment of material facilities, external to a man; though the faculty of appreciating them is internal and personal.

External and internal goods.

A man's *non-material* goods fall into two classes. One consists of his own qualities and faculties for action and for enjoyment; such for instance as business ability, professional skill, or the faculty of deriving recreation from reading or

music. All these lie within himself and are called *internal*. II, II, 1.
The second class are called *external* because they consist of
relations beneficial to him with other people. Such, for
instance, were the labour dues and personal services of
various kinds which the ruling classes used to require from
their serfs and other dependents. But these have passed
away; and the chief instances of such relations beneficial to
their owner now-a-days are to be found in the good will and
business connection of traders and professional men[1].

Again, goods may be *transferable* or *non-transferable*. *Transfer-*
Among the latter are to be classed a person's qualities and *non-trans-*
faculties for action and enjoyment (*i.e.* his internal goods); *ferable*
also such part of his business connection as depends on *goods.*
personal trust in him and cannot be transferred, as part
of his vendible good will; also the advantages of climate,
light, air, and his privileges of citizenship and rights and
opportunities of making use of public property[2].

Those goods are *free*, which are not appropriated and *Free goods.*
are afforded by Nature without requiring the effort of man.
The land in its original state was a free gift of nature. But
in settled countries it is not a free good from the point of
view of the individual. Wood is still free in some Brazilian
forests. The fish of the sea are free generally: but some
sea fisheries are jealously guarded for the exclusive use of
members of a certain nation, and may be classed as national

---

[1] For, in the words in which Hermann begins his masterly analysis of wealth,
"Some Goods are *internal*, others *external*, to the individual. An internal good is
that which he finds in himself given to him by nature, or which he educates in
himself by his own free action, such as muscular strength, health, mental attain-
ments. Everything that the outer world offers for the satisfaction of his wants is an
external good to him."

[2] The above classification of goods may be expressed thus:—

$$
\text{Goods are}
\begin{cases}
\text{external}
\begin{cases}
\text{material}
\begin{cases}
\text{transferable} \\
\text{non-transferable}
\end{cases} \\
\text{personal}
\begin{cases}
\text{transferable} \\
\text{non-transferable}
\end{cases}
\end{cases} \\
\text{internal-personal-non-transferable.}
\end{cases}
$$

Another arrangement is more convenient for some purposes:—

$$
\text{Goods are}
\begin{cases}
\text{material-external}
\begin{cases}
\text{transferable} \\
\text{non-transferable}
\end{cases} \\
\text{personal}
\begin{cases}
\text{external}
\begin{cases}
\text{transferable} \\
\text{non-transferable}
\end{cases} \\
\text{internal-non-transferable.}
\end{cases}
\end{cases}
$$

property. Oyster beds that have been planted by man are not free in any sense; those that have grown naturally are free in every sense if they are not appropriated; if they are private property they are still free gifts from the point of view of the nation. But, since the nation has allowed its rights in them to become vested in private persons, they are not free from the point of view of the individual; and the same is true of private rights of fishing in rivers. But wheat grown on free land and the fish that have been landed from free fisheries are not free: for they have been acquired by labour.

A person's wealth § 2. We may now pass to the question which classes of a man's goods are to be reckoned as part of his wealth. The question is one as to which there is some difference of opinion, but the balance of argument as well as of authority seems clearly to incline in favour of the following answer:—

is his stock of two classes of goods, When a man's *wealth* is spoken of simply, and without any interpretation clause in the context, it is to be taken to be his stock of two classes of goods.

material goods, In the first class are those material goods to which he has (by law or custom) private rights of property, and which are therefore transferable and exchangeable. These it will be remembered include not only such things as land and houses, furniture and machinery, and other material things which may be in his single private ownership, but also any shares in public companies, debenture bonds, mortgages and other obligations which he may hold requiring others to pay money or goods to him. On the other hand, the debts which he owes to others may be regarded as negative wealth; and they must be subtracted from his gross possessions before his true net wealth can be found.

Services and other goods, which pass out of existence in the same instant that they come into it, are, of course, not part of the stock of wealth[1].

and such immaterial external In the second class are those immaterial goods which belong to him, are external to him, and serve directly as

---

[1] That part of the value of the share in a trading company which is due to the personal reputation and connection of those who conduct its affairs ought properly to come under the next head as external personal goods. But this point is not of much practical importance.

the means of enabling him to acquire material goods. Thus
it excludes all his own personal qualities and faculties, even
those which enable him to earn his living; because they are
Internal. And it excludes his personal friendships, in so far
as they have no direct business value. But it includes his
business and professional connections, the organization of
his business, and—where such things exist—his property in
slaves, in labour dues, etc.

goods as are used to obtain material goods.

This use of the term Wealth is in harmony with the
usage of ordinary life: and, at the same time, it includes
those goods, and only those, which come clearly within the
scope of economic science, as defined in Book I.; and which
may therefore be called *economic goods*. For it includes all
those things, external to a man, which (i) belong to him,
and do not belong equally to his neighbours, and therefore
are distinctly his; and which (ii) are directly capable of a
money measure,—a measure that represents on the one side
the efforts and sacrifices by which they have been called into
existence, and, on the other, the wants which they satisfy[1].

The two classes together constitute economic goods.

§ 3. A broader view of wealth may indeed be taken for
some purposes; but then recourse must be had to a special interpretation clause, to prevent confusion. Thus, for instance,
the carpenter's skill is as direct a means of enabling him to
satisfy other people's material wants, and therefore indirectly
his own, as are the tools in his work-basket; and perhaps
it may be convenient to have a term which will include
it as part of wealth in a broader use. Pursuing the lines
indicated by Adam Smith[2], and followed by most continental

A broader use of the term wealth is sometimes required.

[1] It is not implied that the owner of transferable goods, if he transferred
them, could always realize the whole money value, which they have for him.
A well-fitting coat, for instance, may be worth the price charged for it by an
expensive tailor to its owner, because he wants it and cannot get it made for less:
but he could not sell it for half that sum. The successful financier who has spent
£50,000 on having a house and grounds made to suit his own special fancy, is
from one point of view right in reckoning them in the inventory of his property at
their cost price: but, should he fail, they will not form an asset to his creditors of
anything like that value.

And in the same way from one point of view we may count the business connection of the solicitor or physician, the merchant or the manufacturer, at the full
equivalent of the income he would lose if he were deprived of it; while yet we
must recognize that its exchange value, *i.e.* the value which he could get for it by
selling it, is much less than that.

[2] Comp. *Wealth of Nations*, Bk. II. ch. II.

II, ii, 4.
Personal wealth.

economists, we may define *personal wealth* so as to include all those energies, faculties, and habits which directly contribute to making people industrially efficient; together with those business connections and associations of any kind, which we have already reckoned as part of wealth in the narrower use of the term. Industrial faculties have a further claim to be regarded as economic in the fact that their value is as a rule capable of some sort of indirect measurement[1].

The question whether it is ever worth while to speak of them as wealth is merely one of convenience, though it has been much discussed as if it were one of principle.

A broad term to include all forms of private wealth.

Confusion would certainly be caused by using the term "wealth" by itself when we desire to include a person's industrial qualities. "Wealth" simply should always mean external wealth only. But little harm, and some good seems likely to arise from the occasional use of the phrase "material and personal wealth."

But we still have to take account of the individual's share of the common wealth.

§ 4. But we still have to take account of those material goods which are common to him with his neighbours; and which therefore it would be a needless trouble to mention when comparing his wealth with theirs; though they may be important for some purposes, and especially for comparisons between the economic conditions of distant places or distant times.

These goods consist of the benefits which he derives from living in a certain place at a certain time, and being a member of a certain state or community; they include civil and military security, and the right and opportunity to make use of public property and institutions of all kinds, such as roads, gaslight, etc., and rights to justice or to a free education. The townsman and the countryman have each of them for nothing many advantages which the other either cannot get at all, or can get only at great expense. Other things being equal, one person has more real wealth in its broadest sense than another, if the place in which the former lives has a better climate, better roads, better water, more

---

[1] "The bodies of men are without doubt the most valuable treasure of a country," said Davenant in the seventeenth century; and similar phrases have been common whenever the trend of political development has made men anxious that the population should increase fast.

wholesome drainage; and again better newspapers, books, II, ii, 5. and places of amusement and instruction. House-room, food and clothing, which would be insufficient in a cold climate, may be abundant in a warm climate: on the other hand, that warmth which lessens men's physical needs, and makes them rich with but a slight provision of material wealth, makes them poor in the energy that procures wealth.

Many of these things are *collective goods*; *i.e.* goods *Collective* which are not in private ownership. And this brings us to *goods.* consider wealth from the social, as opposed to the individual point of view.

§ 5. Let us then look at those elements of the wealth of *In a broad* a nation which are commonly ignored when estimating the *view of* wealth of the individuals composing it. The most obvious *wealth* forms of such wealth are public material property of all kinds, such as roads and canals, buildings and parks, gasworks and waterworks; though unfortunately many of them have been secured not by public savings, but by public borrowings, and there is the heavy "negative" wealth of a large debt to be set against them.

But the Thames has added more to the wealth of England *account* than all its canals, and perhaps even than all its railroads. *must be* And though the Thames is a free gift of nature (except in so *free goods* far as its navigation has been improved), while the canal is *and of* the work of man, yet we ought for many purposes to reckon the Thames a part of England's wealth.

German economists often lay stress on the non-material *the organi-* elements of national wealth; and it is right to do this in *society or* some problems relating to national wealth, but not in all. *the State.* Scientific knowledge indeed, wherever discovered, soon becomes the property of the whole civilized world, and may be considered as cosmopolitan rather than as specially national wealth. The same is true of mechanical inventions and of many other improvements in the arts of production; and it is true of music. But those kinds of literature which lose their force by translation, may be regarded as in a special sense the wealth of those nations in whose language they are written. And the organization of a free and well-ordered

State is to be regarded for some purposes as an important element of national wealth.

But national wealth includes the individual as well as the collective property of its members. And in estimating the aggregate sum of their individual wealth, we may save some trouble by omitting all debts and other obligations due to one member of a nation from another. For instance, so far as the English national debt and the bonds of an English railway are owned within the nation, we can adopt the simple plan of counting the railway itself as part of the national wealth, and neglecting railway and government bonds altogether. But we still have to deduct for those bonds etc. issued by the English Government or by private Englishmen, and held by foreigners; and to add for those foreign bonds etc. held by Englishmen[1].

Debts from one member of a nation to another may be omitted.

---

[1] The value of a business may be to some extent due to its having a monopoly, either a complete monopoly, secured perhaps by a patent; or a partial monopoly, owing to its wares being better known than others which are really equally good; and in so far as this is the case the business does not add to the real wealth of the nation. If the monopoly were broken down, the diminution of national wealth due to the disappearance of its value would generally be more than made up, partly by the increased value of rival businesses, and partly by the increased purchasing power of the money representing the wealth of other members of the community. (It should, however, be added that in some exceptional cases, the price of a commodity may be lowered in consequence of its production being monopolized: but such cases are very rare, and may be neglected for the present.)

Again, business connections and trade reputations add to the national wealth, only in so far as they bring purchasers into relation with those producers who will meet their real wants most fully for a given price; or in other words, only in so far as they increase the extent to which the efforts of the community as a whole meet the wants of the community as a whole. Nevertheless when we are estimating national wealth, not directly but indirectly as the aggregate of individual wealth, we must allow for these businesses at their full value, even though this partly consists of a monopoly which is not used for the public benefit. For the injury they do to rival producers was allowed for in counting up the values of the businesses of those rivals; and the injury done to consumers by raising the price of the produce, which they buy, was allowed for in reckoning the purchasing power of their means, so far as this particular commodity is concerned.

A special case of this is the organization of credit. It increases the efficiency of production in the country, and thus adds to national wealth. And the power of obtaining credit is a valuable asset to any individual trader. If, however, any accident should drive him out of business, the injury to national wealth is something less than the whole value of that asset; because some part at least of the business, which he would have done, will now be done by others with the aid of some part at least of the capital which he would have borrowed.

There are similar difficulties as to how far money is to be reckoned as part of national wealth; but to treat them thoroughly would require us to anticipate a good deal of the theory of money.

Cosmopolitan wealth differs from national wealth much as that differs from individual wealth. In reckoning it, debts due from members of one nation to those of another may conveniently be omitted from both sides of the account. Again, just as rivers are important elements of national wealth, the ocean is one of the most valuable properties of the world. The notion of cosmopolitan wealth is indeed nothing more than that of national wealth extended over the whole area of the globe.

Individual and national rights to wealth rest on the basis of civil and international law, or at least of custom that has the force of law. An exhaustive investigation of the economic conditions of any time and place requires therefore an inquiry into law and custom; and economics owes much to those who have worked in this direction. But its boundaries are already wide; and the historical and juridical bases of the conceptions of property are vast subjects which may best be discussed in separate treatises.

§ 6. The notion of *Value* is intimately connected with that of Wealth; and a little may be said about it here. "The word *value*" says Adam Smith "has two different meanings, and sometimes expresses the utility of some particular object and sometimes the power of purchasing other goods which the possession of that object conveys." But experience has shown that it is not well to use the word in the former sense.

The value, that is the exchange value, of one thing in terms of another at any place and time, is the amount of that second thing which can be got there and then in exchange for the first. Thus the term value is relative, and expresses the relation between two things at a particular place and time.

Civilized countries generally adopt gold or silver or both as money. Instead of expressing the values of lead and tin, and wood, and corn and other things in terms of one another, we express them in terms of money in the first instance; and call the value of each thing thus expressed its *price*. If we know that a ton of lead will exchange for fifteen sovereigns at any place and time, while a ton of tin will exchange for

II, II, 6. ninety sovereigns, we say that their prices then and there are £15 and £90 respectively, and we know that the value of a ton of tin in terms of lead is six tons then and there.

The price of every thing rises and falls from time to time and place to place; and with every such change the purchasing power of money changes so far as that thing goes. If the purchasing power of money rises with regard to some things, and at the same time falls equally with regard to equally important things, its general purchasing power (or its power of purchasing things in general) has remained stationary. This phrase conceals some difficulties, which we must study later on. But meanwhile we may take it in its popular sense, which is sufficiently clear; and we may throughout this volume neglect possible changes in the general purchasing power of money. Thus the price of anything will be taken as representative of its exchange value relatively to things in general, or in other words as representative of its general purchasing power[1].

But if inventions have increased man's power over nature very much, then the real value of money is better measured for some purposes in labour than in commodities. This difficulty however will not much affect our work in the present volume, which is only a study of the "Foundations" of economics.

---

[1] As Cournot points out (*Principes Mathématiques de la Théorie des Richesses*, ch. II.), we get the same sort of convenience from assuming the existence of a standard of uniform purchasing power by which to measure value, that astronomers do by assuming that there is a "mean sun" which crosses the meridian at uniform intervals, so that the clock can keep pace with it; whereas the actual sun crosses the meridian sometimes before and sometimes after noon as shown by the clock.

CHAPTER III.

PRODUCTION. CONSUMPTION. LABOUR. NECESSARIES.

§ 1. MAN cannot create material things. In the mental II, III, 1. and moral world indeed he may produce new ideas; but when he is said to produce material things, he really only produces utilities; or in other words, his efforts and sacrifices result in changing the form or arrangement of matter to adapt it better for the satisfaction of wants. All that he can do in the physical world is either to readjust matter so as to make it more useful, as when he makes a log of wood into a table; or to put it in the way of being made more useful by nature, as when he puts seed where the forces of nature will make it burst out into life[1].

Man cannot produce matter, but only utilities inherent in matter.

It is sometimes said that traders do not produce: that while the cabinet-maker produces furniture, the furniture-dealer merely sells what is already produced. But there is no scientific foundation for this distinction. They both produce utilities, and neither of them can do more: the furniture-dealer moves and rearranges matter so as to make it more serviceable than it was before, and the carpenter does nothing more. The sailor or the railway-man who carries coal above ground produces it, just as much as the miner who carries it underground; the dealer in fish helps to move on fish from where it is of comparatively little use to where it is of greater use, and the fisherman does no more. It is true that there are often more traders than are necessary; and that, whenever that is the case, there is a

The trader produces utilities.

---

[1] Bacon, *Novum Organon* IV., says "Ad opera nil aliud potest homo quam ut corpora naturalia admoveat et amoveat, reliqua natura intus agit" (quoted by Bonar, *Philosophy and Political Economy*, p. 249).

II, III, 1.   waste. But there is also waste if there are two men to a plough which can be well worked by one man; in both cases all those who are at work produce, though they·may produce but little. Some writers have revived the mediæval attacks on trade on the ground that it does not produce. But they have not aimed at the right mark. They should have attacked the imperfect organization of trade, particularly of retail trade[1].

Man can consume, as he can produce, only utilities.   *Consumption* may be regarded as negative production. Just as man can produce only utilities, so he can consume nothing more. He can produce services and other immaterial products, and he can consume them. But as his production of material products is really nothing more than a rearrangement of matter which gives it new utilities; so his consumption of them is nothing more than a disarrangement of matter, which diminishes or destroys its utilities. Often indeed when he is said to consume things, he does nothing more than to hold them for his use, while, as Senior says, they "are destroyed by those numerous gradual agents which we call collectively *time*[2]." As the "producer" of wheat is he who puts seed where nature will make it grow, so the "consumer" of pictures, of curtains, and even of a house or a yacht does little to wear them out himself; but he uses them while time wastes them.

Consumers' and producers' goods.   Another distinction to which some prominence has been given, but which is vague and perhaps not of much practical use, is that between *consumers' goods* (called also *consumption goods*, or again *goods of the first order*), such as food, clothes, etc., which satisfy wants *directly* on the one hand; and, on the other hand, *producers' goods* (called also *production goods*, or again *instrumental*, or again *intermediate goods*), such as ploughs and looms and raw cotton, which satisfy wants *indirectly* by contributing towards the production of the first class of goods[3].

[1] Production, in the narrow sense, changes the form and nature of products. Trade and transport change their external relations.

[2] *Political Economy*, p. 54. Senior would like to substitute the verb "to use" for the verb "to consume."

[3] Thus flour to be made into a cake when already in the house of the consumer, is treated by some as a consumers' good; while not only the flour, but the cake itself is treated as a producers' good when in the hand of the confectioner.

§ 2. All labour is directed towards producing some effect. II, III, 2.
For though some exertions are taken merely for their own Nearly all
sake, as when a game is played for amusement, they are not labour is in
some sense
counted as labour. We may define *labour* as any exertion productive.
of mind or body undergone partly or wholly with a view to
some good other than the pleasure derived directly from the
work[1]. And if we had to make a fresh start it would be
best to regard all labour as productive except that which
failed to promote the aim towards which it was directed,
and so produced no utility. But in all the many changes
which the meaning of the word "productive" has undergone,
.it has had special reference to stored-up wealth, to the
comparative neglect and sometimes even to the exclusion
of immediate and transitory enjoyment[2]; and an almost
unbroken tradition compels us to regard the central notion

Carl Menger (*Volkswirthschaftslehre*, ch. I. § 2) says bread belongs to the first
order, flour to the second, a flour mill to the third order and so on. It appears
that if a railway train carries people on a pleasure excursion, also some tins of
biscuits, and milling machinery and some machinery that is used for making
milling machinery; then the train is at one and the same time a good of the first,
second, third and fourth orders.

[1] This is Jevons' definition (*Theory of Political Economy*, ch. v.), except
that he includes only painful exertions. But he himself points out how painful
idleness often is. Most people work more than they would if they considered
only the direct pleasure resulting from the work; but in a healthy state, pleasure
predominates over pain in a great part even of the work that is done for hire.
Of course the definition is elastic; an agricultural labourer working in his
garden in the evening thinks chiefly of the fruit of his labours; a mechanic
returning home after a day of sedentary toil finds positive pleasure in his garden
work, but he too cares a good deal about the fruit of his labour; while a rich
man working in like manner, though he may take a pride in doing it well, will
probably care little for any pecuniary saving that he effects by it.

[2] Thus the Mercantilists who regarded the precious metals, partly because
they were imperishable, as wealth in a fuller sense than anything else, regarded
as unproductive or "sterile" all labour that was not directed to producing goods
for exportation in exchange for gold and silver. The Physiocrats thought
all labour sterile which consumed an equal value to that which it produced;
and regarded the agriculturist as the only productive worker, because his labour
alone (as they thought) left behind it a net surplus of stored-up wealth. Adam
Smith softened down the Physiocratic definition; but still he considered that
agricultural labour was more productive than any other. His followers discarded
this distinction; but they have generally adhered, though with many differences
in points of detail, to the notion that productive labour is that which tends to
increase accumulated wealth; a notion which is implied rather than stated in the
celebrated chapter of *The Wealth of Nations* which bears the title, "On the
Accumulation of Capital, or on Productive and Unproductive Labour." (Comp.
Travers Twiss, *Progress of Political Economy*, Sect. VI., and the discussions on
the word Productive in J. S. Mill's *Essays*, and in his *Principles of Political
Economy*.)

II, III, 2.

But that labour is generally said to be specially productive which provides for the wants of the future rather than the present.

of the word as relating to the provision for the wants of the future rather than those of the present. It is true that all wholesome enjoyments, whether luxurious or not, are legitimate ends of action both public and private; and it is true that the enjoyment of luxuries affords an incentive to exertion, and promotes progress in many ways. But if the efficiency and energy of industry are the same, the true interest of a country is generally advanced by the subordination of the desire for transient luxuries to the attainment of those more solid and lasting resources which will assist industry in its future work, and will in various ways tend to make life larger. This general idea has been in solution, as it were, in all stages of economic theory; and has been precipitated by different writers into various hard and fast distinctions by which certain trades have been marked off as productive and certain others as unproductive.

The work of domestic servants is not necessarily unproductive.

For instance, many writers even of recent times have adhered to Adam Smith's plan of classing domestic servants as unproductive. There is doubtless in many large houses a superabundance of servants, some of whose energies might with advantage to the community be transferred to other uses: but the same is true of the greater part of those who earn their livelihood by distilling whisky; and yet no economist has proposed to call them unproductive. There is no distinction in character between the work of the baker who provides bread for a family, and that of the cook who boils potatoes. If the baker should be a confectioner, or fancy baker, it is probable that he spends at least as much of his time as the domestic cook does, on labour that is unproductive in the popular sense of providing unnecessary enjoyments.

Provisional definition of productive.

Whenever we use the word *Productive* by itself, it is to be understood to mean *productive of the means of production, and of durable sources of enjoyment*. But it is a slippery term, and should not be used where precision is needed[1].

---

[1] Among the means of production are included the necessaries of labour but not ephemeral luxuries; and the maker of ices is thus classed as unproductive whether he is working for a pastry-cook, or as a private servant in a country house. But a bricklayer engaged in building a theatre is classed as productive. No doubt the division between permanent and ephemeral sources of enjoyment is vague

If ever we want to use it in a different sense, we must II, III, 3.
say so: for instance we may speak of labour as *productive of*
necessaries, etc.

Productive consumption, when employed as a technical *Productive*
term, is commonly defined as the use of wealth in the *consump-*
tion.
production of further wealth; and it should properly include
not all the consumption of productive workers, but only that
which is necessary for their efficiency. The term may perhaps be useful in studies of the accumulation of material
wealth. But it is apt to mislead. For consumption is the
end of production; and all wholesome consumption is productive of benefits, many of the most worthy of which do
not directly contribute to the production of material wealth[1].

§ 3. This brings us to consider the term Necessaries. Neces-
It is common to distinguish necessaries, comforts, and things
luxuries; the first class including all things required to wants that
meet wants which *must* be satisfied, while the latter consist *must be*
of things that meet wants of a less urgent character. But But this
here again there is a troublesome ambiguity. When we say ambiguous.
that a want *must* be satisfied, what are the consequences
which we have in view if it is not satisfied? Do they

and unsubstantial. But this difficulty exists in the nature of things and cannot be
completely evaded by any device of words. We can speak of an increase of tall
men relatively to short, without deciding whether all those above five feet nine
inches are to be classed as tall, or only those above five feet ten. And we can
speak of the increase of productive labour at the expense of unproductive without
fixing on any rigid, and therefore arbitrary line of division between them. If such
an artificial line is required for any particular purpose, it must be drawn explicitly
for the occasion. But in fact such occasions seldom or never occur.

[1] All the distinctions in which the word Productive is used are very thin and
have a certain air of unreality. It would hardly be worth while to introduce them
now: but they have a long history; and it is probably better that they should
dwindle gradually out of use, rather than be suddenly discarded.

The attempt to draw a hard and fast line of distinction where there is no
real discontinuity in nature has often done more mischief, but has perhaps
never led to more quaint results, than in the rigid definitions which have been
sometimes given of this term Productive. Some of them for instance lead to
the conclusion that a singer in an opera is unproductive, that the printer of the
tickets of admission to the opera is productive; while the usher who shows
people to their places is unproductive, unless he happens to sell programmes, and
then he is productive. Senior points out that "a cook is not said to *make* roast
meat but to *dress* it; but he is said to *make* a pudding....A tailor is said to *make*
cloth into a coat, a dyer is not said to *make* undyed cloth into dyed cloth. The
change produced by the dyer is perhaps greater than that produced by the tailor,
but the cloth in passing through the tailor's hands changes its name; in passing
through the dyer's it does not: the dyer has not produced a *new name*, nor
consequently a *new thing*." *Pol. Econ.* pp. 51, 2.

II, III, 3.   include death? Or do they extend only to the loss of strength and vigour? In other words, are necessaries the things which are necessary for life, or those which are necessary for efficiency?

The term Necessaries is elliptical.

The term Necessaries, like the term Productive, has been used elliptically, the subject to which it refers being left to be supplied by the reader; and since the implied subject has varied, the reader has often supplied one which the writer did not intend, and thus misunderstood his drift. In this, as in the preceding case, the chief source of confusion can be removed by supplying explicitly in every critical place that which the reader is intended to understand.

Necessaries for existence and for efficiency.

The older use of the term Necessaries was limited to those things which were sufficient to enable the labourers, taken one with another, to support themselves and their families. Adam Smith and the more careful of his followers observed indeed variations in the standard of comfort and "decency": and they recognized that differences of climate and differences of custom make things necessary in some cases, which are superfluous in others[1]. But Adam Smith was influenced by reasonings of the Physiocrats: they were based on the condition of the French people in the eighteenth century, most of whom had no notion of any necessaries beyond those which were required for mere existence. In happier times, however, a more careful analysis has made it evident that there is for each rank of industry, at any time and place, a more or less clearly defined income which is necessary for merely sustaining its members; while there is another and larger income which is necessary for keeping it in full efficiency[2].

[1] Compare Carver, *Principles of Political Economy*, p. 474; which called my attention to Adam Smith's observation that customary decencies are in effect necessaries.

[2] Thus in the South of England population has increased during the last hundred years at a fair rate, allowance being made for migration. But the efficiency of labour, which in earlier times was as high as that in the North of England, has sunk relatively to the North; so that the low-waged labour of the South is often dearer than the more highly-paid labour of the North. We cannot thus say whether the labourers in the South have been supplied with necessaries, unless we know in which of these two senses the word is used. They have had the bare necessaries for existence and the increase of numbers, but apparently they have not had the necessaries for efficiency. It must however be remembered that the strongest labourers in the South have constantly migrated to the North; and that the energies of those in the North have been raised by their larger share of

It may be true that the wages of any industrial class II, III, 4. might have sufficed to maintain a higher efficiency, if they *Account* had been spent with perfect wisdom. But every estimate of *must be taken* necessaries must be relative to a given place and time; and *of the conditions* unless there be a special interpretation clause to the contrary, *of place* it may be assumed that the wages will be spent with just *and time and of the* that amount of wisdom, forethought, and unselfishness, which *habits of living.* prevails in fact among the industrial class under discussion. With this understanding we may say that the income of any class in the ranks of industry is below its *necessary* level, *Neces-* when any increase in their income would in the course of *saries.* time produce a more than proportionate increase in their efficiency. Consumption may be economized by a change of habits, but any stinting of necessaries is wasteful[1].

§ 4. Some detailed study of the necessaries for efficiency *Illustra-* of different classes of workers will have to be made, when we *tion. Ne-* *cessaries of* come to inquire into the causes that determine the supply of *unskilled* efficient labour. But it will serve to give some definiteness *labour.* to our ideas, if we consider here what are the necessaries for the efficiency of an ordinary agricultural or of an unskilled town labourer and his family, in England, in this generation. They may be said to consist of a well-drained dwelling with several rooms, warm clothing, with some changes of under-clothing, pure water, a plentiful supply of cereal food, with a moderate allowance of meat and milk, and a little tea, etc., some education and some recreation, and lastly, sufficient freedom for his wife from other work to enable her to perform properly her maternal and her household duties. If in any district unskilled labour is deprived of any of these

economic freedom and of the hope of rising to a higher position. See Mackay in *Charity Organization Journal*, Feb. 1891.

[1] If we considered an individual of exceptional abilities we should have to take account of the fact that there is not likely to be the same close correspondence between the real value of his work for the community and the income which he earns by it, that there is in the case of an ordinary member of any industrial class. And we should have to say that all his consumption is strictly productive and necessary, so long as by cutting off any part of it he would diminish his efficiency by an amount that is of more real value to him or the rest of the world than he saved from his consumption. If a Newton or a Watt could have added a hundredth part to his efficiency by doubling his personal expenditure, the increase in his consumption would have been truly productive. As we shall see later on, such a case is analogous to additional cultivation of rich land that bears a high rent: it may be profitable though the return to it is less than in proportion to the previous outlay.

II, III, 4.

There is waste when any one consumes less than is necessary. Conventional necessaries.

things, its efficiency will suffer in the same way as that of a horse that is not properly tended, or a steam-engine that has an inadequate supply of coals. All consumption up to this limit is strictly productive consumption: any stinting of this consumption is not economical, but wasteful.

In addition, perhaps, some consumption of alcohol and tobacco, and some indulgence in fashionable dress are in many places so habitual, that they may be said to be *conventionally necessary*, since in order to obtain them the average man and woman will sacrifice some things which are necessary for efficiency. Their wages are therefore less than are practically necessary for efficiency, unless they provide not only for what is strictly necessary consumption, but include also a certain amount of conventional necessaries[1].

The consumption of conventional necessaries by productive workers is commonly classed as productive consumption; but strictly speaking it ought not to be; and in critical passages a special interpretation clause should be added to say whether or not they are included.

It should however be noticed that many things which are rightly described as superfluous luxuries, do yet, to some extent, take the place of necessaries; and to that extent their consumption is productive when they are consumed by producers[2].

[1] Compare the distinction between "Physical and Political Necessaries" in James Steuart's *Inquiry*, A.D. 1767, II. XXI.

[2] Thus a dish of green peas in March, costing perhaps ten shillings, is a superfluous luxury: but yet it is wholesome food, and does the work perhaps of three pennyworth of cabbage; or even, since variety undoubtedly conduces to health, a little more than that. So it may be entered perhaps at the value of fourpence under the head of necessaries, and at that of nine shillings and eightpence under that of superfluities; and its consumption may be regarded as strictly productive to the extent of one-fortieth. In exceptional cases, as for instance when the peas are given to an invalid, the whole ten shillings may be well spent, and reproduce their own value.

For the sake of giving definiteness to the ideas it may be well to venture on estimates of necessaries, rough and random as they must be. Perhaps at present prices the strict necessaries for an average agricultural family are covered by fifteen or eighteen shillings a week, the conventional necessaries by about five shillings more. For the unskilled labourer in the town a few shillings must be added to the strict necessaries. For the family of the skilled workman living in a town we may take twenty-five or thirty shillings for strict necessaries, and ten shillings for conventional necessaries. For a man whose brain has to undergo great continuous strain the strict necessaries are perhaps two hundred or two hundred and fifty pounds a year if he is a bachelor: but more than twice as much if he has an expensive family to educate. His conventional necessaries depend on the nature of his calling.

CHAPTER IV.

INCOME. CAPITAL.

§ 1. In a primitive community each family is nearly self- II, IV, 1.
sufficing, and provides most of its own food and clothing and Income in its broad use.
even household furniture. Only a very small part of the
income, or comings in, of the family is in the form of
money; when one thinks of their income at all, one reckons
in the benefits which they get from their cooking utensils,
just as much as those which they get from their plough:
one draws no distinction between their capital and the rest
of their accumulated stock, to which the cooking utensils
and the plough alike belong[1].

But with the growth of a money economy there has been Corresponding to money-income,
a strong tendency to confine the notion of income to those
incomings which are in the form of money; including
"payments in kind" (such as the free use of a house, free
coals, gas, water), which are given as part of an employee's
remuneration, and in lieu of money payments.

In harmony with this meaning of Income, the language we have trade capital.
of the market-place commonly regards a man's capital
as that part of his wealth which he devotes to acquiring
an income in the form of money; or, more generally, to
acquisition (*Erwerbung*) by means of trade. It may be
convenient sometimes to speak of this as his *trade capital*;

---

[1] This and similar facts have led some people to suppose not only that some
parts of the modern analysis of distribution and exchange are inapplicable to a
primitive community; which is true: but also that there are no important parts
of it that are applicable; which is not true. This is a striking instance of the
dangers that arise from allowing ourselves to become the servants of words,
avoiding the hard work that is required for discovering unity of substance underlying variety of form.

which may be defined to consist of those external goods which a person uses in his trade, either holding them to be sold for money or applying them to produce things that are to be sold for money. Among its conspicuous elements are such things as the factory and the business plant of a manufacturer; that is, his machinery, his raw material, any food, clothing, and house-room that he may hold for the use of his employees, and the goodwill of his business.

Its most conspicuous elements.

To the things in his possession must be added those to which he has a right and from which he is drawing income: including loans which he has made on mortgage or in other ways, and all the command over capital which he may hold under the complex forms of the modern "money market." On the other hand debts owed by him must be deducted from his capital.

This definition of capital from the individual or business point of view is firmly established in ordinary usage; and it will be assumed throughout the present treatise whenever we are discussing problems relating to business in general, and in particular to the supply of any particular group of commodities for sale in open market. Income and capital will be discussed from the point of view of private business in the first half of the chapter; and afterwards the social point of view will be considered.

Net income.

§ 2. If a person is engaged in business, he is sure to have to incur certain outgoings for raw material, the hire of labour, etc. And, in that case, his true or *net income* is found by deducting from his gross income "the outgoings that belong to its production[1]."

Anything which a person does for which he is paid directly or indirectly in money, swells his nominal income; while no services that he performs for himself are commonly reckoned as adding to his nominal income. But, though it is best generally to neglect them when they are trivial, account should for consistency be taken of them, when they are of a kind which people commonly pay for having done for them. Thus a woman who makes her own clothes or a man who digs in his own garden or repairs his own house, is earning

[1] See a report of a Committee of the British Association, 1878, on the Income Tax.

income; just as would the dressmaker, gardener or carpenter II, IV, 2.
who might be hired to do the work.

In this connection we may introduce a term of which we *Pro-visional definition of net advantages.* shall have to make frequent use hereafter. The need for it arises from the fact that every occupation involves other disadvantages besides the fatigue of the work required in it, and every occupation offers other advantages besides the receipt of money wages. The true reward which an occupation offers to labour has to be calculated by deducting the money value of all its disadvantages from that of all its advantages; and we may describe this true reward as the *net advantages* of the occupation.

The payment made by a borrower for the use of a loan *Interest of capital.* for, say, a year is expressed as the ratio which that payment bears to the loan, and is called *interest*. And this term is also used more broadly to represent the money equivalent of the whole income which is derived from capital. It is commonly expressed as a certain percentage on the "capital" sum of the loan. Whenever this is done the capital must not be regarded as a stock of things in general. It must be regarded as a stock of one particular thing, money, which is taken to represent them. Thus £100 may be lent at four per cent., that is for an interest of £4 yearly. And, if a man employs in business a capital stock of goods of various kinds which are estimated as worth £10,000 in all; then £400 a year may be said to represent interest at the rate of four per cent. on that capital, on the supposition that the aggregate money value of the things which constitute it has remained unchanged. He would not, however, be willing to continue the business unless he expected his total net gains from it to exceed interest on his capital at the *Profits.* current rate. These gains are called *profits*.

The command over goods to a given money value, which *Free or floating capital.* can be applied to any purpose, is often described as "free" or "floating" capital[1].

---

[1] Professor Clark has made the suggestion to distinguish between *Pure Capital* and *Capital Goods*: the former is to correspond to a waterfall which remains stationary; while Capital Goods are the particular things which enter and leave the business, as particular drops pass through the waterfall. He would of course connect interest with pure capital, not with capital goods.

When a man is engaged in business, his profits for the year are the excess of his receipts from his business during the year over his outlay for his business. The difference between the value of his stock of plant, material, etc. at the end and at the beginning of the year is taken as part of his receipts or as part of his outlay, according as there has been an increase or decrease of value. What remains of his profits after deducting interest on his capital at the current rate (allowing, where necessary, for insurance) is generally called his *earnings of undertaking* or *management*. The ratio in which his profits for the year stand to his capital is spoken of as his *rate of profits*. But this phrase, like the corresponding phrase with regard to interest, assumes that the money value of the things which constitute his capital has been estimated: and such an estimate is often found to involve great difficulties.

When any particular thing, as a house, a piano, or a sewing machine is lent out, the payment for it is often called *Rent*. And economists may follow this practice without inconvenience when they are regarding the income from the point of view of the individual trader. But, as will be argued presently, the balance of advantage seems to lie in favour of reserving the term Rent for the income derived from the free gifts of nature, whenever the discussion of business affairs passes from the point of view of the individual to that of society at large. And for that reason, the term *Quasi-rent* will be used in the present volume for the income derived from machines and other appliances for production made by man. That is to say, any particular machine may yield an income which is of the nature of a rent, and which is sometimes called a Rent; though on the whole, there seems to be some advantage in calling it a Quasi-rent. But we cannot properly speak of the interest yielded by a machine. If we use the term "interest" at all, it must be in relation not to the machine itself, but to its money *value*. For instance if the work done by a machine which cost £100 is worth £4 a year net, that machine is yielding a quasi-rent of £4 which is equivalent to interest at four per cent. on its original cost: but if the machine is worth only £80 now, it

is yielding five per cent. on its present value. This however II, IV, 3,
raises some difficult questions of principle, which will be
discussed in Book V.

§ 3. Next to consider some details relating to capital.
It has been classed as Consumption capital, and Auxiliary or
Instrumental capital: and though no clear distinction can
be drawn between the two classes, it may sometimes be
convenient to use the terms, with the understanding that
they are vague. Where definiteness is necessary, the terms
should be avoided; and explicit enumerations should be
given. The general notion of the distinction which the
terms are designed to suggest, can be gathered from the
following approximate definitions.

Consumption capital consists of goods in a form to satisfy *Con-*
wants directly; that is, goods which afford a direct sus- *sumption capital.*
tenance to the workers, such as food, clothes, house-room, etc.

Auxiliary, or *instrumental, capital* is so called because it *Auxiliary*
consists of all the goods that aid labour in production. *or instru-*
Under this head come tools, machines, factories, railways, *mental capital.*
docks, ships, etc.; and raw materials of all kinds.

But of course a man's clothes assist him in his work and
are instrumental in keeping him warm; and he derives a
direct benefit from the shelter of his factory as he does from
the shelter of his house[1].

We may follow Mill in distinguishing *circulating capital* *Circu-*
"which fulfils the whole of its office in the production in *lating* and
which it is engaged, by a single use," from *fixed capital* *fixed capital.*
"which exists in a durable shape and the return to which is
spread over a period of corresponding duration[2]."

§ 4. The customary point of view of the business man *Transition*
is that which is most convenient for the economist to adopt *to the social*
when discussing the production of goods for a market, and *point of view of*
the causes which govern their exchange value. But there is *income.*
a broader point of view which the business man, no less than

---

[1] See above II. III. 1.

[2] Adam Smith's distinction between fixed and circulating capital turned on
the question whether the goods "yield a profit without changing masters" or not.
Ricardo made it turn on whether they are "of slow consumption or require to be
frequently reproduced"; but he truly remarks that this is "a division not essential,
and in which the line of demarcation cannot be accurately drawn." Mill's modification is generally accepted by modern economists.

the economist, must adopt when he studies the causes which govern the material wellbeing of the community as a whole. Ordinary conversation may pass from one point of view to another without any formal note of the change: for if a misunderstanding arises it soon becomes manifest; and confusion is cut short by a question or by a volunteered explanation. But the economist may take no risks of that sort: he must make prominent any change in his point of view or in his uses of terms. His path might have seemed smoother for the time, if he had passed silently from one use to another: but in the long run better progress is made by a clear indication of the meaning attached to each term in every doubtful case[1].

Let us then during the remainder of this chapter deliberately adopt the *social*, in contrast with the individual point of view: let us look at the production of the community as a whole, and at its total net income available for all purposes. That is, let us revert nearly to the point of view of a primitive people, who are chiefly concerned with the production of desirable things, and with their direct uses; and who are little concerned with exchange and marketing.

In practical matters theoretical completeness may be purchased at too great a cost. From this point of view income is regarded as including all the benefits which mankind derive at any time from their efforts, in the present and in the past, to turn nature's resources to their best account. The pleasure derived from the beauties of the rainbow, or the sweet taste of the fresh morning air, are left out of the reckoning, not because they are unimportant, nor because the estimate would in any way be vitiated by including them; but solely because reckoning them in would serve no good purpose, while it would add greatly to the length of our sentences and the prolixity of our discussions. For a similar reason it is not worth while to take separate account of the simple services which nearly every one renders to himself, such as putting on his clothes; though there are a few persons who choose to pay others to do such things for them. Their exclusion involves no principle; and time spent by some controversial writers on discussing it has been wasted. It simply follows the maxim *De minimis*

---

[1] Compare above II. i. 3.

non curat lex. A driver who, not noticing a pool in his way, splashes a passer by is not held to have done him legal injury; though there is no distinction in principle between his act and that of another, who by a similar lack of attention, did serious harm to someone else.

A man's present labour yields him income directly, when devoted to his own use; and he looks to be paid for it in some form or another if he devotes it as a matter of business to the service of others. Similarly any useful thing which he has made or acquired in the past, or which has been handed down to him, under the existing institutions of property, by others who have so made or acquired it, is generally a source of material benefit to him directly or indirectly. If he applies it in business, this income generally appears in the form of money. But a broader use of this term is occasionally needed, which embraces the whole income of benefits of every sort which a person derives from the ownership of property however applied: it includes for instance the benefits which he gets from the use of his own piano, equally with those which a piano dealer would win by letting out a piano on hire. The language of common life while averse to so broad a use of the term Income as this even when discussing social problems, yet habitually includes a certain number of forms of income, other than money income.

The Income Tax Commissioners count a dwelling-house inhabited by its owner as a source of taxable income, though it yields its income of comfort directly. They do this, not on any abstract principle; but partly because of the practical importance of house-room, partly because the ownership of a house is commonly treated in a business fashion, and partly because the real income accruing from it can easily be separated off and estimated. They do not claim to establish any absolute distinction in kind between the things which their rule includes, and those which it excludes.

Jevons, regarding the problem from a purely mathematical point of view, was justified in classing all commodities in the hands of consumers as capital. But some writers, while developing this suggestion with great ingenuity, have treated it as a great principle; and that appears to be an error in

ɪɪ, ɪ., 6. judgment. A true sense of proportion requires us not to
burden our work with the incessant enumeration of details
of secondary importance, of which no account is taken in
customary discourse, and which cannot even be described
without offending against popular conventions.

The corre-
lation of
income and
capital.
§ 5. This brings us to consider the use of the term
capital from the point of view of inquiries into the material
wellbeing of society as a whole. Adam Smith said that
a person's capital is *that part of his stock from which he
expects to derive an income*. And almost every use of the
term capital, which is known to history, has corresponded
more or less closely to a parallel use of the term Income:
in almost every use, capital has been that part of a man's
stock from which he expects to derive an income.

By far the most important use of the term Capital in
general, *i.e.* from the social point of view, is in the inquiry
how the three agents of production, land (that is, natural
agents), labour and capital, contribute to producing the
national income (or the national dividend, as it will be called
later on); and how that income is distributed among the
three agents. And this is an additional reason for making
the terms Capital and Income correlative from the social,
as we did from the individual point of view.

Meaning
in this
treatise of
the terms
Capital
and *Land*
from the
social point
of view.
Accordingly it is proposed in this treatise to count as
part of capital from the social point of view all things other
than land, which yield income that is generally reckoned as
such in common discourse; together with similar things in
public ownership, such as government factories: the term
Land being taken to include all free gifts of nature, such as
mines, fisheries, etc., which yield income.

Thus it will include all things held for trade purposes,
whether machinery, raw material or finished goods; theatres
and hotels; home farms and houses: but not furniture or
clothes owned by those who use them. For the former are
and the latter are not commonly regarded as yielding income
by the world at large, as is shown by the practice of the
income tax commissioners.

This usage of the term is in harmony with the common
practice of economists of treating social problems in broad

outline to start with, and reserving minor details for later II, IV, 6. consideration: it is in harmony also with their common practice of taking Labour to include those activities, and those only, which are regarded as the source of income in this broader use of the term. Labour together with capital and land thus defined are the sources of all that income of which account is commonly taken in reckoning up the National Income[1].

§ 6. Social income may be estimated by adding together Elements of social income in danger of being counted twice or of being omitted. the incomes of the individuals in the society in question, whether it be a nation or any other group of persons. We must however not count the same thing twice. If we have counted a carpet at its full value, we have already counted the values of the yarn and the labour that were used in making it; and these must not be counted again. And further, if the carpet was made of wool that was in stock at the beginning of the year, the value of that wool must be deducted from the value of the carpet before the net income of the year is reached; while similar deduction must be made for the wear and tear of machinery and other plant used in making it. This is required by the general rule, with which we started, that true or net income is found by deducting from gross income the outgoings that belong to its production.

But if the carpet is cleaned by domestic servants or at steam scouring works, the value of the labour spent in cleaning it must be counted in separately; for otherwise the results of this labour would be altogether omitted from the inventory of those newly-produced commodities and conveniences which constitute the real income of the country. The work of domestic servants is always classed as "labour" in the technical sense; and since it can be assessed *en bloc* at the value of their remuneration in money and in kind without being enumerated in detail, its inclusion raises no great

---

[1] Just as for practical purposes it is better not to encumber ourselves with specifying the "income" of benefit which a man derives from the labour of brushing his hat in the morning, so it is better to ignore the element of capital vested in his brush. But no such consideration arises in a merely abstract discussion: and therefore the logical simplicity of Jevons' dictum that commodities in the hands of consumers are capital has some advantages and no disadvantages for mathematical versions of economic doctrines.

II, IV, 7. statistical difficulty. There is however some inconsistency in omitting the heavy domestic work which is done by women and other members of the household, where no servants are kept.

Again, suppose a landowner with an annual income of £10,000 hires a private secretary at a salary of £500, who hires a servant at wages of £50. It may seem that if the incomes of all these three persons are counted in as part of the net income of the country, some of it will be counted twice over, and some three times. But this is not the case. The landlord transfers to his secretary, in return for his assistance, part of the purchasing power derived from the produce of land; and the secretary again transfers part of this to his servant in return for his assistance. The farm produce the value of which goes as rent to the landlord, the assistance which the landlord derives from the work of the secretary, and that which the secretary derives from the work of the servant are independent parts of the real net income of the country; and therefore the £10,000 and the £500 and the £50 which are their money measures, must all be counted in when we are estimating the income of the country. But if the landlord makes an allowance of £500 a year to his son, that must not be counted as an independent income; because no services are rendered for it. And it would not be assessed to the Income tax.

As the *net* payments on account of interest etc. due to an individual—*net, i.e.* after deducting those due from him to others—are part of his income, so the money and other things received *net* by a nation from other countries are part of its income.

§ 7. The money income, or inflow, of wealth gives a measure of a nation's prosperity, which, untrustworthy as it is, is yet in some respects better than that afforded by the money value of its stock of wealth.

For income consists chiefly of commodities in a form to give pleasure directly; while the greater part of national wealth consists of the means of production, which are of service to the nation only in so far as they contribute to producing commodities ready for consumption. And further, though this is a minor point, consumable commodities, being

National income is a better measure of general economic prosperity than national wealth.

more portable, have more nearly uniform prices all the world II, IV, 8. over than the things used in producing them: the prices of an acre of good land in Manitoba and Kent differ more than those of a bushel of wheat in the two places.

But if we look chiefly at the income of a country we must allow for the depreciation of the sources from which it is derived. More must be deducted from the income derived from a house if it is made of wood, than if it is made of stone; a stone house counts for more towards the real richness of a country than a wooden house which gives equally good accommodation. Again, a mine may yield for a time a large income, but be exhausted in a few years: in that case, it must be counted as equivalent to a field, or a fishery, which yields a much smaller annual income, but will yield that income permanently.

§ 8. In purely abstract, and especially in mathematical, reasoning the terms Capital and Wealth are used as synonymous almost perforce, except that "land" proper may for some purposes be omitted from Capital. But there is a clear tradition that we should speak of Capital when considering things as agents of production; and that we should speak of Wealth when considering them as results of production, as subjects of consumption and as yielding pleasures of possession. Thus the chief *demand* for capital arises from its productiveness, from the services which it renders, for instance, in enabling wool to be spun and woven more easily than by the unaided hand, or in causing water to flow freely wherever it is wanted instead of being carried laboriously in pails; (though there are other uses of capital, as for instance when it is lent to a spendthrift, which cannot easily be brought under this head). On the other hand the *supply* of capital is controlled by the fact that, in order to accumulate it, men must act prospectively: they must "wait" and "save," they must sacrifice the present to the future.

At the beginning of this Book it was argued that the economist must forego the aid of a complete set of technical terms. He must make the terms in common use serve his purpose in the expression of precise thought, by the aid of qualifying adjectives or other indications in the context. If

Prospectiveness and productiveness control the demand for capital and the supply of it.

he arbitrarily assigns a rigid exact use to a word which has several more or less vague uses in the market place, he confuses business men, and he is in some danger of committing himself to untenable positions. The selection of a normal use for such terms as Income and Capital must therefore be tested by actually working with it[1].

[1] A short forecast of some of this work may be given here. It will be seen how Capital needs to be considered in regard *both* to the embodied aggregate of the benefits derivable from its use, *and* to the embodied aggregate of the costs of the efforts and of the saving needed for its production; and it will be shown how these two aggregates tend to balance. Thus in V. IV., which may be taken as in some sense a continuation of the present chapter, they will be seen balancing directly in the forecasts of an individual Robinson Crusoe; and—for the greater part at least—in terms of money in the forecasts of a modern business man. In either case both sides of the account must be referred to the same date of time; those that come after that date being "discounted" back to it; and those that come before being "accumulated" up to it.

A similar balancing in regard to the benefits and the costs of capital at large will be found to be a chief corner stone of social economy: although it is true that in consequence of the unequal distribution of wealth, accounts cannot be made up from the social point of view with that clearness of outline that is attainable in the case of an individual whether a Robinson Crusoe, or a modern business man.

In every part of our discussion of the causes that govern the accumulation and the application of productive resources, it will appear that there is no universal rule that the use of roundabout methods of production is more efficient than direct methods; that there are some conditions under which the investment of effort in obtaining machinery and in making costly provision against future wants is economical in the long run, and others in which it is not: and that capital is accumulated in proportion to the prospectiveness of man on the one hand, and on the other to the absorption of capital by those roundabout methods, which are sufficiently productive to remunerate their adoption. . . .

BOOK III.

ON WANTS AND THEIR SATISFACTION.

CHAPTER I.

INTRODUCTORY.

§ I. The older definitions of economics described it as the science which is concerned with the production, the distribution, the exchange, and the consumption of wealth. Later experience has shown that the problems of distribution and exchange are so closely connected, that it is doubtful whether anything is to be gained by the attempt to keep them separate. There is however a good deal of general reasoning with regard to the relation of demand and supply which is required as a basis for the practical problems of value, and which acts as an underlying backbone, giving unity and consistency to the main body of economic reasoning. Its very breadth and generality mark it off from the more concrete problems of distribution and exchange to which it is subservient; and therefore it is put together in Book V. on "The General Theory of Demand and Supply" which prepares the way for "Distribution and Exchange, or Value."

But first comes the present Book III., a study of Wants and their satisfaction, *i.e.* of demand and consumption. . . .

Several causes are bringing into prominence the study of consumption.

The first cause.

The second cause.

§ 2. Until recently the subject of demand or consumption has been somewhat neglected. For important as is the inquiry how to turn our resources to the best account, it is not one which lends itself, so far as the expenditure of private individuals is concerned, to the methods of economics. The common sense of a person who has had a large experience of life will give him more guidance in such a matter than he can gain from subtle economic analyses; and until recently economists said little on the subject, because they really had not much to say that was not the common property of all sensible people. But recently several causes have combined to give the subject a greater prominence in economic discussions.

The first of these is the growing belief that harm was done by Ricardo's habit of laying disproportionate stress on the side of cost of production, when analysing the causes that determine exchange value. For although he and his chief followers were aware that the conditions of demand played as important a part as those of supply in determining value, yet they did not express their meaning with sufficient clearness, and they have been misunderstood by all but the most careful readers.

Secondly, the growth of exact habits of thought in economics is making people more careful to state distinctly the premises on which they reason. This increased care is partly due to the application by some writers of mathematical language and mathematical habits of thought. It is indeed doubtful whether much has been gained by the use of complex mathematical formulæ. But the application of mathematical habits of thought has been of great service; for it has led people to refuse to consider a problem until they are quite sure what the problem is; and to insist on knowing what is, and what is not intended to be assumed before proceeding further.

This has in its turn compelled a more careful analysis of all the leading conceptions of economics, and especially of demand; for the mere attempt to state clearly how the demand for a thing is to be measured opens up new aspects of the main problems of economics. And though the theory of demand is yet in its infancy, we can already see that it may be possible to collect and arrange statistics of consumption in such a way as to throw light on difficult questions of great importance to public wellbeing. III, I, 2.

Lastly, the spirit of the age induces a closer attention to the question whether our increasing wealth may not be made to go further than it does in promoting the general wellbeing; and this again compels us to examine how far the exchange value of any element of wealth, whether in collective or individual use, represents accurately the addition which it makes to happiness and wellbeing. *The third cause.*

We will begin this Book with a short study of the variety of human wants, considered in their relation to human efforts and activities. For the progressive nature of man is one whole. It is only temporarily and provisionally that we can with profit isolate for study the economic side of his life; and we ought to be careful to take together in one view the whole of that side. There is a special need to insist on this just now, because the reaction against the comparative neglect of the study of wants by Ricardo and his followers shows signs of being carried to the opposite extreme. It is important still to assert the great truth on which they dwelt somewhat too exclusively; viz. that while wants are the rulers of life among the lower animals, it is to changes in the forms of efforts and activities that we must turn when in search for the keynotes of the history of mankind. *We will begin with a study of wants in relation to efforts*

CHAPTER II.

WANTS IN RELATION TO ACTIVITIES.

The wants of the savage are few;

§ 1. HUMAN wants and desires are countless in number and very various in kind: but they are generally limited and capable of being satisfied. The uncivilized man indeed has not many more than the brute animal; but every step in his progress upwards increases the variety of his needs together with the variety in his methods of satisfying them. He desires not merely larger *quantities* of the things he has been accustomed to consume, but better qualities of those things; he desires a greater choice of things, and things that will satisfy new wants growing up in him.

but civilization brings with it a desire for variety for its own sake.

Thus though the brute and the savage alike have their preferences for choice morsels, neither of them cares much for variety for its own sake. As, however, man rises in civilization, as his mind becomes developed, and even his animal passions begin to associate themselves with mental activities, his wants become rapidly more subtle and more various; and in the minor details of life he begins to desire change for the sake of change, long before he has consciously escaped from the yoke of custom. The first great step in this direction comes with the art of making a fire: gradually he gets to accustom himself to many different kinds of food and drink cooked in many different ways; and before long monotony begins to become irksome to him, and he finds it a great hardship when accident compels him to live for a long time exclusively on one or two kinds of food.

As a man's riches increase, his food and drink become III, II, 2.
more various and costly; but his appetite is limited by Man's
nature, and when his expenditure on food is extravagant it capacity
is more often to gratify the desires of hospitality and display is limited,
than to indulge his own senses.

This brings us to remark with Senior that "Strong as is but not his
the desire for variety, it is weak compared with the desire distinc-
for distinction: a feeling which if we consider its universality, tion;
and its constancy, that it affects all men and at all times,
that it comes with us from the cradle and never leaves us
till we go into the grave, may be pronounced to be the most
powerful of human passions." This great half-truth is well
illustrated by a comparison of the desire for choice and
various food with that for choice and various dress.

§ 2. That need for dress which is the result of natural which is
causes varies with the climate and the season of year, and a source of
little with the nature of a person's occupations. But in dress for costly
conventional wants overshadow those which are natural. dress.
Thus in many of the earlier stages of civilization the
sumptuary mandates of Law and Custom have rigidly
prescribed to the members of each caste or industrial grade,
the style and the standard of expense up to which their dress
must reach and beyond which they may not go; and part of
the substance of these mandates remains now, though subject
to rapid change. In Scotland, for instance, in Adam Smith's
time many persons were allowed by custom to go abroad
without shoes and stockings who may not do so now; and
many may still do it in Scotland who might not in England.
Again, in England now a well-to-do labourer is expected to
appear on Sunday in a black coat and, in some places, in a
silk hat; though these would have subjected him to ridicule
but a short time ago. There is a constant increase both in
that variety and expensiveness which custom requires as
a minimum, and in that which it tolerates as a maximum;
and the efforts to obtain distinction by dress are extending themselves throughout the lower grades of English
society.

But in the upper grades, though the dress of women is
still various and costly, that of men is simple and inexpensive

III, II, 3, 4. as compared with what it was in Europe not long ago, and is to-day in the East. For those men who are most truly distinguished on their own account, have a natural dislike to seem to claim attention by their dress; and they have set the fashion[1].

House room.

§ 3. House room satisfies the imperative need for shelter from the weather: but that need plays very little part in the effective demand for house room. For though a small but well-built cabin gives excellent shelter, its stifling atmosphere, its necessary uncleanliness, and its want of the decencies and the quiet of life are great evils. It is not so much that they cause physical discomfort as that they tend to stunt the faculties, and limit people's higher activities. With every increase in these activities the demand for larger house room becomes more urgent[2].

And therefore relatively large and well-appointed house room is, even in the lowest social ranks, at once a "necessary for efficiency[3]," and the most convenient and obvious way of advancing a material claim to social distinction. And even in those grades in which everyone has house room sufficient for the higher activities of himself and his family, a yet further and almost unlimited increase is desired as a requisite for the exercise of many of the higher social activities.

Wants resulting from activities.

§ 4. It is, again, the desire for the exercise and development of activities, spreading through every rank of society, which leads not only to the pursuit of science, literature and

---

[1] A woman may display wealth, but she may not display only her wealth, by her dress; or else she defeats her ends. She must also suggest some distinction of character as well as of wealth; for though her dress may owe more to her dressmaker than to herself, yet there is a traditional assumption that, being less busy than man with external affairs, she can give more time to taking thought as to her dress. Even under the sway of modern fashions, to be "well dressed"—not "expensively dressed"—is a reasonable minor aim for those who desire to be distinguished for their faculties and abilities; and this will be still more the case if the evil dominion of the wanton vagaries of fashion should pass away. For to arrange costumes beautiful in themselves, various and well-adapted to their purposes, is an object worthy of high endeavour; it belongs to the same class, though not to the same rank in that class, as the painting of a good picture.

[2] It is true that many active-minded working men prefer cramped lodgings in a town to a roomy cottage in the country; but that is because they have a strong taste for those activities for which a country life offers little scope.

[3] See Book II. ch. III. § 3.

art for their own sake, but to the rapidly increasing III, II, 4.
demand for the work of those who pursue them as pro-
fessions. Leisure is used less and less as an opportunity
for mere stagnation; and there is a growing desire for
those amusements, such as athletic games and travelling,
which develop activities rather than indulge any sensuous
craving[1].

For indeed the desire for excellence for its own sake, is Gradations
almost as wide in its range as the lower desire for distinction. of the
Just as the desire for distinction graduates down from the excellence.
ambition of those who may hope that their names will be in
men's mouths in distant lands and in distant times, to the
hope of the country lass that the new ribbon she puts on for
Easter may not pass unnoticed by her neighbours; so the
desire for excellence for its own sake graduates down from
that of a Newton, or a Stradivarius, to that of the fisherman
who, even when no one is looking and he is not in a hurry,
delights in handling his craft well, and in the fact that she is
well built and responds promptly to his guidance. Desires
of this kind exert a great influence on the supply of the
highest faculties and the greatest inventions; and they are
not unimportant on the side of demand. For a large part of
the demand for the most highly skilled professional services
and the best work of the mechanical artisan, arises from the
delight that people have in the training of their own faculties,
and in exercising them by aid of the most delicately adjusted
and responsive implements.

Speaking broadly therefore, although it is man's wants In a
in the earliest stages of his development that give rise to healthy
his activities, yet afterwards each new step upwards is to be activities
regarded as the development of new activities giving rise to the way
new wants, rather than of new wants giving rise to new wants.
activities.

We see this clearly if we look away from healthy conditions of life, where new activities are constantly being

---

[1] As a minor point it may be noticed that those drinks which stimulate the
mental activities are largely displacing those which merely gratify the senses.
The consumption of tea is increasing very fast, while that of alcohol is stationary;
and there is in all ranks of society a diminishing demand for the grosser and more
immediately stupefying forms of alcohol.

III, ii, 4. developed; and watch the West Indian negro, using his new freedom and wealth not to get the means of satisfying new wants, but in idle stagnation that is not rest; or again look at that rapidly lessening part of the English working classes, who have no ambition and no pride or delight in the growth of their faculties and activities, and spend on drink whatever surplus their wages afford over the bare necessaries of a squalid life.

The theory of wants can claim no supremacy over the theory of efforts.

It is not true therefore that "the Theory of Consumption is the scientific basis of economics[1]." For much that is of chief interest in the science of wants, is borrowed from the science of efforts and activities. These two supplement one another; either is incomplete without the other. But if either, more than the other, may claim to be the interpreter of the history of man, whether on the economic side or any other, it is the science of activities and not that of wants; and McCulloch indicated their true relations when, discussing "the progressive nature of man[2]," he said:—"The gratification of a want or a desire is merely a step to some new pursuit. In every stage of his progress he is destined to contrive and invent, to engage in new undertakings; and when these are accomplished to enter with fresh energy upon others."

From this it follows that such a discussion of demand as is possible at this stage of our work, must be confined to an elementary analysis of an almost purely formal kind. The higher study of consumption must come after, and not before, the main body of economic analysis; and, though it may have its beginning within the proper domain of

---

[1] This doctrine is laid down by Banfield, and adopted by Jevons as the key of his position. It is unfortunate that here as elsewhere Jevons' .delight in stating his case strongly has led him to a conclusion, which not only is inaccurate, but does mischief by implying that the older economists were more at fault than they really were. Banfield says "the first proposition of the theory of consumption is that the satisfaction of every lower want in the scale creates a desire of a higher character." And if this were true, the above doctrine, which he bases on it, would be true also. But, as Jevons points out (*Theory*, 2nd Ed. p. 59), it is not true: and he substitutes for it the statement that the satisfaction of a lower want permits a higher want to manifest itself. That is a true and indeed an identical proposition: but it affords no support to the claims of the Theory of Consumption to supremacy.

[2] *Political Economy*, ch. II.

economics, it cannot find its conclusion there, but must III, II, 4.
extend far beyond[1].

[1] The formal classification of Wants is a task not without interest; but it is
not needed for our purposes. The basis of most modern work in this direction
is to be found in Hermann's *Staatswirthschaftliche Untersuchungen*, Ch. II., where
wants are classified as "absolute and relative, higher and lower, urgent and capable
of postponement, positive and negative, direct and indirect, general and particular,
constant and interrupted, permanent and temporary, ordinary and extraordinary,
present and future, individual and collective, private and public."

Some analysis of wants and desires is to be found in the great majority of
French and other Continental treatises on economics even of the last generation;
but the rigid boundary which English writers have ascribed to their science
has excluded such discussions. And it is a characteristic fact that there is no
allusion to them in Bentham's *Manual of Political Economy*, although his profound
analysis of them in the *Principles of Morals and Legislation* and in the *Table of
the Springs of Human Action* has exercised a wide-spread influence. Hermann
had studied Bentham; and on the other hand Banfield, whose lectures were
perhaps the first ever given in an English University that owed much directly to
German economic thought, acknowledges special obligations to Hermann. In
England the way was prepared for Jevons' excellent work on the theory
of wants, by Bentham himself; by Senior, whose short remarks on the subject
are pregnant with far-reaching hints; by Banfield, and by the Australian Hearn.
Hearn's *Plutology or Theory of the Efforts to satisfy Human Wants* is at once
simple and profound: it affords an admirable example of the way in which
detailed analysis may be applied to afford a training of a very high order for the
young, and to give them an intelligent acquaintance with the economic conditions
of life, without forcing upon them any particular solution of those more difficult
problems on which they are not yet able to form an independent judgment. At
about the same time as Jevons' *Theory* appeared, Carl Menger gave a great impetus
to the subtle and interesting studies of wants and utilities by the Austrian school of
economists: they had already been initiated by von Thünen, as is indicated in the
Preface to this Volume.

CHAPTER III.

GRADATIONS OF CONSUMERS' DEMAND.

The consumers' demand governs traders' demand.

§ 1. WHEN a trader or a manufacturer buys anything to be used in production, or be sold again, his demand is based on his anticipations of the profits which he can derive from it. These profits depend at any time on speculative risks and on other causes, which will need to be considered later on. But in the long run the price which a trader or manufacturer can afford to pay for a thing depends on the prices which consumers will pay for it, or for the things made by aid of it. The ultimate regulator of all demand is therefore consumers' demand. And it is with that almost exclusively that we shall be concerned in the present Book.

Utility and Want are used as correlative terms, having no ethical or prudential connotations.

Utility is taken to be correlative to Desire or Want. It has been already argued that desires cannot be measured directly, but only indirectly by the outward phenomena to which they give rise: and that in those cases with which economics is chiefly concerned the measure is found in the price which a person is willing to pay for the fulfilment or satisfaction of his desire. He may have desires and aspirations which are not consciously set for any satisfaction: but for the present we are concerned chiefly with those which do so aim; and we assume that the resulting satisfaction corresponds in general fairly well to that which was anticipated when the purchase was made[1].

---

[1] It cannot be too much insisted that to measure directly, or *per se*, either desires or the satisfaction which results from their fulfilment is impossible, if not inconceivable. If we could, we should have two accounts to make up, one of desires, and the other of realized satisfactions. And the two might differ considerably. For, to say nothing of higher aspirations, some of those desires with which economics is chiefly concerned, and especially those connected with emulation, are impulsive; many result from the force of habit; some are morbid and

There is an endless variety of wants, but there is a limit to each separate want. This familiar and fundamental tendency of human nature may be stated in the *law of satiable wants* or *of diminishing utility* thus:—The *total utility* of a thing to anyone (that is, the total pleasure or other benefit it yields him) increases with every increase in his stock of it, but not as fast as his stock increases. If his stock of it increases at a uniform rate the benefit derived from it increases at a diminishing rate. In other words, the additional benefit which a person derives from a given increase of his stock of a thing, diminishes with every increase in the stock that he already has.

That part of the thing which he is only just induced to purchase may be called his *marginal purchase,* because he is on the margin of doubt whether it is worth his while to incur the outlay required to obtain it. And the utility of his marginal purchase may be called the *marginal utility* of the thing to him. Or, if instead of buying it, he makes the thing himself, then its marginal utility is the utility of that part which he thinks it only just worth his while to make. And thus the law just given may be worded: —

The marginal utility of a thing to anyone diminishes with every increase in the amount of it he already has.

Margin notes: III, III, 1. The law of satiable wants or diminishing utility. Total utility. Marginal purchase. Marginal utility.

lead only to hurt; and many are based on expectations that are never fulfilled. (See above I. II. 3, 4.) Of course many satisfactions are not common pleasures, but belong to the development of a man's higher nature, or to use a good old word, to his *beatification*; and some may even partly result from self-abnegation. (See I. II. 1.) The two direct measurements then might differ. But as neither of them is possible, we fall back on the measurement which economics supplies, of the motive or moving force to action: and we make it serve, with all its faults, *both* for the desires which prompt activities and for the satisfactions that result from them. (Compare "Some remarks on Utility" by Prof. Pigou in the *Economic Journal* for March, 1903.)

III, III, 2.

It is implied that the consumer's character is unchanged.

There is however an implicit condition in this law which should be made clear. It is that we do not suppose time to be allowed for any alteration in the character or tastes of the man himself. It is therefore no exception to the law that the more good music a man hears, the stronger is his taste for it likely to become; that avarice and ambition are often insatiable; or that the virtue of cleanliness and the vice of drunkenness alike grow on what they feed upon. For in such cases our observations range over some period of time; and the man is not the same at the beginning as at the end of it. If we take a man as he is, without allowing time for any change in his character, the marginal utility of a thing to him diminishes steadily with every increase in his supply of it[1].

Translation of the law into terms of price.

§ 2. Now let us translate this law of diminishing utility into terms of price. Let us take an illustration from the case of a commodity such as tea, which is in constant demand and which can be purchased in small quantities. Suppose, for instance, that tea of a certain quality is to be had at 2s. per lb. A person might be willing to give 10s. for a single pound once a year rather than go without it altogether; while if he could have any amount of it for nothing he would perhaps not care to use more than 30 lbs. in the year. But as it is, he buys perhaps 10 lbs. in the year; that is to say, the difference between the satisfaction which he gets from buying 9 lbs. and 10 lbs. is enough for him to be willing to pay 2s. for it: while the fact that he does not buy an eleventh pound, shows that he does not think that it would

---

[1] It may be noticed here, though the fact is of but little practical importance, that a small quantity of a commodity may be insufficient to meet a certain special want; and then there will be a more than proportionate increase of pleasure when the consumer gets enough of it to enable him to attain the desired end. Thus, for instance, anyone would derive less pleasure in proportion from ten pieces of wall paper than from twelve, if the latter would, and the former would not, cover the whole of the walls of his room. Or again a very short concert or a holiday may fail of its purpose of soothing and recreating: and one of double length might be of more than double total utility. This case corresponds to the fact, which we shall have to study in connection with the tendency to diminishing return, that the capital and labour already applied to any piece of land may be so inadequate for the development of its full powers, that some further expenditure on it even with the existing arts of agriculture would give a more than proportionate return; and in the fact that an improvement in the arts of agriculture may resist that tendency, we shall find an analogy to the condition just mentioned in the text as implied in the law of diminishing utility.

be worth an extra 2*s.* to him. That is, 2*s.* a pound measures III, III, 3.
the utility to him of the tea which lies at the margin or
terminus or end of his purchases; it measures the marginal
utility to him. If the price which he is just willing to pay *Marginal*
for any pound be called his *demand price*, then 2*s.* is his *demand price.*
marginal demand price. And our law may be worded:—

The larger the amount of a thing that a person has the
less, other things being equal (*i.e.* the purchasing power of
money, and the amount of money at his command being
equal), will be the price which he will pay for a little more
of it: or in other words his marginal demand price for it
diminishes.

His demand becomes *efficient*, only when the price which
he is willing to offer reaches that at which others are willing
to sell.

This last sentence reminds us that we have as yet taken
no account of changes in the marginal utility of money, or
general purchasing power. At one and the same time, a
person's material resources being unchanged, the marginal
utility of money to him is a fixed quantity, so that the
prices he is just willing to pay for two commodities are to
one another in the same ratio as the utility of those two
commodities.

§ 3. A greater utility will be required to induce him to The
buy a thing if he is poor than if he is rich. We have seen *marginal utility of*
how the clerk with £100 a year will walk to business in a *money is greater for*
heavier rain than the clerk with £300 a year[1]. But although *the poor than the*
the utility, or the benefit, that is measured in the poorer *rich.*
man's mind by twopence is greater than that measured by it
in the richer man's mind; yet if the richer man rides a
hundred times in the year and the poorer man twenty times,
then the utility of the hundredth ride which the richer man
is only just induced to take is measured to him by twopence;
and the utility of the twentieth ride which the poorer man is
only just induced to take is measured to him by twopence.
For each of them the marginal utility is measured by twopence; but this marginal utility is greater in the case of the
poorer man than in that of the richer.

[1] See I. II. 2.

III, III, 4.

In other words, the richer a man becomes the less is the marginal utility of money to him; every increase in his resources increases the price which he is willing to pay for any given benefit. And in the same way every diminution of his resources increases the marginal utility of money to him, and diminishes the price that he is willing to pay for any benefit.

A more definite expression for the demand of an individual.

§ 4. To obtain complete knowledge of demand for anything, we should have to ascertain how much of it he would be willing to purchase at each of the prices at which it is likely to be offered; and the circumstance of his demand for, say, tea can be best expressed by a list of the prices which he is willing to pay; that is, by his several demand prices for different amounts of it. (This list may be called his *demand schedule*.)

Thus for instance we may find that he would buy

6 lbs. at 50d. per lb.	10 lbs. at 24d. per lb.
7 " 40 "	11 " 21 "
8 " 33 "	12 " 19 "
9 " 28 "	13 " 17 "

If corresponding prices were filled in for all intermediate amounts we should have an exact statement of his demand[1]. We cannot express a person's demand for a thing

[1] Such a demand schedule may be translated, on a plan now coming into familiar use, into a curve that may be called his *demand curve*. Let Ox and Oy be drawn the one horizontally, the other vertically. Let an inch measured along Ox represent 10 lbs. of tea, and an inch measured along Oy represent 40d.

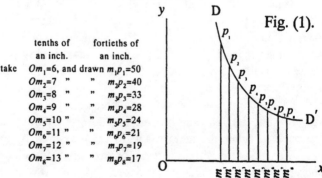

take

$Om_1 = 6$, and drawn $m_1p_1 = 50$
$Om_2 = 7$ " " $m_2p_2 = 40$
$Om_3 = 8$ " " $m_3p_3 = 33$
$Om_4 = 9$ " " $m_4p_4 = 28$
$Om_5 = 10$ " " $m_5p_5 = 24$
$Om_6 = 11$ " " $m_6p_6 = 21$
$Om_7 = 12$ " " $m_7p_7 = 19$
$Om_8 = 13$ " " $m_8p_8 = 17$

Fig. (1).

m_1 being on Ox m_1p_1 being drawn vertically from m_1; and so for the others.

by the "amount he is willing to buy," or by the "intensity of his eagerness to buy a certain amount," without reference to the prices at which he would buy that amount and other amounts. We can represent it exactly only by lists of the prices at which he is willing to buy different amounts[1].

When we say that a person's demand for anything increases, we mean that he will buy more of it than he would before at the same price, and that he will buy as much of it as before at a higher price. A general increase in his demand is an increase throughout the whole list of prices at which he is willing to purchase different amounts of it, and not merely that he is willing to buy more of it at the current prices[2].

III, III, 4.

The meaning of the term *increase of demand*.

Then $p_1 p_2 \ldots p_8$ are points on his demand curve for tea; or as we may say *demand points*. If we could find demand points in the same manner for every possible quantity of tea, we should get the whole continuous curve DD' as shown in the figure. This account of the demand schedule and curve is provisional; several difficulties connected with it are deferred to chapter v.

[1] Thus Mill says that we must "mean by the word demand, the quantity demanded, and remember that this is not a fixed quantity, but in general varies according to the value." (*Principles*, III. II. 4.) This account is scientific in substance; but it is not clearly expressed and it has been much misunderstood. Cairnes prefers to represent "demand as the desire for commodities and services, seeking its end by an offer of general purchasing power, and supply as the desire for general purchasing power, seeking its end by an offer of specific commodities or services." He does this in order that he may be able to speak of a ratio, or equality, of demand and supply. But the quantities of two desires on the part of two different persons cannot be compared directly; their measures may be compared, but not they themselves. And in fact Cairnes is himself driven to speak of supply as "limited by the quantity of specific commodities offered for sale, and demand by the quantity of purchasing power offered for their purchase." But sellers have not a fixed quantity of commodities which they offer for sale unconditionally at whatever price they can get: buyers have not a fixed quantity of purchasing power which they are ready to spend on the specific commodities, however much they pay for them. Account must then be taken in either case of the relation between quantity and price, in order to complete Cairnes' account, and when this is done it is brought back to the lines followed by Mill. He says, indeed, that "Demand, as defined by Mill, is to be understood as measured, not, as my definition would require, by the quantity of purchasing power offered in support of the desire for commodities, but by the quantity of commodities for which such purchasing power is offered." It is true that there is a great difference between the statements, "I will buy twelve eggs," and "I will buy a shilling's worth of eggs." But there is no substantive difference between the statement, "I will buy twelve eggs at a penny each, but only six at three halfpence each," and the statement, "I will spend a shilling on eggs at a penny each, but if they cost three halfpence each I will spend ninepence on them." But while Cairnes' account when completed becomes substantially the same as Mill's, its present form is even more misleading. (See an article by the present writer on *Mill's Theory of Value* in the *Fortnightly Review* for April, 1876.)

[2] We may sometimes find it convenient to speak of this as *a raising of his*

III, III, 5.

Transition to the demand of a group of persons, or market.

The demand on the part of any individual for some things is discontinuous.

§ 5. So far we have looked at the demand of a single individual. And in the particular case of such a thing as tea, the demand of a single person is fairly representative of the general demand of a whole market: for the demand for tea is a constant one; and, since it can be purchased in small quantities, every variation in its price is likely to affect the amount which he will buy. But even among those things which are in constant use, there are many for which the demand on the part of any single individual cannot vary continuously with every small change in price, but can move only by great leaps.. For instance, a small fall in the price of hats or watches will not affect the action of every one; but it will induce a few persons, who were in doubt whether or not to get a new hat or a new watch, to decide in favour of doing so.

There are many classes of things the need for which on the part of any individual is inconstant, fitful, and irregular. There can be no list of individual demand prices for wedding-cakes, or the services of an expert surgeon. But the economist has little concern with particular incidents in the lives of individuals. He studies rather "the course of action that may be expected under certain conditions from the members of an industrial group," in so far as the motives of that action are measurable by a money price; and in these broad results the variety and the fickleness of individual action are merged in the comparatively regular aggregate of the action of many.

But the aggregate demand of many persons shows a fall of demand price for every increase in quantity.

In large markets, then—where rich and poor, old and young, men and women, persons of all varieties of tastes, temperaments and occupations are mingled together,—the peculiarities in the wants of individuals will compensate one another in a comparatively regular gradation of total demand. Every fall, however slight in the price of a commodity in general use, will, other things being equal, increase the total sales of it; just as an unhealthy autumn increases the mortality of a large town, though many persons are

---

demand schedule. Geometrically it is represented by raising his demand curve, or, what comes to the same thing, moving it to the right, with perhaps some modification of its shape.

uninjured by it. And therefore if we had the requisite III, III, 5.
knowledge, we could make a list of prices at which each
amount of it could find purchasers in a given place during,
say, a year.

The total demand. in the place for, say, tea, is the sum
of the demands of all the individuals there. Some will be
richer and some poorer than the individual consumer whose
demand we have just written down; some will have a
greater and others a smaller liking for tea than he has.
Let us suppose that there are in the place a million purchasers of tea, and that their average consumption is equal
to his at each several price. Then the demand of that place
is represented by the same list of prices as before, if we write
a million pounds of tea instead of one pound[1].

There is then one general *law of demand*:—The greater The
the amount to be sold, the smaller must be the price at *demand.*
which it is offered in order that it may find purchasers; or,
in other words, the amount demanded increases with a fall
in price, and diminishes with a rise in price. There will not
be any uniform relation between the fall in price and the
increase of demand. A fall of one-tenth in the price may
increase the sales by a twentieth or by a quarter, or it may
double them. But as the numbers in the left-hand column
of the demand schedule increase, those in the right-hand
column will always diminish[2].

---

[1] The demand is represented by the same curve as before, only an inch
measured along Ox now represents ten million pounds instead of ten pounds. And
a formal definition of the demand curve for a
market may be given thus:—The demand curve for
any commodity in a market during any given unit of
time is the locus of demand points for it. That is to
say, it is a curve such that if from any point P on it,
a straight line PM be drawn perpendicular to Ox,
PM represents the price at which purchasers will be
forthcoming for an amount of the commodity represented by OM.

[2] That is, if a point moves along the curve away
from Oy it will constantly approach Ox. Therefore
if a straight line PT be drawn touching the curve at P and meeting Ox in T, the
angle PTx is an obtuse angle. It will be found convenient to have a short way of
expressing this fact; which may be done by saying that PT is *inclined negatively*.
Thus the one universal rule to which the demand curve conforms is that it is
inclined negatively throughout the whole of its length.

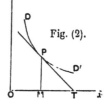

Fig. (2).

III, III, 6.

The price will measure the marginal utility of the commodity to each purchaser individually: we cannot speak of price as measuring marginal utility in general, because the wants and circumstances of different people are different.

The influence on demand of the growth of a rival commodity.

§ 6. The demand prices in our list are those at which various quantities of a thing can be sold in a market *during a given time and under given conditions*. If the conditions vary in any respect the prices will probably require to be changed; and this has constantly to be done when the desire for anything is materially altered by a variation of custom, or by a cheapening of the supply of a rival commodity, or by the invention of a new one. For instance, the list of demand prices for tea is drawn out on the assumption that the price of coffee is known; but a failure of the coffee harvest would raise the prices for tea. The demand for gas is liable to be reduced by an improvement in electric lighting; and in the same way a fall in the price of a particular kind of tea may cause it to be substituted for an inferior but cheaper variety[1].

Relation of the following to the preceding chapter.

Our next step will be to consider the general character of demand in the cases of some important commodities ready for immediate consumption. We shall thus be continuing the inquiry made in the preceding chapter as to the

[1] It is even conceivable, though not probable, that a simultaneous and proportionate fall in the price of all teas may diminish the demand for some particular kind of it; if it happens that those whom the increased cheapness of tea leads to substitute a superior kind for it are more numerous than those who are led to take it in the place of an inferior kind. The question where the lines of division between different commodities should be drawn must be settled by convenience of the particular discussion. For some purposes it may be best to regard Chinese and Indian teas, or even Souchong and Pekoe teas, as different commodities; and to have a separate demand schedule for each of them. While for other purposes it may be best to group together commodities as distinct as beef and mutton, or even as tea and coffee, and to have a single list to represent the demand for the two combined; but in such a case of course some convention must be made as to the number of ounces of tea which are taken as equivalent to a pound of coffee.

Again, a commodity may be simultaneously demanded for several uses (for instance there may be a "composite demand" for leather for making shoes and portmanteaus); the demand for a thing may be conditional on there being a supply of some other thing without which it would not be of much service (thus there may be a "joint demand" for raw cotton and cotton-spinners' labour). Again, the demand for a commodity on the part of dealers who buy it only with the purpose of selling it again, though governed by the demand of the ultimate consumers in the background, has some peculiarities of its own. But all such points may best be discussed at a later stage.

variety and satiability of wants; but we shall be treating III, III, 6. it from a rather different point of view, viz. that of price-statistics[1].

[1] A great change in the manner of economic thought has been brought about during the present generation by the general adoption of semi-mathematical language for expressing the relation between small increments of a commodity on the one hand, and on the other hand small increments in the aggregate price that will be paid for it: and by formally describing these small increments of price as measuring corresponding small increments of pleasure. The former, and by far the more important, step was taken by Cournot (*Recherches sur les Principes Mathématiques de la Théorie des Richesses*, 1838); the latter by Dupuit (*De la Mesure d'utilité des travaux publics* in the *Annales des Ponts et Chaussées*, 1844), and by Gossen (*Entwickelung der Gesetze des menschlichen Verkehrs*, 1854). But their work was forgotten; part of it was done over again, developed and published almost simultaneously by Jevons and by Carl Menger in 1871, and by Walras a little later. Jevons almost at once arrested public attention by his brilliant lucidity and interesting style. He applied the new name *final utility* so ingeniously as to enable people who knew nothing of mathematical science to get clear ideas of the general relations between the small increments of two things that are gradually changing in causal connection with one another. His success was aided even by his faults. For under the honest belief that Ricardo and his followers had rendered their account of the causes that determine value hopelessly wrong by omitting to lay stress on the law of satiable wants, he led many to think he was correcting great errors; whereas he was really only adding very important explanations. He did excellent work in insisting on a fact which is none the less important, because his predecessors, and even Cournot, thought it too obvious to be explicitly mentioned, viz. that the diminution in the amount of a thing demanded in a market indicates a diminution in the intensity of the desire for it on the part of individual consumers, whose wants are becoming satiated. But he has led many of his readers into a confusion between the provinces of Hedonics and Economics, by exaggerating the applications of his favourite phrases, and speaking (*Theory*, 2nd Edn. p. 105) without qualification of the price of a thing as measuring its final utility not only to an individual, which it can do, but also to "a trading body," which it cannot do. These points are developed later on in Appendix I. on Ricardo's Theory of value. It should be added that Prof. Seligman has shown (*Economic Journal*, 1903, pp. 356–363) that a long-forgotten Lecture, delivered by Prof. W. F. Lloyd at Oxford in 1833, anticipated many of the central ideas of the present doctrine of utility.

An excellent bibliography of Mathematical Economics is given by Prof. Fisher as an appendix to Bacon's translation of Cournot's *Researches*, to which the reader may be referred for a more detailed account of the earlier mathematical writings on economics, as well as of those by Edgeworth, Pareto, Wicksteed, Auspitz, Lieben and others. Pantaleoni's *Pure Economics*, amid much excellent matter, makes generally accessible for the first time the profoundly original and vigorous, if somewhat abstract, reasonings of Gossen.

CHAPTER IV.

THE ELASTICITY OF WANTS.

§ 1. WE have seen that the only universal law as to a person's desire for a commodity is that it diminishes, other things being equal, with every increase in his supply of that commodity. But this diminution may be slow or rapid. If it is slow the price that he will give for the commodity will not fall much in consequence of a considerable increase in his supply of it; and a small fall in price will cause a comparatively large increase in his purchases. But if it is rapid, a small fall in price will cause only a very small increase in his purchases. In the former case his willingness to purchase the thing stretches itself out a great deal under the action of a small inducement: the elasticity of his wants, we may say, is great. In the latter case the extra inducement given by the fall in price causes hardly any extension of his desire to purchase: the elasticity of his demand is small. If a fall in price from say 16d. to 15d. per lb. of tea would much increase his purchases, then a rise in price from 15d. to 16d. would much diminish them. That is, when the demand is elastic for a fall in price, it is elastic also for a rise.

And as with the demand of one person so with that of a whole market. And we may say generally:—The *elasticity* (or *responsiveness*) *of demand* in a market is great or small according as the amount demanded increases much or little for a given fall in price, and diminishes much or little for a given rise in price[1].

[1] We may say that the elasticity of demand is one, if a small fall in price will cause an equal proportionate increase in the amount demanded: or as we may say roughly, if a fall of one per cent. in price will increase the sales by one per cent.; that it is two or a half, if a fall of one per cent. in price makes an increase of two or one half per cent. respectively in the amount demanded; and so on. (This statement is rough; because 98 does not bear exactly the same proportion to 100 that 100 does to 102.) The elasticity of demand can be best traced in the demand curve with the aid of the following rule. Let a straight line touching the

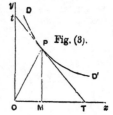

Fig. (3).

§ 2. The price which is so high relatively to the poor man as to be almost prohibitive, may be scarcely felt by the rich; the poor man, for instance, never tastes wine, but the very rich may drink as much of it as he has a fancy for, without giving himself a thought of its cost. We shall therefore get the clearest notion of the law of the elasticity of demand by considering one class of society at a time. Of course there are many degrees of richness among the rich, and poverty among the poor; but for the present we may neglect these minor subdivisions.

III, IV, 2.

The general law of variation of the elasticity of demand, and its consequent responsiveness to changes of price.

When the price of a thing is very high relatively to any class, they will buy but little of it; and in some cases custom and habit may prevent them from using it freely even after its price has fallen a good deal. It may still remain set apart for a limited number of special occasions, or for use in extreme illness, etc. But such cases, though not infrequent, do not form the general rule; and anyhow as soon as it has been taken into common use, any considerable fall in its price causes a great increase in the demand for it. The elasticity of demand is great for high prices, and great, or at least considerable, for medium prices; but it declines as the price falls; and gradually fades away if the fall goes so far that satiety level is reached.

This rule appears to hold with regard to nearly all commodities and with regard to the demand of every class; save only that the level at which high prices end and low prices begin, is different for different classes; and so again is the level at which low prices end and very low prices begin. There are however many varieties in detail; arising chiefly from the fact that there are some commodities with

curve at any point P meet Ox in T and Oy in t, then *the measure of the elasticity at the point P is the ratio of PT to Pt.*

If PT were twice Pt, a fall of 1 per cent. in price would cause an increase of 2 per cent., in the amount demanded; the elasticity of demand would be two. If PT were one-third of Pt, a fall of 1 per cent. in price would cause an increase of 1/3 per cent. in the amount demanded; the elasticity of demand would be one-third; and so on. Another way of looking at the same result is this:—the elasticity at the point P is measured by the ratio of PT to Pt, that is of MT to MO (PM being drawn perpendicular to Om); and therefore *the elasticity is equal to one when the angle TPM is equal to the angle OPM; and it always increases when the angle TPM increases relatively to the angle OPM, and vice versâ. . . .*

III, IV, 2. which people are easily satiated, and others—chiefly things used for display—for which their desire is almost unlimited. For the latter the elasticity of demand remains considerable, however low the price may fall, while for the former the demand loses nearly all its elasticity as soon as a low price has once been reached[1].

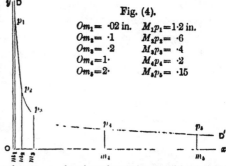

[1] Let us illustrate by the case of the demand for, say, green peas in a town in which all vegetables are bought and sold in one market. Early in the season perhaps 100 lb. a day will be brought to market and sold at 1s. per lb., later on 500 lb. will be brought and sold at 6d., later on 1,000 lb. at 4d., later still 5,000 at 2d., and later still 10,000 at 1½d. Thus demand is represented in fig. (4), an inch along Ox representing 5,000 lbs. and an inch along Oy representing 10d.

Fig. (4).

$Om_1 = \cdot02$ in. $M_1p_1 = 1\cdot2$ in.
$Om_2 = \cdot1$ $M_2p_2 = \cdot6$
$Om_3 = \cdot2$ $M_3p_3 = \cdot4$
$Om_4 = 1\cdot$ $M_4p_4 = \cdot2$
$Om_5 = 2\cdot$ $M_5p_5 = \cdot15$

Then a curve through $p_1p_2...p_5$, found as shown above, will be the total demand curve. But this total demand will be made up of the demands of the rich, the middle class and the poor. The amounts that they will severally demand may perhaps be represented by the following schedules:—

At price in pence per lb.	rich	Number of lbs. bought by middle class	poor	Total
12	100	0	0	100
6	300	200	0	500
4	500	400	100	1,000
2	800	2,500	1,700	5,000
1½	1,000	4,000	5,000	10,000

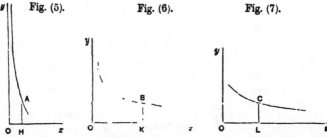

Fig. (5).   Fig. (6).   Fig. (7).

These schedules are translated into curves figs. (5), (6), (7), showing the demands of the rich, the middle class and the poor represented on the same scale as fig. (4). Thus for instance AH, BK and CL each represents a price of 2d. and is ·2 inches in length; $OH = \cdot16$ in. representing 800 lb., $OK = \cdot5$ in. representing 2,500 lb. and $OL = \cdot34$ in. representing 1,700 lb., while $OH + OK + OL = 1$ inch, i.e. $= Om_4$ in fig. (4) as they should do. This may serve as an example of the way in which

§ 3. There are some things the current prices of which III, IV, 3. in this country are very low relatively even to the poorer classes; such are for instance salt, and many kinds of savours and flavours, and also cheap medicines. It is doubtful whether any fall in price would induce a considerable increase in the consumption of these.

Illustrations drawn from the demand for particular commodities.

The current prices of meat, milk and butter, wool, tobacco, imported fruits, and of ordinary medical attendance, are such that every variation in price makes a great change in the consumption of them by the working classes, and the lower half of the middle classes; but the rich would not much increase their own personal consumption of them however cheaply they were to be had. In other words, the direct demand for these commodities is very elastic on the part of the working and lower middle classes, though not on the part of the rich. But the working class is so numerous that their consumption of such things as are well within their reach is much greater than that of the rich; and therefore the aggregate demand for all things of the kind is very elastic. A little while ago sugar belonged to this group of commodities: but its price in England has now fallen so far as to be low relatively even to the working classes, and the demand for it is therefore not elastic[1].

The current prices of wall-fruit, of the better kinds of fish, and other moderately expensive luxuries are such as to make the consumption of them by the middle class increase much with every fall in price; in other words, the middle class demand for them is very elastic: while the demand on the several partial demand curves, drawn to the same scale, can be superimposed horizontally on one another to make the total demand curve representing the aggregate of the partial demand.

[1] We must however remember that the character of the demand schedule for any commodity depends in a great measure on whether the prices of its rivals are taken to be fixed or to alter with it. If we separated the demand for beef from that for mutton, and supposed the price of mutton to be held fixed while that for beef was raised, then the demand for beef would become extremely elastic. For any slight fall in the price of beef would cause it to be used largely in the place of mutton and thus lead to a very great increase of its consumption: while on the other hand even a small rise in price would cause many people to eat mutton to the almost entire exclusion of beef. But the demand schedule for all kinds of fresh meat taken together, their prices being supposed to retain always about the same relation to one another, and to be not very different from those now prevailing in England, shows only a moderate elasticity. And similar remarks apply to beet-root and cane-sugar. Compare the note on p. 100.

III, iv, 4. part of the rich and on the part of the working class is much less elastic, the former because it is already nearly satiated, the latter because the price is still too high.

The current prices of such things as rare wines, fruit out of season, highly skilled medical and legal assistance, are so high that there is but little demand for them except from the rich: but what demand there is, often has considerable elasticity. Part of the demand for the more expensive kinds of food is really a demand for the means of obtaining social distinction, and is almost insatiable[1].

The demand for necessaries. § 4. The case of necessaries is exceptional. When the price of wheat is very high, and again when it is very low, the demand has very little elasticity: at all events if we assume that wheat, even when scarce, is the cheapest food for man; and that, even when most plentiful, it is not consumed in any other way. We know that a fall in the price of the quartern loaf from 6d. to 4d. has scarcely any effect in increasing the consumption of bread. With regard to the other end of the scale it is more difficult to speak with certainty, because there has been no approach to a scarcity in England since the repeal of the corn laws. But, availing ourselves of the experience of a less happy time, we may suppose that deficits in the supply of 1, 2, 3, 4, or 5 tenths would cause a rise in price of 3, 8, 16, 28, or 45 tenths respectively[2]. Much greater variations in prices indeed than this have not been uncommon. Thus wheat sold in London

---

[1] See above ch. ii. § 1. In April 1894, for instance, six plovers' eggs, the first of the season, were sold in London at 10s. 6d. each. The following day there were more, and the price fell to 5s.; the next day to 3s. each; and a week later to 4d.

[2] This estimate is commonly attributed to Gregory King. Its bearing on the law of demand is admirably discussed by Lord Lauderdale (*Inquiry*, pp. 51-3). It is represented in fig. (8) by the curve DD', the point A corresponding to the ordinary price. If we take account of the fact that where the price of wheat is very low, it may be used, as it was for instance in 1834, for feeding cattle and sheep and pigs and for brewing and distilling, the lower part of the curve would take a shape somewhat like that of the dotted line in the figure. And if we assume that when the price is very high, cheaper substitutes can be got for it, the upper part of the curve would take a shape similar to that of the upper dotted line.

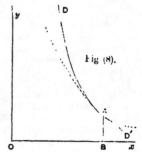

Fig. (8).

for ten shillings a bushel in 1335, but in the following year it III, IV, 4.
sold for ten pence[1].

There may be even more violent changes than this in Commo-
dities some
the price of a thing which is not necessary, if it is perishable part of the
and the demand for it is inelastic: thus fish may be very consump-
tion of
dear one day, and sold for manure two or three days later. which is
necessary.

Water is one of the few things the consumption of which
we are able to observe at all prices, from the very highest
down to nothing at all. At moderate prices the demand for
it is very elastic. But the uses to which it can be put are
capable of being completely filled: and as its price sinks
towards zero the demand for it loses its elasticity. Nearly
the same may be said of salt. Its price in England is so low
that the demand for it as an article of food is very inelastic:
but in India the price is comparatively high and the demand
is comparatively elastic.

The price of house-room, on the other hand, has never
fallen very low except when a locality is being deserted by
its inhabitants. Where the condition of society is healthy,
and there is no check to general prosperity, there seems
always to be an elastic demand for house-room, on account
both of the real conveniences and the social distinction
which it affords. The desire for those kinds of clothing
which are not used for the purpose of display, is satiable:
when their price is low the demand for them has scarcely
any elasticity.

The demand for things of a higher quality depends much Influence
of sensi-
on sensibility: some people care little for a refined flavour bility and
in their wine provided they can get plenty of it: others acquired
tastes and
crave a high quality, but are easily satiated. In the ordinary distastes.
working class districts the inferior and the better joints are
sold at nearly the same price: but some well-paid artisans
in the north of England have developed a liking for the
best meat, and will pay for it nearly as high a price as can
be got in the west end of London, where the price is kept
artificially high by the necessity of sending the inferior
joints away for sale elsewhere. Use also gives rise to

---

[1] *Chronicon Preciosum* (A.D. 1745) says that the price of wheat in London was
as low as 2s. a quarter in 1336: and that at Leicester it sold at 40s. on a Saturday,
and at 14s. on the following Friday.

III, IV, 4. acquired distastes as well as to acquired tastes. Illustrations which make a book attractive to many readers, will repel those whose familiarity with better work has rendered them fastidious. A person of high musical sensibility in a large town will avoid bad concerts: though he might go to them gladly if he lived in a small town, where no good concerts are to be heard, because there are not enough persons willing to pay the high price required to cover their expenses. The effective demand for first-rate music is elastic only in large towns; for second-rate music it is elastic both in large and small towns.

Influence of variety of uses.

Generally speaking those things have the most elastic demand, which are capable of being applied to many different uses. Water for instance is needed first as food, then for cooking, then for washing of various kinds and so on. When there is no special drought, but water is sold by the pailful, the price may be low enough to enable even the poorer classes to drink as much of it as they are inclined, while for cooking they sometimes use the same water twice over, and they apply it very scantily in washing. The middle classes will perhaps not use any of it twice for cooking; but they will make a pail of water go a good deal further for washing purposes than if they had an unlimited supply at command. When water is supplied by pipes, and charged at a very low rate by meter, many people use as much of it even for washing as they feel at all inclined to do; and when the water is supplied not by meter but at a fixed annual charge, and is laid on in every place where it is wanted, the use of it for every purpose is carried to the full satiety limit[1].

[1] Thus the general demand of any one person for such a thing as water is the aggregate (or *compound*, see V. VI. 3) of his demand for it for each use; in the same way as the demand of a group of people of different orders of wealth for a commodity, which is serviceable in only one use, is the aggregate of the demands of each member of the group. Again, just as the demand of the rich for peas is considerable even at a very high price, but loses all elasticity at a price that is still high relatively to the consumption of the poor; so the demand of the individual for water to drink is considerable even at a very high price, but loses all elasticity at a price that is still high relatively to his demand for it for the purpose of cleaning up the house. And as the aggregate of a number of demands on the part of different classes of people for peas retains elasticity over a larger range of price than will that of any one individual, so the demand of an individual for water for many uses retains elasticity over a larger range of prices than his demand for it for any one use. Compare an article by J. B. Clark on *A Universal Law of Economic Variation* in the *Harvard Journal of Economics*, Vol. VIII.

On the other hand, demand is, generally speaking, very III, IV, 5.
inelastic, firstly, for absolute necessaries (as distinguished Inelastic
from conventional necessaries and necessaries for efficiency); demand.
and secondly, for some of those luxuries of the rich which do
not absorb much of their income.

§ 5. So far we have taken no account of the difficulties Difficulties
of getting exact lists of demand prices, and interpreting statistical
them correctly. The first which we have to consider arises study; The
from the element of *time*, the source of many of the greatest Time.
difficulties in economics.

Thus while a list of demand prices represents the changes
in the price at which a commodity can be sold consequent on
changes in the amount offered for sale, *other things being
equal*; yet other things seldom are equal in fact over
periods of time sufficiently long for the collection of full and
trustworthy statistics. There are always occurring disturbing
causes whose effects are commingled with, and cannot easily
be separated from, the effects of that particular cause which
we desire to isolate. This difficulty is aggravated by the fact
that in economics the full effects of a cause seldom come at
once, but often spread themselves out after it has ceased to
exist.

To begin with, the purchasing power of money is con- Changes in
tinually changing, and rendering necessary a correction of chasing
the results obtained on our assumption that money retains power of
a uniform value. This difficulty can however be overcome
fairly well, since we can ascertain with tolerable accuracy
the broader changes in the purchasing power of money.

Next come the changes in the general prosperity and in whether
the total purchasing power at the disposal of the community or tem-
at large. The influence of these changes is important, but porary.
perhaps less so than is generally supposed. For when the
wave of prosperity is descending, prices fall, and this increases
the resources of those with fixed incomes at the expense of
those whose incomes depend on the profits of business. The
downward fluctuation of prosperity is popularly measured
almost entirely by the conspicuous losses of this last class;
but the statistics of the total consumption of such commodities as tea, sugar, butter, wool, etc. prove that the total

III, IV, 6. purchasing power of the people does not meanwhile fall
very fast. Still there is a fall, and the allowance to be made
for it must be ascertained by comparing the prices and the
consumption of as many things as possible.

Next come the changes due to the gradual growth of
population and wealth. For these an easy numerical correction can be made when the facts are known[1].

Gradual
changes in
habits and
in the
familiarity
with new
things and
new ways
of using
them.

§ 6. Next, allowance must be made for changes in fashion,
and taste and habit[2], for the opening out of new uses of a
commodity, for the discovery or improvement or cheapening
of other things that can be applied to the same uses with
it. In all these cases there is great difficulty in allowing for
the time that elapses between the economic cause and its
effect. For time is required to enable a rise in the price
of a commodity to exert its full influence on consumption.
Time is required for consumers to become familiar with
substitutes that can be used instead of it, and perhaps for
producers to get into the habit of producing them in sufficient
quantities. Time may be also wanted for the growth of habits
of familiarity with the new commodities and the discovery of
methods of economizing them.

[1] When a statistical table shows the gradual growth of the consumption of
a commodity over a long series of years, we may want to compare the percentage
by which it increases in different years. This can be
done pretty easily with a little practice. But when the
figures are expressed in the form of a statistical diagram,
it cannot easily be done, without translating the diagram
back into figures; and this is a cause of the disfavour in
which many statisticians hold the graphic method. But
by the knowledge of one simple rule the balance can be
turned, so far as this point goes, in favour of the graphic
method. The rule is as follows:—Let the quantity of a
commodity consumed (or of trade carried, or of tax levied
etc.) be measured by horizontal lines parallel to Ox, fig.

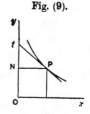

Fig. (9).

(9), while the corresponding years are in the usual manner ticked off in descending
order at equal distances along Oy. To measure the rate of growth at any point P,
put a ruler to touch the curve at P. Let it meet Oy in t, and let N be the point
on Oy at the same vertical height as P: then the number of years marked off
along Oy by the distance Nt is the inverse of the fraction by which the amount is
increasing annually. That is, if Nt is 20 years, the amount is increasing at the rate
of $\frac{1}{20}$, i.e. of 5 per cent. annually; if Nt is 25 years, the increase is $\frac{1}{25}$ or 4 per
cent. annually; and so on. See a paper by the present writer in the Jubilee
number of the *Journal of the London Statistical Society*, June 1885; also Note
IV. in the Mathematical Appendix.

[2] For illustrations of the influence of fashion see articles by Miss Foley in the
Economic Journal, Vol. III., and Miss Heather Bigg in the *Nineteenth Century*,
Vol. XXIII.

For instance when wood and charcoal became dear in III, IV, 6.
England, familiarity with coal as a fuel grew slowly, fireplaces Illus-
were but slowly adapted to its use, and an organized traffic trations.
in it did not spring up quickly even to places to which it
could be easily carried by water: the invention of processes
by which it could be used as a substitute for charcoal in
manufacture went even more slowly, and is indeed hardly
yet complete. Again, when in recent years the price of coal
became very high, a great stimulus was given to the invention
of economies in its use, especially in the production of iron
and steam; but few of these inventions bore much practical
fruit till after the high price had passed away. Again, when
a new tramway or suburban railway is opened, even those
who live near the line do not get into the habit of making
the most of its assistance at once; and a good deal more
time elapses before many of those whose places of business
are near one end of the line change their homes so as to live
near the other end. Again, when petroleum first became
plentiful few people were ready to use it freely; gradually
petroleum and petroleum lamps have become familiar to
all classes of society: too much influence would therefore be
attributed to the fall in price which has occurred since then,
if it were credited with all the increase of consumption.

Another difficulty of the same kind arises from the fact Some
that there are many purchases which can easily be put off demands
for a short time, but not for a long time. This is often the can be
more easily
case with regard to clothes and other things which are worn postponed
out gradually, and which can be made to serve a little than
others.
longer than usual under the pressure of high prices. For
instance, at the beginning of the cotton famine the recorded
consumption of cotton in England was very small. This was
partly because retail dealers reduced their stock, but chiefly
because people generally made shift to do as long as they
could without buying new cotton goods. In 1864 however
many found themselves unable to wait longer; and a good
deal more cotton was entered for home consumption in that
year, though the price was then much higher, than in either
of the preceding years. For commodities of this kind then a
sudden scarcity does not immediately raise the price fully

III, IV, 7. up to the level, which properly corresponds to the reduced
supply. Similarly after the great commercial depression in
the United States in 1873 it was noticed that the boot trade
revived before the general clothing trade; because there is a
great deal of reserve wear in the coats and hats that are
thrown aside in prosperous times as worn out, but not so
much in the boots.

Imperfec-
tions of
statistics.
§ 7. The above difficulties are fundamental: but there
are others which do not lie deeper than the more or less
inevitable faults of our statistical returns.

We desire to obtain, if possible, a series of prices
at which different amounts of a commodity can find
purchasers during a given time in a market. A perfect
market is a district, small or large, in which there are many
buyers and many sellers all so keenly on the alert and so well
acquainted with one another's affairs that the price of a commodity is always practically the same for the whole of the
district. But independently of the fact that those who buy
for their own consumption, and not for the purposes of trade,
are not always on the look out for every change in the market,
there is no means of ascertaining exactly what prices are paid
in many transactions. Again, the geographical limits of a
market are seldom clearly drawn, except when they are
marked out by the sea or by custom-house barriers; and no
country has accurate statistics of commodities produced in
it for home consumption.

Increase of
dealers'
stocks
mistaken
for increase
of con-
sumption.
Again, there is generally some ambiguity even in such
statistics as are to be had. They commonly show goods
as entered for consumption as soon as they pass into the
hands of dealers; and consequently an increase of dealers'
stocks cannot easily be distinguished from an increase of
consumption. But the two are governed by different causes.
A rise of prices tends to check consumption; but if the rise
is expected to continue, it will probably, as has already been
noticed, lead dealers to increase their stocks[1].

[1] In examining the effects of taxation, it is customary to compare the amounts
entered for consumption just before and just after the imposition of the tax. But
this is untrustworthy. For dealers anticipating the tax lay in large stocks just
before it is imposed, and need to buy very little for some time afterwards. And
vice versâ when a tax is lowered. Again, high taxes lead to false returns. For

Next it is difficult to insure that the commodities referred III, IV, 8.
to are always of the same quality. After a dry summer what Changes of
wheat there is, is exceptionally good; and the prices for the quality.
next harvest year appear to be higher than they really are.
It is possible to make allowance for this, particularly now
that dry Californian wheat affords a standard. But it is
almost impossible to allow properly for the changes in quality
of many kinds of manufactured goods. This difficulty occurs
even in the case of such a thing as tea: the substitution in
recent years of the stronger Indian tea for the weaker Chinese
tea has made the real increase of consumption greater than
that which is shown by the statistics.

NOTE ON STATISTICS OF CONSUMPTION.

§ 8. General Statistics of consumption are published by many Inductive
Governments with regard to certain classes of commodities. But study of
partly for the reasons just indicated they are of very little service in demand is
helping us to trace either a causal connection between variations in difficult;
prices and variations in the amounts which people will buy, or in the could
distribution of different kinds of consumption among the different further it
classes of the community. analysing

As regards the first of these objects, viz. the discovery of the laws their own
connecting variations in consumption consequent on variations in price, accounts.
there seems much to be gained by working out a hint given by Jevons
(*Theory*, pp. 11, 12) with regard to shopkeepers' books. A shopkeeper,
or the manager of a co-operative store, in the working man's quarter
of a manufacturing town has often the means of ascertaining with
tolerable accuracy the financial position of the great body of his
customers. He can find out how many factories are at work, and for
how many hours in the week, and he can hear about all the important
changes in the rate of wages: in fact he makes it his business to do
so. And as a rule his customers are quick in finding out changes in
the price of things which they commonly use. He will therefore often
find cases in which an increased consumption of a commodity is
brought about by a fall in its price, the cause acting quickly, and
acting alone without any admixture of disturbing causes. Even where

instance, the nominal importation of molasses into Boston increased fiftyfold in
consequence of the tax being lowered by the Rockingham Ministry in 1766, from
6d. to 1d. per gallon. But this was chiefly due to the fact that with the tax
at 1d., it was cheaper to pay the duty than to smuggle.

III, IV, 8. disturbing causes are present, he will often be able to allow for their
influence. For instance, he will know that as the winter comes on,
the prices of butter and vegetables rise; but the cold weather makes
people desire butter more and vegetables less than before: and therefore
when the prices of both vegetables and butter rise towards the winter, he
will expect a greater falling off of consumption in the case of vegetables
than should properly be attributed to the rise in price taken alone, but
a less falling off in the case of butter. If however in two neighbouring
winters his customers have been about equally numerous, and in receipt
of about the same rate of wages; and if in the one the price of butter
was a good deal higher than in the other, then a comparison of his books
for the two winters will afford a very accurate indication of the influence
of changes in price on consumption. Shopkeepers who supply other
classes of society must occasionally be in a position to furnish similar
facts relating to the consumption of their customers.

Consumption by the poor of cheap things may suggest the probable variations in its consumption by the rich if it became very dear.   If a sufficient number of tables of demand by different sections of
society could be obtained, they would afford the means of estimating
indirectly the variations in total demand that would result from extreme
variations in price, and thus attaining an end which is inaccessible by
any other route. For, as a general rule, the price of a commodity
fluctuates within but narrow limits; and therefore statistics afford us
no direct means of guessing what the consumption of it would be, if
its price were either fivefold or a fifth part of what it actually is. But
we know that its consumption would be confined almost entirely to the
rich if its price were very high; and that, if its price were very low, the
great body of its consumption would in most cases be among the working classes. If then the present price is very high relatively to the
middle or to the working classes, we may be able to infer from the
laws of their demand at the present prices what would be the demand
of the rich if the price were so raised so as to be very high relatively
even to their means. On the other hand, if the present price is moderate relatively to the means of the rich, we may be able to infer from
their demand what would be the demand of the working classes if the
price were to fall to a level which is moderate relatively to their means.
It is only by thus piecing together fragmentary laws of demand that
we can hope to get any approach to an accurate law relating to widely
different prices. (That is to say, the general demand curve for a commodity cannot be drawn with confidence except in the immediate
neighbourhood of the current price, until we are able to piece it together out of the fragmentary demand curves of different classes of
society. Compare the Second Section of this Chapter.)

When some progress has been made in reducing to definite law the
demand for commodities that are destined for immediate consumption,
then, but not till then, will there be use in attempting a similar task
with regard to those secondary demands which are dependent on these
—the demands namely for the labour of artisans and others who take

part in the production of things for sale; and again the demand for machines, factories, railway material and other instruments of production. The demand for the work of medical men, of domestic servants and of all those whose services are rendered direct to the consumer is similar in character to the demand for commodities for immediate consumption, and its laws may be investigated in the same manner.

It is a very important, but also difficult task to ascertain the proportions in which the different classes of society distribute their expenditure between necessaries, comforts and luxuries; between things that provide only present pleasure, and those that build up stores of physical and moral strength; and lastly between those which gratify the lower wants and those which stimulate and educate the higher wants. Several endeavours have been made in this direction on the Continent during the last fifty years; and latterly the subject has been investigated with increasing vigour not only there but also in America and in England[1].

III, iv, 8.

Another method is to collect budgets of individuals in different classes.

[1] A single table made out by the great statistician Engel for the consumption of the lower, middle and working classes in Saxony in 1857, may be quoted here; because it has acted as a guide and a standard of comparison to later inquiries. It is as follows:—

Items of Expenditure.	Proportions of the Expenditure of the Family of—		
	1. Workman with an Income of 45*l.* to 60*l.* a Year.	2. Workman with an Income of 90*l.* to 120*l.*	3. Middle-Class person with an Income of 150*l.* to 200*l.*
1. Food only	62·0 per cent.	55·0 per cent.	50·0 per cent.
2. Clothing	16·0 „	18·0 „	18·0 „
3. Lodging	12·0 „	12·0 „	12·0 „
4. Light and fuel	5·0 „	5·0 „	5·0 „
5. Education	2·0 „	3·5 „	5·5 „
6. Legal protection	1·0 „	2·0 „	3·0 „
7. Care of health	1·0 „	2·0 „	3·0 „
8. Comfort and recreation	1·0 „	2·5 „	3·5 „
Totals	100·0 per cent.	100·0 per cent.	100·0 per cent.

Working-men's budgets have often been collected and compared. But like all other figures of the kind they suffer from the facts that those who will take the trouble to make such returns voluntarily are not average men, that those who keep careful accounts are not average men; and that when accounts have to be supplemented by the memory, the memory is apt to be biassed by notions as to how the money ought to have been spent, especially when the accounts are put together specially for another's eye. This border-ground between the provinces of domestic and public economy is one in which excellent work may be done by many who are disinclined for more general and abstract speculations.

Information bearing on the subject was collected long ago by Harrison, Petty, Cantillon (whose lost Supplement seems to have contained some workmen's budgets), Arthur Young, Malthus and others. Working-men's budgets were collected by Eden at the end of the last century; and there is much miscellaneous information on the expenditure of the working classes in subsequent Reports of

III, IV, 8. Commissions on Poor-relief, Factories, etc. Indeed almost every year sees some important addition from public or private sources to our information on these subjects.

It may be noted that the method of le Play's monumental *Les Ouvriers Européens* is the *intensive* study of all the details of the domestic life of a few carefully chosen families. To work it well requires a rare combination of judgment in selecting cases, and of insight and sympathy in interpreting them. At its best, it is the best of all: but in ordinary hands it is likely to suggest more untrustworthy general conclusions, than those obtained by the *extensive* method of collecting more rapidly very numerous observations, reducing them as far as possible to statistical form, and obtaining broad averages in which inaccuracies and idiosyncrasies may be trusted to counteract one another to some extent.

CHAPTER V.

CHOICE BETWEEN DIFFERENT USES OF THE SAME THING. IMMEDIATE AND DEFERRED USES.

§ 1. THE primitive housewife finding that she has a limited number of hanks of yarn from the year's shearing, considers all the domestic wants for clothing and tries to distribute the yarn between them in such a way as to contribute as much as possible to the family wellbeing. She will think she has failed if, when it is done, she has reason to regret that she did not apply more to making, say, socks, and less to vests. That would mean that she had miscalculated the points at which to suspend the making of socks and vests respectively; that she had gone too far in the case of vests, and not far enough in that of socks; and that therefore at the points at which she actually did stop, the utility of yarn turned into socks was greater than that of yarn turned into vests. But if, on the other hand, she hit on the right points to stop at, then she made just so many socks and vests that she got an equal amount of good out of the last bundle of yarn that she applied to socks, and the last she applied to vests. This illustrates a general principle, which may be expressed thus:—

If a person has a thing which he can put to several uses, he will distribute it among these uses in such a way that it has the same marginal utility in all. For if it had a greater marginal utility in one use than another, he would

III, v, 1.

The distribution of a person's means between the gratification of different wants.

III, v, 2. gain by taking away some of it from the second use and
applying it to the first[1].

But a
person may
have too
much of
one thing
for all uses,
and too
little of
another.

One great disadvantage of a primitive economy, in which
there is but little free exchange, is that a person may easily
have so much of one thing, say wool, that when he has
applied it to every possible use, its marginal utility in each
use is low: and at the same time he may have so little of
some other thing, say wood, that its marginal utility for him
is very high. Meanwhile some of his neighbours may be in
great need of wool, and have more wood than they can turn
to good account. If each gives up that which has for him
the lower utility and receives that which has the higher, each
will gain by the exchange. But to make such an adjustment
by barter, would be tedious and difficult.

Barter is
a partial
remedy.

The difficulty of barter is indeed not so very great
where there are but a few simple commodities each capable
of being adapted by domestic work to several uses; the
weaving wife and the spinster daughters adjusting rightly
the marginal utilities of the different uses of the wool, while
the husband and the sons do the same for the wood.

Money
can be
distributed
so as to
have equal
marginal
utilities in
each use.

§ 2. But when commodities have become very numerous
and highly specialized, there is an urgent need for the free
use of money, or general purchasing power; for that alone
can be applied easily in an unlimited variety of purchases.
And in a money-economy, good management is shown by so
adjusting the margins of suspense on each line of expenditure
that the marginal utility of a shilling's worth of goods on
each line shall be the same. And this result each one will
attain by constantly watching to see whether there is anything on which he is spending so much that he would gain
by taking a little away from that line of expenditure and
putting it on some other line.

Illustra-
tions.

Thus, for instance, the clerk who is in doubt whether to
ride to town, or to walk and have some little extra indulgence

---

[1] Our illustration belongs indeed properly to domestic production rather than
to domestic consumption. But that was almost inevitable; for there are very
few things ready for immediate consumption which are available for many
different uses. And the doctrine of the distribution of means between different
uses has less important and less interesting applications in the science of
demand than in that of supply. See *e.g.* V. III. 3.

at his lunch, is weighing against one another the (marginal)
utilities of two different modes of spending his money. And
when an experienced housekeeper urges on a young couple
the importance of keeping accounts carefully; a chief motive
of the advice is that they may avoid spending impulsively a
great deal of money on furniture and other things; for, though
some quantity of these is really needful, yet when bought
lavishly they do not give high (marginal) utilities in proportion to their cost. And when the young pair look over their
year's budget at the end of the year, and find perhaps that
it is necessary to curtail their expenditure somewhere, they
compare the (marginal) utilities of different items, weighing
the loss of utility that would result from taking away a
pound's expenditure here, with that which they would lose
by taking it away there: they strive to adjust their parings
down so that the aggregate loss of utility may be a minimum,
and the aggregate of utility that remains to them may be a
maximum[1].

§ 3. The different uses between which a commodity is
distributed need not all be present uses; some may be
present and some future. A prudent person will endeavour
to distribute his means between all their several uses, present
and future, in such a way that they will have in each the
same marginal utility. But in estimating the present marginal utility of a distant source of pleasure a twofold allowance
must be made; firstly, for its uncertainty (this is an *objective*
property which all well-informed persons would estimate in
the same way); and secondly, for the difference in the value
to them of a distant as compared with a present pleasure
(this is a *subjective* property which different people would

---

[1] The working-class budgets which were mentioned in Ch. IV. § 8 may render
most important services in helping people to distribute their resources wisely
between different uses, so that the marginal utility for each purpose shall be the
same. But the vital problems of domestic economy relate as much to wise action
as to wise spending. The English and the American housewife make limited
means go a less way towards satisfying wants than the French housewife does,
not because they do not know how to buy, but because they cannot produce as
good finished commodities out of the raw material of inexpensive joints, vegetables
etc., as she can. Domestic economy is often spoken of as belonging to the science
of consumption: but that is only half true. The greatest faults in domestic
economy, among the sober portion of the Anglo-Saxon working-classes at all events,
are faults of production rather than of consumption.

III, v, 3.   estimate in different ways according to their individual
characters, and their circumstances at the time).

Future
benefits
are "dis-
counted,"
at different
rates.

If people regarded future benefits as equally desirable
with similar benefits at the present time, they would probably endeavour to distribute their pleasures and other
satisfactions evenly throughout their lives. They would
therefore generally be willing to give up a present pleasure
for the sake of an equal pleasure in the future, provided they
could be certain of having it. But in fact human nature is
so constituted that in estimating the "present value" of a
future benefit most people generally make a second deduction
from its future value, in the form of what we may call a
"discount," that increases with the period for which the
benefit is deferred. One will reckon a distant benefit at
nearly the same value which it would have for him if it were
present; while another who has less power of realizing the
future, less patience and self-control, will care comparatively
little for any benefit that is not near at hand. And the
same person will vary in his mood, being at one time
impatient, and greedy for present enjoyment; while at
another his mind dwells on the future, and he is willing to
postpone all enjoyments that can conveniently be made to
wait. Sometimes he is in a mood to care little for anything
else: sometimes he is like the children who pick the plums
out of their pudding to eat them at once, sometimes like
those who put them aside to be eaten last. And, in any
case, when calculating the rate at which a future benefit
is discounted, we must be careful to make allowance for the
pleasures of expectation.

Desire for
lasting
sources of
enjoyment
and for
ownership.

The rates at which different people discount the future
affect not only their tendency to save, as the term is ordinarily understood, but also their tendency to buy things
which will be a lasting source of pleasure rather than those
which give a stronger but more transient enjoyment; to buy
a new coat rather than to indulge in a drinking bout, or to
choose simple furniture that will wear well, rather than
showy furniture that will soon fall to pieces.

It is in regard to these things especially that the pleasure
of possession makes itself felt. Many people derive from

the mere feeling of ownership a stronger satisfaction than III, v, 4.
they derive from ordinary pleasures in the narrower sense
of the term: for example, the delight in the possession of
land will often induce people to pay for it so high a price that
it yields them but a very poor return on their investment.
There is a delight in ownership for its own sake; and there
is a delight in ownership on account of the distinction it
yields. Sometimes the latter is stronger than the former,
sometimes weaker; and perhaps no one knows himself or
other people well enough to be able to draw the line quite
certainly between the two.

§ 4. As has already been urged, we cannot compare the But we
quantities of two benefits, which are enjoyed at different really
times even by the same person. When a person postpones a estimate
pleasure-giving event he does not postpone the pleasure; but *quantity*
he gives up a present pleasure and takes in its place another, benefit.
or an expectation of getting another at a future date: and
we cannot tell whether he expects the future pleasure to be
greater than the one which he is giving up, unless we know
all the circumstances of the case. And therefore, even
though we know the rate at which he discounts future
pleasurable events, such as spending £1 on immediate gratifications, we yet do not know the rate at which he discounts
future pleasures[1].

[1] In classifying some pleasures as more *urgent* than others, it is often forgotten that the postponement of a pleasurable event may alter the circumstances
under which it occurs, and therefore alter the character of the pleasure itself. For
instance it may be said that a young man discounts at a very high rate the
pleasure of the Alpine tours which he hopes to be able to afford himself when he
has made his fortune. He would much rather have them now, partly because
they would give him much greater pleasure now.
Again, it may happen that the postponement of a pleasurable event involves
an unequal distribution in Time of a certain good, and that the Law of Diminution of Marginal Utility acts strongly in the case of this particular good. For
instance, it is sometimes said that the pleasures of eating are specially urgent;
and it is undoubtedly true that if a man goes dinnerless for six days in the week
and eats seven dinners on the seventh, he loses very much; because when postponing six dinners, he does not postpone the pleasures of eating six separate
dinners, but substitutes for them the pleasure of one day's excessive eating.
Again, when a person puts away eggs for the winter he does not expect that they
will be better flavoured then than now; he expects that they will be scarce, and
that therefore their utility will be higher than now. This shows the importance
of drawing a clear distinction between discounting a future pleasure, and discounting the pleasure derived from the future enjoyment of a certain amount of
a commodity. For in the latter case we must make separate allowance for

III, v, 4.
An
artificial
measure
of the
rate of
discount
of future
benefits.

We can however get an artificial measure of the rate at which he discounts future benefits by making two assumptions. These are, firstly, that he expects to be about as rich at the future date as he is now; and secondly, that his capacity for deriving benefit from the things which money will buy will on the whole remain unchanged, though it may have increased in some directions and diminished in others. On these assumptions, if he is willing, but only just willing, to spare a pound from his expenditure now with the certainty of having (for the disposal of himself or his heirs) a guinea one year hence, we may fairly say that he discounts future benefits that are perfectly secure (subject only to the conditions of human mortality) at the rate of five per cent. per annum. And on these assumptions the rate at which he discounts future (certain) benefits, will be the rate at which he can discount money in the money market[1].

differences between the marginal utilities of the commodity at the two times: but in the former this has been allowed for once in estimating the amount of the pleasure; and it must not be allowed for again.

[1] It is important to remember that, except on these assumptions there is no direct connection between the rate of discount on the loan of money, and the rate at which future pleasures are discounted. A man may be so impatient of delay that a certain promise of a pleasure ten years hence will not induce him to give up one close at hand which he regards as a quarter as great. And yet if he should fear that ten years hence money may be so scarce with him (and its marginal utility therefore so high) that half-a-crown then may give him more pleasure or save him more pain than a pound now, he will save something for the future even though he have to hoard it, on the same principle that he might store eggs for the winter. But we are here straying into questions that are more closely connected with Supply than with Demand. We shall have to consider them again from different points of view in connection with the Accumulation of Wealth, and later again in connection with the causes that determine the Rate of Interest.

We may however consider here how to measure numerically the present value of a future pleasure, on the supposition that we know, (i) its amount, (ii) the date at which it will come, if it comes at all, (iii) the chance that it will come, and (iv) the rate at which the person in question discounts future pleasures.

If the probability that a pleasure will be enjoyed is three to one, so that three chances out of four are in its favour, the value of its expectation is three-fourths of what it would be if it were certain: if the probability that it will be enjoyed were only seven to five, so that only seven chances out of twelve are in its favour, the value of its expectation is only seven-twelfths of what it would be if the event were certain, and so on. [This is its actuarial value: but further allowance may have to be made for the fact that the true value to anyone of an uncertain gain is generally less than its actuarial value (see the note on p. 209).] If the anticipated pleasure is both uncertain and distant, we have a twofold deduction to make from its full value. We will suppose, for instance, that a person would give 10s. for a gratification if it were present and certain, but that

So far we have considered each pleasure singly; but a
great many of the things which people buy are durable, *i.e.*
are not consumed in a single use; a durable good, such as a
piano, is the probable source of many pleasures, more or
less remote; and its value to a purchaser is the aggregate of
the usance, or worth to him of all these pleasures,
allowance being made for their uncertainty and for their
distance[1].

III, v, 4.
___
Future
pleasures
expected
from the
ownership
of durable
commodi-
ties.

it is due a year hence, and the probability of its happening then is three to one. Suppose also that he discounts the future at the rate of twenty per cent. per annum. Then
the value to him of the anticipation of it is $\frac{3}{4} \times \frac{80}{100} \times 10s.$ i.e. 6s. Compare the
Introductory chapter of Jevons' *Theory of Political Economy.*

[1] Of course this estimate is formed by a rough instinct; and in any attempt to
reduce it to numerical accuracy . . . , we must recollect what has been said, in this
and the preceding Section, as to the impossibility of comparing accurately pleasures
or other satisfactions that do not occur at the same time; and also as to the assumption of uniformity involved in supposing the discount of future pleasures to obey the
exponential law.

CHAPTER VI.

VALUE AND UTILITY.

§ 1. WE may now turn to consider how far the price which is actually paid for a thing represents the benefit that arises from its possession. This is a wide subject on which economic science has very little to say, but that little is of some importance.

We have already seen that the price which a person pays for a thing can never exceed, and seldom comes up to that which he would be willing to pay rather than go without it: so that the satisfaction which he gets from its purchase generally exceeds that which he gives up in paying away its price; and he thus derives from the purchase a surplus of satisfaction. The excess of the price which he would be willing to pay rather than go without the thing, over that which he actually does pay, is the economic measure of this surplus satisfaction. It may be called *consumer's surplus*.

It is obvious that the consumer's surpluses derived from some commodities are much greater than from others. There are many comforts and luxuries of which the prices are very much below those which many people would pay rather than go entirely without them; and which therefore afford a very great consumer's surplus. Good instances are matches, salt, a penny newspaper, or a postage-stamp.

This benefit, which he gets from purchasing at a low price things for which he would rather pay a high price than go without them, may be called the benefit which he derives

from his *opportunities*, or from his *environment*; or, to recur III, vi, 2.
to a word that was in common use a few generations ago, from from his
his *conjuncture*. Our aim in the present chapter is to apply *environ-ment* or
the notion of consumer's surplus as an aid in estimating *conjunc-ture.*
roughly some of the benefits which a person derives from his
environment or his conjuncture[1].

§ 2. In order to give definiteness to our notions, let us Con-sumer's
consider the case of tea purchased for domestic consumption. surplus in
Let us take the case of a man, who, if the price of tea relation to the demand
were 20*s*. a pound, would just be induced to buy one pound of an in-dividual.
annually; who would just be induced to buy two pounds if
the price were 14*s*., three pounds if the price were 10*s*., four
pounds if the price were 6*s*., five pounds if the price were
4*s*., six pounds if the price were 3*s*., and who, the price
being actually 2*s*., does purchase seven pounds. We have to
investigate the consumer's surplus which he derives from his
power of purchasing tea at 2*s*. a pound.

The fact that he would just be induced to purchase one
pound if the price were 20*s*., proves that the total enjoyment
or satisfaction which he derives from that pound is as great as
that which he could obtain by spending 20*s*. on other things.
When the price falls to 14*s*., he could, if he chose, continue
to buy only one pound. He would then get for 14*s*. what
was worth to him at least 20*s*.; and he will obtain a surplus
satisfaction worth to him at least 6*s*., or in other words a
consumer's surplus of at least 6*s*. But in fact he buys a
second pound of his own free choice, thus showing that he
regards it as worth to him at least 14*s*., and that this
represents the *additional* utility of the second pound to him.
He obtains for 28*s*. what is worth to him at least 20*s*. + 14*s*.;
i.e. 34*s*. His surplus satisfaction is at all events not diminished
by buying it, but remains worth at least 6*s*. to him. The

---

[1] This term is a familiar one in German economics, and meets a need which is
much felt in English economics. For "opportunity" and "environment," the only
available substitutes for it, are sometimes rather misleading. By *Conjunctur*, says
Wagner (*Grundegung*, Ed. iii. p. 387), "we understand the sum total of the
technical, economic, social and legal conditions; which, in a mode of national
life (*Volkswirthschaft*) resting upon division of labour and private property,—
especially private property in land and other material means of production—
determine the demand for and supply of goods, and therefore their exchange
value: this determination being as a rule, or at least in the main, *independent* of
the will of the owner, of his activity and his remissness."

III, VI, 2. total utility of the two pounds is worth at least 34*s*., his consumer's surplus is at least 6*s*.[1] The fact that each additional purchase reacts upon the utility of the purchases which he had previously decided to make *has already been allowed for in making out the schedule and must not be counted a second time.*

When the price falls to 10*s*., he might, if he chose, continue to buy only two pounds; and obtain for 20*s*. what

---

[1] Some further explanations may be given of this statement; though in fact they do little more than repeat in other words what has already been said. The significance of the condition in the text that he buys the second pound of his own free choice is shown by the consideration that if the price of 14*s*. had been offered to him on the condition that he took two pounds, he would then have to elect between taking one pound for 20*s*. or two pounds for 28*s*.: and then his taking two pounds would not have proved that he thought the second pound worth more than 8*s*. to him. But as it is, he takes a second pound paying 14*s*. unconditionally for it; and that proves that it is worth at least 14*s*. to him. (If he can get buns at a penny each, but seven for sixpence; and he elects to buy seven, we know that he is willing to give up his sixth penny for the sake of the sixth and the seventh buns: but we cannot tell how much he would pay rather than go without the seventh bun only.)

It is sometimes objected that as he increases his purchases, the urgency of his need for his earlier purchases is diminished, and their utility falls; therefore we ought to continually redraw the earlier parts of our list of demand prices at a lower level, as we pass along it towards lower prices (*i.e.* to redraw at a lower level our demand curve as we pass along it to the right). But this misconceives the plan on which the list of prices is made out. The objection would have been valid, if the demand price set against each number of pounds of tea represented the *average* utility of that number. For it is true that, if he would pay just 20*s*. for one pound, and just 14*s*. for a second, then he would pay just 34*s*. for the two; *i.e.* 17*s*. each on the average. And if our list had had reference to the *average* prices he would pay, and had set 17*s*. against the second pound; then no doubt we should have had to redraw the list as we passed on. For when he has bought a third pound the average utility to him of each of the three will be less than that of 17*s*.; being in fact 14*s*. 8*d*. if, as we go on to assume, he would pay just 10*s*. for a third pound. But this difficulty is entirely avoided on the plan of making out demand prices which is here adopted; according to which his second pound is credited, not with the 17*s*. which represents the average value per pound of the two pounds; but with the 14*s*., which represents the *additional* utility which a second pound has for him. For that remains unchanged when he has bought a third pound, of which the additional utility is measured by 10*s*.

The first pound was probably worth to him more than 20*s*. All that we know is that it was not worth less to him. He probably got some small surplus even on that. Again, the second pound was probably worth more than 14*s*. to him. All that we know is that it was worth at least 14*s*. and not worth 20*s*. to him. He would get therefore at this stage a surplus satisfaction of at least 6*s*., probably a little more. A ragged edge of this kind, as mathematicians are aware, always exists when we watch the effects of considerable changes, as that from 20*s*. to 14*s*. a pound. If we had begun with a very high price, had descended by practically infinitesimal changes of a farthing per pound, and watched infinitesimal variations in his consumption of a small fraction of a pound at a time, this ragged edge would have disappeared.

was worth to him at least 34s., and derive a surplus satis- III, VI, 2.
faction worth at least 14s. But in fact he prefers to buy a
third pound: and as he does this freely, we know that he
does not diminish his surplus satisfaction by doing it. He
now gets for 30s. three pounds; of which the first is worth
to him at least 20s., the second at least 14s., and the third at
least 10s. The total utility of the three is worth at least
44s., his consumer's surplus is at least 14s., and so on.

When at last the price has fallen to 2s. he buys seven
pounds, which are severally worth to him not less than 20,
14, 10, 6, 4, 3, and 2s. or 59s. in all. This sum measures
their total utility to him, and his consumer's surplus is (at
least) the excess of this sum over the 14s. he actually does
pay for them, i.e. 45s. This is the excess value of the
satisfaction he gets from buying the tea over that which he
could have got by spending the 14s. in extending a little his
purchase of other commodities, of which he had just not
thought it worth while to buy more at their current prices;
and any further purchases of which at those prices would
not yield him any consumer's surplus. In other words,
he derives this 45s. worth of surplus enjoyment from his
conjuncture, from the adaptation of the environment to
his wants in the particular matter of tea. If that adaptation
ceased, and tea could not be had at any price, he would have
incurred a loss of satisfaction at least equal to that which he
could have got by spending 45s. more on extra supplies of
things that were worth to him only just what he paid for
them[1].

[1] Prof. Nicholson (*Principles of Political Economy*, Vol. I and *Economic Journal*, Vol. IV.) has raised objections to the notion of consumers' surplus, which have been answered by Prof. Edgeworth in the same Journal. Prof. Nicholson says:—"Of what avail is it to say that the utility of an income of (say) £100 a year is worth (say) £1000 a year?" There would be no avail in saying that. But there might be use, when comparing life in Central Africa with life in England, in saying that, though the things which money will buy in Central Africa may on the average be as cheap there as here, yet there are so many things which cannot be bought there at all, that a person with a thousand a year there is not so well off as a person with three or four hundred a year here. If a man pays 1d. toll on a bridge, which saves him an additional drive that would cost a shilling, we do not say that the penny is worth a shilling, but that the penny together with the advantage offered him by the bridge (the part it plays in his conjuncture) is worth a shilling for that day. Were the bridge swept away on a day on which he needed it, he would be in at least as bad a position as if he had been deprived of eleven pence.

VALUE AND UTILITY

§ 3. In the same way if we were to neglect for the moment the fact that the same sum of money represents different amounts of pleasure to different people, we might measure the surplus satisfaction which the sale of tea affords, say, in the London market, by the aggregate of the sums by which the prices shown in a complete list of demand prices for tea exceeds its selling price[1].

[1] Let us then consider the demand curve DD' for tea in any large market.

Let OH be the amount which is sold there at the price HA annually, a year being taken as our unit of time. Taking any point M in OH let us draw MP vertically upwards to meet the curve in P and cut a horizontal line through A in R. We will suppose the several lbs. numbered in the order of the eagerness of the several purchasers: the eagerness of the purchaser of any lb. being measured by the price he is just willing to pay for that lb. The figure informs us that OM can be sold at the price PM; but that at any higher price

Fig. (10).

not quite so many lbs. can be sold. There must be then some individual who will buy more at the price PM, than he will at any higher price; and we are to regard the OMth lb. as sold to this individual. Suppose for instance that PM represents 4*s.*, and that OM represents a million lbs. The purchaser described in the text is just willing to buy his fifth lb of tea at the price 4*s.*, and the OMth or millionth lb. may be said to be sold to him. If AH and therefore RM represent 2*s.*, the consumers' surplus derived from the OMth lb. is the excess of PM or 4*s.* which the purchaser of that lb. would have been willing to pay for it over RM the 2*s.* which he actually does pay for it. Let us suppose that a very thin vertical parallelogram is drawn of which the height is PM and of which the base is the distance along Ox that measures the single unit or lb. of tea. It will be convenient henceforward to regard price as measured not by a mathematical straight line without thickness, as PM; but by a very thin parallelogram, or as it may be called a thick straight line, of which the breadth is in every case equal to the distance along Ox which measures a unit or lb. of tea. Thus we should say that the total satisfaction derived from the OMth lb. of tea is represented (or, on the assumption made in the last paragraph of the text is measured) by the thick straight line MP; that the price paid for this lb. is represented by the thick straight line MR and the consumers' surplus derived from this lb. by the thick straight line RP. Now let us suppose that such thin parallelograms, or thick straight lines, are drawn from all positions of M between O and H, one for each lb. of tea. The thick straight lines thus drawn, as MP is, from Ox up to the demand curve will each represent the aggregate of the satisfaction derived from a lb. of tea; and taken together thus occupy and exactly fill up the whole area $DOHA$. Therefore we may say that the area $DOHA$ represents the aggregate of the satisfaction derived from the consumption of tea. Again, each of the straight lines drawn, as MR is, from Ox upwards as far as AC represents the price that actually is paid for a lb. of tea. These straight lines together make up the area $COHA$; and therefore this area represents the total price paid for tea. Finally each of the straight lines drawn as RP is from AC upwards as far as the demand curve, represents the consumers' surplus derived from the corresponding lb. of tea. These straight lines together make up the area DCA; and therefore this area represents the total consumers' surplus that is derived from tea when the price is

This analysis, with its new names and elaborate machinery, appears at first sight laboured and unreal. On closer study it will be found to introduce no new difficulties and to make no new assumptions; but only to bring to light difficulties and assumptions that are latent in the common language of the market-place. For in this, as in other cases, the apparent simplicity of popular phrases veils a real complexity, and it is the duty of science to bring out that latent complexity; to face it; and to reduce it as far as possible: so that in later stages we may handle firmly difficulties that could not be grasped with a good grip by the vague thought and language of ordinary life.

It is a common saying in ordinary life that the real worth of things to a man is not gauged by the price he pays for them: that, though he spends for instance much more on tea than on salt, yet salt is of greater real worth to him; and that this would be clearly seen if he were entirely deprived of it. This line of argument is but thrown into precise technical form when it is said that we cannot trust the marginal utility of a commodity to indicate its total utility. If some ship-wrecked men, expecting to wait a year before they were rescued, had a few pounds of tea and the same number of pounds of salt to divide between them, the salt would be the more highly prized; because the marginal utility of an ounce of salt, when a person expects to get only a few of them in the year is greater than that of tea under like circumstances. But, under ordinary circumstances, the price of salt being low, every one buys so much of it that an additional pound would bring him little additional satisfaction: the total utility of salt to him is very great indeed, and yet its marginal utility is low. On the other hand, since tea is costly, most people use less of it and let the water stay on it rather longer than they would, if it could be got at nearly as low a price

III, vi, 3.

This analysis aims only at giving definite expression to familiar notions.

AH. But it must be repeated that this geometrical measurement is only an aggregate of the measures of benefits which are not all measured on the same scale except on the assumption just made in the text. Unless that assumption is made the area only represents an aggregate of satisfactions, the several amounts of which are not exactly measured. On that assumption only, its area measures the volume of the total *net* satisfaction derived from the tea by its various purchasers.

III, vi, 3. as salt can. Their desire for it is far from being satiated: its marginal utility remains high, and they may be willing to pay as much for an additional ounce of it as they would for an additional pound of salt. The common saying of ordinary life with which we began suggests all this: but not in an exact and definite form, such as is needed for a statement which will often be applied in later work. The use of technical terms at starting adds nothing to knowledge: but it puts familiar knowledge in a firm compact shape, ready to serve as the basis for further study[1].

In regard to different people allowance may have to be made where necessary for differences of sensibility

Or the real worth of a thing might be discussed with reference not to a single person but to people in general; and thus it would naturally be assumed that a shilling's worth of gratification to one Englishman might be taken as equivalent with a shilling's worth to another, "to start with," and "until cause to the contrary were shown." But everyone would know that this was a reasonable course only on the supposition that the consumers of tea and those of salt belonged to the same classes of people; and included people of every variety of temperament[2].

and for differences of wealth:

This involves the consideration that a pound's worth of satisfaction to an ordinary poor man is a much greater thing than a pound's worth of satisfaction to an ordinary rich man: and if instead of comparing tea and salt, which are

---

[1] Harris On Coins 1757, says "Things in general are valued, not according to their real uses in supplying the necessities of men; but rather in proportion to the land, labour and skill that are requisite to produce them. It is according to this proportion nearly, that things or commodities are exchanged one for another; and it is by the said scale, that the intrinsic values of most things are chiefly estimated. Water is of great use, and yet ordinarily of little or no value; because in most places, water flows spontaneously in such great plenty, as not to be withheld within the limits of private property; but all may have enough, without other expense than that of bringing or conducting it, when the case so requires. On the other hand, diamonds being very scarce, have upon that account a great value, though they are but little use."

[2] There might conceivably be persons of high sensibility who would suffer specially from the want of either salt or tea: or who were generally sensitive, and would suffer more from the loss of a certain part of their income than others in the same station of life. But it would be assumed that such differences between individuals might be neglected, since we were considering in either case the average of large numbers of people; though of course it might be necessary to consider whether there were some special reason for believing, say, that those who laid most store by tea were a specially sensitive class of people. If it could, then a separate allowance for this would have to be made before applying the results of economical analysis to practical problems of ethics or politics.

both used largely by all classes, we compared either of them III, vi, 8.
with champagne or pineapples, the correction to be made on
this account would be more than important: it would change
the whole character of the estimate. In earlier generations
many statesmen, and even some economists, neglected to
make adequate allowance for considerations of this class,
especially when constructing schemes of taxation; and their
words or deeds seemed to imply a want of sympathy with
the sufferings of the poor; though more often they were due
simply to want of thought.

On the whole however it happens that by far the greater
number of the events with which economics deals, affect in but it is
about equal proportions all the different classes of society; so seldom needed in
that if the money measures of the happiness caused by two considering large
events are equal, there is not in general any very great groups of people.
difference between the amounts of the happiness in the two
cases. And it is on account of this fact that the exact
measurement of the consumers' surplus in a market has
already much theoretical interest, and may become of high
practical importance.

It will be noted however that the demand prices of each
commodity, on which our estimates of its total utility and
consumers' surplus are based, assume that *other things remain
equal*, while its price rises to scarcity value: and when the
total utilities of two commodities which contribute to the
same purpose are calculated on this plan, we cannot say that
the total utility of the two together is equal to the sum of
the total utilities of each separately[1].

---

[1] Some ambiguous phrases in earlier editions appear to have suggested to
some readers the opposite opinion. But the task of adding together the total
utilities of all commodities, so as to obtain the aggregate of the total utility of all
wealth, is beyond the range of any but the most elaborate mathematical formulæ.
An attempt to treat it by them some years ago convinced the present writer that
even if the task be theoretically feasible, the result would be encumbered by so
many hypotheses as to be practically useless.

Attention has already (pp. 100, 105) been called to the fact that for some
purposes such things as tea and coffee must be grouped together as one commodity: and it is obvious that, if tea were inaccessible, people would increase
their consumption of coffee, and *vice versâ*. The loss that people would suffer
from being deprived both of tea and coffee would be greater than the sum of
their losses from being deprived of either alone: and therefore the total utility of
tea and coffee is greater than the sum of the total utility of tea calculated on the

It is
seldom
necessary
to take
account of
changes in
the pur-
chaser's
command
of money.

§ 4. The substance of our argument would not be affected if we took account of the fact that, the more a person spends on anything the less power he retains of purchasing more of it or of other things, and the greater is the value of money to him (in technical language every fresh expenditure increases the marginal value of money to him). But though its substance would not be altered, its form would be made more intricate without any corresponding gain; for there are very few practical problems, in which the corrections to be made under this head would be of any importance[1].

There are however some exceptions. For instance, as Sir R. Giffen has pointed out, a rise in the price of bread makes so large a drain on the resources of the poorer labouring families and raises so much the marginal utility of money to them, that they are forced to curtail their consumption of meat and the more expensive farinaceous foods: and, bread being still the cheapest food which they can get and will take, they consume more, and not less of it. But such cases are rare; when they are met with, each must be treated on its own merits.

supposition that people can have recourse to coffee, and that of coffee calculated on a like supposition as to tea. This difficulty can be theoretically evaded by grouping the two "rival" commodities together under a common demand schedule. On the other hand, if we have calculated the total utility of fuel with reference to the fact that without it we could not obtain hot water to obtain the beverage tea from tea leaves, we should count something twice over if we added to that utility the total utility of tea leaves, reckoned on a similar plan. Again the total utility of agricultural produce includes that of ploughs; and the two may not be added together; though the total utility of ploughs may be discussed in connection with one problem, and that of wheat in connection with another. Other aspects of these two difficulties are examined in V. vi.

Prof. Patten has insisted on the latter of them in some able and suggestive writings. But his attempt to express the aggregate utility of all forms of wealth seems to overlook many difficulties.

[1] In mathematical language the neglected elements would generally belong to the second order of small quantities; and the legitimacy of the familiar scientific method by which they are neglected would have seemed beyond question, had not Prof. Nicholson challenged it. A short reply to him has been given by Prof. Edgeworth in the *Economic Journal* for March 1894; and a fuller reply by Prof. Barone in the *Giornale degli Economisti* for Sept. 1894; of which some account is given by Mr Sanger in the *Economic Journal* for March 1895. . . .

It has already been remarked that we cannot guess at all III, vi, 5.
accurately how much of anything people would buy at
prices very different from those which they are accustomed
to pay for it: or in other words, what the demand prices for
it would be for amounts very different from those which
are commonly sold. Our list of demand prices is therefore
highly conjectural except in the neighbourhood of the customary price; and the best estimates we can form of the
whole amount of the utility of anything are liable to large
error. But this difficulty is not important practically. For
the chief applications of the doctrine of consumers' surplus
are concerned with such changes in it as would accompany
changes in the price of the commodity in question in the
neighbourhood of the customary price: that is, they require
us to use only that information with which we are fairly
well supplied. These remarks apply with special force to
necessaries[1].

§ 5. There remains another class of considerations which
are apt to be overlooked in estimating the dependence of wellbeing upon material wealth. Not only does a person's happi-

We can seldom obtain a complete list of demand prices: nor do we often need them.

Elements of collective wealth are apt to be overlooked.

---

[1] The notion of consumers' surplus may help us a little now; and, when our statistical knowledge is further advanced, it may help us a great deal to decide how
much injury would be done to the public by an additional tax of 6d. a pound on tea,
or by an addition of ten per cent. to the freight charges of a railway: and the value
of the notion is but little diminished by the fact that it would not help us much to
estimate the loss that would be caused by a tax of 30s. a pound on tea, or a tenfold
rise in freight charges.

Reverting to our last diagram, we may express this by saying that, if A is the point
on the curve corresponding to the amount that is wont to be sold in the market, data can
be obtained sufficient for drawing the curve with tolerable correctness for some distance
on either side of A; though the curve can seldom be drawn with any approach to accuracy right up to D. But this is practically unimportant, because in the chief practical
applications of the theory of value we should seldom make any use of a knowledge of
the whole shape of the demand curve if we had it. We need just what we can get, that is,
a fairly correct knowledge of its shape in the neighbourhood of A. We seldom require to
ascertain the total area DCA; it is sufficient for most of our purposes to know the
changes in this area that would be occasioned by moving A through small distances
along the curve in either direction. Nevertheless it will save trouble to assume provisionally, as in pure theory we are at liberty to do, that the curve is completely drawn.

There is however a special difficulty in estimating the whole of the utility of commodities some supply of which is necessary for life. If any attempt is made to do it, the best plan
is perhaps to take that necessary supply for granted, and estimate the total utility only of that
part of the commodity which is in excess of this amount. But we must recollect that the desire
for anything is much dependent on the difficulty of getting substitutes for it. . . .

ness often depend more on his own physical, mental and moral health than on his external conditions: but even among these conditions many that are of chief importance for his real happiness are apt to be omitted from an inventory of his wealth. Some are free gifts of nature; and these might indeed be neglected without great harm if they were always the same for everybody; but in fact they vary much from place to place. More of them however are elements of collective wealth which are often omitted from the reckoning of individual wealth; but which become important when we compare different parts of the modern civilized world, and even more important when we compare our own age with earlier times.

So-called consumers' associations belong to the subject of Production.

Collective action for the purposes of securing common wellbeing, as for instance in lighting and watering the streets, will occupy us much towards the end of our inquiries. Cooperative associations for the purchase of things for personal consumption have made more progress in England than elsewhere: but those for purchasing the things wanted for trade purposes by farmers and others, have until lately been backward in England. Both kinds are sometimes described as Consumers' associations; but they are really associations for economizing effort in certain branches of business, and belong to the subject of Production rather than Consumption.

We are here concerned with large incomes rather than large possessions.

§ 6. When we speak of the dependence of wellbeing on material wealth, we refer to the flow or stream of wellbeing as measured by the flow or stream of incoming wealth and the consequent power of using and consuming it. A person's stock of wealth yields by its usance and in other ways an income of happiness, among which of course are to be counted the pleasures of possession: but there is little direct connection between the aggregate amount of that stock and his aggregate happiness. And it is for that reason that we have throughout this and preceding chapters spoken of the rich, the middle classes and the poor as having respectively large, medium and small incomes—not possessions.

In accordance with a suggestion made by Daniel Bernoulli, we may regard the satisfaction which a person derives from his income as commencing when he has enough to support life, and afterwards as increasing by equal amounts with every equal successive percentage that is added to his income; and *vice versâ* for loss of income[1].

III, vi, 6.
——
Bernoulli's suggestion.

But after a time new riches often lose a great part of their charms. Partly this is the result of familiarity; which makes people cease to derive much pleasure from accustomed comforts and luxuries, though they suffer greater pain from their loss. Partly it is due to the fact that with increased riches there often comes either the weariness of age, or at least an increase of nervous strain; and perhaps even habits of living that lower physical vitality, and diminish the capacity for pleasure.

The edge of enjoyment is blunted by familiarity.

[1] That is to say, if £30 represent necessaries, a person's satisfaction from his income will begin at that point; and when it has reached £40, an additional £1 will add a tenth to the £10 which represents its happiness-yielding power. But if his income were £100, that is £70 above the level of necessaries, an additional £7 would be required to add as much to his happiness as £1 if his income were £40: while if his income were £10,000, an additional £1000 would be needed to produce an equal effect. . . . Of course such estimates are very much at random, and unable to adapt themselves to the varying circumstances of individual life. As we shall see later, the systems of taxation which are now most widely prevalent follow generally on the lines of Bernoulli's suggestion. Earlier systems took from the poor very much more than would be in accordance with that plan; while the systems of graduated taxation, which are being foreshadowed in several countries, are in some measure based on the assumption that the addition of one per cent. to a very large income adds less to the wellbeing of its owner than an addition of one per cent. to smaller incomes would, even after Bernoulli's correction for necessaries has been made.

It may be mentioned in passing that from the general law that the utility to anyone of an additional £1 diminishes with the number of pounds he already has, there follow two important practical principles. The first is that gambling involves an economic loss, even when conducted on perfectly fair and even terms. For instance, a man who having £600 makes a fair even bet of £100, has now an expectation of happiness equal to half that derived from £700, and half that derived from £500; and this is less than the certain expectation of the happiness derived from £600, because by hypothesis the difference between the happiness got from £600 and £500 is greater than the difference between the happiness got from £700 and £600. The second principle, the direct converse of the first, is that a theoretically fair insurance against risks is always an economic gain. But of course every insurance office, after calculating what is a theoretically fair premium, has to share in addition to it enough to pay profits on its own capital, and to cover its own expenses of working, among which are often to be reckoned very heavy items for advertising and for losses by fraud. The question whether it is advisable to pay the premium which insurance offices practically do charge, is one that must be decided for each case on its own merits.

III, VI, 6.

The value of leisure and rest.

In every civilized country there have been some followers of the Buddhist doctrine that a placid serenity is the highest ideal of life; that it is the part of the wise man to root out of his nature as many wants and desires as he can; that real riches consist not in the abundance of goods but in the paucity of wants. At the other extreme are those who maintain that the growth of new wants and desires is always beneficial because it stimulates people to increased exertions. They seem to have made the mistake, as Herbert Spencer says, of supposing that life is for working, instead of working for life[1].

The excellence of a moderate income obtained by moderate work.

The truth seems to be that as human nature is constituted, man rapidly degenerates unless he has some hard work to do, some difficulties to overcome; and that some strenuous exertion is necessary for physical and moral health. The fulness of life lies in the development and activity of as many and as high faculties as possible. There is intense pleasure in the ardent pursuit of any aim, whether it be success in business, the advancement of art and science, or the improvement of the condition of one's fellow-beings. The highest constructive work of all kinds must often alternate between periods of over-strain and periods of lassitude and stagnation; but for ordinary people, for those who have no strong ambitions, whether of a lower or a higher kind, a moderate income earned by moderate and fairly steady work offers the best opportunity for the growth of those habits of body, mind, and spirit in which alone there is true happiness.

Expenditure for the sake of display.

There is some misuse of wealth in all ranks of society. And though, speaking generally, we may say that every increase in the wealth of the working classes adds to the fulness and nobility of human life, because it is used chiefly in the satisfaction of real wants; yet even among the artisans in England, and perhaps still more in new countries, there are signs of the growth of that unwholesome desire for wealth as a means of display which has been the chief bane of the well-to-do classes in every civilized country. Laws against luxury have been futile; but it would be a gain if the moral sentiment of the community could induce people to avoid

[1] See his lecture on *The Gospel of Relaxation.*

all sorts of display of individual wealth. There are indeed III,VI, 6.
true and worthy pleasures to be got from wisely ordered The
magnificence: but they are at their best when free from any superior
nobility
taint of personal vanity on the one side and envy on the of the
collective
other; as they are when they centre round public buildings, over the
private use
public parks, public collections of the fine arts, and public of wealth.
games and amusements. So long as wealth is applied to
provide for every family the necessaries of life and culture,
and an abundance of the higher forms of enjoyment for
collective use, so long the pursuit of wealth is a noble aim;
and the pleasures which it brings are likely to increase
with the growth of those higher activities which it is used
to promote.

When the necessaries of life are once provided, everyone The
tasteful
should seek to increase the beauty of things in his possession purchaser
rather than their number or their magnificence. An im- educates
the pro-
provement in the artistic character of furniture and clothing ducer.
We thus
trains the higher faculties of those who make them, and is approach
the fringe
a source of growing happiness to those who use them. But of broad
inquiries,
if instead of seeking for a higher standard of beauty, we which
spend our growing resources on increasing the complexity must be
deferred.
and intricacy of our domestic goods, we gain thereby no true
benefit, no lasting happiness. The world would go much
better if everyone would buy fewer and simpler things, and
would take trouble in selecting them for their real beauty;
being careful of course to get good value in return for his
outlay, but preferring to buy a few things made well by
highly paid labour rather than many made badly by low
paid labour.

But we are exceeding the proper scope of the present
Book; the discussion of the influence on general wellbeing
which is exerted by the mode in which each individual
spends his income is one of the more important of those
applications of economic science to the art of living.

BOOK V.

GENERAL RELATIONS OF DEMAND, SUPPLY AND VALUE.

CHAPTER I.

INTRODUCTORY. ON MARKETS.

§ 1. A business firm grows and attains great strength, and afterwards perhaps stagnates and decays; and at the turning point there is a balancing or equilibrium of the forces of life and decay. . . . And as we reach to the higher stages of our work, we shall need ever more and more to think of economic forces as resembling those which make a young man grow in strength, till he reaches his prime; after which he gradually becomes stiff and inactive, till at last he sinks to make room for other and more vigorous life. But to prepare the way for this advanced study we want first to look at a simpler balancing of forces which corresponds rather to the mechanical equilibrium of a stone hanging by an elastic string, or of a number of balls resting against one another in a basin.

V, i, 1.

Biological and mechanical notions of the balancing of opposed forces.

We have now to examine the general relations of demand and supply; especially those which are connected with that adjustment of price, by which they are maintained in "equilibrium." This term is in common use and may be used for the present without special explanation. But there are many difficulties connected with it, which can only be handled gradually: and indeed they will occupy our attention during a great part of this Book.

Scope of this book.

V, I, 2.   Illustrations will be taken now from one class of economic problems and now from another, but the main course of the reasoning will be kept free from assumptions which specially belong to any particular class.

Thus it is not descriptive, nor does it deal constructively with real problems. But it sets out the theoretical backbone of our knowledge of the causes which govern value, and thus prepares the way for the construction which is to begin in the following Book. It aims not so much at the attainment of knowledge, as at the power to obtain and arrange knowledge with regard to two opposing sets of forces, those which impel man to economic efforts and sacrifices, and those which hold him back.

Markets described only provisionally here   We must begin with a short and provisional account of markets: for that is needed to give precision to the ideas in this and the following Books. But the organization of markets is intimately connected both as cause and effect with money, credit, and foreign trade; a full study of it must therefore be deferred to a later volume, where it will be taken in connection with commercial and industrial fluctuations, and with combinations of producers and of merchants, of employers and employed.

Definition of a market.   § 2. When demand and supply are spoken of in relation to one another, it is of course necessary that the markets to which they refer should be the same. As Cournot says, "Economists understand by the term *Market*, not any particular market place in which things are bought and sold, but the whole of any region in which buyers and sellers are in such free intercourse with one another that the prices of the same goods tend to equality easily and quickly[1]." Or again as Jevons says:—"Originally a market was a public place in a town where provisions and other objects were exposed for sale; but the word has been generalized, so as to mean any body of persons who are in intimate business relations and carry on extensive transactions in any commodity. A great city may contain as many markets as there are important branches of trade, and these markets may or

[1] *Recherches sur les Principes Mathématiques de la Théorie des Richesses*, ch. IV. See also above III. IV. 7.

may not be localized. The central point of a market is the v, i, 3.
public exchange, mart or auction rooms, where the traders
agree to meet and transact business.   In London the Stock
Market, the Corn Market, the Coal Market, the Sugar Market,
and many others are distinctly localized; in Manchester the
Cotton Market, the Cotton Waste Market, and others. But
this distinction of locality is not necessary. The traders
may be spread over a whole town, or region of country, and
yet make a market, if they are, by means of fairs, meetings,
published price lists, the post-office or otherwise, in close
communication with each other[1]."

Thus the more nearly perfect a market is, the stronger
is the tendency for the same price to be paid for the same
thing at the same time in all parts of the market: but of
course if the market is large, allowance must be made for
the expense of delivering the goods to different purchasers;
each of whom must be supposed to pay in addition to the
market price a special charge on account of delivery[2].

§ 3. In applying economic reasonings in practice it is Boundaries
often difficult to ascertain how far the movements of supply of a market.
and demand in any one place are influenced by those in
another. It is clear that the general tendency of the
telegraph, the printing-press and steam traffic is to extend
the area over which such influences act and to increase their
force. The whole Western World may, in a sense, be re- Instances
garded as one market for many kinds of stock exchange of very wide
securities, for the more valuable metals, and to a less extent markets.
for wool and cotton and even wheat; proper allowance being
made for expenses of transport, in which may be included taxes
levied by any customs houses through which the goods have
to pass. For in all these cases the expenses of transport,
including customs duties, are not sufficient to prevent buyers
from all parts of the Western World from competing with
one another for the same supplies.

There are many special causes which may widen or General
narrow the market of any particular commodity: but nearly conditions which

[1] *Theory of Political Economy*, ch. iv.
[2] Thus it is common to see the prices of bulky goods quoted as delivered "free
on board" (f. o. b.) any vessel in a certain port, each purchaser having to make
his own reckoning for bringing the goods home.

V, I, 4. all those things for which there is a very wide market are in

affect the universal demand, and capable of being easily and exactly

extent described. Thus for instance cotton, wheat, and iron satisfy
of the

market for wants that are urgent and nearly universal. They can
a thing.

Suitability be easily described, so that they can be bought and sold
for grading

and by persons at a distance from one another and at a distance

sampling. also from the commodities. If necessary, samples can be

taken of them which are truly representative: and they can

even be "graded," as is the actual practice with regard to

grain in America, by an independent authority; so that

the purchaser may be secure that what he buys will come

up to a given standard, though he has never seen a sample

of the goods which he is buying and perhaps would not

be able himself to form an opinion on it if he did[1].

Porta-   Commodities for which there is a very wide market must
bility.

also be such as will bear a long carriage: they must be some-

what durable, and their value must be considerable in pro-

portion to their bulk. A thing which is so bulky that its

price is necessarily raised very much when it is sold far away

from the place in which it is produced, must as a rule have a

narrow market. The market for common bricks for instance

is practically confined to the near neighbourhood of the

kilns in which they are made: they can scarcely ever bear

a long carriage by land to a district which has any kilns of

its own. But bricks of certain exceptional kinds have mar-

kets extending over a great part of England.

The   § 4. Let us then consider more closely the markets for
conditions

of highly things which satisfy in an exceptional way these conditions
organized

markets of being in general demand, cognizable and portable. They

are, as we have said, stock exchange securities and the more

valuable metals.

Illustrated Any one share or bond of a public company, or any bond
by refer-

ence to of a government is of exactly the same value as any other
stock

exchanges. of the same issue: it can make no difference to any purchaser

---

[1] Thus the managers of a public or private "elevator," receive grain from
a farmer, divide it into different grades, and return to him certificates for as
many bushels of each grade as he has delivered. His grain is then mixed with
those of other farmers; his certificates are likely to change hands several times
before they reach a purchaser who demands that the grain shall be actually
delivered to him; and little or none of what that purchaser receives may have
come from the farm of the original recipient of the certificate.

which of the two he buys. Some securities, principally those V, I, 4. of comparatively small mining, shipping, and other companies, require local knowledge, and are not very easily dealt in except on the stock exchanges of provincial towns in their immediate neighbourhood. But the whole of England is one market for the shares and bonds of a large English railway. In ordinary times a dealer will sell, say, Midland Railway shares, even if he has not them himself; because he knows they are always coming into the market, and he is sure to be able to buy them.

But the strongest case of all is that of securities which are called "international," because they are in request in every part of the globe. They are the bonds of the chief governments, and of very large public companies such as those of the Suez Canal and the New York Central Railway. For bonds of this class the telegraph keeps prices at almost exactly the same level in all the stock exchanges of the world. If the price of one of them rises in New York or in Paris, in London or in Berlin, the mere news of the rise tends to cause a rise in other markets; and if for any reason the rise is delayed, that particular class of bonds is likely soon to be offered for sale in the high priced market under telegraphic orders from the other markets, while dealers in the first market will be making telegraphic purchases in other markets. These sales on the one hand, and purchases on the other, strengthen the tendency which the price has to seek the same level everywhere; and unless some of the markets are in an abnormal condition, the tendency soon becomes irresistible.

On the stock exchange also a dealer can generally make sure of selling at nearly the same price as that at which he buys; and he is often willing to buy first class stocks at a half, or a quarter, or an eighth, or in some cases even a six-teenth per cent. less than he offers in the same breath to sell them at. If there are two securities equally good, but one of them belongs to a large issue of bonds, and the other to a small issue by the same government, so that the first is constantly coming on the market, and the latter but seldom, then the dealers will on this account alone require a larger

V, I, 5. margin between their selling price and their buying price in
the latter case than in the former[1]. This illustrates well the
great law, that the larger the market for a commodity the
smaller generally are the fluctuations in its price, and the
lower is the percentage on the turnover which dealers charge
for doing business in it.

The world market for the precious metals.

Stock exchanges then are the pattern on which markets
have been, and are being formed for dealing in many kinds
of produce which can be easily and exactly described, are
portable and in general demand. The material commodities
however which possess these qualities in the highest degree
are gold and silver. For that very reason they have been
chosen by common consent for use as money, to represent the
value of other things: the world market for them is most
highly organized, and will be found to offer many subtle
illustrations of the actions of the laws which we are now
discussing.

§ 5. At the opposite extremity to international stock
exchange securities and the more valuable metals are, firstly,
things which must be made to order to suit particular
individuals, such as well-fitting clothes; and, secondly, perishable and bulky goods, such as fresh vegetables, which can
seldom be profitably carried long distances. The first can
scarcely be said to have a wholesale market at all; the
conditions by which their price is determined are those of
retail buying and selling, and the study of them may be
postponed[2].

Putting aside cases of retail dealing,

[1] In the case of shares of very small and little known companies, the difference
between the price at which a dealer is willing to buy and that at which he will sell
may amount to from five per cent. or more of the selling value. If he buys, he
may have to carry this security a long time before he meets with any one who
comes to take it from him, and meanwhile it may fall in value: while if he
undertakes to deliver a security which he has not himself got and which does not
come on the market every day, he may be unable to complete his contract without
much trouble and expense.

[2] A man may not trouble himself much about small retail purchases: he may
give half-a-crown for a packet of paper in one shop which he could have got
for two shillings in another. But it is otherwise with wholesale prices. A
manufacturer cannot sell a ream of paper for six shillings while his neighbour is
selling it at five. For those whose business it is to deal in paper know almost
exactly the lowest price at which it can be bought, and will not pay more than
this. The manufacturer has to sell at about the market price, that is at about the
price at which other manufacturers are selling at the same time.

There are indeed wholesale markets for the second class, but they are confined within narrow boundaries; we may find our typical instance in the sale of the commoner kinds of vegetables in a country town. The market-gardeners in the neighbourhood have probably to arrange for the sale of their vegetables to the townspeople with but little external interference on either side. There may be some check to extreme prices by the power on the one side of selling, and on the other of buying elsewhere; but under ordinary circumstances the check is inoperative, and it may happen that the dealers in such a case are able to combine, and thus fix an artificial monopoly price; that is, a price determined with little direct reference to cost of production, but chiefly by a consideration of what the market will bear.

V, I, 5.

we pass to a market which seems to be narrowly confined,

On the other hand, it may happen that some of the market-gardeners are almost equally near a second country town, and send their vegetables now to one and now to the other; and some people who occasionally buy in the first town may have equally good access to the second. The least variation in price will lead them to prefer the better market; and thus make the bargainings in the two towns to some extent mutually dependent. It may happen that this second town is in close communication with London or some other central market, so that its prices are controlled by the prices in the central market; and in that case prices in our first town also must move to a considerable extent in harmony with them. As news passes from mouth to mouth till a rumour spreads far away from its forgotten sources, so even the most secluded market is liable to be influenced by changes of which those in the market have no direct cognizance, changes that have had their origin far away and have spread gradually from market to market.

though even this is subject to indirect influences from great distances.

Thus at the one extreme are world markets in which competition acts directly from all parts of the globe; and at the other those secluded markets in which all direct competition from afar is shut out, though indirect and transmitted competition may make itself felt even in these; and about midway between these extremes lie the great majority of the markets which the economist and the business man have to study.

Limita-
tions of
market
with
regard
to time
affect the
nature of
the causes
of which
we have
to take
account.

§ 6. Again, markets vary with regard to the period of time which is allowed to the forces of demand and supply to bring themselves into equilibrium with one another, as well as with regard to the area over which they extend. And this element of Time requires more careful attention just now than does that of Space. For the nature of the equilibrium itself, and that of the causes by which it is determined, depend on the length of the period over which the market is taken to extend. We shall find that if the period is short, the supply is limited to the stores which happen to be at hand: if the period is longer, the supply will be influenced, more or less, by the cost of producing the commodity in question; and if the period is very long, this cost will in its turn be influenced, more or less, by the cost of producing the labour and the material things required for producing the commodity. These three classes of course merge into one another by imperceptible degrees. We will begin with the first class; and consider in the next chapter those temporary equilibria of demand and supply, in which "supply" means in effect merely the stock available at the time for sale in the market; so that it cannot be directly influenced by the cost of production.

CHAPTER II.

TEMPORARY EQUILIBRIUM OF DEMAND AND SUPPLY.

§ 1. The simplest case of balance or equilibrium between desire and effort is found when a person satisfies one of his wants by his own direct work. When a boy picks blackberries for his own eating, the action of picking is probably itself pleasurable for a while; and for some time longer the pleasure of eating is more than enough to repay the trouble of picking. But after he has eaten a good deal, the desire for more diminishes; while the task of picking begins to cause weariness, which may indeed be a feeling of monotony rather than of fatigue. Equilibrium is reached when at last his eagerness to play and his disinclination for the work of picking counterbalance the desire for eating. The satisfaction which he can get from picking fruit has arrived at its *maximum*: for up to that time every fresh picking has added more to his pleasure than it has taken away; and after that time any further picking would take away from his pleasure more than it would add.

In a casual bargain that one person makes with another, as for instance when two backwoodsmen barter a rifle for a canoe, there is seldom anything that can properly be called an equilibrium of supply and demand: there is probably a margin of satisfaction on either side; for probably the one would be willing to give something besides the rifle for the canoe, if he could not get the canoe otherwise; while the

V, II, 2. other would in case of necessity give something besides the canoe for the rifle.

The case of systematic barter may be deferred. It is indeed possible that a true equilibrium may be arrived at under a system of barter; but barter, though earlier in history than buying and selling, is in some ways more intricate; and the simplest cases of a true equilibrium value are found in the markets of a more advanced state of civilization.

Market for unique or rare things. We may put aside as of little practical importance a class of dealings which has been much discussed. They relate to pictures by old masters, rare coins and other things, which cannot be "graded" at all. The price at which each is sold, will depend much on whether any rich persons with a fancy for it happen to be present at its sale. If not, it will probably be bought by dealers who reckon on being able to sell it at a profit; and the variations in the price for which the same picture sells at successive auctions, great as they are, would be greater still if it were not for the steadying influence of professional purchasers.

Illustration from a local corn-market of a true though temporary equilibrium. § 2. Let us then turn to the ordinary dealings of modern life; and take an illustration from a corn-market in a country town, and let us assume for the sake of simplicity that all the corn in the market is of the same quality. The amount which each farmer or other seller offers for sale at any price is governed by his own need for money in hand, and by his calculation of the present and future conditions of the market with which he is connected. There are some prices which no seller would accept, some which no one would refuse. There are other intermediate prices which would be accepted for larger or smaller amounts by many or all of the sellers. Everyone will try to guess the state of the market and to govern his actions accordingly. Let us suppose that in fact there are not more than 600 quarters, the holders of which are willing to accept as low a price as 35s.; but that holders of another hundred would be tempted by 36s.; and holders of yet another three hundred by 37s. Let us suppose also that a price of 37s. would tempt buyers for only 600 quarters; while another hundred could be sold at 36s., and

yet another two hundred at 35s. These facts may be put out
in a table thus:—

At the price	Holders will be willing to sell	Buyers will be willing to buy
37s.	1000 quarters,	600 quarters.
36s.	700 „	700 „
35s.	600 „	900 „

Of course some of those who are really willing to take 36s.
rather than leave the market without selling, will not show
at once that they are ready to accept that price. And in like
manner buyers will fence, and pretend to be less eager than
they really are. So the price may be tossed hither and
thither like a shuttlecock, as one side or the other gets the
better in the "higgling and bargaining" of the market. But
unless they are unequally matched; unless, for instance, one
side is very simple or unfortunate in failing to gauge the
strength of the other side, the price is likely to be never very
far from 36s.; and it is nearly sure to be pretty close to 36s.
at the end of the market. For if a holder thinks that the
buyers will really be able to get at 36s. all that they care to
take at that price, he will be unwilling to let slip past him
any offer that is well above that price.

Buyers on their part will make similar calculations; and
if at any time the price should rise considerably above 36s.
they will argue that the supply will be much greater than
the demand at that price: therefore even those of them who
would rather pay that price than go unserved, wait; and by
waiting they help to bring the price down. On the other
hand, when the price is much below 36s., even those sellers
who would rather take the price than leave the market with
their corn unsold, will argue that at that price the demand
will be in excess of the supply: so they will wait, and by
waiting help to bring the price up.

The price of 36s. has thus some claim to be called the true
equilibrium price: because if it were fixed on at the beginning, and adhered to throughout, it would exactly equate
demand and supply (i.e. the amount which buyers were
willing to purchase at that price would be just equal to that
for which sellers were willing to take that price); and because

V, II, 3.   every dealer who has a perfect knowledge of the circumstances of the market expects that price to be established. If he sees the price differing much from 36s. he expects that a change will come before long, and by anticipating it he helps it to come quickly.

It is not indeed necessary for our argument that any dealers should have a thorough knowledge of the circumstances of the market. Many of the buyers may perhaps underrate the willingness of the sellers to sell, with the effect that for some time the price rules at the highest level at which any buyers can be found; and thus 500 quarters may be sold before the price sinks below 37s. But afterwards the price must begin to fall and the result will still probably be that 200 more quarters will be sold, and the market will close on a price of about 36s. For when 700 quarters have been sold, no seller will be anxious to dispose of any more except at a higher price than 36s., and no buyer will be anxious to purchase any more except at a lower price than 36s. In the same way if the sellers had underrated the willingness of the buyers to pay a high price, some of them might begin to sell at the lowest price they would take, rather than have their corn left on their hands, and in this case much corn might be sold at a price of 35s.; but the market would probably close on a price of 36s. and a total sale of 700 quarters[1].

The latent assumption, that the dealers' willingness to spend money is nearly constant throughout,

§ 3. In this illustration there is a latent assumption which is in accordance with the actual conditions of most markets; but which ought to be distinctly recognized in order to prevent its creeping into those cases in which it is not justifiable. We tacitly assumed that the sum which purchasers were willing to pay, and which sellers were willing to take, for the seven hundredth quarter would not be affected by the question whether the earlier bargains had been made at a high or a low rate. We allowed for the diminution in the buyers' need of corn [its marginal utility to them] as the amount bought increased. But we did not allow for any appreciable change in their unwillingness to part with money

---

[1] A simple form of the influence which opinion exerts on the action of dealers, and therefore on market price, is indicated in this illustration: we shall be much occupied with more complex developments of it later on.

[its marginal utility]; we assumed that that would be prac- V, ii, 3.
tically the same whether the early payments had been at a
high or a low rate.

This assumption is justifiable with regard to most of the *is generally valid as to a corn-market;* market dealings with which we are practically concerned.
When a person buys anything for his own consumption, he
generally spends on it a small part of his total resources;
while when he buys it for the purposes of trade, he looks to
re-selling it, and therefore his potential resources are not
diminished. In either case there is no appreciable change in
his willingness to part with money. There may indeed be
individuals of whom this is not true; but there are sure to
be present some dealers with large stocks of money at their
command; and their influence steadies the market[1].

The exceptions are rare and unimportant in markets for *but in a labour market the exceptions are often important.* commodities; but in markets for labour they are frequent and
important. When a workman is in fear of hunger, his need
of money [its marginal utility to him] is very great; and, if
at starting, he gets the worst of the bargaining, and is
employed at low wages, it remains great, and he may go
on selling his labour at a low rate. That is all the more
probable because, while the advantage in bargaining is likely

---

[1] For instance a buyer is sometimes straitened for want of ready money, and
has to let offers pass by him in no way inferior to others which he has gladly
accepted: his own funds being exhausted, he could not perhaps borrow except on
terms that would take away all the profit that the bargains had at first sight
offered. But if the bargain is really a good one, some one else, who is not so
straitened, is nearly sure to get hold of it.

Again, it is possible that several of those who had been counted as ready to
sell corn at a price of 36s. were willing to sell only because they were in urgent
need of a certain amount of ready money; if they succeeded in selling some corn
at a high price, there might be a perceptible diminution in the marginal utility of
ready money to them; and therefore they might refuse to sell for 36s. a quarter
all the corn which they would have sold if the price had been 36s. throughout.
In this case the sellers in consequence of getting an advantage in bargaining at
the beginning of the market might retain to the end a price higher than *the*
equilibrium price. The price at which the market closed would be *an* equilibrium
price; and though not properly described as *the* equilibrium price, it would be
very unlikely to diverge widely from that price.

Conversely, if the market had opened much to the disadvantage of the sellers
and they had sold some corn very cheap, so that they remained in great want of
ready money, the final utility of money to them might have remained so high that
they would have gone on selling considerably below 36s. until the buyers had been
supplied with all that they cared to take. The market would then close without
the true equilibrium price having ever been reached, but a very near approach
would have been made to it.

to be pretty well distributed between the two sides of a market for commodities, it is more often on the side of the buyers than on that of the sellers in a market for labour. Another difference between a labour market and a market for commodities arises from the fact that each seller of labour has only one unit of labour to dispose of. These are two among many facts, in which we shall find, as we go on, the explanation of much of that instinctive objection which the working classes have felt to the habit of some economists, particularly those of the employer class, of treating labour simply as a commodity and regarding the labour market as like every other market; whereas in fact the differences between the two cases, though not fundamental from the point of view of theory, are yet clearly marked, and in practice often very important.

This difference has important results in theory and in practice.

The theory of buying and selling becomes therefore much more complex when we take account of the dependence of marginal utility on amount in the case of money as well as of the commodity itself. The practical importance of this consideration is not very great. . . . In barter a person's stock of either commodity exchanged needs to be adjusted closely to his individual wants. If his stock is too large he may have no good use for it. If his stock is too small he may have some difficulty in finding any one who can conveniently give him what he wants and is also in need of the particular things of which he himself has a superfluity. But any one who has a stock of general purchasing power, can obtain any thing he wants as soon as he meets with any one who has a superfluity of that thing: he needs not to hunt about till he comes across "the double coincidence" of a person who can spare what he wants, and also wants what he can spare. Consequently every one, and especially a professional dealer, can afford to keep command over a large stock of money; and can therefore make considerable purchases without depleting his stock of money or greatly altering its marginal value.

CHAPTER III.

EQUILIBRIUM OF NORMAL DEMAND AND SUPPLY.

§ 1. WE have next to inquire what causes govern supply prices, that is prices which dealers are willing to accept for different amounts. In the last chapter we looked at the affairs of only a single day; and supposed the stocks offered for sale to be already in existence. But of course these stocks are dependent on the amount of wheat sown in the preceding year; and that, in its turn, was largely influenced by the farmers' guesses as to the price which they would get for it in this year. This is the point at which we have to work in the present chapter.

Even in the corn-exchange of a country town on a market-day the equilibrium price is affected by calculations of the future relations of production and consumption; while in the leading corn-markets of America and Europe dealings for future delivery already predominate and are rapidly weaving into one web all the leading threads of trade in corn throughout the whole world. Some of these dealings in "futures" are but incidents in speculative manœuvres; but in the main they are governed by calculations of the world's consumption on the one hand, and of the existing stocks and coming harvests in the Northern and Southern hemispheres on the other. Dealers take account of the areas sown with each kind of grain, of the forwardness and weight of the crops, of the supply of things which can be used as substitutes for grain, and of the things for which grain can be used as a substitute. Thus, when buying or selling barley, they take account of the supplies of such things as sugar, which can be used as substitutes for it in brewing, and again of all the various feeding stuffs, a scarcity of which might raise the value of barley for consumption on the farm. If it is thought that the growers of any kind of grain in any part of the world have been losing money, and are likely to sow a less area for a future harvest; it is argued that prices are likely to rise as soon as that harvest comes into sight, and its shortness is manifest to all. Anticipations of that rise exercise an influence on present sales for future delivery, and that in its turn influences cash prices; so that these prices are indirectly affected by estimates of the expenses of producing further supplies.

and we are now to consider slow and gradual adjustments of supply and demand.

But in this and the following chapters we are specially concerned with movements of price ranging over still longer periods than those for which the most far-sighted dealers in futures generally make their reckoning: we have to consider the volume of production adjusting itself to the conditions of the market, and the normal price being thus determined at the position of stable equilibrium of normal demand and normal supply.

The account of supply price carried a little further.

§ 2. In this discussion we shall have to make frequent use of the terms *cost* and *expenses* of production; and some provisional account of them must be given before proceeding further.

We may revert to the analogy between the supply price and the demand price of a commodity. Assuming for the moment that the efficiency of production depends solely upon the exertions of the workers, we saw [in Book IV] that "the price required to call forth the exertion necessary for producing any given amount of a commodity may be called the supply price for that amount, with reference of course to a given unit of time." But now we have to take account of the fact that the production of a commodity generally requires many different kinds of labour and the use of capital in many forms. The exertions of all the different

kinds of labour that are directly or indirectly involved in *V, III, 2.*
making it; together with the abstinences or rather the
waitings required for saving the capital used in making it:
all these efforts and sacrifices together will be called the
real cost of production of the commodity. The sums of *Real and*
money that have to be paid for these efforts and sacrifices *money cost of*
will be called either its *money cost of production*, or, for *production.*
shortness, its *expenses of production*; they are the prices *Expenses*
which have to be paid in order to call forth an adequate *of pro-*
duction.
supply of the efforts and waitings that are required for
making it; or, in other words, they are its supply price[1].

The analysis of the expenses of production of a commodity might be carried backward to any length; but it is
seldom worth while to go back very far. It is for instance
often sufficient to take the supply prices of the different
kinds of raw materials used in any manufacture as ultimate
facts, without analysing these supply prices into the several
elements of which they are composed; otherwise indeed the
analysis would never end. We may then arrange the things
that are required for making a commodity into whatever
groups are convenient, and call them its *factors of production*. *Factors of*
Its expenses of production when any given amount of it is *production.*
produced are thus the supply prices of the corresponding
quantities of its factors of production. And the sum of
these is the supply price of that amount of the commodity.

---

[1] Mill and some other economists have followed the practice of ordinary life in
using the term Cost of production in two senses, sometimes to signify the difficulty
of producing a thing, and sometimes to express the outlay of money that has to
be incurred in order to induce people to overcome this difficulty and produce it.
But by passing from one use of the term to the other without giving explicit
warning, they have led to many misunderstandings and much barren controversy.
The attack on Mill's doctrine of Cost of Production in relation to Value, which is
made in Cairnes' *Leading Principles*, was published just after Mill's death; and
unfortunately his interpretation of Mill's words was generally accepted as au-
thoritative, because he was regarded as a follower of Mill. But in an article by
the present writer on "Mill's Theory of Value" (*Fortnightly Review*, April 1876)
it is argued that Cairnes had mistaken Mill's meaning, and had really seen not
more but less of the truth than Mill had done.

The expenses of production of any amount of a raw commodity may best be
estimated with reference to the "margin of production" at which no rent is paid.
But this method of speaking has great difficulties with regard to commodities
that obey the law of increasing return. It seemed best to note this point in
passing: it will be fully discussed later on, chiefly in ch. XII.

There
is great
variety
in the
relative
importance
of different
elements
of cost of
production.

§ **3.** The typical modern market is often regarded as that in which manufacturers sell goods to wholesale dealers at prices into which but few trading expenses enter. But taking a broader view, we may consider that the supply price of a commodity is the price at which it will be delivered for sale to that group of persons whose demand for it we are considering; or, in other words, in the market which we have in view. On the character of that market will depend how many trading expenses have to be reckoned to make up the supply price[1]. For instance, the supply price of wood in the neighbourhood of Canadian forests often consists almost exclusively of the price of the labour of lumber men: but the supply price of the same wood in the wholesale London market consists in a large measure of freights; while its supply price to a small retail buyer in an English country town is more than half made up of the charges of the railways and middlemen who have brought what he wants to his doors, and keep a stock of it ready for him. Again, the supply price of a certain kind of labour may for some purposes be divided up into the expenses of rearing, of general education and of special trade education. The possible combinations are numberless; and though each may have incidents of its own which will require separate treatment in the complete solution of any problem connected with it, yet all such incidents may be ignored, so far as the general reasonings of this Book are concerned.

In calculating the expenses of production of a commodity we must take account of the fact that changes in the amounts produced are likely, even when there is no new invention, to be accompanied by changes in the relative quantities of its several factors of production. For instance, when the scale of production increases, horse or steam power is likely to be substituted for manual labour; materials are likely to be brought from a greater distance and in greater quantities, thus increasing those expenses of production which

---

[1] We have already (II. III.) noticed that the economic use of the term "production" includes the production of new utilities by moving a thing from a place in which it is less wanted to a place in which it is more wanted, or by helping consumers to satisfy their needs.

correspond to the work of carriers, middlemen and traders V, III, 4.
of all kinds.

As far as the knowledge and business enterprise of the *The prin-*
producers reach, they in each case choose those factors of *ciple of*
production which are best for their purpose; the sum of the *tion.*
supply prices of those factors which are used is, as a rule,
less than the sum of the supply prices of any other set of
factors which could be substituted for them; and whenever
it appears to the producers that this is not the case, they
will, as a rule, set to work to substitute the less expensive
method. And further on we shall see how in a somewhat
similar way society substitutes one undertaker for another
who is less efficient in proportion to his charges. We may
call this, for convenience of reference, *The principle of
substitution.*

The applications of this principle extend over almost
every field of economic inquiry.

§ 4. The position then is this: we are investigating the The posi-
equilibrium of normal demand and normal supply in their tion from
most general form; we are neglecting those features which which we
                                                           start.
are special to particular parts of economic science, and are
confining our attention to those broad relations which are
common to nearly the whole of it. Thus we assume that We assume
the forces of demand and supply have free play; that there is free play
no close combination among dealers on either side, but each for demand
                                                             and supply
acts for himself, and there is much free competition; that is, in the
buyers generally compete freely with buyers, and sellers market.
compete freely with sellers. But though everyone acts for
himself, his knowledge of what others are doing is supposed
to be generally sufficient to prevent him from taking a lower
or paying a higher price than others are doing This is
assumed provisionally to be true both of finished goods and
of their factors of production, of the hire of labour and of the
borrowing of capital. We have already inquired to some
extent, and we shall have to inquire further, how far these
assumptions are in accordance with the actual facts of life.
But meanwhile this is the supposition on which we proceed;
we assume that there is only one price in the market at one

and the same time; it being understood that separate allowance is made, when necessary, for differences in the expense of delivering goods to dealers in different parts of the market; including allowance for the special expenses of retailing, if it is a retail market.

General conditions of demand.

In such a market there is a demand price for each amount of the commodity, that is, a price at which each particular amount of the commodity can find purchasers in a day or week or year. The circumstances which govern this price for any given amount of the commodity vary in character from one problem to another; but in every case the more of a thing is offered for sale in a market the lower is the price at which it will find purchasers; or in other words, the demand price for each bushel or yard diminishes with every increase in the amount offered.

The unit of time may be chosen according to the circumstances of each particular problem: it may be a day, a month, a year, or even a generation: but in every case it must be short relatively to the period of the market under discussion. It is to be assumed that the general circumstances of the market remain unchanged throughout this period; that there is, for instance, no change in fashion or taste, no new substitute which might affect the demand, no new invention to disturb the supply.

The conditions of supply will vary with the length of time to which reference is made.

The conditions of normal supply are less definite; and a full study of them must be reserved for later chapters. They will be found to vary in detail with the length of the period of time to which the investigation refers; chiefly because both the material capital of machinery and other business plant, and the immaterial capital of business skill and ability and organization, are of slow growth and slow decay.

But we may provisionally regard normal supply price as the expenses of production,

Let us call to mind the "representative firm," whose economies of production, internal and external, are dependent on the aggregate volume of production of the commodity that it makes; and, postponing all further study of the nature of this dependence, let us assume that the normal supply price of any amount of that commodity may be taken to be its normal expenses of production (including *gross* earnings of management) by that firm. That is, let us assume that this is the price the expectation of which will just suffice to maintain the existing aggregate amount of production; some firms meanwhile rising and increasing their output, and others falling and diminishing theirs; but the aggregate production remaining unchanged. A price higher than this would increase the growth of the rising firms, and slacken, though it might not arrest, the decay of the falling firms; with the net result of an increase in the aggregate production. On the other hand, a price lower than this would hasten the decay of the falling firms, and slacken the growth of the rising firms; and on the whole diminish production: and a rise or fall of price would affect in like manner though perhaps not in an equal degree those great joint-stock companies which often stagnate, but seldom die.

§ 5. To give definiteness to our ideas let us take an illustration from the woollen trade. Let us suppose that a person well acquainted with the woollen trade sets himself to inquire what would be the normal supply price of a certain number of millions of yards annually of a particular kind of cloth. He would have to reckon (i) the price of the wool, coal, and other materials which would be used up in making it, (ii) wear-and-tear and depreciation of the buildings, machinery and other fixed capital, (iii) interest and insurance on all the capital, (iv) the wages of those who work in the factories, and (v) the gross earnings of management (including insurance against loss), of those who undertake the risks, who engineer and superintend the working. He would of course estimate the supply prices of all these different factors of production of the cloth with reference to the amounts of each of them that would be wanted, and on the supposition that the conditions of supply would be normal; and he would add them all together to find the supply price of the cloth.

Let us suppose a list of supply prices (or a supply schedule) made on a similar plan to that of our list of demand prices[1]: the supply price of each amount of the commodity in a year, or any other unit of time, being

V, III, 5.
including gross earnings of management, of a representative firm.

The construction of the list of prices at which a thing can be supplied; or its supply schedule.

1 See III. III. 4.

160   EQUILIBRIUM OF NORMAL DEMAND AND SUPPLY

V, III, 5.   written against that amount[1]. As the flow, or (annual) amount of the commodity increases, the supply price may either increase or diminish; or it may even alternately increase and diminish[2]. For if nature is offering a sturdy resistance to man's efforts to wring from her a larger supply of raw material, while at that particular stage there is no great room for introducing important new economies into the manufacture, the supply price will rise; but if the volume of production were greater, it would perhaps be profitable to substitute largely machine work for hand work and steam power for muscular force; and the increase in the volume of production would have diminished the expenses of production of the commodity of our representative

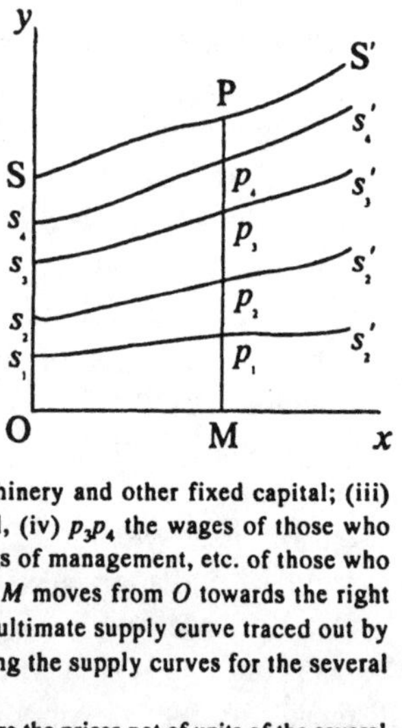

[1] Measuring, as in the case of the demand curve, amounts of the commodity along Ox and prices parallel to Oy, we get for each point M along Ox a line MP drawn at right angles to it measuring the supply price for the amount OM, the extremity of which, P, may be called a *supply point*; this price MP being made up of the supply prices of the several factors of production for the amount OM. The locus of P may be called the *supply curve*.

Fig 18.*

Suppose, for instance, that we classify the expenses of production of our representative firm, when an amount OM of cloth is being produced under the heads of (i) Mp_1, the supply price of the wool and other circulating capital which would be consumed in making it, (ii) p_1p_2 the corresponding wear-and-tear and depreciation on buildings, machinery and other fixed capital; (iii) p_2p_3 the interest and insurance on all the, capital, (iv) p_3p_4 the wages of those who work in the factory, and (v) p_4P the gross earnings of management, etc. of those who undertake the risks and direct the work. Thus as M moves from O towards the right p_1, p_2, p_3, p_4 will each trace out a curve, and the ultimate supply curve traced out by P will be thus shown as obtained by superimposing the supply curves for the several factors of production of the cloth.

It must be remembered that these supply prices are the prices not of units of the several factors but of those amounts of the several factors which are required for producing a yard of the cloth. Thus, for instance, p_3p_4 is the supply price not of any fixed amount of labour but of that amount of labour which is employed in making a yard where there is an aggregate production of OM yards. (See above, § 3.) We need not trouble ourselves to consider just here whether the ground-rent of the factory must be put into a class by itself: this belongs to a group of questions which will be discussed later. We are taking no notice of rates and taxes, for which he would of course have to make his account.

[2] That is, a point moving along the supply curve towards the right may either rise or fall, or even it may alternately rise and fall; in other words, the supply curve may be inclined positively or negatively, or even at some parts of its course it may be inclined positively and at others negatively. (See footnote on p. 99.)

[*Figures 11–17 are in Book IV.]

firm. But those cases in which the supply price falls as the V, III, 6.
amount increases involve special difficulties of their own;
and they are postponed to chapter XII. of this Book.

§ 6. When therefore the amount produced (in a unit of *What is*
time) is such that the demand price is greater than the *meant by*
supply price, then sellers receive more than is sufficient to *brium.*
make it worth their while to bring goods to market to that
amount; and there is at work an active force tending to
increase the amount brought forward for sale. On the other
hand, when the amount produced is such that the demand
price is less than the supply price, sellers receive less than is
sufficient to make it worth their while to bring goods to
market on that scale; so that those who were just on the
margin of doubt as to whether to go on producing are decided
not to do so, and there is an active force at work tending to
diminish the amount brought forward for sale. When the
demand price is equal to the supply price, the amount
produced has no tendency either to be increased or to be
diminished; it is in equilibrium.

When demand and supply are in equilibrium, the amount *Equi-*
of the commodity which is being produced in a unit of time *librium-amount*
may be called the *equilibrium-amount*, and the price at which *and equi-*
it is being sold may be called the *equilibrium-price.* *librium-price.*

Such an equilibrium is *stable*; that is, the price, if dis- *Stable*
placed a little from it, will tend to return, as a pendulum *equilibria,*
oscillates about its lowest point; and it will be found to be a *the*
characteristic of stable equilibria that in them the demand *conditions under*
price is greater than the supply price for amounts just less *which they*
than the equilibrium amount, and *vice versâ.* For when the *occur.*
demand price is greater than the supply price, the amount
produced tends to increase. Therefore, if the demand price
is greater than the supply price for amounts just less than
an equilibrium amount; then, if the scale of production
is temporarily diminished somewhat below that equilibrium
amount, it will tend to return; thus the equilibrium is stable
for displacements in that direction. If the demand price is
greater than the supply price for amounts just less than the
equilibrium amount, it is sure to be less than the supply
price for amounts just greater: and therefore, if the scale of

V, III, 6.

production is somewhat increased beyond the equilibrium position, it will tend to return; and the equilibrium will be stable for displacements in that direction also.

Oscillations about a position of stable equilibrium

When demand and supply are in stable equilibrium, if any accident should move the scale of production from its equilibrium position, there will be instantly brought into play forces tending to push it back to that position; just as, if a stone hanging by a string is displaced from its equilibrium position, the force of gravity will at once tend to bring it back to its equilibrium position. The movements of the scale of production about its position of equilibrium will be of a somewhat similar kind[1].

are seldom rhythmical.

But in real life such oscillations are seldom as rhythmical as those of a stone hanging freely from a string; the comparison would be more exact if the string were supposed to hang in the troubled waters of a mill-race, whose stream was at one time allowed to flow freely, and at another partially cut off. Nor are these complexities sufficient to illustrate all the disturbances with which the economist and the merchant alike are forced to concern themselves. If the person holding the string swings his hand with movements partly rhythmical and partly arbitrary, the illustration will not outrun the difficulties of some very real and practical problems of value. For indeed the demand and supply schedules do not

[1] Compare V. I. 1. To represent the equilibrium of demand and supply geometrically we may draw the demand and supply curves together as in Fig. 19. If then OR represents the rate at which production is being actually carried on, and Rd the demand price is greater than Rs the supply price, the production is exceptionally profitable, and will be increased. R, the *amount-index*, as we may call it, will move to the right. On the other hand, if Rd is less than Rs, R will move to the left. If Rd is equal to Rs, that is, if R is vertically under a point of intersection of the curves, demand and supply are in equilibrium.

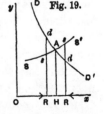
Fig. 19.

This may be taken as the typical diagram for stable equilibrium for a commodity that obeys the law of diminishing return. But if we had made SS' a horizontal straight line, we should have represented the case of "constant return," in which the supply price is the same for all amounts of the commodity. And if we had made SS' inclined negatively, but less steeply than DD' (the necessity for this condition will appear more fully later on), we should have got a case of stable equilibrium for a commodity which obeys the law of increasing return. In either case the above reasoning remains unchanged without the alteration of a word or a letter; but the last case introduces difficulties which we have arranged to postpone.

in practice remain unchanged for a long time together, but V, III, 6.
are constantly being changed; and every change in them
alters the equilibrium amount and the equilibrium price,
and thus gives new positions to the centres about which the
amount and the price tend to oscillate.

These considerations point to the great importance of Loose con-
the element of time in relation to demand and supply, to the nection
study of which we now proceed. We shall gradually dis- supply
cover a great many different limitations of the doctrine that price and
the price at which a thing can be produced represents its real cost of
real cost of production, that is, the efforts and sacrifices significance
which have been directly and indirectly devoted to its pro- of the
duction. For, in an age of rapid change such as this, the Normal
equilibrium of normal demand and supply does not thus equilibrium
correspond to any distinct relation of a certain aggregate of long run.
pleasures got from the consumption of the commodity and
an aggregate of efforts and sacrifices involved in producing
it: the correspondence would not be exact, even if normal
earnings and interest were exact measures of the efforts
and sacrifices for which they are the money payments. This
is the real drift of that much quoted, and much-misunder-
stood doctrine of Adam Smith and other economists that
the normal, or "natural," value of a commodity is that
which economic forces tend to bring about *in the long run*.
It is the average value which economic forces would bring
about if the general conditions of life were stationary for a
run of time long enough to enable them all to work out
their full effect.

But we cannot foresee the future perfectly The unexpected may happen; and the existing tendencies may be
modified before they have had time to accomplish what
appears now to be their full and complete work. The fact
that the general conditions of life are not stationary is the
source of many of the difficulties that are met with in
applying economic doctrines to practical problems.

Of course Normal does not mean Competitive. Market
prices and Normal prices are alike brought about by a multitude of influences, of which some rest on a moral basis

V, III, 7. and some on a physical; of which some are competitive and some are not. It is to the persistence of the influences considered, and the time allowed for them to work out their effects that we refer when contrasting Market and Normal price, and again when contrasting the narrower and the broader use of the term Normal price[1].

Influences of utility and cost of production on value.

§ 7. The remainder of the present volume will be chiefly occupied with interpreting and limiting this doctrine that the value of a thing tends in the long run to correspond to its cost of production. In particular the notion of equilibrium, which has been treated rather slightly in this chapter, will be studied more carefully in chapters v. and XII. of this Book: and some account of the controversy whether "cost of production" or "utility" governs value will be given in Appendix I. But it may be well to say a word or two here on this last point.

We might as reasonably dispute whether it is the upper or the under blade of a pair of scissors that cuts a piece of paper, as whether value is governed by utility or cost of production. It is true that when one blade is held still, and the cutting is effected by moving the other, we may say with careless brevity that the cutting is done by the second; but the statement is not strictly accurate, and is to be excused only so long as it claims to be merely a popular and not a strictly scientific account of what happens.

The former preponderates in market values;

In the same way, when a thing already made has to be sold, the price which people will be willing to pay for it will be governed by their desire to have it, together with the amount they can afford to spend on it. Their desire to have it depends partly on the chance that, if they do not buy it, they will be able to get another thing like it at as low a price: this depends on the causes that govern the supply of it, and this again upon cost of production. But it may so happen that the stock to be sold is practically fixed. This, for instance, is the case with a fish market, in which the value of fish for the day is governed almost exclusively by the stock on the slabs in relation to the demand: and if a person chooses to take the stock for granted, and say that the price

---

[1] See above pp. 34—36.

is governed by demand, his brevity may perhaps be excused V, III, 7. so long as he does not claim strict accuracy. So again it may be pardonable, but it is not strictly accurate to say that the varying prices which the same rare book fetches, when sold and resold at Christie's auction room, are governed exclusively by demand.

Taking a case at the opposite extreme, we find some the latter commodities which conform pretty closely to the law of $\frac{\text{in normal}}{\text{values.}}$ constant return; that is to say, their average cost of production will be very nearly the same whether they are produced in small quantities or in large. In such a case the normal level about which the market price fluctuates will be this definite and fixed (money) cost of production. If the demand happens to be great, the market price will rise for a time above the level; but as a result production will increase and the market price will fall: and conversely, if the demand falls for a time below its ordinary level.

In such a case, if a person chooses to neglect market fluctuations, and to take it for granted that there will anyhow be enough demand for the commodity to insure that some of it, more or less, will find purchasers at a price equal to this cost of production, then he may be excused for ignoring the influence of demand, and speaking of (normal) price as governed by cost of production—provided only he does not claim scientific accuracy for the wording of his doctrine, and explains the influence of demand in its right place.

Thus we may conclude that, *as a general rule*, the shorter the period which we are considering, the greater must be the share of our attention which is given to the influence of demand on value; and the longer the period, the more important will be the influence of cost of production on value. For the influence of changes in cost of production takes as a rule a longer time to work itself out than does the influence of changes in demand. The actual value at any time, the market value as it is often called, is often more influenced by passing events and by causes whose action is fitful and short lived, than by those which work persistently. But in long periods these fitful and irregular

V, III, 7.

causes in large measure efface one another's influence; so that in the long run persistent causes dominate value completely. Even the most persistent causes are however liable to change. For the whole structure of production is modified, and the relative costs of production of different things are permanently altered, from one generation to another.

The business man is concerned with money costs; but the evolution of normal value with real costs.

When considering costs from the point of view of the capitalist employer, we of course measure them in money; because his direct concern with the efforts needed for the work of his employees lies in the money payments he must make. His concern with the real costs of their effort and of the training required for it is only indirect, though a monetary assessment of his own labour is necessary for some problems, as will be seen later on. But when considering costs from the social point of view, when inquiring whether the cost of attaining a given result is increasing or diminishing with changing economic conditions, then we are concerned with the real costs of efforts of various qualities, and with the real cost of waiting. If the purchasing power of money, in terms of effort has remained about constant, and if the rate of remuneration for waiting has remained about constant, then the money measure of costs corresponds to the real costs: but such a correspondence is never to be assumed lightly. These considerations will generally suffice for the interpretation of the term Cost in what follows, even where no distinct indication is given in the context.

CHAPTER IV.

THE INVESTMENT AND DISTRIBUTION OF RESOURCES.

§ 1. THE first difficulty to be cleared up in our study of normal values, is the nature of the motives which govern the investment of resources for a distant return. It will be well to begin by watching the action of a person who neither buys what he wants nor sells what he makes, but works on his own behalf; and who therefore balances the efforts and sacrifices which he makes on the one hand against the pleasures which he expects to derive from their fruit on the other, without the intervention of any money payments at all.

V, IV, 1.

The policy of investment for a distant return may be clearly seen in the case of a man who makes a thing for his own use.

Let us then take the case of a man who builds a house for himself on land, and of materials, which nature supplies gratis; and who makes his implements as he goes, the labour of making them being counted as part of the labour of building the house. He would have to estimate the efforts required for building on any proposed plan; and to allow almost instinctively an amount increasing in geometrical proportion (a sort of compound interest) for the period that would elapse between each effort and the time when the house would be ready for his use. The utility of the house to him when finished would have to compensate him not only for the efforts, but for the waitings[1].

---

[1] For he might have applied these efforts, or efforts equivalent to them, to producing immediate gratifications; and if he deliberately chose the deferred gratifications, it would be because, even after allowing for the disadvantages of waiting, he regarded them as outweighing the earlier gratifications which he could have substituted for them. The motive force then tending to deter him from building the house would be his estimate of the aggregate of these efforts, the evil or discommodity of each being increased in geometrical proportion (a sort of compound interest) according to the corresponding interval of waiting. The motive on the other hand impelling him to build it, would be expectation of the satisfaction which he would have from the house when completed; and that again might be resolved into the aggregate of many satisfactions more or less remote,

If the two motives, one deterring, the other impelling, seemed equally balanced, he would be on the margin of doubt. Probably the gain would much more than outweigh the "real" cost with regard to some part of the house. But as he turned over more and more ambitious plans, he would at last find the advantages of any further extension balanced by the efforts and waitings required for making it; and that extension of the building would be on the outer limit, or margin of profitableness of the investment of his capital.

There would probably be several ways of building parts of the house; some parts for instance might almost equally well be built of wood or of rough stones: the investment of capital on each plan for each part of the accommodation would be compared with the advantages offered thereby, and each would be pushed forward till the outer limit or margin of profitableness had been reached. Thus there would be a great many margins of profitableness: one corresponding to each kind of plan on which each kind of accommodation might be provided.

§ 2. This illustration may serve to keep before us the way in which the efforts and sacrifices which are the real cost of production of a thing, underlie the expenses which are its money cost. But, as has just been remarked, the modern business man commonly takes the payments which he has to make, whether for wages or raw material, as he finds them; without staying to inquire how far they are an accurate measure of the efforts and sacrifices to which they correspond. His expenditure is generally made piece-meal; and the longer he expects to wait for the fruit of any outlay, the richer must that fruit be in order to compensate him. The anticipated fruit may not be certain; and in that case he will have to allow for the risk of failure. After making that allowance, the fruit of the outlay must be expected to exceed the outlay itself by an amount which, independently of his own remuneration, increases   at   compound   interest   in   proportion

Transition to the investment of capital by the modern undertaker of business enterprises.

and more or less certain, which he expected to derive from its use. If he thought that this aggregate of discounted values of satisfactions that it would afford him, would be more than a recompense to him for all the efforts and waitings which he had undergone, he would decide to build. . . .

to the time of waiting[1]. Under this head are to be entered
the heavy expenses, direct and indirect, which every business
must incur in building up its connection.

For brevity we may speak of any element of outlay (allow- *Accumula-*
ance being made for the remuneration of the undertaker *tion of past and dis-*
himself) when increased by compound interest in this way, *counting of future*
as *accumulated*; just as we used the term *discounted* to outlays
represent the present value of a future gratification. Each *and receipts.*
element of outlay has then to be accumulated for the time
which will elapse between its being incurred and its bearing
fruit; and the aggregate of these accumulated elements is
the total outlay involved in the enterprise. The balance
between efforts and the satisfactions resulting from them may
be made up to any day that is found convenient. But whatever day is chosen, one simple rule must be followed:—Every
element whether an effort or a satisfaction, which dates from
a time anterior to that day, must have compound interest for
the interval accumulated upon it: and every element, which
dates from a time posterior to that day, must have compound
interest for the interval discounted from it. If the day be
anterior to the beginning of the enterprise, then every
element must be discounted. But if, as is usual in such
cases, the day be that when the efforts are finished, and the
house is ready for use; then the efforts must carry compound
interest up to that day, and the satisfactions must all be
discounted back to that day.

Waiting is an element of cost as truly as effort is, and it
is entered in the cost when accumulated: it is therefore of
course not counted separately. Similarly, on the converse
side, whatever money or command over satisfaction "comes
in" at any time is part of the income of that time: if the
time is before the day for which accounts are balanced up,
then it must be accumulated up to that day; if after, it must
be discounted back. If, instead of being converted to immediate enjoyment, it is used as a stored up source of future

---

[1] We may, if we choose, regard the price of the business undertaker's own
work as part of the original outlay, and reckon compound interest on it together
with the rest. Or we may substitute for compound interest a sort of "compound
profit." The two courses are not strictly convertible: and at a later stage we shall
find that in certain cases the first is to be preferred, and in others the second.

income, that later income must not be counted as an additional return to the investment[1].

If the enterprise were, say, to dig out a dock-basin on a contract, the payment for which would be made without fail when the work was finished; and if the plant used in the work might be taken to be worn out in the process, and valueless at the end of it; then the enterprise would be just remunerative if this aggregate of outlays, accumulated up to the period of payment, were just equal to that payment.

But, as a rule, the proceeds of the sales come in gradually; and we must suppose a balance-sheet struck, looking both backwards and forwards. Looking backwards we should sum up the net outlays, and add in accumulated compound interest on each element of outlay. Looking forwards we should sum up all net incomings, and from the value of each subtract compound interest for the period during which it would be deferred. The aggregate of the net incomings so discounted would be balanced against the aggregate of the accumulated outlays: and if the two were just equal, the business would be just remunerative. In calculating the outgoings the head of the business must reckon in the value of his own work[2].

[1] In the aggregate the income from the saving will in the ordinary course be larger in amount than the saving by the amount of the interest that is the reward of saving. But, as it will be turned to account in enjoyment later than the original saving could have been, it will be discounted for a longer period (or accumulated for a shorter); and if entered in the balance sheet of the investment in place of the original saving, it would stand for exactly the same sum. (Both the original income which was saved and the subsequent income earned by it are assessed to income tax; on grounds similar to those which make it expedient to levy a larger income tax from the industrious than from the lazy man.) . . .

[2] Almost every trade has its own difficulties and its own customs connected with the task of valuing the capital that has been invested in a business, and of allowing for the depreciation which that capital has undergone from wear-and-tear, from the influence of the elements, from new inventions, and from changes in the course of trade. These two last causes may temporarily raise the value of some kinds of fixed capital, at the same time that they are lowering that of others. And people whose minds are cast in different moulds, or whose interests in the matter point in different directions, will often differ widely on the question what part of the expenditure required for adapting buildings and plant to changing conditions of trade, may be regarded as an investment of new capital; and what ought to be set down as charges incurred to balance depreciation, and treated as expenditure deducted from the current receipts, before determining the net profits or true income earned by the business. These difficulties, and the consequent differences of opinion, are greatest of all with regard to the investment of capital

§ 3. At the beginning of his undertaking, and at every V, IV, 3.
successive stage, the alert business man strives so to modify The
his arrangements as to obtain better results with a given principle
expenditure, or equal results with a less expenditure. In tution.
other words, he ceaselessly applies the principle of substitution, with the purpose of increasing his profits; and, in so
doing, he seldom fails to increase the total efficiency of
work, the total power over nature which man derives from
organization and knowledge.

Every locality has incidents of its own which affect in
various ways the methods of arrangement of every class of
business that is carried on in it: and even in the same place
and the same trade no two persons pursuing the same aims
will adopt exactly the same routes. The tendency to variation is a chief cause of progress; and the abler are the
undertakers in any trade the greater will this tendency be.
In some trades, as for instance cotton-spinning, the possible
variations are confined within narrow limits; no one can hold
his own at all who does not use machinery, and very nearly
the latest machinery, for every part of the work. But in
others, as for instance in some branches of the wood and
metal trades, in farming, and in shopkeeping, there can be
great variations. For instance, of two manufacturers in the
same trade, one will perhaps have a larger wages bill and the
other heavier charges on account of machinery; of two retail
dealers one will have a larger capital locked up in stock and
the other will spend more on advertisements and other means
of building up the immaterial capital of a profitable trade
connection. And in minor details the variations are numberless.

Each man's actions are influenced by his special opportunities and resources, as well as by his temperament and
in building up a business connection, and the proper method of appraising the
goodwill of a business, or its value "as a going concern." On the whole of this
subject see Matheson's *Depreciation of Factories and their Valuation*.

Another group of difficulties arises from changes in the general purchasing
power of money. If that has fallen, or, in other words, if there has been a rise of
general prices. the value of a factory may appear to have risen when it has really
remained stationary. Confusions arising from this source introduce greater errors
into estimates of the real profitableness of different classes of business than would
at first sight appear probable. But all questions of this kind must be deferred till
we have discussed the theory of money.

V, IV, 4.

The margin of profitableness is not a mere point on any one route, but a line intersecting all routes.

his associations: but each, taking account of his own means, will push the investment of capital in his business in each several direction until what appears in his judgment to be the outer limit, or margin, of profitableness is reached; that is, until there seems to him no good reason for thinking that the gains resulting from any further investment in that particular direction would compensate him for his outlay. The margin of profitableness, even in regard to one and the same branch or sub-branch of industry, is not to be regarded as a mere point on any one fixed line of possible investment; but as a boundary line of irregular shape cutting one after another every possible line of investment.

§ 4. This principle of substitution is closely connected with, and is indeed partly based on, that tendency to a diminishing rate of return from any excessive application of resources or of energies in any given direction, which is in accordance with general experience. It is thus linked up with the broad tendency of a diminishing return to increased applications of capital and labour to land in old countries which plays a prominent part in classical economics. And it is so closely akin to the principle of the diminution of marginal utility that results in general from increased expenditure, that some applications of the two principles are almost identical. It has already been observed that new methods of production bring into existence new commodities, or lower the price of old commodities so as to bring them within the reach of increased numbers of consumers: that on the other hand changes in the methods and volume of consumption cause new developments of production, and new distribution of the resources of production: and that though some methods of consumption which contribute most to man's higher life, do little if anything towards furthering the production of material wealth, yet production and consumption are intimately correlated[1]. But now we are to consider more in detail how the distribution of the resources of production between different industrial undertakings is the counterpart and reflex of the distribution of the

[1] See pp. 84—91, and 64—67.

consumers' purchases between different classes of com- V, IV, 4.
modities[1].

Let us revert to the primitive housewife, who having "a The distrib-
limited number of hanks of yarn from the year's shearing, ution of
considers all the domestic wants for clothing and tries to resources in domestic
distribute the yarn between them in such a way as to con- economy.
tribute as much as possible to the family wellbeing. She
will think she has failed if, when it is done, she has reason
to regret that she did not apply more to making, say, socks,
and less to vests. But if, on the other hand, she hit on the
right points to stop at, then she made just so many socks
and vests that she got an equal amount of good out of the
last bundle of yarn that she applied to socks, and the last
she applied to vests[2]." If it happened that two ways of
making a vest were open to her, which were equally satisfactory as regards results, but of which one, while using up
a little more yarn, involved a little less trouble than the
other; then her problems would be typical of those of the
larger business world. They would include first decisions
as to the relative urgency of various ends; secondly, decisions as to the relative advantages of various means of
attaining each end; thirdly, decisions, based on these two
sets of decisions, as to the margin up to which she could
most profitably carry the application of each means
towards each end.

These three classes of decisions have to be taken on a The distrib-
larger scale by the business man, who has more complex ution of
balancings and adjustments to make before reaching each resources in business
decision. Let us take an illustration from the building economy.
trade. Let us watch the operations of a "speculative Illustration
builder" in the honourable sense of the term: that is, from the
a man who sets out to erect honest buildings in antici- building
pation of general demand; who bears the penalty of trade.
any error in his judgment; and who, if his judgment is

---

[1] The substance of part of this section was placed in VI. I. 7 in earlier editions.
But it seems to be needed here in preparation for the central chapters of Book V.
[2] See III. v. 1.

approved by events, benefits the community as well as himself. Let him be considering whether to erect dwelling houses, or warehouses, or factories or shops. He is trained to form at once a fairly good opinion as to the method of working most suitable for each class of building, and to make a rough estimate of its cost. He estimates the cost of various sites adapted for each class of building: and he reckons in the price that he would have to pay for any site as a part of his capital expenditure, just as he does the expense to which he would be put for laying foundations in it, and so on. He brings this estimate of cost into relation with his estimate of the price he is likely to get for any given building, together with its site. If he can find no case in which the demand price exceeds his outlays by enough to yield him a good profit, with some margin against risks, he may remain idle. Or he may possibly build at some risk in order to keep his most trusty workmen together, and to find some occupation for his plant and his salaried assistance: but more on this later on.

Suppose him now to have decided that (say) villa residences of a certain type, erected on a plot of ground which he can buy, are likely to yield him a good profit. The main end to be sought being thus settled, he sets himself to study more carefully the means by which it is to be obtained, and, in connection with that study, to consider possible modifications in the details of his plans.

Given the general character of the houses to be built, he will have to consider in what proportions to use various materials—brick, stone, steel, cement, plaster, wood, etc., with a view to obtaining the result which will contribute most, in proportion to its cost, to the efficiency of the house in gratifying the artistic taste of purchasers and in ministering to their comfort. In thus deciding what is the best distribution of his resources between various commodities, he is dealing with substantially the same problem as the primitive housewife, who has to consider the most economic distribution of her yarn between the various needs of her household. Like her, he has to reflect that the yield of benefit which any particular use gave would be relatively large up

to a certain point, and would then gradually diminish. Like V, IV, 5.
her, he has so to distribute his resources that they have the
same marginal utility in each use: he has to weigh the loss
that would result from taking away a little expenditure here,
with the gain that would result from adding a little there. In
effect both of them work on lines similar to those which
guide the farmer in so adjusting the application of his capital and labour to land, that no field is stinted of extra cultivation to which it would have given a generous return, and
none receives so great an expenditure as to call into strong
activity the tendency to diminishing return in agriculture[1].

Thus it is that the alert business man, as has just been said,
"pushes the investment of capital in his business in each several direction until what appears in his judgment to be the
outer limit, or margin, of profitableness is reached; that is,
until there seems to him no good reason for thinking that the
gains resulting from any further investment in that particular
direction would compensate him for his outlay." He never
assumes that roundabout methods will be remunerative in the
long run. But he is always on the look out for roundabout
methods that promise to be more effective in proportion to
their cost than direct methods: and he adopts the best of them,
if it lies within his means. . . .

* * * *

§ 5. Some technical terms relating to costs may be considered here. When investing his capital in providing the
means of carrying on an undertaking, the business man looks
to being recouped by the price obtained for its various prod- *Prime cost.*
ucts; and he expects to be able under normal conditions to
charge for each of them a sufficient price; that is, one which
will not only cover the *special, direct,* or *prime cost,* but also
bear its proper share of the general expenses of the business;
and these we may call its general, or *supplementary cost.*
These two elements together make its *total cost.*

There are great variations in the usage of the term
Prime cost in business. But it is taken here in a narrow

[1] See above III. III. 1. . . .

V, IV, 6. sense. Supplementary costs are taken to include standing charges on account of the durable plant in which much of the capital of the business has been invested, and also the salaries of the upper employees: for the charges to which the business is put on account of their salaries cannot generally be adapted quickly to changes in the amount of work there is for them to do. There remains nothing but the (money) cost of the raw material used in making the commodity and the wages of that part of the labour spent on it which is paid by the hour or the piece and the extra wear-and-tear of plant. This is the special cost which a manufacturer has in view, when his works are not fully employed, and he is calculating the lowest price at which it will be worth his while to accept an order, irrespectively of any effect that his action may have in spoiling the market for future orders, and trade being slack at the time. But in fact he must as a rule take account of this effect: the price at which it is just worth his while to produce, even when trade is slack, is in practice generally a good deal above this prime cost, as we shall see later on[1].

The division between prime and supplementary costs varies with the duration of the undertaking. Illustration from wages and salaries.

§ 6. Supplementary cost must generally be covered by the selling price to some considerable extent in the short run. And they must be completely covered by it in the long run; for, if they are not, production will be checked. Supplementary costs are of many different kinds; and some of them differ only in degree from prime costs. For instance, if an engineering firm is in doubt whether to accept an order at a rather low price for a certain locomotive, the absolute prime costs include the value of the raw material and the wages of the artisans and labourers employed on the locomotive. But there is no clear rule as to the salaried staff: for, if work is slack, they will probably have some time on their hands; and their salaries will therefore commonly be classed among general or supplementary costs. The line of division is

---

[1] Especially in V. IX. "There are many systems of Prime Cost in vogue...we take Prime Cost to mean, as in fact the words imply, only the original or direct cost of production; and while in some trades it may be a matter of convenience to include in the cost of production a proportion of indirect expenses, and a charge for depreciation on plant and buildings, in no case should it comprise interest on capital or profit." (Garcke and Fells, *Factory Accounts*, ch. I.)

however often blurred over. For instance, foremen and other V, IV, 6. trusted artisans are seldom dismissed merely because of a temporary scarcity of work; and therefore an occasional order may be taken to fill up idle time, even though its price does not cover their salaries and wages. That is they may not be regarded as prime costs in such a case. But, of course the staff in the office can be in some measure adjusted to variations in the work of the firm by leaving vacancies unfilled and even by weeding out inefficient men during slack times; and by getting extra help or putting out some of the work in busy times.

If we pass from such tasks to larger and longer tasks, *Illustration from* as for instance the working out a contract to deliver a great *outlay on* number of locomotives gradually over a period of several *plant.* years, then most of the office work done in connection with that order must be regarded as special to it: for if it had been declined and nothing else taken in its place, the expenses under the head of salaries could have been reduced almost to a proportionate extent.

The case is much stronger when we consider a fairly steady market for any class of staple manufactures extending over a long time. For then the outlay incurred for installing specialized skill and organization, the permanent office staff, and the durable plant of the workshops can all be regarded as part of the costs necessary for the process of production. That outlay will be increased up to a margin at which the branch of manufacture seems in danger of growing too fast for its market.

In the next chapter the argument of Chapter III. and of *This influence* this chapter is continued. It is shown in more detail how *of the* those costs which most powerfully act on supply and therefore *element of time is* on price, are limited to a narrow and arbitrary group in the *further developed* case of a single contract for, say, a locomotive; but are much *in Chs. v.* fuller, and correspond much more truly to the broad features *and VIII.—x.* of industrial economy in the case of a continuous supply to a fairly steady general market: the influence of cost of production on value does not show itself clearly except in relatively long periods; and it is to be estimated with regard to a whole process of production rather than a particular

V, IV, 6. locomotive, or a particular parcel of goods. And a similar
study is made in Chapters VIII.—X. of variations in the
character of those prime and supplementary costs which
consist of charges for interest (or profits) on investments in
agents of production, according as the periods of the market
under consideration are long or short.

The distinction between prime and supplementary costs operates even where neither are reckoned in money.   Meanwhile it may be noticed that the distinction between
prime and supplementary costs operates in every phase of
civilization, though it is not likely to attract much attention
except in a capitalistic phase. Robinson Crusoe had to do
only with real costs and real satisfactions: and an old-
fashioned peasant family, which bought little and sold little,
arranged its investments of present "effort and waiting" for
future benefits on nearly the same lines. But, if either were
doubting whether it was worth while to take a light ladder
on a trip to gather wild fruits, the prime costs alone would
be weighed against the expected benefits: and yet the ladder
would not have been made, unless it had been expected to
render sufficient service in the aggregate of many little tasks,
to remunerate the cost of making it. In the long run it
had to repay its total costs, supplementary as well as prime.

Even the modern employer has to look at his own labour
as a real cost in the first instance. He may think that a
certain enterprise is likely to yield a surplus of money
incomings over money outgoings (after proper allowances for
risks and for discountings of future happenings); but that
the surplus will amount to less than the money equivalent
of the trouble and worry that the enterprise will cause to
himself: and, in that case, he will avoid it[1].

---

[1] The Supplementary costs, which the owner of a factory expects to be able to
add to the prime costs of its products, are the source of the quasi-rents which it will
yield to him. If they come up to his expectation, then his business so far yields
good profits: if they fall much short of it, his business tends to go to the bad.
But his statement bears only on long-period problems of value: and in that
connection the difference between Prime and Supplementary costs has no special
significance. The importance of the distinction between them is confined to short-
period problems.

CHAPTER V.

EQUILIBRIUM OF NORMAL DEMAND AND SUPPLY, CON-
TINUED, WITH REFERENCE TO LONG AND SHORT
PERIODS.

§ 1. THE variations in the scope of the term *Normal*, V, v, 1.
according as the periods of time under discussion are long or The
short, were indicated in Chapter III. We are now ready to difficulties discussed
study them more closely. in this chapter

In this case, as in others, the economist merely brings to as to the element of
light difficulties that are latent in the common discourse of time are
life, so that by being frankly faced they may be thoroughly latent in ordinary
overcome. For in ordinary life it is customary to use the discourse,
word Normal in different senses, with reference to different
periods of time; and to leave the context to explain the
transition from one to another. The economist follows this
practice of every-day life: but, by taking pains to indicate
the transition, he sometimes seems to have created a compli-
cation which in fact he has only revealed.

Thus, when it is said that the price of wool on a certain where the use of
day was abnormally high though the average price for the the term
year was abnormally low, that the wages of coal-miners were Normal is elastic.
abnormally high in 1872 and abnormally low in 1879, that
the (real) wages of labour were abnormally high at the end
of the fourteenth century and abnormally low in the middle
of the sixteenth; everyone understands that the scope of the
term normal is not the same in these various cases.

The best illustrations of this come from manufactures
where the plant is long-lived, and the product is short-lived.

v, v, 1.
―

When a new textile fabric is first introduced into favour, and there is very little plant suitable for making it, its normal price for some months may be twice as high as those of other fabrics which are not less difficult to make, but for making which there is an abundant stock of suitable plant and skill. Looking at long periods we may say that its normal price is on a par with that of the others: but if during the first few months a good deal of it were offered for sale in a bankrupt's stock we might say that its price was abnormally low even when it was selling for half as much again as the others. Everyone takes the context as indicating the special use of the term in each several case; and a formal interpretation clause is seldom necessary, because in ordinary conversation misunderstandings can be nipped in the bud by question and answer. But let us look at this matter more closely.

Illustration from the cloth trade.

We have noticed[1] how a cloth manufacturer would need to calculate the expenses of producing all the different things required for making cloth with reference to the amounts of each of them that would be wanted; and on the supposition in the first instance that the conditions of supply would be normal. But we have yet to take account of the fact that he must give to this term a wider or narrower range, according as he was looking more or less far ahead.

Thus in estimating the wages required to call forth an adequate supply of labour to work a certain class of looms, he might take the current wages of similar work in the neighbourhood: or he might argue that there was a scarcity of that particular class of labour in the neighbourhood, that its current wages there were higher than in other parts of England, and that looking forward over several years so as to allow for immigration, he might take the normal rate of wages at a rather lower rate than that prevailing there at the time. Or lastly, he might think that the wages of weavers all over the country were abnormally low relatively to others of the same grade, in consequence of a too sanguine view having been taken of the prospects of the trade half a generation ago. He might argue that this branch of work

[1] V. III. 5.

was overcrowded, that parents had already begun to choose V, v, 1.
other trades for their children which offered greater net
advantages and yet were not more difficult; that in consequence a few years would see a falling-off in the supply
of labour suited for his purpose; so that looking forward a
long time he must take normal wages at a rate rather higher
than the present average[1].

Again, in estimating the normal supply price of wool, he
would take the average of several past years. He would
make allowance for any change that would be likely to
affect the supply in the immediate future; and he would
reckon for the effect of such droughts as from time to time
occur in Australia and elsewhere; since their occurrence is
too common to be regarded as abnormal. But he would not
allow here for the chance of our being involved in a great
war, by which the Australian supplies might be cut off;
he would consider that any allowance for this should come
under the head of extraordinary trade risks, and not enter
into his estimate of the normal supply price of wool.

He would deal in the same way with the risk of civil
tumult or any violent and long-continued disturbance of the
labour market of an unusual character; but in his estimate
of the amount of work that could be got out of the machinery,
etc. under normal conditions, he would probably reckon for
minor interruptions from trade disputes such as are continually occurring, and are therefore to be regarded as
belonging to the regular course of events, that is as not
abnormal.

In all these calculations he would not concern himself
specially to inquire how far mankind are under the exclusive
influence of selfish or self-regarding motives. He might be
aware that anger and vanity, jealousy and offended dignity
are still almost as common causes of strikes and lockouts,
as the desire for pecuniary gain: but that would not enter

---

[1] There are indeed not many occasions on which the calculations of a business
man for practical purposes need to look forward so far, and to extend the range
of the term Normal over a whole generation: but in the broader applications of
economic science it is sometimes necessary to extend the range even further, and
to take account of the slow changes that in the course of centuries affect the
supply price of the labour of each industrial grade.

V, V, 2. into his calculations. All that he would want to know about them would be whether they acted with sufficient regularity for him to be able to make a reasonably good allowance for their influence in interrupting work and raising the normal supply price of the goods[1].

The complex problem of value must be broken up.

§ 2. The element of time is a chief cause of those difficulties in economic investigations which make it necessary for man with his limited powers to go step by step; breaking up a complex question, studying one bit at a time, and at last combining his partial solutions into a more or less complete solution of the whole riddle. In breaking it up, he segregates those disturbing causes, whose wanderings happen to be inconvenient, for the time in a pound called *Cæteris Paribus*. The study of some group of tendencies is isolated by the assumption *other things being equal*: the existence of other tendencies is not denied, but their disturbing effect is neglected for a time. The more the issue is thus narrowed, the more exactly can it be handled: but also the less closely does it correspond to real life. Each exact and firm handling of a narrow issue, however, helps towards treating broader issues, in which that narrow issue is contained, more exactly than would otherwise have been possible. With each step more things can be let out of the pound; exact discussions can be made less abstract, realistic discussions can be made less inexact than was possible at an earlier stage[2].

Fiction of a stationary state.

Our first step towards studying the influences exerted by the element of time on the relations between cost of production and value may well be to consider the famous fiction of the "Stationary state" in which those influences would be but little felt; and to contrast the results which would be found there with those in the modern world.

This state obtains its name from the fact that in it the

---

[1] Compare I. II. 7.

[2] As has been explained in the Preface, pp. vi—ix, this volume is concerned mainly with normal conditions; and these are sometimes described as Statical. But in the opinion of the present writer the problem of normal value belongs to economic Dynamics: partly because Statics is really but a branch of Dynamics, and partly because all suggestions as to economic rest, of which the hypothesis of a Stationary state is the chief, are merely provisional, used only to illustrate particular steps in the argument, and to be thrown aside when that is done.

general conditions of production and consumption, of distri- v, v, 2. bution and exchange remain motionless; but yet it is full of movement; for it is a mode of life. The average age of the population may be stationary; though each individual is growing up from youth towards his prime, or downwards to old age. And the same amount of things per head of the population will have been produced in the same ways by the same classes of people for many generations together; and therefore this supply of the appliances for production will have had full time to be adjusted to the steady demand.

Of course we might assume that in our stationary state every business remained always of the same size, and with the same trade connection. But we need not go so far as that; it will suffice to suppose that firms rise and fall, but that the "representative" firm remains always of about the same size, as does the representative tree of a virgin forest, and that therefore the economies resulting from its own resources are constant: and since the aggregate volume of production is constant, so also are those economies resulting from subsidiary industries in the neighbourhood, etc. [That is, its internal and external economies are both constant. The price, the expectation of which just induced persons to enter the trade, must be sufficient to cover in the long run the cost of building up a trade connection; and a proportionate share of it must be added in to make up the total cost of production.]

In a stationary state then the plain rule would be that In a cost of production governs value. Each effect would be stationary attributable mainly to one cause; there would not be much doctrine complex action and reaction between cause and effect. would be simple. Each element of cost would be governed by "natural" laws, subject to some control from fixed custom. There would be no reflex influence of demand; no fundamental difference between the immediate and the later effects of economic causes. There would be no distinction between long-period and short-period normal value, at all events if we supposed that in that monotonous world the harvests themselves were uniform: for the representative firm being always of the same size, and always doing the same class of business to the

V, v, 3.   same extent and in the same way, with no slack times, and no specially busy times, its normal expenses by which the normal supply price is governed would be always the same. The demand lists of prices would always be the same, and so would the supply lists; and normal price would never vary.

But in the real world a simple doctrine of value is worse than none.   But nothing of this is true in the world in which we live. Here every economic force is constantly changing its action, under the influence of other forces which are acting around it. Here changes in the volume of production, in its methods, and in its cost are ever mutually modifying one another; they are always affecting and being affected by the character and the extent of demand. Further all these mutual influences take time to work themselves out, and, as a rule, no two influences move at equal pace. In this world therefore every plain and simple doctrine as to the relations between cost of production, demand and value is necessarily false: and the greater the appearance of lucidity which is given to it by skilful exposition, the more mischievous it is. A man is likely to be a better economist if he trusts to his common sense, and practical instincts, than if he professes to study the theory of value and is resolved to find it easy.

Modifications of the fiction of a stationary state bring us nearer to real life and help to break up a complex problem.   § 3. The Stationary state has just been taken to be one in which population is stationary. But nearly all its distinctive features may be exhibited in a place where population and wealth are both growing, provided they are growing at about the same rate, and there is no scarcity of land: and provided also the methods of production and the conditions of trade change but little; and above all, where the character of man himself is a constant quantity. For in such a state by far the most important conditions of production and consumption, of exchange and distribution will remain of the same quality, and in the same general relations to one another, though they are all increasing in volume[1].

This relaxation of the rigid bonds of a purely stationary state brings us one step nearer to the actual conditions of

---

[1] See below, V. XI. 6; and compare Keynes, *Scope and Method of Political Economy*, VI. 2.

life: and by relaxing them still further we get nearer still. We thus approach by gradual steps towards the difficult problem of the interaction of countless economic causes. In the stationary state all the conditions of production and consumption are reduced to rest: but less violent assumptions are made by what is, not quite accurately, called the *statical* method. By that method we fix our minds on some central point: we suppose it for the time to be reduced to a *stationary* state; and we then study in relation to it the forces that affect the things by which it is surrounded, and any tendency there may be to equilibrium of these forces. A number of these partial studies may lead the way towards a solution of problems too difficult to be grasped at one effort.

§ 4. We may roughly classify problems connected with fishing industries as those which are affected by very quick changes, such as uncertainties of the weather; or by changes of moderate length, such as the increased demand for fish caused by the scarcity of meat during the year or two following a cattle plague; or lastly, we may consider the great increase during a whole generation of the demand for fish which might result from the rapid growth of a high-strung artisan population making little use of their muscles. *Illustration from the fishing trade.*

The day to day oscillations of the price of fish resulting from uncertainties of the weather, etc., are governed by practically the same causes in modern England as in the supposed stationary state. The changes in the general economic conditions around us are quick; but they are not quick enough to affect perceptibly the short-period normal level about which the price fluctuates from day to day: and they may be neglected [impounded in *cæteris paribus*] during a study of such fluctuations. *Day to day oscillations.*

Let us then pass on; and suppose a great increase in the general demand for fish, such for instance as might arise from a disease affecting farm stock, by which meat was made a dear and dangerous food for several years together. We now impound fluctuations due to the weather in *cæteris* *An increase in the amount demanded generally raises short-period supply price;*

V, V, 4.   *paribus,* and neglect them provisionally: they are so quick
that they speedily obliterate one another, and are therefore
not important for problems of this class. And for the opposite reason we neglect variations in the numbers of those
who are brought up as seafaring men: for these variations
are too slow to produce much effect in the year or two during
which the scarcity of meat lasts. Having impounded these
two sets for the time, we give our full attention to such
influences as the inducements which good fishing wages will
offer to sailors to stay in their fishing homes for a year or
two, instead of applying for work on a ship. We consider
what old fishing boats, and even vessels that were not
specially made for fishing, can be adapted and sent to fish
for a year or two. The normal price for any given daily
supply of fish, which we are now seeking, is the price which
will *quickly* call into the fishing trade capital and labour
enough to obtain that supply in a day's fishing of average
good fortune; the influence which the price of fish will have
upon capital and labour available in the fishing trade being
governed by rather narrow causes such as these. This new
level about which the price oscillates during these years
of exceptionally great demand, will obviously be higher than
before. Here we see an illustration of the almost universal
law that the term Normal being taken to refer to a short
period of time *an increase in the amount demanded raises
the normal supply* price. This law is almost universal even
as regards industries which in long periods follow the
tendency to increasing return[1].

but not
necessarily
long-period
supply
price.

But if we turn to consider the normal supply price with
reference to a *long period* of time, we shall find that it is
governed by a different set of causes, and with different
results. For suppose that the disuse of meat causes a
permanent distaste for it, and that an increased demand
for fish continues long enough to enable the forces by which
its supply is governed to work out their action fully (of course
oscillation from day to day and from year to year would continue: but we may leave them on one side). The source of
supply in the sea might perhaps show signs of exhaustion, and

[1] See V. XI. 1.

the fishermen might have to resort to more distant coasts and   V, v, 4.
to deeper waters, Nature giving a Diminishing Return to the
increased application of capital and labour of a given order of
efficiency. On the other hand, those might turn out to be right
who think that man is responsible for but a very small part of
the destruction of fish that is constantly going on; and in that
case a boat starting with equally good appliances and an
equally efficient crew would be likely to get nearly as good a
haul after the increase in the total volume of the fishing trade
as before. In any case the normal cost of equipping a good
boat with an efficient crew would certainly not be higher, and
probably be a little lower after the trade had settled down to
its now increased dimensions than before. For since fishermen require only trained aptitudes, and not any exceptional
natural qualities, their number could be increased in less than
a generation to almost any extent that was necessary to meet
the demand; while the industries connected with building
boats, making nets, etc. being now on a larger scale would be
organized more thoroughly and economically. If therefore the
waters of the sea showed no signs of depletion of fish, an
increased supply could be produced at a lower price after a
time sufficiently long to enable the normal action of economic causes to work itself out: and, the term Normal being
taken to refer to a long period of time, the normal price of
fish would decrease with an increase in demand[1].

[1] Tooke (*History of Prices*, Vol. I. p. 104) tells us: "There are particular articles
of which the demand for naval and military purposes forms so large a proportion to
the total supply, that no diminution of consumption by individuals can keep pace
with the immediate increase of demand by government; and consequently, the
breaking out of a war tends to raise the price of such articles to a great relative
height. But even of such articles, if the consumption were not on a progressive scale
of increase so rapid that the supply, with all the encouragement of a relatively high
price, could not keep pace with the demand, the tendency is (supposing no impedi-
ment, natural or artificial, to production or importation) to occasion such an increase
of quantity, as to reduce the price to nearly the same level as that from which it had
advanced. And accordingly it will be observed, by reference to the table of prices,
that salt-petre, hemp, iron, etc., after advancing very considerably under the influence of a greatly extended demand for military and naval purposes, tended downwards again whenever that demand was not progressively and rapidly increasing."
Thus a continuously progressive increase in demand may raise the supply price of a
thing even for several years together; though a steady increase of demand for that
thing, at a rate not too great for supply to keep pace with it, would lower price.

V, v, 5
———
Average
and normal
prices.

Thus we may emphasize the distinction already made between average price and normal price. An average may be taken of the prices of any set of sales extending over a day or a week or a year or any other time: or it may be the average of sales at any time in many markets; or it may be the average of many such averages. But the conditions which are normal to any one set of sales are not likely to be exactly those which are normal to the others: and therefore it is only by accident that an average price will be a normal price; that is, the price which any one set of conditions tends to produce. In a stationary state alone, as we have just seen, the term normal always means the same thing: there, but only there, "average price" and "normal price" are convertible terms[1].

Restate-
ment of the
main
result.

§ 5. To go over the ground in another way. Market values are governed by the relation of demand to stocks actually in the market; with more or less reference to "future" supplies, and not without some influence of trade combinations.

Nature of
marginal
production.

But the current supply is in itself partly due to the action of producers in the past; and this action has been determined on as the result of a comparison of the prices which they expect to get for their goods with the expenses to which they will be put in producing them. The range of expenses of which they take account depends on whether they are merely considering the extra expenses of certain extra production with their existing plant, or are considering whether to lay down new plant for the purpose. In the case, for instance, of an order for a single locomotive, which was discussed a little while ago[2], the question of readjusting the plant to demand would hardly arise: the main question would be whether more work could conveniently be got out of the existing plant. But in view of an order for a large number of locomotives to be delivered gradually over a series of years, some extension of plant "specially" made for the

---

[1] V. III. 6. The distinction will be yet further discussed in V. XII. . . . . See also Keynes, *Scope and Method of Political Economy*, ch. VII.
[2] Pp. 176–83.

purpose, and therefore truly to be regarded as prime marginal V, v, 5.
costs would almost certainly be carefully considered.

Whether the new production for which there appears
to be a market be large or small, the general rule will be
that unless the price is expected to be very low that portion
of the supply which can be most easily produced, with but
small prime costs, will be produced: that portion is not
likely to be on the margin of production. As the expectations of price improve, an increased part of the production
will yield a considerable surplus above prime costs, and the
margin of production will be pushed outwards. Every increase in the price expected will, as a rule, induce some
people who would not otherwise have produced anything, to
produce a little; and those, who have produced something
for the lower price, will produce more for the higher price.
That part of their production with regard to which such
persons are on the margin of doubt as to whether it is worth
while for them to produce it at the price, is to be included
together with that of the persons who are in doubt whether
to produce at all; the two together constitute the marginal
production at that price. The producers, who are in doubt
whether to produce anything at all, may be said to lie
altogether on the margin of production (or, if they are
agriculturists, on the margin of cultivation). But as a rule
they are very few in number, and their action is less important
than that of those who would in any case produce something.

The general drift of the term normal supply price is The
always the same whether the period to which it refers is general drift of
short or long; but there are great differences in detail. the term
In every case reference is made to a certain given rate of supply
aggregate production; that is, to the production of a certain price for
aggregate amount daily or annually. In every case the long
price is that the expectation of which is sufficient and only periods.
just sufficient to make it worth while for people to set themselves to produce that aggregate amount; in every case
the cost of production is marginal; that is, it is the cost of
production of those goods which are on the margin of not
being produced at all, and which would not be produced if
the price to be got for them were expected to be lower.

V, v, 6.

But the causes which determine this margin vary with the length of the period under consideration. For short periods people take the stock of appliances for production as practically fixed; and they are governed by their expectations of demand in considering how actively they shall set themselves to work those appliances. In long periods they set themselves to adjust the flow of these appliances to their expectations of demand for the goods which the appliances help to produce. Let us examine this difference closely.

For short periods the stock of appliances of production are practically fixed, but their employment varies with demand.

§ 6. The immediate effect of the expectation of a high price is to cause people to bring into active work all their appliances of production, and to work them full time and perhaps overtime. The supply price is then the money cost of production of that part of the produce which forces the undertaker to hire such inefficient labour (perhaps tired by working overtime) at so high a price, and to put himself and others to so much strain and inconvenience that he is on the margin of doubt whether it is worth his while to do it or not. The immediate effect of the expectation of a low price is to throw many appliances for production out of work, and slacken the work of others; and if the producers had no fear of spoiling their markets, it would be worth their while to produce for a time for any price that covered the prime costs of production and rewarded them for their own trouble.

But, as it is, they generally hold out for a higher price; each man fears to spoil his chance of getting a better price later on from his own customers; or, if he produces for a large and open market, he is more or less in fear of incurring the resentment of other producers, should he sell needlessly at a price that spoils the common market for all. The marginal production in this case is the production of those whom a little further fall of price would cause, either from a regard to their own interest or by formal or informal agreement with other producers, to suspend production for fear of further spoiling the market. The price which, for these reasons, producers are just on the point of refusing, is the true marginal supply price for short periods. It is nearly always above, and generally very much above the special or prime cost for raw materials, labour and wear-and-tear of

plant, which is immediately and directly involved by getting   V, v, 6.
a little further use out of appliances which are not fully
employed. This point needs further study.

In a trade which uses very expensive plant, the prime *Where*
cost of goods is but a small part of their total cost; and an *there is much fixed*
order at much less than their normal price may leave a large *capital, prices can*
surplus above their prime cost. But if producers accept *fall far below their*
such orders in their anxiety to prevent their plant from *normal level*
being idle, they glut the market and tend to prevent prices *without*
from reviving. In fact however they seldom pursue this *reaching special or*
policy constantly and without moderation. If they did, they *prime cost;*
might ruin many of those in the trade, themselves perhaps
among the number; and in that case a revival of demand
would find little response in supply, and would raise violently
the prices of the goods produced by the trade. Extreme
variations of this kind are in the long run beneficial neither
to producers nor to consumers; and general opinion is not
altogether hostile to that code of trade morality which con-
demns the action of anyone who "spoils the market" by
being too ready to accept a price that does little more than
cover the prime cost of his goods, and allows but little on
account of his general expenses[1].

For example, if at any time the prime cost, in the
narrowest sense of the word, of a bale of cloth is £100; and
if another £100 are needed to make the cloth pay its due
share of the general expenses of the establishment, including
normal profits to its owners, then the practically effective
supply price is perhaps not very likely to fall below £150
under ordinary conditions, even for short periods; though of
course a few special bargains may be made at lower prices
without much affecting the general market.

---

[1] Where there is a strong combination, tacit or overt, producers may sometimes regulate the price for a considerable time together with very little reference
to cost of production. And if the leaders in that combination were those who had
the best facilities for production, it might be said, in apparent though not in real
contradiction to Ricardo's doctrines, that the price was governed by that part of
the supply which was most easily produced. But as a fact, those producers whose
finances are weakest, and who are bound to go on producing to escape failure,
often impose their policy on the rest of the combination: insomuch that it is
a common saying, both in America and England, that the weakest members of a
combination are frequently its rulers.

V, v, 6.

but such
a fall is
opposed
by many
causes,
mostly
indirect.
Thus, although nothing but prime cost enters *necessarily and directly* into the supply price for short periods, it is yet true that supplementary costs also exert some influence indirectly. A producer does not often isolate the cost of each separate small parcel of his output; he is apt to treat a considerable part of it, even in some cases the whole of it, more or less as a unit. He inquires whether it is worth his while to add a certain new line to his present undertakings, whether it is worth while to introduce a new machine and so on. He treats the extra output that would result from the change more or less as a unit beforehand; and afterwards he quotes the lowest prices, which he is willing to accept, with more or less reference to the whole cost of that extra output regarded as a unit.

The
marginal
unit is a
whole
process of
production
rather than
a parcel of
goods.
In other words he regards an increase in his processes of production, rather than an individual parcel of his products, as a unit in most of his transactions. And the analytical economist must follow suit, if he would keep in close touch with actual conditions. These considerations tend to blur the sharpness of outline of the theory of value: but they do not affect its substance[1].

General
conclu-
sions as
to short
periods.
To sum up then as regards short periods. The supply of specialized skill and ability, of suitable machinery and other material capital, and of the appropriate industrial organization has not time to be fully adapted to demand; but the producers have to adjust their supply to the demand as best they can with the appliances already at their disposal. On the one hand there is not time materially to increase those appliances if the supply of them is deficient; and on the other, if the supply is excessive, some of them must remain imperfectly employed, since there is not time for the supply to be much reduced by gradual decay, and by conversion to other uses. Variations in the particular income

---

[1] This general description may suffice for most purposes: but in chapter XI. there will be found a more detailed study of that extremely complex notion, a marginal increment in the processes of production by a representative firm; together with a fuller explanation of the necessity of referring our reasonings to the circumstances of a representative firm, especially when we are considering industries which show a tendency to increasing return.

derived from them do not *for the time* affect perceptibly the supply; and do not directly affect the price of the commodities produced by them. The income is a surplus of total receipts over prime cost; [that is, it has something of the nature of a rent as will be seen more clearly in chapter VIII.]. But unless it is sufficient to cover in the long run a fair share of the general costs of the business, production will gradually fall off. In this way a controlling influence over the relatively quick movements of supply price during short periods is exercised by causes in the background which range over a long period; and the fear of "spoiling the market" often makes those causes act more promptly than they otherwise would.

§ 7. In long periods on the other hand all investments of capital and effort in providing the material plant and the organization of a business, and in acquiring trade knowledge and specialized ability, have time to be adjusted to the incomes which are expected to be earned by them: and the estimates of those incomes therefore directly govern supply, and are the true long-period normal supply price of the commodities produced.

In long periods the flow of appliances for production is adjusted to the demand for the products of those appliances.

A great part of the capital invested in a business is generally spent on building up its internal organization and its external trade connections. If the business does not prosper all that capital is lost, even though its material plant may realize a considerable part of its original cost. And anyone proposing to start a new business in any trade must reckon for the chance of this loss. If himself a man of normal capacity for that class of work, he may look forward ere long to his business being a representative one, in the sense in which we have used this term, with its fair share of the economies of production on a large scale. If the net earnings of such a representative business seem likely to be greater than he could get by similar investments in other trades to which he has access, he will choose this trade. Thus that investment of capital in a trade, on which the price of the commodity produced by it depends in the long run, is governed by estimates on the one hand of the outgoings required to build up and to work a representative

V, v, 8.   firm, and on the other of the incomings, spread over a long
period of time, to be got by such a price.

At any particular moment some businesses will be rising
and others falling: but when we are taking a broad view of
the causes which govern normal supply price, we need not
trouble ourselves with these eddies on the surface of the great
tide. Any particular increase of production may be due to
some new manufacturer who is struggling against difficulties,
working with insufficient capital, and enduring great priva-
tions in the hope that he may gradually build up a good
business. Or it may be due to some wealthy firm which by
enlarging its premises is enabled to attain new economies,
and thus obtain a larger output at a lower proportionate
cost: and, as this additional output will be small relatively
to the aggregate volume of production in the trade, it will
not much lower the price; so that the firm will reap great
gains from its successful adaptation to its surroundings.
But while these variations are occurring in the fortunes of
individual businesses, there may be a steady tendency of the
long-period normal supply price to diminish, as a direct
consequence of an increase in the aggregate volume of production.

There is
no sharp
division
between
long and
short
periods.

§ 8. Of course there is no hard and sharp line of division
between "long" and "short" periods. Nature has drawn no
such lines in the economic conditions of actual life; and in
dealing with practical problems they are not wanted. Just
as we contrast civilized with uncivilized races, and establish
many general propositions about either group, though no
hard and fast division can be drawn between the two; so we
contrast long and short periods without attempting any rigid
demarcation between them. If it is necessary for the purposes of any particular argument to divide one case sharply
from the other, it can be done by a special interpretation
clause: but the occasions on which this is necessary are
neither frequent nor important.

Classifi-
cation of
problems
of value
by the
periods to
which they
refer.

Four classes stand out. In each, price is governed by
the relations between demand and supply. As regards
market prices, Supply is taken to mean the stock of the
commodity in question which is on hand, or at all events "in

sight." As regards *normal* prices, when the term Normal is
taken to relate to *short* periods of a few months or a year,
Supply means broadly what can be produced for the price
in question with the existing stock of plant, personal and
impersonal, in the given time. As regards *normal* prices,
when the term Normal is to refer to *long* periods of several
years, Supply means what can be produced by plant, which
itself can be remuneratively produced and applied within the
given time; while lastly, there are very gradual or *Secular*
movements of normal price, caused by the gradual growth
of knowledge, of population and of capital, and the changing
conditions of demand and supply from one generation to
another[1].

[1] Compare the first section of this chapter. Of course the periods required to
adapt the several factors of production to the demand may be very different; the
number of skilled compositors, for instance, cannot be increased nearly as fast as
the supply of type and printing-presses. And this cause alone would prevent any
rigid division being made between long and short periods. But in fact a theoretically perfect long period must give time enough to enable not only the factors of
production of the commodity to be adjusted to the demand, but also the factors
of production of those factors of production to be adjusted and so on; and this,
when carried to its logical consequences, will be found to involve the supposition
of a stationary state of industry, in which the requirements of a future age can
be anticipated an indefinite time beforehand. Some such assumption is indeed
unconsciously implied in many popular renderings of Ricardo's theory of value, if
not in his own versions of it; and it is to this cause more than any other that we
must attribute that simplicity and sharpness of outline, from which the economic
doctrines in fashion in the first half of this century derived some of their seduc-
tive charm, as well as most of whatever tendency they may have to lead to false
practical conclusions.

Relatively short and long period problems go generally on similar lines. In
both use is made of that paramount device, the partial or total isolation for
special study of some set of relations. In both opportunity is gained for analysing
and comparing similar episodes, and making them throw light upon one another;
and for ordering and co-ordinating facts which are suggestive in their similarities,
and are still more suggestive in the differences that peer out through their similarities. But there is a broad distinction between the two cases. In the relatively
short-period problem no great violence is needed for the assumption that the
forces not specially under consideration may be taken for the time to be inactive.
But violence is required for keeping broad forces in the pound of *Cæteris Paribus*
during, say, a whole generation, on the ground that they have only an indirect
bearing on the question in hand. For even indirect influences may produce great
effects in the course of a generation, if they happen to act cumulatively; and it is
not safe to ignore them even provisionally in a practical problem without special
study. Thus the uses of the statical method in problems relating to very long
periods are dangerous; care and forethought and self-restraint are needed at every
step. The difficulties and risks of the task reach their highest point in connection
with industries which conform to the law of Increasing Return; and it is just
in connection with those industries that the most alluring applications of the

The remainder of the present volume is chiefly concerned with the third of the above classes: that is, with the normal relations of wages, profits, prices, etc., for rather long periods. But occasionally account has to be taken of changes that extend over very many years. . . .

method are to be found. . . .

But an answer may be given here to the objection that since "the economic world is subject to continual changes; and is becoming more complex, . . . the longer the run the more hopeless the rectification": so that to speak of that position which value tends to reach in the long run is to treat "variables as constants." (Devas, *Political Economy*, Book IV. ch v.) It is true that we do treat variables *provisionally* as constants. But it is also true that this is the only method by which science has ever made any great progress in dealing with complex and changeful matter, whether in the physical or moral world. See above V. v. 2.

CHAPTER VI.

JOINT AND COMPOSITE DEMAND. JOINT AND COMPOSITE SUPPLY.

§ 1. BREAD satisfies man's wants directly: and the demand for it is said to be direct. But a flour mill and an oven satisfy wants only indirectly, by helping to make bread, etc., and the demand for them is said to be indirect. More generally: —

The demand for raw materials and other means of production is *indirect* and is *derived* from the direct demand for those directly serviceable products which they help to produce.

Indirect or derived demand.

The services of the flour mill and the oven are joined together in the ultimate product, bread: the demand for them is therefore called a joint demand. Again, hops and malt are complementary to one another; and are joined together in the common destination of ale: and so on. Thus the demand for each of several complementary things is derived from the services which they *jointly* render in the production of some ultimate product, as for instance a loaf of bread, a cask of ale. In other words there is a *joint demand* for the services which any of these things render in helping to produce a thing which satisfies wants directly and for which there is therefore a direct demand: the direct demand for the finished product is in effect split up into many derived demands for the things used in producing it[1].

Joint demand.

[1] Compare III. III. 6. It will be recollected that the things in a form ready for immediate use have been called *goods of the first order*, or *consumers' goods*;

To take another illustration, the direct demand for houses gives rise to a joint demand for the labour of all the various building trades, and for bricks, stone, wood, etc. which are factors of production of building work of all kinds, or as we may say for shortness, of new houses. The demand for any one of these, as for instance the labour of plasterers, is only an indirect or derived demand.

Illustration taken from a labour dispute in the building trade.
Let us pursue this last illustration with reference to a class of events that are of frequent occurrence in the labour market; the period over which the disturbance extends being short, and the causes of which we have to take account as readjusting demand and supply being only such as are able to operate within that short period.

This case has important practical bearings, which give it a special claim on our attention; but we should notice that, referring as it does to short periods, it is an exception to our general rule of selecting illustrations in this and the neighbouring chapters from cases in which there is time enough for the full long-period action of the forces of supply to be developed.

Let us then suppose that the supply and demand for building being in equilibrium, there is a strike on the part of one group of workers, say the plasterers, or that there is some other disturbance to the supply of plasterers' labour. In order to isolate and make a separate study of the demand for that factor, we suppose firstly that the general conditions of the demand for new houses remain unchanged (that is, that the demand schedule for new houses remains valid); and secondly we assume that there is no change in the general conditions of supply of the other factors, two of which are of course the business faculties and the business organizations of the master builders; (that is, we assume that their lists of supply prices also remain valid). Then a temporary check to

and that things used as factors of production of other goods have been called *producers' goods*, or *goods of the second and higher orders* or *intermediate goods*: also that it is difficult to say when goods are really finished; that many things are commonly treated as finished consumers' goods before they are really ready for consumption, *e.g.* flour. See II. III. 1. The vagueness of the notion of *instrumental goods*, regarded as things the value of which is derived from that of their products, is indicated in II. IV. 13.

the supply of plasterers' labour will cause a proportionate V, VI, 1.
check to the amount of building: the demand price for the
diminished number of houses will be a little higher than
before; and the supply prices for the other factors of production will not be greater than before[1]. Thus new houses
can now be sold at prices which exceed by a good margin the
sum of the prices at which these other requisites for the
production of houses can be bought; and that margin gives
the limit to the possible rise of the price that will be offered
for plasterers' labour, on the supposition that plasterers'
labour is indispensable. The different amounts of this
margin, corresponding to different checks to the supply of
plasterers' labour, are governed by the general rule that:—
The price that will be offered for any thing used in producing *Law of*
a commodity is, for each separate amount for the commodity, *derived demand.*
limited by the excess of the price at which that amount of
the commodity can find purchasers, over the sum of the
prices at which the corresponding supplies of the other
things needed for making it will be forthcoming.

To use technical terms, the demand schedule for any
factor of production of a commodity can be *derived* from
that for the commodity by subtracting from the demand
price of each separate amount of the commodity the sum
of the supply prices for corresponding amounts of the other
factors[2].

[1] This is at any rate true under all ordinary conditions: there will be less
extra charges for overtime; and the price of the labour of carpenters, bricklayers
and others is likely rather to go down than to go up, and the same is true of bricks
and other building materials.

[2] The broad account given in the text may suffice for most purposes; and the
general reader should perhaps omit the remaining footnotes to this chapter.

It must be remembered that this Derived schedule has no validity except
on the suppositions that we are isolating this one factor for separate study;
that its own conditions of supply are disturbed; that there is at the time no
independent disturbance affecting any other element in the problem; and that
therefore in the case of each of the other factors of production the selling price
may be taken to coincide always with the supply price.

In illustrating this by a diagram, it will be well, for the sake of shortness of
wording, to divide the expenses of production of a commodity into the supply
prices of two things of which it is made; let us then regard the supply price of
a knife as the sum of the supply prices of its blade and handle, and neglect the
expense of putting the two together. Let *ss'* be the supply curve for handles and
SS' that for knives; so that *M* being any point on *Ox*, and *MqQ* being drawn vertically to cut *ss'* in *q* and *SS'* in *Q*, *Mq* is the supply price for *OM* handles, *qQ* is
the supply price for *OM* blades and *MQ* the supply price for *OM* knives. Let *DD'*

Cautions as
to the prac-
tical appli-
cations of
the theory.

§ 2. When however we come to apply this theory to the actual conditions of life, it will be important to remember that if the supply of one factor is disturbed, the supply of others is likely to be disturbed also. In particular, when the factor of which the supply is disturbed is one class of labour, as that of the plasterers, the employers' earnings generally act as a buffer. That is to say, the loss falls in the first

the demand curve for knives cut *SS'* in *A,* and *AaB* be drawn vertically as in the figure. Then in equilibrium *OB* knives are sold at a price *BA of* which *Ba* goes for the handle and *aA* for the blade.

(In this illustration we may suppose that sufficient time is allowed to enable the forces which govern supply price to work themselves out fully; and we are at liberty therefore to make our supply curves inclined negatively. This change will not affect the argument; but on the whole it is best to take our typical instance with the supply curve inclined positively.)

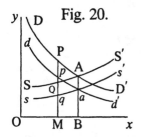

Fig. 20.

Now let us suppose that we want to isolate for separate study the demand for knife handles.

Accordingly we suppose that the demand for knives and the supply of blades conform to the laws indicated by their respective curves: also that the supply curve for handles still remains in force and represents the circumstances of normal supply of handles, although the supply of handles is temporarily disturbed. Let *MQ* cut *DD'* in *P*, then *MP* is the demand price for *OM* knives and *Qq* is the supply price for *OM* blades. Take a point *p* in *MP* such that *Pp* is equal to *Qq*, and therefore *Mp* is the excess of *MP* over *Qq*; then *Mp* is the demand price for *OM* handles. Let *dd'* be the locus of *p* obtained by giving *M* successive positions along *Ox* and finding the corresponding positions of *p*; then *dd'* is the derived demand curve for handles. Of course it passes though *a*. We may now neglect all the rest of the figure except the curves *dd'*, *ss'*; and regard them as representing the relations of demand for and supply of handles, other things being equal, that is to say, in the absence of any disturbing cause which affects the law of supply of blades and the law of demand for knives. *Ba* is then the equilibrium price of handles, about which the market price oscillates, in the manner investigated in the preceding chapter, under the influence of demand and supply, of which the schedules are represented by *dd'* and *ss'*. It has already been remarked that the ordinary demand and supply curves have no practical value except in the immediate neighbourhood of the point of equilibrium. And the same remark applies with even greater force to the equation of derived demand.

[Since *Mp - Mq = MP - MQ*; therefore *A* being a point of stable equilibrium, the equilibrium at *a* also is stable. But this statement needs to be somewhat qualified if the supply curves are negatively inclined. . . .]

In the illustration that has just been worked out the unit of each of the factors remains unchanged whatever be the amount of the commodity produced; for one blade and one handle are always required for each knife; but when a change in the amount of the commodity produced occasions a change in the amount of each factor that is required for the production of a unit of the commodity, the demand and supply curves for the factor got by the above process are not expressed in terms of fixed units of the factor. They must be translated back into fixed units before they are available for general use. . . .

instance on them; but by discharging some of their work- V, VI, 2.
men and lowering the wages of others, they ultimately
distribute a great part of it among the other factors of production. The details of the process by which this is effected
are various, and depend on the action of trade combinations,
on the higgling and bargaining of the market, and on other
causes with which we are not just at present concerned.

Let us inquire what are the conditions, under which a Conditions
check to the supply of a thing that is wanted not for direct under
which a
use, but as a factor of production of some commodity, may check to
supply may
cause a very great rise in its price. The first condition is raise much
the price of
that the factor itself should be essential, or nearly essential a requisite
of produc-
to the production of the commodity, no good substitute being tion.
available at a moderate price.

The second condition is that the commodity in the production of which it is a necessary factor, should be one for
which the demand is stiff and inelastic; so that a check to
its supply will cause consumers to offer a much increased
price for it rather than go without it; and this of course
includes the condition that no good substitutes for the commodity are available at a price but little higher than its
equilibrium price. If the check to house building raises the
price of houses very much, builders, anxious to secure the
exceptional profits, will bid against one another for such
plasterers' labour as there is in the market[1].

The third condition is that only a small part of the
expenses of production of the commodity should consist of
the price of this factor. Since the plasterer's wages are but
a small part of the total expenses of building a house, a rise
of even 50 per cent. in them would add but a very small
percentage to the expenses of production of a house and
would check demand but little[2].

---

[1] We have to inquire under what conditions the ratio pM to aB will be the
greatest, pM being the demand price for the factor in question corresponding to
a supply reduced from OB to OM, that is reduced by the given amount BM. The
second condition is that PM should be large; and since the elasticity of demand is
measured by the ratio which BM bears to the excess of PM over AB, the greater
PM is, the smaller, other things being equal, is the elasticity of demand.

[2] The third condition is that when PM exceeds AB in a given ratio, pM shall
be caused to exceed Ba in a large ratio: and other things being equal, that requires
Ba to be but a small part of BA.

The fourth condition is that even a small check to the amount demanded should cause a considerable fall in the supply prices of other factors of production; as that will increase the margin available for paying a high price for this one[1]. If, for instance, bricklayers and other classes of workmen, or the employers themselves cannot easily find other things to do, and cannot afford to remain idle, they may be willing to work for much lower earnings than before, and this will increase the margin available for paying higher wages to plasterers. These four conditions are independent, and the effects of the last three are cumulative.

Moderating influence of the principle of substitution,

The rise in plasterers' wages would be checked if it were possible either to avoid the use of plaster, or to get the work done tolerably well and at a moderate price by people outside the plasterers' trade: the tyranny, which one factor of production of a commodity might in some cases exercise over the other factors through the action of derived demand, is tempered by the principle of substitution[2].

and of the power of modifying the proportions which the several factors of production of a commodity bear to one another.

Again, an increased difficulty in obtaining one of the factors of a finished commodity can often be met by modifying the character of the finished product. Some plasterers' labour may be indispensable; but people are often in doubt how much plaster work it is worth while to have in their houses, and if there is a rise in its price they will have less of it. The intensity of the satisfaction of which they would be deprived if they had a little less of it, is its marginal utility; the price which they are just willing to pay in order to have it, is the true demand price for plasterers' work up to the amount which is being used.

So again there is a joint demand for malt and hops in ale. But their proportions can be varied. A higher price can be

---

[1] That is, if Qq had been smaller than it is, Pp would have been smaller and Mp would have been larger. . . .

[2] It is shown in Böhm-Bawerk's excellent *Grundzüge der Theorie des wirtshaftlichen Güterwerts (Jahrbuch für Nationalökonomie und Statistik,* vol. XIII. p. 59) that if all but one of the factors of production of a commodity have available substitutes in unlimited supply, by which their own price is rigidly fixed, the derived demand price for the remaining factor will be the excess of the demand price for the finished product over the sum of the supply prices thus fixed for the remaining factors. This is an interesting special case of the law given in the text.

got for an ale which differs from others only in containing V, VI, 3.
more hops; and this excess price represents the demand for
hops.

The relations between plasterers, bricklayers, etc., are
representative of much that is both instructive and
romantic in the history of alliances and conflicts between
trades-unions in allied trades. But the most numerous
instances of joint demand are those of the demand for a raw
material and the operatives who work it up; as for instance
cotton or jute or iron or copper, and those who work up
these several materials. Again, the relative prices of different articles of food vary a good deal with the supply of
skilled cooks' labour: thus for instance many kinds of meat
and many parts of vegetables which are almost valueless in
America, where skilled cooks are rare and expensive, have
a good value in France, where the art of cooking is widely
diffused.

§ 3. We have already[1] discussed the way in which the *Composite*
aggregate demand for any commodity is compounded of *or aggre-*
the demands of the different groups of people who may *gate*
need it. But we now may extend this notion of *composite* *demand.*
demand to requisites of production which are needed by
several groups of producers.

Nearly every raw material and nearly every kind of labour is *Rival*
applied in many different branches of industry, and contributes to *demands.*
the production of a great variety of commodities. Each of these
commodities has its own direct demand; and from that the derived
demand for any of the things used in making it can be found, and
the thing is "distributed between its various uses" in the manner
which we have already discussed[2]. The various uses are rivals, or
competitors with one another; and the corresponding derived
demands are *rival* or *competitive demands* relatively to one
another. But in relation to the supply of the product, they co-
operate with one another; being "compounded" into the total
demand that carries off the supply: in just the same way as the
partial demands of several classes of society for a finished

[1] See above, III. IV. 2, 4.
[2] See III. V.

commodity are aggregated, or compounded together into the total demand for it[1].

§ 4. We may now pass to consider the case of *joint products*: *i.e.* of things which cannot easily be produced separately; but are joined in a common origin, and may therefore be said to have *joint supply*, such as beef and hides, or wheat and straw[2]. This case corresponds to that of things which have a joint demand, and it may be discussed almost in the same words, by merely substituting "demand" for "supply," and *vice versâ*. As there is a joint demand for things joined in a common destination: so there is a joint supply of things which have a common origin. The single supply of the common origin is split up into so many derived supplies of the things that proceed from it[3].

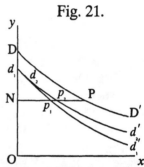

Fig. 21.

[1] Thus, let a factor of production have three uses. Let $d_1 d_1'$ *be* the demand curve for it in its first use. From N any point on Oy draw Np_1 horizontally to cut $d_1 d_1'$ in p_1; then Np_1 is the amount that is demanded for the first use at price ON. Produce Np_1 to p_2, and further on to P making $p_1 p_2$ and $p_2 P$ of such lengths as to represent the amounts of the factor demanded at price ON for the second and third uses respectively. As N moves along Oy let p_2 trace out the curve $d_2 d_2'$ and let P trace out the curve DD'. Thus $d2d_2'$ would be the demand curve for the factor if it had only its first and second uses. DD' is its demand curve for all three uses. It is immaterial in what order we take the several uses. In the case represented, the demand for the second use begins at a lower price and that for the third use begins at a higher price than does the demand for the first use. . . .

[2] Professor Dewsnup (*American Economic Review, Supplement* 1914, p. 89) suggests that things should be described as joint products, when their "total costs of production by a single plant are less than the sum of the costs of their production by separate plants." This definition is less general than that reached at the end of this section; but it is convenient for some special uses.

[3] If it is desired to isolate the relations of demand and supply for a joint product, the derived supply price is found in just the same way as the derived demand price for a factor of production was found in the parallel case of demand. Other things must be assumed to be equal (that is, the supply schedule for the whole process of production must be assumed to remain in force and so must the demand schedule for each of the joint products except that to be isolated). The derived supply price is then found by the rule that it must equal the excess of the supply price for the whole process of production over the sum of the demand prices of all the other joint products; the prices being taken throughout with reference to corresponding amounts.

We may again illustrate by a simple example in which it is assumed that the

For instance, since the repeal of the Corn Laws much of the wheat consumed in England has been imported, of course without any straw. This has caused a scarcity and a consequent rise in the price of straw, and the farmer who grows wheat looks to the straw for a great part of the value of the crop. The value of straw then is high in countries which import wheat, and low in those which export wheat. In the same way the price of mutton in the wool-producing districts of Australia was at one time very low. The wool was exported, the meat had to be consumed at home; and as there was no great demand for it, the price of the wool had to defray almost the whole of the joint expenses of production of the wool and the meat. Afterwards the low price of meat gave a stimulus to the industries of preserving meat for exportation, and now its price in Australia is higher.

There are very few cases of joint products the cost of production of both of which together is exactly the same as that of one of them alone. So long as any product of a business has a market value, it is almost sure to have devoted to it some special care and expense, which would be diminished, or dispensed with if the demand for that product were to fall very much. Thus, for instance, if straw were valueless, farmers would exert themselves more than they do to make the ear bear as large a proportion as possible to the stalk. Again, the importation of foreign wool has caused English

V, VI, 4.

If the proportions of joint products can be modified,

relative amounts of the two joint products are unalterable. Let *SS'* be the supply curve for bullocks which yield meat and leather in fixed quantities; *dd'* the demand curve for their carcases, that is, for the meat derived from them. *M* being any point on *Ox* draw *Mp* vertically to cut *dd'* in *p*, and produce it to *P* so that *pP* represents the demand price for *OM* hides. Then *MP* is the demand price for *OM* bullocks, and *DD'* the locus of *P* is the demand curve for bullocks: it may be called the total demand curve. Let *DD'* cut *SS'* in *A*; and draw *AaB* as in the figure. Then in equilibrium *OB* bullocks are produced and sold at the price *BA* of which *Ba* goes for the carcase and *aA* for the hide.

Let *MP* cut *SS'* in *Q*. From *QM* cut off *Qq* equal to *Pp*; then *q* is a point on the derived supply curve for carcases. For if we assume that the selling price of *OM* hides is always equal to the corresponding demand price *Pp*, it follows that since it costs *QM* to produce each of *OM* bullocks there remains a price *QM - Pp*, that is *qM*, to be borne by each of the *OM* carcases. Then *ss'* the locus of *q*, and *dd'* are the supply and demand curves for carcases. . . .

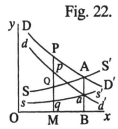

Fig. 22.

their several costs may be discovered.

sheep to be adapted by judicious crossing and selection so as to develop heavy weights of good meat at an early age, even at the expense of some deterioration of their wool. It is only when one of two things produced by the same process is valueless, unsaleable, and yet does not involve any expense for its removal, that there is no inducement to attempt to alter its amount; and, it is only in these exceptional cases that we have no means of assigning its separate supply price to each of the joint products. For when it is possible to modify the proportions of these products, we can ascertain what part of the whole expense of the process of production would be saved, by so modifying these proportions as slightly to diminish the amount of one of the joint products without affecting the amounts of the others. That part of the expense is the expense of production of the marginal element of that product; it is the supply price of which we are in search.

But these are exceptional cases. It more frequently happens that a business, or even an industry finds its advantage in using a good deal of the same plant, technical skill, and business organization for several classes of products. In such cases the cost of anything used for several purposes has to be defrayed by its fruits in all of them: but there is seldom any rule of nature to determine either the relative importance of these uses, or the proportions in which the total cost should be distributed among them: much depends on the changing features of markets[1].

Composite supply.

§ 5. We may pass to the problem of *composite supply* which is analogous to that of composite demand. A demand can often be satisfied by any one of several routes, according to the principle of substitution. These various routes are rivals or competitors with one another; and the corresponding supplies of commodities are *rival*, or *competitive* supplies relatively to one another. But in relation to the demand they co-operate with one another; being "compounded" into the total supply that meets the demand[2].

---

[1] A little more is said on this subject in the next chapter: it is discussed fully in the forthcoming work on *Industry and Trade*.

[2] The latter phrase "competing commodities" is used by Prof. Fisher in his

If the causes which govern their production are nearly the
same, they may for many purposes be treated as one commodity[1].
For instance, beef and mutton may be treated as varieties of one
commodity for many purposes; but they must be treated as separate for others, as for instance for those in which the question of
the supply of wool enters. Rival things are however often not finished commodities, but factors of production: for instance, there
are many rival fibres which are used in making ordinary printing
paper. We have just noticed how the fierce action of derived
demand for one of several complementary supplies, as *e.g.* for
the supply of plasterers' labour, was liable to be moderated,
when the demand was met by the competitive supply of a rival
thing, which could be substituted for it[2].

brilliant *Mathematical Investigations in the theory of value and prices*, which throw
much light on the subjects discussed in the present chapter.

[1] Comp. Jevons, *l. c.* pp. 145, 6. See also above, footnotes on pp. 100, 105.

[2] The want which all the rivals tend to satisfy is met by a composite supply, the
total supply at any price being the sum of the partial supplies at that price.

Thus, for instance, N being any point on Oy draw Nq_1q_2Q parallel to Ox such
that Nq_1, q_1q_2 and q_2Q are respec-
tively the amounts of the first,
second and third of those rivals
which can be supplied at the price
ON. Then NQ is the total composite
supply at that price, and the locus
of Q is the total supply curve of the
means of satisfying the want in
question. Of course the units of the
several things which are rivals
must be so taken that each of them
satisfies the same amount of want.
In the case represented in the

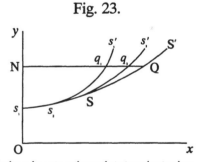

Fig. 23.

figure small quantities of the first rival can be put on the market at a price too low
to call forth any supply of the other two, and small quantities of the second at a price
too low to call forth any of the third. . . .

Continued rivalry is as a rule possible only when none of the rivals has its supply governed by the law of increasing return. The equilibrium is stable only when none of them is able
to drive the others out; and this is the case when all of them conform to the law of diminishing
return; because then if one did obtain a temporary advantage and its use increased, its supply
price would rise, and then the others would begin to undersell it. But if one of them conformed
to the law of increasing return, the rivalry would soon cease; for whenever it happened to gain
a temporary advantage over its rivals its increased use would lower its supply price and therefore increase its sale—its supply price would then be further lowered, and so on: thus its advantage over its rivals would be continually increased until it had driven them out of the field. It
is true that there are apparent exceptions to this rule; and things which conform to the law of
increasing return do sometimes seem to remain for a long time in the field as

V, VI, 6.

Instances
of intricate
relations
between
the values
of different
things.

§ 6. All the four chief problems which have been discussed in this chapter have some bearing on the causes
that govern the value of almost every commodity: and
many of the most important cross connections between the
values of different commodities are not obvious at first sight.
Thus when charcoal was generally used in making iron,
the price of leather depended in some measure on that of
iron; and the tanners petitioned for the exclusion of foreign
iron in order that the demand on the part of English iron
smelters for oak charcoal might cause the production of
English oak to be kept up, and thus prevent oak bark from
becoming dear[1]. This instance may serve to remind us of
the way in which an excessive demand for a thing may
cause its sources of supply to be destroyed, and thus render
scarce any joint products that it may have: for the demand
for wood on the part of the ironmakers led to a relentless
destruction of many forests in England. Again, an excessive
demand for lamb was assigned as a cause of the prevailing
scarcity of sheep some years ago; while some argued on the
contrary that the better the price to be got for spring lamb
sold to the rich, the more profitable would be the production
of sheep, and the cheaper would mutton be for the people.
The fact is that an increase of demand may have opposite
effects according as it does or does not act so suddenly as to
prevent producers from adapting their action to it.

Again, the development of railways and other means of
communication for the benefit of one trade, as for instance
wheat growing in some parts of America and silver mining
in others, greatly lowers some of the chief expenses of
production of nearly every other product of those districts.
Again, the prices of soda, and bleaching materials and other

rivals: such is the case perhaps with different kinds of sewing machines and of
electric lights. But in these cases the things do not really satisfy the same wants,
they appeal to slightly different needs or tastes; there is still some difference of
opinion as to their relative merits; or else perhaps some of them are patented or
in some other way have become the monopoly of particular firms. In such cases
custom and the force of advertising may keep many rivals in the field for a long
time; particularly if the producers of those things which are really the best in
proportion to their expenses of production are not able effectively to advertise
and push their wares by travellers and other agencies.
[1] Toynbee (*Industrial Revolution*, p. 80).

products of industries, the chief raw material of which is
salt, move up and down relatively to one another with
almost every improvement in the various processes which
are used in those industries; and every change in those
prices affects the prices of many other goods, for the various products of the salt industries are more or less important factors in many branches of manufacture.

Again, cotton and cotton-seed oil are joint products, and
the recent fall in the price of cotton is largely due to the
improved manufacture and uses of cotton-seed oil: and further, as the history of the cotton famine shows, the price of
cotton largely affects that of wool, linen and other things of
its own class; while cotton-seed oil is ever opening up new
rivalries with things of its own class. Again, many new
uses have been found for straw in manufacture; and these
inventions are giving value to straw that used to be burnt in
the West of America, and tend to hinder the rise in the marginal cost of producing wheat[1].

[1] Again, since sheep and oxen compete for the use of land, leather and cloth
compete in indirect demand for the use of a factor of production. But also in the
upholsterer's shop they compete as supplying means for meeting the same want.
There is thus a composite demand on the part of upholsterer and shoemaker for
leather; and also for cloth when the upper part of a shoe is made of cloth: the shoe
offers a joint demand for cloth and leather, they offering complementary supplies:
and so on, in endless complications. . . . The Austrian doctrine of "imputed value"
has something in common with that of derived value given in this chapter.
Whichever phrase be used, it is important that we should recognise the continuity
between the old doctrine of value and the new; and that we should treat imputed or
derived values merely as elements which take their place with many others in the
broad problem of distribution and exchange. The new phrases merely give the means
of applying to the ordinary affairs of life, some of that precision of expression which
is the special property of mathematical language. Producers have always to consider
how the demand for any raw material in which they are interested is dependent on
the demand for the things in making which it is used, and how it is influenced by
every change that affects them; and this is really a special case of the problem of
ascertaining the efficient strength of any one of the forces, which contribute to a
common result. In mathematical language this common result is called a *function* of
the various forces: and the (marginal) contribution, which any of them is making to
it, is represented by the (small) change in the result which would result from a
(small) change in that force; that is by the *differential coefficient* of the result with
regard to that force. In other words, the imputed value, or the derived value of a
factor of production, if used for only one product, is the differential coefficient of
that product with regard to that factor; and so on in successive complications. . . .
(Some objections to parts of Prof. Wieser's doctrine of imputed values are well
urged by Prof. Edgeworth, *Economic Journal*, Vol. V. pp. 279–85.)

CHAPTER VII.

PRIME AND TOTAL COST IN RELATION TO JOINT PRODUCTS. COST OF MARKETING. INSURANCE AGAINST RISK. COST OF REPRODUCTION.

Supplementary costs of joint products. Difficulty arising when one branch of a business supplies a raw material to another.

§ 1. WE may now return to the consideration of prime and supplementary costs, with special reference to the proper distribution of the latter between the joint products of a business.

It often happens that a thing made in one branch of a business is used as a raw material in another, and then the question of the relative profitableness of the two branches can be accurately ascertained only by an elaborate system of book-keeping by double entry; though in practice it is more common to rely on rough estimates made by an almost instinctive guess. Some of the best illustrations of this difficulty are found in agriculture, especially when the same farm combines permanent pasture and arable land worked on long rotation[1].

Difficulties as to the joint products of the same business,

Another difficult case is that of the shipowner who has to apportion the expenses of his ship between heavy goods and goods that are bulky but not heavy. He tries, as far as may be, to get a mixed cargo of both kinds; and an important element in the struggle for existence of rival ports is the disadvantage under which those ports lie which are able to offer a cargo only of bulky or only of heavy goods: while

---

[1] There is scope for applications of mathematical or semi-mathematical analyses, such as are indicated in the last chapter, to some of the chief practical difficulties of book-keeping by double entry in different trades.

a port whose chief exports are weighty but not bulky, attracts to its neighbourhood industries which make for export goods that can be shipped from it at low freights. The Staffordshire Potteries, for example, owe part of their success to the low freights at which their goods are carried by ships sailing from the Mersey with iron and other heavy cargoes.

But there is free competition in the shipowning trade, and it has great powers of variation as regards the size and shape of ships, the routes which they take, and the whole method of trading; and thus in many ways the general principle can be applied, that the relative proportions of the joint products of a business should be so modified that the marginal expenses of production of either product should be equal to its marginal demand price[1]. Or, in other words, the amount of carrying power for each kind of cargo has a constant tendency to move towards equilibrium at a point at which the demand price for that amount in a normal state of trade is just sufficient to cover the expenses of providing it; these expenses being reckoned so as to include not only its (money) prime cost, but also all those general expenses of the business which are in the long run incurred on its account, whether directly or indirectly[2].

In some branches of manufacture it is customary to make a first approximation to the total cost of producing any class of goods, by assuming that their share of the general expenses of the business is proportionate either to their prime cost, or to the special labour bill that is incurred in making them. Corrections can then be made to meet such cases as those of goods which require either more or less than an average share of space or light, or of the use of expensive machinery; and so on.

V, VII, 1.

are often overcome through the power of varying the details of the plan of production.

A first approximation is sometimes got by treating supplementary as proportional to prime cost.

---

[1] Compare ch. VI. § 4.

[2] Of course this does not apply to railway rates. For a railway company having little elasticity as to its methods of working, and often not much competition from outside, has no inducement to endeavour to adjust the charges which it makes for different kinds of traffic to their cost to itself. In fact though it may ascertain the prime cost in each case easily enough, it cannot determine accurately what are the relative total costs of fast and slow traffic, of short and long distance traffic, of light and heavy traffic; nor again of extra traffic when its lines and its trains are crowded and when they are nearly empty.

V, vii, 2.

The difficulty of assigning to each branch of a business its share of the expenses of marketing

§ 2. There are two elements of the general expenses of a business, the sharing of which between the different branches requires some special attention. They are the expense of marketing and that of insurance against risk.

Some kinds of goods are easily marketed; there is a steady demand for them, and it is always safe to make them for stock. But for that very reason competition cuts their price "very fine," and does not allow a large margin above the direct cost of making them. Sometimes the tasks of making and selling them can be rendered almost automatic, so as to require very little to be charged on their account under the heads of the expenses of management and marketing. But in practice it is not uncommon to charge such goods with even less than the small share that would properly fall to them, and to use them as a means of obtaining and maintaining a business connection, that will facilitate the marketing of other classes of goods, the production of which cannot so well be reduced to routine; for as to these there is not so close a competition. Manufacturers, especially in trades connected with furniture and dress, and retailers in almost all trades, frequently find it best to use certain of their goods as a means of advertising others, and to charge the first with less and the second with more than their proportionate share of Supplementary expenses. In the former class they put those goods which are so uniform in character and so largely consumed that nearly all purchasers know their value well, in the second those with regard to which purchasers think more of consulting their fancy than of buying at the lowest possible price.

becomes very great when the law of increasing return acts strongly;

All difficulties of this kind are much increased by that instability of supply price, which results whenever the tendency to increasing return is acting strongly. We have seen that in seeking the normal supply price in such cases we must select as representative a business which is managed with normal ability and so as to get its fair share of the economies, both internal and external, resulting from industrial organization: also that these economies, though they fluctuate with the fortunes of particular businesses, yet increase generally when the aggregate production increases.

Now it is obvious that if a manufacturer makes a commodity
the increased production of which would put largely increased
internal economies within his reach, it is worth his while to
sacrifice a great deal in order to push its sales in a new
market. If he has a large capital, and the commodity is one
in much demand, his expenditure for this purpose may be
very great, even exceeding that which he devotes directly to
the manufacture: and if, as is likely, he is pushing at the
same time several other commodities, nothing more than a
very rough guess can be made as to what share of this
expenditure should be charged to the sales of each of them
in the current year, and what share should be charged to the
connection which he is endeavouring to build up for them in
the future.

In fact when the production of a commodity conforms to *especially when the* the law of increasing return in such a way as to give a very *production* great advantage to large producers, it is apt to fall almost *falls into the hands* entirely into the hands of a few large firms; and then the *of a few large firms.* normal marginal supply price cannot be isolated on the plan just referred to, because that plan assumes the existence of a great many competitors with businesses of all sizes, some of them being young and some old, some in the ascending and some in the descending phase. The production of such a commodity really partakes in a great measure of the nature of a monopoly; and its price is likely to be so much influenced by the incidents of the campaign between rival producers, each struggling for an extension of territory, as scarcely to have a true normal level.

Economic progress is constantly offering new facilities for *Economies in produc-* marketing goods at a distance: it not only lowers cost of *tion are* carriage, but what is often more important, it enables pro- *balanced* ducers and consumers in distant places to get in touch with *by local facilities* one another. In spite of this, the advantages of the producer *for marketing.* who lives on the spot are very great in many trades; they often enable him to hold his own against competitors at a distance whose methods of production are more economical. He can sell in his own neighbourhood as cheaply as they can, because though the cost of making is greater for his goods than for theirs, he escapes much of the cost which they incur for marketing. But time is on the side of the more economic methods of production; his distant competitors will gradually get a stronger footing in the place, unless he or some new man adopts their improved methods.

It remains to make a closer study of the relation in which insurance against the risks of a business stands to the supply price of any particular commodity produced in it.

An insurance cannot be effected at moderate rates against all business risks.

§ 3. The manufacturer and the trader commonly insure against injury by fire and loss at sea; and the premiums which they pay are among the general expenses, a share of which has to be added to the prime cost in order to determine the total cost of their goods. But no insurance can be effected against the great majority of business risks.

Even as regards losses by fire and sea, insurance companies have to allow for possible carelessness and fraud; and must therefore, independently of all allowances for their own expenses and profits, charge premiums considerably higher than the true equivalent of the risks run by the buildings or the ships of those who manage their affairs well. The injury done by fire or sea however is likely, if it occurs at all, to be so very great that it is generally worth while to pay this extra charge; partly for special trade reasons, but chiefly because the total utility of increasing wealth increases less than in proportion to its amount. But the greater part of business risks are so inseparably connected with the general management of the business that an insurance company which undertook them would really make itself responsible for the business: and in consequence every firm has to act as its own insurance office with regard to them. The charges to which it is put under this head are part of its general expenses, and a share of them has to be added to the prime cost of each of its products.

But here there are two difficulties. In some cases insurance against risk is apt to be left out of account altogether, in others it is apt to be counted twice over. Thus a large shipowner sometimes declines to insure his ships with the underwriters: and sets aside part at least of

the premiums that he might have paid to them, to build up V, vii, 3.
an insurance fund of his own. But he must still, when Caution
calculating the total cost of working a ship, add to its prime against overlook-
cost a charge on account of insurance. And he must do the ing certain insurance
same thing, in some form or other, with regard to those risks expenses,
against which he could not buy an insurance policy on
reasonable terms even if he wanted to. At times, for instance, some of his ships will be idle in port, or will earn
only nominal freights: and to make his business remunerative in the long run he must, in some form or other, charge
his successful voyages with an insurance premium to make
up for his losses on those which are unsuccessful.

In general, however, he does this, not by making a formal and against counting
entry in his accounts under a separate head, but by the others
simple plan of taking the average of successful and unsuccess- twice over.
ful voyages together; and when that has once been done,
insurance against these risks cannot be entered as a separate
item in cost of production, without counting the same thing
twice over. Having decided to run these risks himself, he is
likely to spend a little more than the average of his competitors, in providing against their occurrence; and this extra
expense enters in the ordinary way into his balance-sheet.
It is really an insurance premium in another form; and
therefore he must not count insurance against this part of
the risk separately, for then he would be counting it twice
over[1].

When a manufacturer has taken the average of his sales
of dress materials over a long time, and bases his future
action on the results of his past experience, he has already
allowed for the risk that the machinery will be depreciated
by new inventions rendering it nearly obsolete, and for
the risk that his goods will be depreciated by changes
in fashion. If he were to allow separately for insurance

---

[1] Again, certain insurance companies in America take risks against fire in
factories at very much less than the ordinary rates, on condition that some
prescribed precautions are taken, such as providing automatic sprinklers and
making the walls and floor solid. The expense incurred in these arrangements
is really an insurance premium; and care must be taken not to count it twice
over. A factory which undertakes its own risks against fire will have to add to
the prime cost of its goods an allowance for insurance at a lower rate, if it is
arranged on this plan, than if built in the ordinary way.

V, vii, 4. against these risks, he would be counting the same thing twice over[1].

But uncertainty is an evil in itself,

§ 4. Thus, though when we have counted up the average receipts of a risky trade, we must not make a separate full allowance for insurance against risk; though there may be something to be allowed as a charge on account of uncertainty. It is true that an adventurous occupation, such as gold mining, has special attractions for some people: the deterrent force of risks of loss in it is less than the attractive force of chances of great gain, even when the value of the latter estimated on the actuarial principle is much less than that of the former; and as Adam Smith pointed out, a risky trade, in which there is an element of romance, often becomes so overcrowded that the average earnings in it are lower than if there were no risks to be run[2]. But in the large majority of cases the influence of risk is in the opposite direction; a railway stock that is certain to pay four per cent. will sell for a higher price than one which is equally likely to pay one or seven per cent. or any intermediate amount.

and an average gain generally counts for less, the more uncertain the elements of which it is made up.

Every trade then has its own peculiarities, but in most cases the evils of uncertainty count for something, though not very much: in some cases a slightly higher average price is required to induce a given outlay, if that average is the mean of widely divergent and uncertain results, than if the adventurer may reckon confidently on a return that differs but little from that average. To the average price therefore we must add a recompense for uncertainty, if that is unusually great; though if we added insurance against risk we should be counting the greater part of that twice over[3].

---

[1] Again, when a farmer has calculated the expenses of raising any particular crop with reference to an average year, he must not count in addition insurance against the risk that the season may be bad, and the crop a failure: for in taking an average year, he has already set off the chances of exceptionally good and bad seasons against one another. When the earnings of a ferryman have been calculated on the average of a year, allowance has already been made for the risk that he may sometimes have to cross the stream with an empty boat.

[2] *Wealth of Nations*, Book I. ch. x.

[3] The evils resulting from the uncertainty involved in great business risks are well shown by von Thünen (*Isolirter Staat*, II. I. p. 82).

§ 5. This discussion of the risks of trade has again
brought before us the fact that the value of a thing, though
it tends to equal its normal (money) cost of production, does
not coincide with it at any particular time, save by accident.
Carey, observing this, suggested that we should speak of
value in relation to (money) cost of reproduction instead of
in relation to cost of production.

The suggestion has, however, no significance so far as
normal values are concerned. For normal cost of production
and normal cost of reproduction are convertible terms; and
no real change is made by saying that the normal value
of a thing tends to equal its normal (money) cost of reproduction instead of its normal (money) cost of production.
The former phrase is less simple than the latter, but means
the same thing.

And no valid argument for the change can be founded on
the fact, which may be readily admitted, that there are some
few cases in which the market value of a thing is nearer its
cost of reproduction than the cost that was actually incurred
in producing that particular thing. The present price of an
iron ship for instance, made before the great recent improvements in the manufacture of iron, might diverge less from
the cost of reproducing it, that is of producing another just
like it by modern methods, than from that which was actually
incurred in producing it. But the price of the old ship
would be less than the cost of reproduction of the ship,
because the art of designing ships has improved as fast as
that of manufacturing iron; and moreover steel has displaced
iron as the material of shipbuilding. It may still be urged
that the price of the ship is equal to that of producing a ship,
which would be equally serviceable, on a modern plan and
by modern methods. But that would not be the same thing
as saying that the value of the ship is equal to its cost of
reproduction; and, as a matter of fact, when, as often
happens, an unexpected scarcity of ships causes freights to
increase very rapidly, those who are anxious to reap the
harvest of profitable trade, will pay for a ship in sailing
order a price much above that for which a shipbuilding firm
would contract to produce another equally good and deliver

it some time hence. Cost of reproduction exerts little direct influence on value, save when purchasers can conveniently wait for the production of new supplies.

Again, there is no connection between cost of reproduction and price in the cases of food in a beleaguered city, of quinine the supply of which has run short in a fever-stricken island, of a picture by Raphael, of a book that nobody cares to read, of an armour-clad ship of obsolete pattern, of fish when the market is glutted, of fish when the market is nearly empty, of a cracked bell, of a dress material that has gone out of fashion, or of a house in a deserted mining village.

*   *   *

The reader, unless already experienced in economic analysis, is recommended to omit the next seven chapters, and pass at once to Chapter XV., which contains a brief summary of this Book. It is true that the four chapters on marginal costs in relation to values, and especially Chapters VIII. and IX., bear upon some difficulties which are latent in the phrase "the net product of labour." . . . But the broad explanation of it given there will suffice provisionally for most purposes; and the intricacies connected with it may be best appreciated at a somewhat advanced stage of economic studies.

CHAPTER VIII.

MARGINAL COSTS IN RELATION TO VALUES.
GENERAL PRINCIPLES.

§ 1. This Chapter and the three following are given to a study of the marginal costs of products in relation to the values of those products on the one hand, and on the other hand to the values of the land, machinery, and other appliances used in making them. *The study relates to normal conditions and long period results.* This fact must ever be borne in mind. The market value of anything may be much above or much below the normal cost of production: and the marginal costs of a particular producer at any time may stand in no close relation to marginal costs under normal conditions[1].

It was indicated at the end of Chapter VI. that no one part of the problem can be isolated from the rest. There are comparatively few things the demand for which is not greatly affected by the demand for other things to the usefulness of which they contribute; and it may even be said that the demand for the majority of articles of commerce is not direct but is derived from the demand for those commodities to the making of which they contribute, as materials or as implements. And again this demand, because it is so derived, is largely dependent on the supply of other things which will work with them in making those commodities. And again the supply of anything available for use in making any commodity is apt to be greatly influenced by the demand for that thing derived from its uses in making other commodities: and so on. These inter-relations can be and must be ignored in rapid and popular discussions on the business

V, VIII, 1.

This and the next three chapters continue the main argument of chapters IV.—VI.

---

[1] Numerous objections have been urged against the important place assigned to marginal costs in modern analysis. But it will be found that most of them rely on arguments, in which statements referring to normal conditions and normal value are controverted by statements relating to abnormal or particular conditions.

Reasons
for dealing
here only
with mate-
rial, imple-
ments, etc.

Restate-
ment of the
principle of
substitu-
tion.

affairs of the world. But no study that makes any claim to thoroughness can escape from a close investigation of them. This requires many things to be borne in mind at the same time: and for that reason economics can never become a simple science[1].

The contribution which this group of chapters aims at making covers little ground: but that ground is difficult: and we shall need to work over it carefully, and from more than one point of view; for it is thickly strewn with pitfalls and stumbling blocks. It deals primarily with the earnings of land, machinery, and other material agents of production. Its main argument applies to the earnings of human beings; but they are influenced by some causes which do not affect the earnings of material agents of production: and the matter in hand is sufficiently difficult without further complicating it by side issues.

§ 2. Let us begin by recalling the action of the principle of substitution. In the modern world nearly all the means of production pass through the hands of employers and other business men, who specialize themselves in organizing the economic forces of population. Each of them chooses in every case those factors of production which seem best for his purpose. And the sum of the prices which he pays for those factors which he uses is, as a rule, less than the sum of the prices which he would have to pay for any other set of factors which could be substituted for them: for, whenever it appears that this is not the case, he will, as a rule, set to work to substitute the less expensive arrangement or process[2].

This statement is in close harmony with such common sayings of every-day life, as that "everything tends to find its own level," that "most men earn just about what they are worth," that "if one man can earn twice as much as another, that shows that his work is worth twice as much," that "machinery will displace manual labour whenever it can do the work cheaper." The principle does not indeed

---

[1] The reader is referred to the footnote on page 209. . . .
[2] Compare V. III. 3; and V. IV. 3,4. . . .

act without hindrance. It may be restricted by custom or V, vɪɪɪ, 2.
law, by professional etiquette or trade-union regulation: it
may be weakened by want of enterprise, or it may be softened
by a generous unwillingness to part with old associates. But
it never ceases to act, and it permeates all the economic
adjustments of the modern world.

Thus there are some kinds of field work for which horse- Illustra-
power is clearly more suitable than steam-power, and *vice* ^tions.^
versâ. If we may now suppose that there have been no great
recent improvements in horse oɾ steam machinery, and that
therefore the experience of the past has enabled farmers
gradually to apply the law of substitution; then, on this
supposition the application of steam-power will have been
pushed just so far that any further use of it in the place
of horse-power would bring no net advantage. There will
however remain a margin on which they could be *indifferently*
applied (as Jevons would have said); and on that margin the
net efficiency of either in adding to the money value of the
total product will be proportionate to the cost of applying it[1].

Similarly, if there are two methods of obtaining the same
result, one by skilled and the other by unskilled labour, that
one will be adopted which is the more efficient in proportion
to its cost. There will be a margin on which either will be
indifferently applied[2]. On that line the efficiency of each
will be in proportion to the price paid for it, account being
taken of the special circumstances of different districts and
of different workshops in the same district. In other words,
the wages of skilled and unskilled labour will bear to one
another the same ratio that their efficiencies do at the
margin of indifference.

Again, there will be a rivalry between hand-power and

---

[1] This margin will vary with local circumstances, as well as with the habits,
inclinations, and resources of individual farmers. The difficulty of applying
steam machinery in small fields and on rugged ground is overcome more
generally in those districts in which labour is scarce than in those in which it is
plentiful; especially if, as is probable, coal is cheaper, and the feed of horses
dearer in the former than the latter.

[2] Skilled manual labour being generally used for special orders and for things
of which not many are required of the same pattern; and unskilled labour aided
by specialized machinery being used for others. The two methods are to be seen
side by side on similar work in every large workshop: but the position of the line
between them will vary a little from one workshop to another.

machine-power similar to that between two different kinds of hand-power or two different kinds of machine-power. Thus hand-power has the advantage for some operations, as, for instance, for weeding out valuable crops that have an irregular growth; horse-power in its turn has a clear advantage for weeding an ordinary turnip field; and the application of each of them will be pushed in each district till any further use of it would bring no net advantage there. On the margin of indifference between hand-power and horse-power their prices must be proportionate to their efficiency; and thus the influence of substitution will tend to establish a direct relation between the wages of labour and the price that has to be paid for horse-power.

The net product at the margin. § 3. As a rule many kinds of labour, of raw material, of machinery and other plant, and of business organization, both internal and external, go to the production of a commodity: and the advantages of economic freedom are never more strikingly manifest than when a business man endowed with genius is trying experiments, at his own risk, to see whether some new method, or combination of old methods, will be more efficient than the old. Every business man indeed, according to his energy and ability, is constantly endeavouring to obtain a notion of the relative efficiency of every agent of production that he employs; as well as of others that might possibly be substituted for some of them. He estimates as best he can how much *net product* (*i.e.* net addition to the value of his total product) will be caused by a certain extra use of any one agent; *net* that is after deducting for any extra expenses that may be indirectly caused by the change, and adding for any incidental savings. He endeavours to employ each agent up to that margin at which its net product would no longer exceed the price he would have to pay for it. He works generally by trained instinct rather than formal calculation; but his processes are substantially similar to those indicated in our study of derived demand; and, from another point of view, they may be described as those which might be reaped by a complex and refined system of book-keeping by double entry[1].

---

[1] The changes, which he desires, may be such as could only be made on a large

We have already fòllowed some simple estimates of this V, VIII, 4.
sort. We have noticed, for instance, how the proportion of Illustration
hops and malt in ale can be varied, how the extra price of the way
which can be got for ale by increasing the quantity of hops in which
in it is a representative of the causes which govern the product of
demand price for hops. Assuming that no further trouble or an agent of
expense of any kind is involved by this additional use of production
hops, and that the expediency of using this extra amount is estimated.
doubtful, the extra value thus given to the ale is the marginal net product of the hops of which we are in search. In
this case, as in most others, the net product is an improvement in quality or a general contribution to the value of the
product; it is not a definite part of the produce which can
be separated from the rest. But in exceptional instances
that can be done[1].

§ 4. The notion of the marginal employment of any The dimin-
agent of production implies a possible tendency to dimin- ishing
ishing return from its increased employment. return from
dispropor-
Excessive applications of any means to the attainment of tionate use
any end are indeed sure to yield diminishing returns in every of any
branch of business; and, one may say, in all the affairs of production,
life. We may take some additional examples of a principle is akin to,
that has already been illustrated[2]. In the manufacture of from,
sewing machines some parts may well be made of cast iron; Dimin-
for others a common kind of steel will suffice; there are yet ishing
others for which a specially expensive steel-compound is land in gen-
needed; and all parts should be finished off more or less eral to
smoothly, so that the machine may work easily. Now if any sive cultivation,
scale; as for instance the substitution of steam-power for hand-power in a certain fac- however
tory; and in that case there would be a certain element of uncertainty and risk in the appropriate.
change. Such breaches of continuity are however inevitable both in production and
consumption if we regard the action of single individuals. But as there is a continuous
demand in a large market for hats and watches and wedding cakes, though no individual buys many of them (see III. III. 5), so there will always be trades in which
small businesses are most economically conducted without steam-power, and larger
businesses with; while businesses of intermediate size are on the margin. Again, even
in large establishments in which steam is already in use, there will always be some
things done by hand-power which are done by steam-power elsewhere; and so on.

[1] See p. 203. . . . See also other illustrations in V. VI. VII. . . .
[2] See V. VI. 4. . . .

one devoted a disproportionate care and expense to the selection of materials for the less important uses, it might truly be said that that expenditure was yielding a rapidly diminishing return; and that he would have done better to give some of it to making his machines work smoothly, or even to producing more machines: and the case might be even worse if he devoted an excessive expenditure to mere brilliancy of finish, and put low grade metal to work for which a higher grade was needed.

This consideration seems at first to simplify economic problems; but on the contrary it is a chief source of difficulty and confusion. For though there is some analogy between all these various tendencies to diminishing return, they yet are not identical. Thus the diminishing return which arises from an ill-proportioned application of the various agents of production into a particular task has little in common with that broad tendency to the pressure of a crowded and growing population on the means of subsistence. The great classical Law of Diminishing Return has its chief application, not to any one particular crop, but to all the chief food crops. It takes for granted that farmers raise, as a rule, those crops for which their land and other resources are best adapted, account being taken of the relative demands for the several crops; and that they distribute their resources appropriately between different routes. It does not attribute to them unlimited intelligence and wisdom, but it assumes that, taking one with another, they have shown a reasonable amount of care and discretion in the distribution of these resources. It refers to a country the whole land of which is already in the hands of active business men, who can supplement their own capital by loans from banks wherever they can show it is likely to be well applied; and asserts that an increase in the total amount of capital applied to agriculture in that country will yield diminishing returns of produce in general. This statement is akin to, but yet quite distinct from, the statement that if any farmer makes a bad distribution of his resources between different plans of cultivation, he will get a markedly diminishing return from those elements of expenditure which he has driven to excess.

For instance, in any given case, there is a certain pro- V, VIII, 4.
portion between the amounts which may with best advantage be spent on ploughing and harrowing, or manuring.
There might be some differences of opinion on the matter,
but only within narrow limits. An inexperienced person who
ploughed many times over land, which was already in fairly
good mechanical condition, while he gave it little or none of
the manure which it was craving, would be generally con-
demned as having so over applied ploughing as to make it
yield a rapidly diminishing return. But this result of the
misapplication of resources has no very close connection
with the tendency of agriculture in an old country to yield a
diminishing return to a general increase of resources well
applied in cultivation: and indeed exactly parallel cases can
be found of a diminishing return to particular resources
when applied in undue proportion, even in industries which
yield an increasing return to increased applications of capital and labour when appropriately distributed[1].

[1] See . . . Carver, *Distribution of Wealth*, ch. II. . . . Mr J. A. Hobson is a vigorous and
suggestive writer on the realistic and social sides of economics: but, as a critic of Ricardian
doctrines, he is perhaps apt to underrate the difficulty of the problems which he discusses.
He argues that if the marginal application of any agent of production be curtailed, that will
so disorganize production that every other agent will be working to less effect than before;
and that therefore the total resulting loss will include not only the true marginal product of
that agent, but also a part of the products due to the other agents: but he appears to have
overlooked the following points:—(1) There are forces constantly at work tending so to
readjust the distribution of resources between their different uses, that any maladjustment
will be arrested before it has gone far: and the argument does not profess to apply to exceptional cases of violent maladjustment. (2) When the adjustment is such as to give the best
results, a slight change in the proportions in which they are applied diminishes the efficiency of that adjustment by a quantity which is very small relatively to that change—in
technical language it is of "the second order of smalls"—; and it may therefore be neglected
relatively to that change. (In pure mathematical phrase, efficiency being regarded as a function of the proportions of the agents; when the efficiency is at its maximum, its differential
coefficient with regard to any one of these proportions is zero.) A grave error would therefore have been involved, if any allowance had been made for those elements which Mr
Hobson asserts to have been overlooked. (3) In economics, as in physics, changes are generally continuous. Convulsive changes may indeed occur, but they must be dealt with separately: and an illustration drawn from a convulsive change can throw no true light on the
processes of normal steady evolution. In the particular problem before us, this precaution is
of special importance: for a violent check to the supply of any one agent of production, may
easily render the work of all other agents practically useless; and therefore it may inflict a
loss out of all proportion to the harm done by a small check to the supply of that agent when
applied up to that margin, at which there was doubt whether the extra net product due to a

V, viii, 5.

Marginal uses and costs do not govern value, but are governed together with value by the general relations of demand and supply.

§ 5. The part played by the net product at the margin of production in the modern doctrine of Distribution is apt to be misunderstood. In particular many able writers have supposed that it represents the marginal use of a thing as *governing* the value of the whole. It is not so; the doctrine says we must *go to the margin to study the action of those forces which govern* the value of the whole: and that is a very different affair. Of course the withdrawal of (say) iron from any of its necessary uses would have just the same influence on its value as its withdrawal from its marginal uses; in the same way as the pressure in a boiler for cooking under high pressure would be affected by the escape of any other steam just as it would by the escape of the steam in one of the safety valves: but in fact the steam does not escape except through the safety valves. In like manner iron, or any other agent of production, is not (under ordinary circumstances) thrown out of use except at points at which its use yields no clear surplus of profit; that is, it is thrown out from its marginal uses only.

Again, the finger of an automatic weighing machine determines, in the sense of *indicating*, the weight sought for. So the escape of steam from a safety valve, governed by a spring representing a pressure of a hundred pounds to the square inch, determines the pressure of steam in the boiler, in the sense of indicating that it has reached a hundred pounds to the inch. The pressure is caused by the heat; the spring in the valve governs the pressure by yielding and letting out some of the steam when its amount is so great, at the existing heat, as to overbear the resistance of the spring.

Similarly, with regard to machinery and other appliances of production made by man, there is a margin through which additional supplies come in after overcoming the resistance of a spring, called "cost of production." For when the supply

small additional application of it would be remunerative. The study of changes in complex quantitative relations is often vitiated by a neglect of this consideration, to which Mr Hobson seems to be prone; as indeed is instanced by his remarks on a "marginal shepherd" in *The Industrial System*, p. 110. See Professor Edgeworth's masterly analyses of the two instances mentioned in this note, *Quarterly Journal of Economics*, 1904, p. 167; and *Scientia*, 1910, pp. 95—100.

of those appliances is so small relatively to the demand that the earnings expected from new supplies are more than sufficient to yield normal interest (or profits, if earnings of management are reckoned in) on their cost of production, besides allowing for depreciation, etc., then the valve opens, and the new supplies come in. When the earnings are less than this, the valve remains shut: and as anyhow the existing supply is always in process of slow destruction by use and the lapse of time, the supply is always shrinking when the valve is closed. The valve is that part of the machinery by which the general relations of demand and supply govern value. But marginal uses do not govern value; because they, together with value, are themselves governed by those general relations.

§ 6. Thus, so long as the resources of an individual producer are in the form of general purchasing power, he will push every investment up to the margin at which he no longer expects from it a higher net return than he could get by investing in some other material, or machine, or advertisement, or in the hire of some additional labour: every investment will, as it were, be driven up to a valve which offers to it a resistance equal to its own expanding force. If he invests in material or in labour, that is soon embodied in some saleable product: the sale replenishes his fluid capital, and that again is invested up to the margin at which any further investment would yield a return so diminished as not to be profitable.

But if he invests in land, or in a durable building or machine, the return which he gets from his investment may vary widely from his expectation. It will be governed by the market for his products, which may change its character largely through new inventions, changes in fashion, etc., during the life of a machine, to say nothing of the perpetual life of land. The incomes which he thus may derive from investments in land and in machinery differ from his individual point of view mainly in the longer life of the land. But in regard to production in general, a dominant difference between the two lies in the fact that the supply of land is fixed (though in a new country, the supply of land utilized

V, VIII, 6.

The terms Interest and Profits are directly applicable to fluid capital;

but only indirectly and on certain definite assumptions to particular embodiments of capital.

in man's service may be increased); while the supply of machines may be increased without limit. And this difference reacts on the individual producer. For if no great new invention renders his machines obsolete, while there is a steady demand for the things made by them, they will be constantly on sale at about their cost of production; and his machines will generally yield him normal profits on that cost of production, with deductions corresponding to their wear and tear.

Thus the rate of interest is a ratio: and the two things which it connects are both sums of money. So long as capital is "free," and the sum of money or general purchasing power over which it gives command is known, the net money income, expected to be derived from it, can be represented at once as bearing a given ratio (four or five or ten per cent.) to that sum. But when the free capital has been invested in a particular thing, its money value cannot as a rule be ascertained except by capitalizing the net income which it will yield: and therefore the causes which govern it are likely to be akin in a greater or less degree to those which govern rents.

The central doctrine of this group of chapters. We are thus brought to the central doctrine of this part of economics, viz.:—"That which is rightly regarded as interest on 'free' or 'floating' capital, or on new investments of capital, is more properly treated as a sort of rent— a *Quasi-rent*—on old investments of capital. And there is no sharp line of division between floating capital and that which has been 'sunk' for a special branch of production, nor between new and old investments of capital; each group shades into the other gradually. And thus even the rent of land is seen, not as a thing by itself, but as the leading species of a large genus; though indeed it has peculiarities of its own which are of vital importance from the point of view of theory as well as of practice[1]."

[1] This statement is reproduced from the Preface to the first edition of the present volume.

CHAPTER IX.

MARGINAL COSTS IN RELATION TO VALUES.
GENERAL PRINCIPLES, CONTINUED.

§ 1. THE incidents of the tenure of land are so complex: V, IX, 1. and so many practical issues connected with them have The essential features of rent proper are seen most clearly in an imaginary instance, raised controversies on side issues of the problem of value, that it will be well to supplement our previous illustration from land. We may take another from an imaginary commodity so chosen that sharp outlines can be assigned to each stage of the problem, without inviting the objection that such sharp outlines are not found in the actual relations between landlord and tenant.

But before entering on this, we may prepare the way for aided by illustrations drawn from the incidence of taxes. using, as we go, illustrations drawn from the incidence of taxation to throw side-lights on the problem of value. For indeed a great part of economic science is occupied with the diffusion throughout the community of economic changes which primarily affect some particular branch of production or consumption; and there is scarcely any economic principle which cannot be aptly illustrated by a discussion of the shifting of the effects of some tax "forwards," *i.e.* towards the ultimate consumer, and away from the producer of raw material and implements of production; or else in the opposite direction, "backwards." But especially is this true of the class of problems now under discussion[1].

It is a general principle that if a tax impinges on Shifting forwards and backwards. anything used by one set of persons in the production of goods or services to be disposed of to other persons, the tax tends to check production. This tends to shift a large

---

[1] The substance of this section is reproduced from answers to questions proposed by the Royal Commission on Local Taxation. See [C. 9528], 1899, pp. 112—126.

V, IX, 1. part of the burden of the tax forwards on to consumers, and a small part backwards on to those who supply the requirements of this set of producers. Similarly, a tax on the consumption of anything is shifted in a greater or less degree backwards on to its producer.

Incidence of a tax on printing. For instance, an unexpected and heavy tax upon printing would strike hard upon those engaged in the trade, for if they attempted to raise prices much, demand would fall off quickly: but the blow would bear unevenly on various classes engaged in the trade. Since printing machines and compositors cannot easily find employment out of the trade, the prices of printing machines and wages of compositors would be kept low for some time. On the other hand, the buildings and steam engines, the porters, engineers, and clerks would not wait for their numbers to be adjusted by the slow process of natural decay to the diminished demand; some of them would be quickly at work in other trades, and very little of the burden would stay long on those of them who remained in the trade. A considerable part of the burden, again, would fall on subsidiary industries, such as those engaged in making paper and type; because the market for their products would be curtailed. Authors and publishers would also suffer a little; because they would be forced either to raise the price of books, with a consequent diminution of sales, or to see a greater proportion of their gross receipts swallowed up by costs. Finally, the total turnover of the booksellers would diminish, and they would suffer a little.

A local tax on printing. So far it has been assumed that the tax spreads its net very wide, and covers every place to which the printing industry in question could be easily transferred. But, if the tax were only local, the compositors would migrate beyond its reach; and the owners of printing houses might bear a larger and not a smaller proportionate share of the burden than those whose resources were more specialized but more mobile. If the local tax were uncompensated by any effect which tended to attract population, part of the burden would be thrown on local bakers, grocers, etc., whose sales would be diminished.

Next suppose the tax to be levied on printing presses V, IX, 2. instead of on printed matter. In that case, if the printers A tax on had no semi-obsolete presses which they were inclined to printing presses. destroy or to leave idle, the tax would not strike marginal production: it would not immediately affect the output of printing, nor therefore its price. It would merely intercept some of the earnings of the presses on the way to the owners, and lower the quasi-rents of the presses. But it would not affect the rate of net profits which was needed to induce people to invest fluid capital in presses: and therefore, as the old presses wore out, the tax would add to marginal expenses, that is to expenses which the producer was free to incur or not as he liked, and which he was in doubt whether to incur. Therefore the supply of printing would be curtailed; its price would rise: and new presses would be introduced only up to the margin at which they would be able, in the judgment of printers generally, to pay the tax and yet yield normal profits on the outlay. When this stage had been reached the distribution of the burden of a tax upon presses would henceforth be nearly the same as that of a tax upon printing: excepting only that there would be more inducement to get a great deal of work out of each press. For instance more of the presses might be made to work double shifts; in spite of the fact that night work involves special expenses.

We now pass to apply these principles of shifting of taxes to our main illustration.

§ 2. Let us suppose that a meteoric shower of a few A limited thousand large stones harder than diamonds fell all in one large place; so that they were all picked up at once, and no stones harder amount of search could find any more. These stones, able to than diamonds. cut every material, would revolutionize many branches of industry; and the owners of them would have a differential advantage in production, that would afford a large producer's surplus. This surplus would be governed wholly by the urgency and volume of the demand for their services on the one hand and the number of the stones on the other hand: it could not be affected by the cost of obtaining a further supply, because none could be had at any price. A cost of production might indeed influence their value indirectly: but it would be the cost of tools made of hard steel and other materials of which the supply can be increased to keep pace with demand. So long as any of the stones were habitually used by intelligent producers for work which could be done equally well by such tools, the value of a stone could not much exceed the cost of producing tools (allowance being made for wear and tear) equally efficient with it in these inferior uses.

The stones, being so hard as not to be affected by wear, would probably be kept in operation during all the working hours of the day. And if their services were very valuable, it might be worth while to keep people working overtime, or even in double or triple shifts, in order to extract the utmost service from them. But the more intensively they were applied, the less net return would be reaped from each additional service forced from them; thus illustrating the law that the intensive working not only of land, but of every other appliance of production is likely to yield a diminishing return if pressed far enough.

The purchaser would expect them to yield interest on their price. The total supply of stones is fixed. But of course any particular manufacturer might obtain almost as many as he liked to pay for: and in the long run he would expect his outlay on them to be returned with interest (or profits, if the remuneration for his own work were not reckoned separately), just in the same way as if he were buying machinery, the total stock of which could be increased indefinitely, so that its price conformed pretty closely to its cost of production.

But the net income which he actually reaped from them would be governed by the value of their services, But when he had once bought the stones, changes in the processes of production or of demand for the things made by their aid, might cause the income yielded by them to become twice as great or only half as great as he had expected. In the latter case it would resemble the income derived from a machine, which had not the latest improvements and could earn only half as much as a new machine of equal cost. The values of the stone and of the machine alike would be reached by capitalizing the income which they were capable of earning, and that income would be governed by the net

value of the services rendered by them. The income V, IX, 2.
earning power and therefore the value of each would be uncon-
independent of its own costs of production, but would be trolled
governed by the general demand for its products in relation supplies
to the general supply of those products. But in the case of on cost.
the machine that supply would be controlled by the cost of
supply of new machines equally efficient with it; and in the
case of the stone there would be no such limit, so long as all
the stones in existence were employed on work that could
not be done by anything else.

This argument may be put in another way. Since any
one, who bought stones, would take them from other
producers, his purchase would not materially affect the
general relations of demand for the services of the stones to
the supply of those services. It would not therefore affect
the price of the stones; which would still be the capitalized
value of the services which they rendered in those uses, in
which the need for them was the least urgent: and to say
that the purchaser expected normal interest on the price
which represented the capitalized value of the services,
would be a circular statement that the value of the services
rendered by stones is governed by the value of those very
services[1].

[1] Such circular reasonings are sometimes nearly harmless: but they always
tend to overlay and hide the real issues. And they are sometimes applied to
illegitimate uses by company promoters; and by advocates of special interests,
who desire to influence the course of legislation in their own favour. For instance
a semi-monopolistic business aggregation or trust is often "over-capitalized." To
effect this a time is chosen, at which the branch of production with which it is
concerned is abnormally prosperous: when perhaps some solid firms are earning
fifty per cent. net on their capital in a single year, and thus making up for lean
years past and to come in which their receipts will do little more than cover
prime costs. Financiers connected with the flotation sometimes even arrange
that the businesses to be offered to the public shall have a good many orders to
fill at specially favourable prices: the loss falling on themselves, or on other
companies which they control. The gains to be secured by semi-monopolistic
selling, and possibly by some further economies in production are emphasized:
and the stock of the trust is absorbed by the public. If ultimately objection to
the conduct of the trust is raised, and especially to the strengthening of its semi-
monopolistic position by a high tariff or any other public favour, the answer is
given that the shareholders are receiving but a moderate return on their investments. Such cases are not uncommon in America. In this country a more
moderate watering of the stock of some railways has been occasionally used
indirectly as a defence of the shareholders against a lowering of rates, that
threatens to reduce dividends on inflated capital below what would be a fair
return on solid capital.

V, IX, 8.

Next suppose that the supply of stones can be increased slowly;

Next let us suppose that the stones were not all found at once but were scattered over the surface of the earth on public ground, and that a laborious search might expect to be rewarded by finding one here and there. Then people would hunt for the stones only up to that point, or margin, at which the probable gain of so doing would in the long run just reward the outlay of labour and capital involved; and in the long run, the normal value of the stones would be such as to maintain equilibrium between demand and supply, the number of the stones gathered annually being in the long run just that for which the normal demand price was equal to the normal supply price.

and lastly that it can be increased quickly, and that the stones are quickly worn out.

Finally, let us bring the case of the stones into accord with that of the lighter machinery and other plant ordinarily used in manufacture, by supposing that the stones were brittle, and were soon destroyed; and that an inexhaustible store existed from which additional supplies could be obtained quickly and certainly at a nearly uniform cost. In this case the value of the stones would always correspond closely to that cost: variations in demand would have but little influence on their price, because even a slight change in price would quickly effect a great change in the stock of them in the market. In this case the income derived from a stone (allowance being made for wear-and-tear) would always adhere closely to interest on its cost of production.

The above string of hypotheses begins with rents proper,

§ 3. This series of hypotheses stretches continuously from the one extreme in which the income derived from the stones is a rent in the strictest sense of the term, to the other extreme in which it is to be classed rather with interest on free or floating capital. In the first extreme case the stones cannot be worn out or destroyed, and no more can be found. They of course tend to be distributed among the various uses to which they are applicable in such a way that there is no use to which an increased supply of them could be applied, without taking them away from some other use in which they were rendering net services at least as valuable. These margins of application of the several uses are thus *governed* by the relation in which the fixed stock of stones stands to the aggregate of demands for them in

different uses. And the margins being thus governed, the
prices that will be paid for their use are *indicated* by the
value of the services which they render at any one of those
margins.

A uniform tax on them, collected from the user, will *and in this*
lower their net service in each use by the same amount: it *case a tax*
will not affect their distribution between several uses; and *remains on*
the owners.
it will fall wholly on the owner, after perhaps some little
delay caused by a frictional resistance to readjustments.

At the opposite extreme of our chain of hypotheses, the *At the*
stones perish so quickly, and are so quickly reproduced at *other ex-*
treme are
about a uniform cost, that variations in the urgency and *incomes*
kept close
volume of the uses to which the stones can be put will be *to interest*
followed so promptly by changes in the stock of them avail- *(or profits)*
on money
able, that those services can never yield much more or much *cost of*
less than normal *interest* on the money cost of obtaining *production*
and here
additional stones. In this case a business man, when making *a tax falls*
his estimates for the cost of any undertaking in which stones *upon users.*
will be used, may enter *interest* (or if he is counting his own
work in, *profits*), for the time during which those stones will
be used (together with wear-and-tear), as part of the prime,
special, or direct expenses of his undertaking. A tax on the
stones under these conditions would fall entirely on any one
who even a little while after the tax had come into force,
gave out a contract for anything in making which the stones
would be used.

Taking an intermediate hypothesis as to the length of *Inter-*
life of the stones and the rapidity with which new supplies *mediate*
stages.
could be obtained; we find that the charges which the
borrower of stones must expect to pay, and the revenue
which the owner of the stones could reckon on deriving from
them at any time, might temporarily diverge some way
from interest (or profits) on their cost. For changes in the
urgency and volume of the uses to which they could be
applied, might have caused the value of the services rendered
by them in their marginal uses to rise or fall a great deal,
even though there had been no considerable change in the
difficulty of obtaining them. And if this rise or fall, arising
from variations in demand, and not from variations in the

V, IX, 3. cost of the stones, is likely to be great during the period of any particular enterprise, or any particular problem of value that is under discussion; then for that discussion the income yielded by the stones is to be regarded as more nearly akin to a rent than to interest on the cost of producing the stones. A tax upon the stones in such a case would tend to diminish the rental which people would pay for their use, and therefore to diminish the inducements towards investing capital and effort in obtaining additional supplies. It would therefore check the supply, and compel those who needed the stones to pay gradually increasing rentals for their use, up to the point at which the rentals fully covered the costs of producing the stones. But the time needed for this re-adjustment might be long: and in the interval a great part of the tax would fall upon the owners of the stones.

Prime costs relatively to long periods become supple-mentary relatively to short; If the life of the stones was long relatively to that process of production in which the stones were used which was under discussion, the stock of stones might be in excess of that needed to do all the work for which they were specially fitted. Some of them might be lying almost idle, and the owner of these stones might make up his estimate of the marginal price for which he was just willing to work without entering in that estimate interest on the value of the stones. That is to say, some costs which would have been classed as prime costs in relation to contracts, or other affairs, which lasted over a long period, would be classed as supplementary costs in relation to a particular affair which would last but a short time, and which came under consideration when business was slack.

It is of course just as essential in the long run that the price obtained should cover general or supplementary costs as that it should cover prime costs. An industry will be driven out of existence in the long run as certainly by failing to return even a moderate interest on capital invested in steam engines, as by failing to replace the price of the coal or the raw material used up from day to day: just as a man's work will be stopped as certainly by depriving him of food as by putting him in chains. But the man can go on working fairly well for a day without food; while if he is

put in chains the check to his work comes at once. So an V, IX, 4.
industry may, and often does, keep tolerably active during
a whole year or even more, in which very little is earned
beyond prime costs, and the fixed plant has "to work for
nothing." But when the price falls so low that it does not
pay for the out of pocket expenses during the year for
wages and raw material, for coal and for lighting, etc., then
the production is likely to come to a sharp stop.

This is the fundamental difference between those incomes and there is
yielded by agents of production which are to be regarded as a corre-
rents or quasi-rents and those which (after allowing for the transition
replacement of wear-and-tear and other destruction) may be from
regarded as interest (or profits) on current investments. The free capital
difference is fundamental, but it is only one of degree. Biology to quasi-
tends to show that the animal and vegetable kingdoms have a embodied
common origin. But yet there are fundamental differences capital.
between mammals and trees; while in a narrower sense the differences between an oak tree and an apple tree are fundamental; and so are in a still narrower sense those between an
apple tree and a rose bush, though they are both classed as
rosaceœ. Thus our central doctrine is that interest on free capital and quasi-rent on an old investment of capital shade into
one another gradually; even the rent of land being Not a thing
by itself, but the leading species of a large genus[1].

§ 4. Again, pure elements are seldom isolated from all Economics
others by nature either in the physical or moral world. Pure physics to
rent in the strict sense of the term is scarcely ever met with: reason
nearly all income from land contains more or less important elements,
elements which are derived from efforts invested in though they
building houses and sheds, in draining the land and so on. are rarely
But economists have learnt to recognize diversity of nature nature.
in those composite things to which the names of rent,
profits, wages etc. are given in popular language; they have
learnt that there is an element of true rent in the composite
product that is commonly called wages, an element of true
earnings in what is commonly called rent and so on. They
have learnt in short to follow the example of the chemist

[1] See above, p. 228.

who seeks for the true properties of each element; and who is thus prepared to deal with the common oxygen or soda of commerce, though containing admixtures of other elements[1].

They recognize that nearly all land in actual use contains an element of capital; that separate reasonings are required for those parts of its value which are, and those which are not, due to efforts of man invested in the land for the purposes of production; and that the results of these reasonings must be combined in dealing with any particular case of that income which commonly goes by the name "rent," but not all of which is rent in the narrower sense of the term. The manner in which the reasonings are to be combined depends on the nature of the problem. Sometimes the mere mechanical "composition of forces" suffices; more often allowance must be made for a quasi-chemical interaction of the various forces; while in nearly all problems of large scope and importance, regard must be had to biological conceptions of growth.

The distinction between differential rents and scarcity rents is not fundamental.

§ 5. Finally a little may be said on a distinction that is sometimes made between "scarcity rents" and "differential rents." In a sense all rents are scarcity rents, and all rents are differential rents. But in some cases it is convenient to estimate the rent of a particular agent by comparing its

---

[1] Professor Fetter seems to ignore this lesson in an article on "The passing of the concept of rent" in the *Quarterly Journal of Economics*, May 1901, p. 419; where he argues that "if only those things which owe nothing to labour are classed as land, and if it is then shown that there is no material thing in settled countries of which this can be said, it follows that everything must be classed as capital." Again he appears to have missed the true import of the doctrines which he assails, when he argues (*ib.* pp. 423–9) against "Extension as the fundamental attribute of land, and the basis of rent." The fact is that its extension (or rather the aggregate of "its space relations") is the chief, though not the only property of land, which causes the income derived from it (in an old country) to contain a large element of true rent: and that the element of true rent, which exists in the income derived from land, or the "rent of land" in the popular use of the term, is in practice so much more important than any others that it has given a special character to the historical development of the Theory of Rent. . . . If meteoric stones of absolute hardness, in high demand and incapable of increase, had played a more important part in the economic history of the world than land, then the elements of true rent which attracted the chief attention of students, would have been associated with the property of hardness; and this would have given a special tone and character to the development of the Theory of Rent. But neither extension nor hardness is a fundamental attribute of all things which yield a true rent. Professor Fetter seems also to have missed the point of the central doctrine as to rents, quasi-rents and interest, given above.

yield to that of an inferior (perhaps a marginal) agent, when similarly worked with appropriate appliances. And in other cases it is best to go straight to the fundamental relations of demand to the scarcity or abundance of the means for the production of those commodities for making which the agent is serviceable.

Suppose for instance that all the meteoric stones in existence were equally hard and imperishable; and that they were in the hands of a single authority: further that this authority decided, not to make use of its monopolistic power to restrict production so as to raise the price of its services artificially, but to work each of the stones to the full extent it could be profitably worked (that is up to the margin of pressure so intensive that the resulting product could barely be marketed at a price which covered, with profits, its expenses without allowing anything for the use of the stone). Then the price of the services rendered by the stones would have been governed by the natural scarcity of the aggregate output of their services in relation to the demand for those services; and the aggregate surplus or rent would most easily be reckoned as the excess of this scarcity price over the aggregate expenses of working the stones. It would therefore generally be regarded as a scarcity rent. But on the other hand it could have been reckoned as the differential excess of the aggregate value of the net services of the stones over that which would have been reached if all their uses had been as unproductive as their marginal uses. And exactly the same would be true if the stones were in the hands of different producers, impelled by competition with one another to work each stone up to the margin at which its further use ceased to be profitable.

This last instance has been so chosen as to bring out the fact that the "differential" as well as the "scarcity" routes for estimating rent are independent of the existence of inferior agents of production: for the differential comparison in favour of the more advantageous uses of the stones can be made by reference to the marginal uses of good stones, as clearly as by reference to the use of inferior stones which are on the margin of not being worth using at all.

V, ix, 5.

The exis-
tence of
inferior
agents does
not raise,
but lowers
the rents of
superior.

In this connection it may be noted that the opinion that the existence of inferior land, or other agents of production, tends to raise the rents of the better agents is not merely untrue. It is the reverse of the truth. For, if the bad land were to be flooded and rendered incapable of producing anything at all, the cultivation of other land would need to be more intensive; and therefore the price of the product would be higher, and rents generally would be higher, than if that land had been a poor contributor to the total stock of produce[1].

Compare Cassel, *Das Recht auf den vollen Arbeitsertrag*, p. 81.

The many misconceptions, that have appeared in the writings even of able economists, as to the nature of a quasi-rent, seem to arise from an inadequate attention to the differences between short periods and long in regard to value and costs. Thus it has been said that a quasi-rent is an "unnecessary profit," and that it is "no part of cost." Quasi-rent is correctly described as an unnecessary profit in regard to short periods, because no "special" or "prime" costs have to be incurred for the production of a machine that, by hypothesis, is already made and waiting for its work. But it is a necessary profit in regard to those other (supplementary) costs which must be incurred in the long run in addition to prime costs; and which in some industries, as for instance sub-marine telegraphy, are very much more important than prime costs. It is no part of cost under any conditions: but the confident expectation of coming quasi-rents is a necessary condition for the investment of capital in machinery, and for the incurring of supplementary costs generally.

Again a quasi-rent has been described as a sort of "conjuncture" or "opportunity" profit; and, almost in the same breath, as no profit or interest at all, but only a rent. For the time being, it is a conjuncture or opportunity income: while in the long run it is expected to, and it generally does, yield a normal rate of interest (or if earnings of management are counted in, of profit) on the free capital, represented by a definite sum of money that was invested in producing it. By definition the rate of interest is a percentage; that is a relation between two numbers. . . . A machine is not a number: its value may be a certain number of pounds or dollars: but that value is estimated, unless the machine be a new one, as the aggregate of its (discounted) earnings, or quasi-rents. If the machine is new, its makers have calculated that this aggregate will appear to probable purchasers as the equivalent of a price which will repay the makers for it: in that case therefore it is as a rule, *both* a cost price, *and* a price which represents an aggregate of (discounted) future incomes. But when the machine is old and partially obsolete in pattern, there is no close relation between its value and its cost of production: its value is then simply the aggregate of the discounted values of the future quasi-rents, which it is expected to earn.

CHAPTER X.

MARGINAL COSTS IN RELATION TO AGRICULTURAL VALUES.

§ 1. WE now pass from general considerations to those relating to land; and we begin with those specially applicable to agricultural land in an old country.

Suppose, that a war, which was not expected to last long, were to cut off part of the food supplies of England. Englishmen would set themselves to raise heavier crops by such extra application of capital or labour as was likely to yield a speedy return; they would consider the results of artificial manures, of the use of clod-crushing machines, and so on; and the more favourable these results were, the less would be the rise in the price of produce in the coming year which they regarded as necessary to make it worth their while to incur additional outlay in these directions. But the war would have very little effect on their action as to those improvements which would not bear fruit till it was over. In any inquiry then as to the causes that will determine the prices of corn during a short period, that fertility which the soil derives from slowly made improvements has to be taken for granted as it then is, almost in the same way as if it had been made by nature. Thus, the income derived from these permanent improvements gives a surplus above the *prime* or *special* costs needed for raising extra produce. But it is not a true surplus, in the same sense that rent proper is; *i.e.* it is not a surplus above the *total* costs of the produce: it is needed to cover the general expenses of the business.

To speak more exactly:—If the extra income derived from improvements that have been made in the land by its individual owner is so reckoned as not to include any benefit which would have been conferred on the land by the general progress of society independently of his efforts and sacrifices; then, as a rule, the whole of it is required to remunerate him for those efforts and sacrifices. He may have underestimated the gains which will result from them; but he is about equally likely to have made an overestimate. If he has estimated them rightly, his interest has urged him to make the investment as soon as it showed signs of being profitable: and in the absence of any special reason to the contrary we may suppose him to have done this. In the long run, then, the net returns to the investment of capital in the land, taking successful and unsuccessful returns together, do not afford more than an adequate motive to such investment. If poorer returns had been expected than those on which people actually based their calculations, fewer improvements would have been made.

That is to say:—for periods which are long in comparison with the time needed to make improvements of any kind, and bring them into full operation, the net incomes derived from them are but the price required to be paid for the efforts and sacrifices of those who make them: the expenses of making them thus directly enter into marginal expenses of production, and take a direct part in governing long-period supply price. But in short periods, that is, in periods short relatively to the time required to make and bring into full bearing improvements of the class in question, no such direct influence on supply price is exercised by the necessity that such improvements should in the long run yield net incomes sufficient to give normal profits on their cost. And therefore when we are dealing with such periods, these incomes may be regarded as quasi-rents which depend on the price of the produce[1].

---

[1] Of course the character and extent of the improvements depends partly on the conditions of land tenure, and the enterprise and ability and command over capital on the part of landlords and tenants which existed at the time and place in question. In this connection we shall find, when we come to study land tenure, that there are large allowances to be made for the special conditions of different places.

It may be noted, however, that rent proper is estimated on the understanding that the original properties of the soil are unimpaired. And when the income

We may conclude then:—(1) The amount of produce raised, and therefore the position of the margin of cultivation (*i.e.* the margin of the profitable application of capital and labour to good and bad land alike) are both governed by the general conditions of demand and supply. They are governed on the one hand by demand; that is, by the numbers of the population who consume the produce, the intensity of their need for it, and their means of paying for it; and on the other hand by supply; that is, by the extent and fertility of the available land, and the numbers and resources of those ready to cultivate it. Thus cost of production, eagerness of demand, margin of production, and price of the produce mutually govern one another: and no circular reasoning is involved in speaking of any one as in part governed by the others. (2) That part of the produce which goes as rent is of course thrown on the market, and acts on prices, in just the same way as any other part. But the general conditions of demand and supply, or their relations to one another, are not affected by the division of the produce into the share of rent and the share needed to render the farmer's expenditure profitable. The amount of that rent is not a governing cause; but is itself governed by the fertility of land, the price of the produce, and the position of the margin: it is the excess of the value of the total returns which capital and labour applied to land do obtain, over those which they would have obtained under circumstances as unfavourable as those on the margin of cultivation. (3) If the cost of production were estimated for parts of the produce which do not come from the margin, a charge on account of rent would of course need to be entered in this estimate; and if this estimate were used in an account of the causes which govern the price of the produce; then the reasoning would be circular. For that, which is wholly an effect, would be reckoned up as part of

V, x, 1.

Summary of relations between marginal costs and value of agricultural produce in general in an old country.

derived from improvements is regarded as a quasi-rent, it is to be understood that they are kept up in full efficiency: if they are being deteriorated, the equivalent of the injury done to them must be deducted from the income they are made to yield before we can arrive at that *Net* income which is to be regarded as their quasi-rent.

That part of the income which is required to cover wear-and-tear bears some resemblance to a royalty, which does no more than cover the injury done to a mine by taking ore out of it.

V, x, 2. the cause of those things of which it is an effect. (4) The cost of production of the marginal produce can be ascertained without reasoning in a circle. The cost of production of other parts of the produce cannot. The cost of production on the margin of the profitable application of capital and labour is that to which the price of the whole produce tends, under the control of the general conditions of demand and supply: it does not govern price, but it focusses the causes which do govern price.

Scarcity without inequalities of fertility gives rise to rent.

§ 2. It has sometimes been suggested that if all land were equally advantageous and all were occupied, the income derived from it would partake of the nature of a monopoly rent: but this seems to be an error. Of course the landowners might conceivably combine to stint production, whether their properties were of equal fertility or not; the raised prices which would thus be obtained for the produce would be monopoly prices; and the incomes of the owners would be monopoly revenues rather than rents. But, with a free market, the revenues from land would be rents, governed by the same causes and in the same way in a country where the land was all of equal advantage, as in those where good and bad land were intermingled[1].

It is, indeed, true that if there were more than enough land, all of about the same fertility, to enable everyone to have as much of it as was needed to give full scope to the capital he was prepared to apply to it, then it could yield no rent. But that merely illustrates the old paradox that water, when abundant, has no market value: for though the services of some part of it are essential to support life, yet everyone can get without effort to that margin of satiety at which any further supplies would be of no service to him. When every cottager has a well from which he can draw as much water as he needs, with no more labour than is required at his neighbour's well, the water in the well has no market value. But let a drought set in, so that the shallow wells are exhausted, and even the deeper wells are threatened, then the owners of those wells can exact a charge for every bucket which they allow anyone to draw for his own use.

[1] Compare V. ix. 5.

The denser population becomes, the more numerous will
be the occasions on which such charges can be made (it
being supposed that no new wells are developed): and at
last every owner of a well may find in it a permanent source
of revenue.

In the same way the scarcity value of land in a new When
country gradually emerges. The early settler exercises no country is
exclusive privilege, for he only does what anyone else is at first
liberty to do. He undergoes many hardships, if not personal and land
dangers; and perhaps he runs some risks that the land may migration
turn out badly, and that he may have to abandon his improve- up to the
ments. On the other hand, his venture may turn out well; margin at
the flow of population may trend his way, and the value of pioneer's
his land may soon give as large a surplus over the normal is just
remuneration of his outlay on it as the fishermen's haul does rewarded.
when they come home with their boat full. But in this there
is no surplus above the rewards needed for his venture. He
has engaged in a risky business which was open to all, and
his energy and good fortune have given him an exceptionally
high reward: anyone else might have taken the same chance
as he did. Thus the income which he expects the land to
afford in the future enters into the calculations of the settler,
and adds to the motives which determine his action when in
doubt as to how far to carry his enterprise. He regards its
"discounted value[1]" as profits on his capital, and as earnings
of his own labour, in so far as his improvements are made
with his own hands.

A settler often takes up land with the expectation that Rent
the produce which it affords while in his possession, will fall a surplus
short of an adequate reward for his hardships, his labour and as demand
his expenditure. He looks for part of his reward to the and the
value of the land itself, which he may perhaps after a while labour
sell to some new-comer who has no turn for the life of a increase.
pioneer. Sometimes even, as the British farmer learns to
his cost, the new settler regards his wheat almost as a
by-product; the main product for which he works is a farm,
the title-deeds to which he will earn by improving the land:
he reckons that its value will steadily rise, not through his

---

[1] Compare III. v. 3 and V. iv. 2.

V, x, 3.   own efforts so much as through the growth of those comforts and resources, and of those markets in which to buy and in which to sell, that are the product of the growing *public* prosperity.

This may be put in another way. People are generally unwilling to face the hardships and isolation of pioneer agriculture, unless they can look forward with some confidence to much higher earnings, measured in terms of the necessaries of life, than they could get at home. Miners cannot be attracted to a rich mine, isolated from other conveniences and varied social opportunities of civilization, except by the promise of high wages: and those who superintend the investment of their own capital in such mines expect very high profits. For similar reasons pioneer farmers require high aggregate gains made up of receipts for the sale of their produce, together with the acquisition of valuable title-deeds, to remunerate them for their labour and endurance of hardships. And the land is peopled up to that margin at which it just yields gains adequate for this purpose, without leaving any surplus for rent, when no charge is made for the land. When a charge is made, immigration spreads only up to that margin, at which the gains will leave a surplus, of the nature of rent, to cover such charges, in addition to rewarding the pioneer's endurance.

Land is but one form of capital to the individual producer.

§ 3. With all this it is to be remembered that land is but a particular form of capital from the point of view of the individual producer. The question whether a farmer has carried his cultivation of a particular piece of land as far as he profitably can; and whether he should try to force more from it, or to take in another piece of land; is of the same kind as the question whether he should buy a new plough, or try to get a little more work out of his present stock of ploughs, using them sometimes when the soil is not in a very favour ble condition, and feeding his horses a little more lavishly. He weighs the net product of a little more land against the other uses to which he could put the capital sum that he would have to expend in order to obtain it: and in like manner he weighs the net product, to be got by working his ploughs under unfavourable circumstances, against

that got by increasing his stock of ploughs, and thus working
under more favourable conditions. That part of his produce
which he is in doubt whether to raise by extra use of his
existing ploughs, or by introducing a new plough, may be
said to be derived from a marginal use of the plough. It
pays nothing *net* (*i.e.* nothing beyond a charge for actual
wear-and-tear) towards the net income earned by the
plough.

So again a manufacturer or trader, owning both land and
buildings, regards the two as bearing similar relations to his
business. Either will afford him aid and accommodation at
first liberally; and afterwards with diminishing return, as he
endeavours to force more and more from them: till at last
he will doubt whether the overcrowding of his workshops or
his storerooms is not so great a source of trouble, that it
would answer his purpose to obtain more space. And when
he comes to decide whether to obtain that space by taking in
an extra piece of land or by building his factory a floor
higher, he weighs the net income to be derived from further
investments in the one against that to be derived from the
other. That part of his production which he just forces out
of his existing appliances (being in doubt whether it would
not be better worth his while to increase those appliances
than to work so intensively those which he has), does not
contribute to the net income which those appliances yield
him. This argument says nothing as to whether the
appliances were made by man, or part of a stock given by
nature; it applies to rents and quasi-rents alike.

But there is this difference from the point of view of Likeness
society. If one person has possession of a farm, there unlikeness
is less land for others to have. His use of it is not in between
addition to, but in lieu of the use of a farm by other and quasi-
people: whereas if he invests in improvements of land or rent.
in buildings on it, he will not appreciably curtail the opportunities of others to invest capital in like improvements.
Thus there is likeness amid unlikeness between land and
appliances made by man. There is unlikeness because land
in an old country is approximately (and in some senses
absolutely) a *permanent and fixed stock*: while appliances

made by man, whether improvements in land, or in buildings, or machinery, etc., are a flow capable of being increased or diminished according to variations in the effective demand for the products which they help in raising. So far there is unlikeness. But on the other hand there is likeness, in that, since some of them cannot be produced quickly, they are a practically *fixed stock for short periods*: and for those periods the incomes derived from them stand in the same relation to the value of the products raised by them, as do true rents[1].

Illustration from the ultimate incidence of a tax on agricultural produce in general. §4. Let us apply these considerations to the supposition that a permanent tax is to be levied on "corn," in the sense in which it was used by the classical economists as short for all agricultural produce. It is obvious that the farmer would try to make the consumer pay some part at least of the tax. But any rise in the price charged to the consumer would check demand, and thus react on the farmer. In order to decide how much of this tax would be shifted on to the consumer, we must study the *margin of profitable expenditure*, whether that be the margin of a little expenditure applied to poor land and land far removed from good markets, or the margin of a large expenditure applied to rich land, and land near to dense industrial districts.

---

[1] The relations between rent and profits engaged the attention of the economists of the last generation; among whom may be specially mentioned Senior and Mill, Hermann and Mangoldt. Senior seemed almost on the point of perceiving that the key of the difficulty was held by the element of time: but here as elsewhere he contented himself with suggestions; he did not work them out. He says (*Political Economy*, p. 129), "for all useful purposes the distinction of profits from rent ceases as soon as the capital from which a given revenue arises has become, whether by gift or by inheritance, the property of a person to whose abstinence and exertions it did not owe its creation." Again, Mill says, *Political Economy*, Book III. ch. v. §4, "Any difference in favour of certain producers or in favour of production in certain circumstances is the source of a gain, which though not called rent unless paid periodically by one person to another, is governed by laws entirely the same with it."

It has been well observed that a speculator, who, without manipulating prices by false intelligence or otherwise, anticipates the future correctly; and who makes his gains by shrewd purchases and sales on the Stock Exchange or in Produce Markets, generally renders a public service by pushing forward production where it is wanted, and repressing it where it is not: but that a speculator in land in an old country can render no such public service, because the stock of land is fixed. At the best he can prevent a site with great possibilities from being devoted to inferior uses in consequence of the haste, ignorance, or impecuniosity of those in control of it.

If only a little corn had been raised near the margin, a ~V, x, 4.~ moderate fall in the net price received by the farmer would not cause a great check to the supply of corn. There would therefore be no great rise in the price paid for it by the consumer; and the consumer would bear very little of the tax. But the surplus value of the corn over its expenses of production would fall considerably. The farmer, if cultivating his own land, would bear the greater part of the tax. And, if he were renting the land, he could demand a great reduction of his rent.

If, on the other hand, a great deal of corn had been raised near the margin of cultivation, the tax would tend to cause a great shrinkage of production. The consequent rise of price would arrest that shrinkage, leaving the farmer in a position to cultivate nearly as intensively as before: and the landlord's rent would suffer but little[1].

Thus, on the one band, a tax which is so levied as to discourage the cultivation of land or the erection of farm buildings on it, tends to be shifted forward on to the consumers of the produce of land. But, on the other hand, a tax on that part of the (annual) value of land, which arises from its position, its extension, its yearly income of sunlight and heat and rain and air, cannot settle anywhere except on the landlord; a lessee being, of course, landlord for the time. This (annual) value of the land is commonly called its "original value" or its "inherent value"; but much of that value is the result of the action of men, though not of its individual holders. For instance, barren heath land may suddenly acquire a high value from the growth of an industrial population near it; though its owners have left it untouched as it was made by nature. It is, therefore, perhaps *The public* more correct to call this part of the annual value of land its *value* of "*public value*"; while that part which can be traced to the *land.* work and outlay of its individual holders may be called its "private value." The old terms "inherent value" and "original value" may however be retained for general use,

---

[1] Of course the adjustments of rent to the true economic surplus from the land are in practice slow and irregular. . . .

with a note of caution as to their partial inaccuracy. And, using another term that has precedent in its favour, we may speak of this annual public value of the land as "true rent."

A tax on the public value of land does not greatly diminish the inducements to cultivate the land highly, nor to erect farm buildings on it. Such a tax therefore does not greatly diminish the supply of agricultural produce offered on the market, nor raise the price of produce; and it is not therefore shifted away from the owners of land.

Implicit assumption that the land is turned to reasonably good account.

This assumes that the true rent of land on which the tax is levied is assessed with reference to its general capabilities, and not to the special use which the owner makes of it: its net product is supposed to be that which could be got by a cultivator of normal ability and enterprise, turning it to good account to the best of his judgment. If an improved method of cultivation develops latent resources of the soil, so as to yield an increased return much in excess of what is required to remunerate the outlay with a good rate of profits; this excess of net return above normal profits belongs properly to true rent: and yet, if it is known, or even expected, that a very heavy special tax on true rent will be made to apply to this excess income, that expectation may deter the owner from making the improvement[1].

Relations between marginal costs and value for any one kind of agricultural produce.

§ 5. A little has been said incidentally of the competition between different branches of industry for the same raw material or appliances for production. But now we have to consider the competition between various branches of agriculture for the same land. This case is simpler than that of urban land, because farming is a single business so far as the main crops are concerned; though the rearing of choice trees (including vines), flowers, vegetables etc. affords scope for various kinds of specialized business ability. The classical economists were therefore justified in provisionally supposing that all kinds of agricultural produce can be regarded as equivalent to certain quantities of corn; and that all the land will be used for agricultural purposes, with the

[1] The exemption of vacant building land from taxes on its full value retards building. . . .

exception of building sites which are a small and nearly V, x, 5.
fixed part of the whole. But when we concentrate our attention on any one product, as for instance, hops, it may seem that a new principle is introduced. That is however not the case. Let us look into this.

Hops are grown in varying rotations with other crops; The marginal costs and value of hops are governed by Substitution in combination with Diminishing Return to cultivation in general.

and the farmer is often in doubt whether he shall grow hops or something else on one of his fields. Thus each crop strives against others for the possession of the land; and if any one crop shows signs of being more remunerative than before relatively to others, the cultivators will devote more of their land and resources to it. The change may be retarded by habit, or diffidence, or obstinacy, or limitations of the cultivator's knowledge; or by the terms of his lease. But it will still be true in the main that each cultivator—to recall once more the dominant principle of substitution— "taking account of his own means, will push the investment of capital in his business in each several direction until what appears in his judgment to be the margin of profitableness is reached; that is, until there seems to him no good reason for thinking that the gains resulting from any further investment in that particular direction would compensate him for his outlay."

Thus in equilibrium, oats and hops and every other crop will yield the same net return to that outlay of capital and labour, which the cultivator is only just induced to apply. For otherwise he would have miscalculated; he would have failed to get the *maximum* reward which his outlay can be made to yield: and it would still be open to him to increase his gains by redistributing his crops, by increasing or diminishing his cultivation of oats or some other crop[1].

---

[1] In so far as the farmer is producing raw material, or even human food, for market, his distribution of resources between different uses is a problem of business economy: in so far as he is producing for his own domestic consumption it is, in part at least, a problem of domestic economy. Compare above V. IV. 4. . . .

Mill (*Principles*, III. XVI. 2), when discussing "joint products," observed that all questions relating to the competition of crops for the possession of particular soils are complicated by the rotation of crops and similar causes; an intricate debit and credit account by double entry needs to be kept between the various

V, x, 5.

Competition of different crops for the same land: the incidence of a special tax on hops.

This brings us to consider taxation in reference to the competition of different crops for the use of the same land. Let us suppose that a tax is imposed on hops, wherever grown; it is not to be a mere local rate or tax. The farmer can evade a part of the pressure of the tax by lessening the intensity of his cultivation of the land which he plants with hops; and a yet further part by substituting another crop on land which he had proposed to devote to hops. He will have recourse to this second plan in so far as he considers that he would get a better result by growing another crop, and selling it free from the tax, than by growing hops and selling them in spite of the tax. In this case the surplus which he could obtain from the land by growing, say, oats upon it would come into his mind when deciding where to set the limit to his production of hops. But even here there would be no simple numerical relation between the surplus, or rent, which the land would yield under oats, and the marginal costs which the price of hops must cover. And a farmer whose land produced hops of exceptionally high quality, and which happened to be in good condition at the time for hops, would have no doubt at all that it was best to grow hops on the land; though in consequence of the tax he might decide to curtail a little his expenditure on it[1].

members of the rotation. Practice and shrewd instinct enable the farmer to do this fairly well. The whole problem might be expressed in simple mathematical phrases. But they would be tedious, and perhaps unfruitful. They would therefore not be serviceable, so long as they remained abstract; though they belong to a class which may ultimately be of good use in the higher science of agriculture, when that has advanced far enough to fill in realistic details.

[1] If for instance he reckoned that he could get a surplus of £30 above his expenses (other than rent) in spite of the tax by growing hops, and a surplus of only £20 above similar expenses by growing any other crop, it could not be truly said that the rent which the field could be made to yield by growing other crops, "entered into" the marginal price of oats. But it is easier to interpret the classical doctrine that "Rent does not enter into cost of production" in a sense in which it is not true, and to scoff at it, than in the sense in which it was intended and is true. It seems best therefore to avoid the phrase.

The ordinary man is offended by the old phrase that rent does not enter into the price of oats; when he sees that an increase in the demand for land for other uses, manifests itself in a rise of the rental value of all land in the neighbourhood; leaves less land free for growing oats; consequently makes it worth while to force larger crops of oats out of the remaining oat-land, and thus raises the marginal expenses of oats and their price. A rise in rent does serve as a medium through which the growing scarcity of land available for hops and other produce obtrudes itself on his notice; and it is not worth while to try to force him to go

Meanwhile the tendency towards a general restriction in the supply of hops would tend to raise their price. If the demand for them were very rigid, and hops of adequate quality could not easily be imported from beyond the range of this special tax, the price might rise by nearly the full amount of the tax. In that case the tendency would be checked, and very nearly as much hops would be grown as before the tax had been levied. And here, as in the case of a tax on printing, recently discussed, the effect of a local tax is in strong contrast to that of a general tax. For unless the local tax covered most of the ground in the country on which good hops could be grown, its effect would be to drive them beyond its boundary: very little revenue would be got from it, local farmers would suffer a good deal, and the public would pay a rather higher price for their hops.

§ 6. The argument of the last section applies, so far as short periods are concerned, to the earning power of farm-buildings and to other quasi-rents. When existing farm-buildings, or other appliances which could be used in pro-ducing one commodity are diverted to producing another because the demand for that is such as to enable them to earn a higher income by producing it, then *for the time* the supply of the first will be less, and its price higher than if the appliances had not been able to earn a higher income by another use. Thus, when appliances are capable of being

V, x, 6.
Contrast between a general and a local tax on hops.

Arguments relating to rent in relation to the value of a single crop extended to quasi-rent of farm-build-ings, etc.

behind these symptoms of the change in conditions to the truly operative causes. It is therefore inexpedient to say that the rent of land does not enter into their price. But it is worse than inexpedient to say that the rent of the land does enter into their price: that is false.

Jevons asks (Preface to *Theory of Political Economy*, p. liv): "If land which has been yielding £2 per acre rent, as pasture, be ploughed up and used for raising wheat, must not the £2 per acre he debited against the expenses of production of wheat?" The answer is in the negative. For there is no connection between this particular sum of £2 and the expenses of production of that wheat which only just pays its way. What should be said is:—"When land capable of being used for producing one commodity is used for producing another, the price of the first is raised by the consequent limitation of its field of production. The price of the second will be the expenses of production (wages and profits) of that part of it which only just pays its way, that which is produced on the margin of profitable expenditure. And if for the purposes of any particular argument we take together the whole expenses of the production on that land, and divide these among the whole of the commodity produced; then the rent which we ought to count in is not that which the land would pay if used for producing the first commodity, but that which it does pay when used for producing the second."

used in more than one branch of agriculture, the marginal cost in each branch will be affected by the extent to which these appliances are called off for work in other branches. Other agents of production will be pushed to more intensive uses in the first branch, in spite of a diminishing return; and the value of its product will rise, because only at a higher value will the price be in equilibrium. The increased earning power of the appliances due to the external demand will appear to be the cause of this increase in value: for it will cause a relative scarcity of the appliances in that branch of production, and therefore raise marginal costs. And from this statement it appears superficially to be a simple transition to the statement that the increased earning power of the appliances enter into those costs which govern value. But the transition is illegitimate. There will be no direct or numerical relation between the increase in the price of the first commodity and the income that the appliances can earn when they have been transferred to the second industry and adapted for service in it.

Parallel case in manufacture.

Similarly, if a tax be put on factories used in one industry, some of them will be diverted to other industries; and consequently the marginal costs and therefore the values of the products in those industries will fall; simultaneously with a temporary fall in net rental values of factories in all uses. But these falls will vary in amount, and there will be no numerical relation between the fall in the prices of the product and in these rents, or rather quasi-rents.

The principles of these two chapters are not applicable to mines.

These principles are not applicable to mines, whether for short periods or for long. A royalty is *not* a rent, though often so called. For, except when mines, quarries, etc., are practically inexhaustible, the excess of their income over their direct outgoings has to be regarded, in part at least, as the price got by the sale of stored-up goods—stored up by nature indeed, but now treated as private property; and therefore the marginal supply price of minerals includes a royalty in addition to the marginal expenses of working the mine. Of course the owner desires to receive the royalty without undue delay; and the contract between him and the lessee often provides, partly for this reason, for

the payment of a rent as well as a royalty. But the royalty V, x, 6.
itself on a ton of coal, when accurately adjusted, represents
that diminution in the value of the mine, regarded as a
source of wealth in the future, which is caused by taking
the ton out of nature's storehouse[1].

[1] ... Adam Smith is attacked by Ricardo for putting rent on the same footing
with wages and profits as parts of (money) cost of production; and no doubt he does
this sometimes. But yet he says elsewhere, "Rent it is to be observed enters into the
composition of the price of commodities in a different way from wages and profit.
High or low wages and profit are the causes of high or low price: high or low rent is
the effect of it. It is because high or low wages and profit must be paid in order to
bring a particular commodity to market that its price is high or low. But it is because
its price is high or low a great deal more, or very little more, or no more than what is
sufficient to pay those wages and profits, that it affords a high rent, or a low rent, or
no rent at all" (*Wealth of Nations*, I. XI.) In this, as in many other instances, he anticipated in one part of his writings truths which in other parts he has seemed to deny.

Adam Smith discusses the "price at which coals can he sold for any considerable
time"; and contends that "the most fertile mine regulates the price of coals at all
other mines in the neighbourhood." His meaning is not clear; but he does not appear
to be referring to any temporary underselling; and he seems to imply that the mines
are leased at so much a year. Ricardo, following on apparently the same lines, comes
to the opposite conclusion that it "is the least fertile mine which regulates price";
which is perhaps nearer the truth than Adam Smith's doctrine. But in fact when the
charge for the use of a mine is mainly in the form of a royalty, neither proposition
seems to be applicable. Ricardo was technically right (or at all events not definitely
wrong) when he said that rent does not enter into the marginal cost of production of
mineral produce. But he ought to have added that if a mine is not practically inexhaustible, the income derived from it is partly rent and partly royalty; and that
though the rent does not, the minimum royalty does enter directly into the expenses
incurred on behalf of every part of the produce, whether marginal or not.

The royalty is of course calculated in regard to those seams in the mine., which
are neither exceptionally rich and easy of working, nor exceptionally poor and difficult. Some seams barely pay the expenses of working them; and some which run
short, or have a bad fault, do not even nearly pay the wages of the labour spent on
them. The whole argument however implicitly assumes the conditions of an old
country. Professor Taussig is probably right when, having in view the circumstances
of a new country (*Principles*, II. p. 98), he "doubts whether any payment at all can
be secured by the owner of the very poorest mine, assuming he has done nothing to
develop it."

CHAPTER XI.

MARGINAL COSTS IN RELATION TO URBAN VALUES.

§ 1. The last three chapters examined the relation in which cost of production stands to the income derived from the ownership of the "original powers" of land and other free gifts of nature, and also to that which is directly due to the investment of private capital. There is a third class, holding an intermediate position between these two, which consists of those incomes, or rather those parts of incomes which are the indirect result of the general progress of society, rather than the direct result of the investment of capital and labour by individuals for the sake of gain. This class has to be studied now, with special reference to the value of urban sites.

We have already noted that, though nature nearly always gives a less than proportionate return, when measured by *the amount* of the produce raised, to increasing applications of capital and labour in the cultivation of land; yet, on the other hand, if the more intensive cultivation is the result of the growth of a non-agricultural population in the neighbourhood, this very concourse of people is likely to raise *the value* of produce. We have seen how this influence opposes, and usually outweighs the action of the law of diminishing return when the produce is measured according to its value to the producer and not according to its amount; the cultivator gets good markets in which to supply his wants, as well as good markets in which to sell, he buys more cheaply while he sells more dearly, and the conveniences and enjoyments of social life are ever being brought more within his reach.

Again, we have seen how the economies which result *V, xi, 1.* from a high industrial organization often depend only to a small extent on the resources of individual firms. Those *internal* economies which each establishment has to arrange for itself are frequently very small as compared with those *external* economies which result from the general progress of the industrial environment; the situation of a business nearly always plays a great part in determining the extent to which it can avail itself of external economies; and the situation value which a site derives from the growth of a rich and active population close to it, or from the opening up of railways and other good means of communication with existing markets, is the most striking of all the influences which changes in the industrial environment exert on cost of production.

If in any industry, whether agricultural or not, two producers have equal facilities in all respects, except that one has a more convenient situation than the other, and can buy or sell in the same markets with less cost of carriage, the differential advantage which his situation gives him is the aggregate of the excess charges for cost of carriage to which his rival is put. And we may suppose that other advantages of situation, such for instance as the near access to a labour market specially adapted to his trade, can be translated in like manner into money values. When this is done, and all are added together we have the money value of the advantages of situation which the first business has over the second: and this becomes its special *situation value*, if the second has no situation value and its site is reckoned merely at agricultural value. The extra income which can be earned on the more favoured site gives rise to what may be called a special situation rent: and the aggregate *site value* of any piece of building land is that which it would have if cleared of buildings and sold in a free market. The "annual site value"—to use a convenient, though not strictly correct form of speaking—is the income which that price would yield at the current rate of interest. It obviously exceeds the

Exceptional cases in which the income derived from advantageous situation is earned by individual effort and outlay.

Illustrations from Saltaire and Pullman City.

special situation value, merely by agricultural value; which is often an almost negligible quantity in comparison[1].

§ 2. It is obvious that the greater part of situation value is "public value." (See above, p. 250.) There are however exceptional cases, which call for notice. Sometimes the settlement of a whole town, or even district is planned on business principles, and carried out as an investment at the expense and risk of a single person or company. The movement may be partly due to philanthropic or religious motives, but its financial basis will in any case be found in the fact that the concourse of numbers is itself a cause of increased economic efficiency. Under ordinary circumstances the chief gains arising from this efficiency would accrue to those who are already in possession of the place: but the chief hopes of commercial success, by those who undertake to colonize a new district or build a new town, are usually founded on securing these gains for themselves.

When, for instance, Mr Salt and Mr Pullman determined to take their factories into the country and to found Saltaire and Pullman City, they foresaw that the land, which they could purchase at its value for agricultural purposes, would obtain the special situation value which town property derives from the immediate neighbourhood of a dense population. And similar considerations have influenced those, who, having fixed upon a site adapted by nature to become a favourite watering-place, have bought the land and spent

---

[1] If we suppose that two farms, which sell in the same market, return severally to equal applications of capital and labour amounts of produce, the first of which exceeds the second by the extra cost of carrying its produce to market, then the rent of the two farms will be the same. (The capital and labour applied to the two farms are here supposed to be reduced to the same money measure, or which comes to the same thing, the two farms are supposed to have equally good access to markets in which to buy.) Again, if we suppose that two mineral springs A and B supplying exactly the same water are capable of being worked each to an unlimited extent at a constant money cost of production; this cost being, say twopence a bottle at A whatever the amount produced by it, and twopence half-penny at B; then those places to which the cost of carriage per bottle from B is a half-penny less than from A, will be the neutral zone for their competition. (If the cost of carriage be proportional to the distance, this neutral zone is a hyperbola of which A and B are foci.) A can undersell B for all places on A's side of it, and *vice versâ*; and each of them will be able to derive a monopoly rent from the sale of its produce within its own area. This is a type of a great many fanciful, but not uninstructive, problems which readily suggest themselves. Compare von Thünen's brilliant researches in *Der isolirte Staat*.

large sums in developing its resources: they have been willing to wait long for any net income from their investment in the hope that ultimately their land would derive a high situation value from the concourse of people attracted to it[1].

In all such cases the yearly income derived from the land (or at all events that part of it which is in excess of the agricultural rent) is for many purposes to be regarded as profits rather than rent. And this is equally true, whether the land is that on which the factory itself at Saltaire or Pullman City is built, or that which affords a high "ground-rent" as the site of a shop or store, whose situation will enable it to do a brisk trade with those who work in the factory. For in such cases great risks have to be run; and in all undertakings in which there are risks of great losses, there must also be hopes of great gains. The normal expenses of production of a commodity must include payment for the ventures required for producing it, sufficient to cause those who are on the margin of doubt whether to venture or not, to regard the probable net amount of their gains—net, that is, after deducting the probable amount of their losses— as compensating them for their trouble and their outlay. And that the gains resulting from such ventures are not much more than sufficient for this purpose is shown by the fact that they are not as yet very common. They are however likely to be more frequent in those industries which are in the hands of very powerful corporations. A large railway company, for instance, can found a Crewe or a New Swindon for manufacturing railway plant without running any great risk[2].

---

[1] Cases of this kind are of course most frequent in new countries. But they are not very rare in old countries: Saltburn is a conspicuous instance; while a more recent instance of exceptional interest is furnished by Letchworth Garden City.

[2] Governments have great facilities for carrying out schemes of this kind, especially in the matter of choosing new sites for garrison towns, arsenals, and establishments for the manufacture of the materials of war. In comparisons of the expenses of production by Government and by private firms, the sites of the Government works are often reckoned only at their agricultural value. But such a plan is misleading. A private firm has either to pay heavy annual charges on account of its site, or to run very heavy risks if it tries to make a town for itself. And therefore in order to prove that Government management is for general

Improvements effected at the joint expense of the landowners concerned.

Somewhat similar instances are those of a group of land-owners who combine to make a railway, the net traffic receipts of which are not expected to pay any considerable interest on the capital invested in making it; but which will greatly raise the value of their land. In such cases part of the increase of their incomes as landowners ought to be regarded as profits on capital which they have invested in the improvement of their land: though the capital has gone towards making a railway instead of being applied directly to their own property.

Other cases of like nature are main drainage schemes, and other plans for improving the general condition of agricultural or town property, in so far as they are carried out by the landowners at their own expense, whether by private agreement or by the levying of special rates on themselves. Similar cases again are found in the investment of capital by a nation in building up its own social and political organization as well as in promoting the education of the people and in developing its sources of material wealth.

Thus that improvement of the environment, which adds to the value of land and of other free gifts of nature, is in a good many cases partly due to the deliberate investment of capital by the owners of the land for the purpose of raising its value; and therefore a portion of the consequent increase of income may be regarded as profits when we are considering long periods. But in many cases it is not so; and any increase in the net income derived from the free gifts of nature which was not brought about by, and did not supply the direct motive to, any special outlay on the part of the landowners, is to be regarded as rent for all purposes.

Analogous cases in the laying out of suburban property.

Cases somewhat analogous to these arise when the owner of a score or more of acres in the neighbourhood of a growing town "develops" them for building. He probably lays out

purposes as efficient and economical as private management, a full charge ought to be made in the balance-sheets of Government factories for the town-value of their sites. In those exceptional branches of production for which a Government can found a manufacturing town without incurring the risks that a private firm would incur in a similar case, that point of advantage may fairly be reckoned as an argument for Governments undertaking those particular businesses.

the roads, decides where houses are to be continuous, and V, xi, 3.
where detached; and prescribes the general style of archi-
tecture, and perhaps the minimum expenditure on each
house; for the beauty of each adds to the general value of
all. This collective value, thus created by him, is of the
nature of public value; and it is dependent, for the greater
part, on that dormant public value, which the site as a whole
derived from the growth of a prosperous town in its neighbourhood. But yet that share of it which results from his
forethought, constructive faculty and outlay, is to be regarded
as the reward of business enterprise, rather than as the
appropriation of public value by a private person.

These exceptional cases must be reckoned with. But the But as a
general rule holds that the amount and character of the value owes
building put upon each plot of land is, in the main (subject to little to the owner of
the local building bylaws), that from which the most profitable the site.
results are anticipated, with little or no reference to its
reaction on the situation value of the neighbourhood. In
other words the site value of the plot is governed by causes
which are mostly beyond the control of him who determines
what buildings shall be put on it: and he adjusts his
expenditure on it to his estimates of the income to be
derived from various descriptions of buildings on it.

§ 3. The owner of building land sometimes builds on it Causes
himself: sometimes he sells it outright: very often he lets that govern
it at a fixed ground-rent for ninety-nine years, after which the capital value of
the land and the buildings on it (which by covenant must be building land.
kept in good repair) revert to his successor in title. Let us
consider what governs the value at which he can sell the
land and the ground-rent at which he can let it.

The capitalized value of any plot of land is the actuarial
"discounted" value of all the net incomes which it is likely
to afford, allowance being made on the one hand for all
incidental expenses, including those of collecting the rents,
and on the other for its mineral wealth, its capabilities of
development for any kind of business, and its advantages,
material, social and æsthetic, for the purposes of residence.
The money equivalent of that social status and those other
personal gratifications which the ownership of land affords,

V, xi, 3.   does not appear in the returns of the money income derived
from it, but does enter into its capital money value[1].

Ground-
rents for
long leases
are based
on esti-
mates of
future true
site values.

Next let us consider what governs the "ground-rent"
which the owner can obtain for a plot which he lets on, say,
a ninety-nine years' building lease. The present discounted
value of all the fixed money payments under that lease tends
to be equal to the present capital value of the land; after
deducting, firstly, for the obligation to return the land with
the buildings on it to the successor in title of the present
owner at the end of the lease, and secondly for the possible
inconvenience of any restrictions on the use of the land
contained in the lease. In consequence of these deductions
the ground-rent would be rather less than the "annual site
value" of the land, if that site value were expected to remain
fixed throughout. But in fact the site value is expected to
rise in consequence of the growth of population, and other
causes: and therefore the ground-rent is generally a little
above the annual site value at the beginning of the lease,
and much below it towards the end[2].

---

[1] The value of agricultural land is commonly expressed as a certain number
of times the current money rental, or in other words a certain "number of years'
purchase" of that rental: and other things being equal it will be the higher, the
more important these direct gratifications are, as well as the greater the chance
that they and the money income afforded by the land will rise. The number of
years' purchase would be increased also by an expected fall either in the future
normal rate of interest or in the purchasing power of money.

The discounted value of a very distant rise in the value of land is much less
than is commonly supposed. For instance, if we take interest at five per cent.
(and higher rates prevailed during the Middle Ages), £1 invested at compound
interest would amount to about £17,000 in 200 years, and £40,000,000,000 in
500 years. Therefore an expenditure by the State of £1 in securing to itself the
reversion of a rise in the value of land which came into operation now for the
first time would have been a bad investment, unless the value of that rise now
exceeded £17,000, if the payment was made 200 years ago; if 500 years ago to
£40,000,000,000. This assumes that it would have been possible to invest a sum
of this dimension at five per cent.: which of course it would not.

[2] A few site-values have fallen in districts which have been deserted by fashion
or trade. But on the other hand annual site values have risen to be many times
as great as the ground-rents in the case of land which was leased when it had no
special situation value, but has since become a chief centre of fashion, or of
trade: and all the more if the lease was granted in the first half of the eighteenth
century, when gold was scarce and the incomes of all classes of the people,
measured in money, were very low. The present discounted value of the return
of property to the ground landlord a hundred years hence, which will then be
worth £1000, is less perhaps than is commonly supposed; though the error is not
so great as in the case of anticipations ranging over many hundred years, which

Among the estimated outgoings on account of any
building, which have to be deducted from its estimated gross
yield before deciding what is the value of the privilege of
erecting it on any given plot of land, are the taxes (central and
local) which may be expected to be levied on the property,
and to be paid by the owner of the property. . . .

§ 4. Let us revert to the fact that the law of diminishing *The rela-*
return applies to the use of land for the purposes of living *tions of*
and working on it in all trades. Of course in the trade of *marginal*
building, as in agriculture, it is possible to apply capital *costs to the*
value of the
too thinly. Just as a homesteader may find that he can raise *product and*
more produce by cultivating only a half of the 160 acres *to the rent*
of the land
allotted to him than by spreading his labour over the whole, *used are*
so even when ground has scarcely any value, a very low *similar in*
house may be dear in proportion to its accommodation. *manufac-*
ture and
But, as in agriculture, there is a certain application of cap- *agriculture.*
ital and labour to the acre which gives the highest return,
and further applications after this give a less return, so it is
in building. The amount of capital per acre which gives the
maximum return varies in agriculture with the nature of the
crops, with the state of the arts of production, and with the
character of the markets to be supplied; and similarly in
building, the capital per square foot which would give the
maximum return, if the site had no scarcity value, varies
with the purpose for which the building is wanted. But
when the site has a scarcity value, it is worth while to go
on applying capital beyond this maximum rather than pay
the extra cost of land required for extending the site. In
places where the value of land is high, each square foot is
made to yield perhaps twice the accommodation, at more
than twice the cost, that it would be made to give, if used
for similar purposes where the value of land is low.

We may apply the phrase *the margin of building* to that
accommodation which it is only just worth while to get

were discussed in a recent note: if interest be taken at three per cent. it is about £50;
if at five per cent., as was the rule three or four generations ago, it is but £8.

from a given site, and which would not be got from it if land
were less scarce. To fix the ideas, we may suppose this accommodation to be given by the top floor of the building[1].

By erecting this floor, instead of spreading the building
over more ground, a saving in the cost of land is effected,
which just compensates for the extra expense and inconvenience of the plan. The accommodation given by this
floor, when allowance has been made for its incidental disadvantages, is only just enough to be worth what it costs
without allowing anything for the rent of land; and the
expenses of production of the things raised on this floor, if
it is part of a factory, are just covered by their price; there
is no surplus for the rent of land. The expenses of production of manufactures may then be reckoned as those of the
goods which are made on the margin of building, so as to
pay no rent for land. That is to say the rent of the land does
not enter into that set of expenses at the margin at which
the action of the forces of demand and supply in governing
value may be most clearly seen.

Suppose, for instance, that a person is planning a hotel
or a factory; and considering how much land to take for the
purpose. If land is cheap he will take much of it; if it is dear
he will take less and build high. Suppose him to calculate
the expenses of building and working his establishment
with frontages of 100 and 110 feet respectively, in ways
equally convenient on the whole to himself, his customers
and employees, and therefore equally profitable to himself.

[1] Houses built in flats are often provided with a lift which is run at the expense
of the owner of the house, and in such cases, at all events in America, the top floor
sometimes lets for a higher rent than any other. If the site is very valuable and the
law does not limit the height of his house in the interest of his neighbours, he may
build very high: but at last he will reach the margin of building. At last he will find
that the extra expenses for foundations and thick walls, and for his lift, together with
some resulting depreciation of the lower floors, make him stand to lose more than be
gains by adding one more floor; the extra accommodation which it only just answers
his purpose to supply is then to be regarded as at the margin of building, even though
the gross rent be greater for the higher floors than for the lower. . . .

But in England bylaws restrain an individual from building so high as to deprive
his near neighbours of air and light. In the course of time those who build high will
be forced to have a good deal of free space about their buildings; and this will render
very high buildings unprofitable.

Let him find that the difference between the two plans, after V, xi, 5.
capitalizing future expenditure, shows an advantage of £500
in favour of the larger area; he will then be inclined to take
the larger if the land is to be got at less than £50 per foot of
frontage, but not otherwise; and £50 will be the marginal
value of land to him. He might have reached this result by
calculating the increased value of the business that could be
done with the same outlay in other respects on the larger
site as compared with the smaller, or again by building on
less expensive ground instead of in a less favourable situation.
But, by whatever route he makes his calculation, its character is similar to that by which he decides whether it is worth
his while to buy business plant of any other kind: and he
regards the net income (allowance being made for depreciation) which he expects to get from either investment as
standing in the same general relation to his business; and if
the advantages of the situation are such, that all the land
available on it can find employments of different kinds in
each of which its marginal use is represented by a capital
value of £50 per foot of frontage, then that will be the current
value of the land.

§ 5. This assumes that the competition for land for The com-
various uses will cause building in each locality and for each factories,
use to be carried up to that margin, at which it is no longer ware-
profitable to apply any more capital to the same site. As houses,
the demand for residential and business accommodation in same land.
a district increases, it becomes worth while to pay a higher
and higher price for land, in order to avoid the expense and
inconvenience of forcing more accommodation from the same
ground area.

For instance, if the value of land in, say, Leeds rises
because of the increased competition for it by shops, warehouses, iron works, etc.; then a woollen manufacturer finding
his expenses of production increased, may move to another
town or into the country; and thus leave the land on which
he used to work to be build over with shops and warehouses,
for which a town situation is more valuable than it is for
factories. For he may think that the saving in the cost of
land that he will make by moving into the country, together

V, xi, 5. with other advantages of the change, will more than counter-balance its disadvantages. In a discussion as to whether it was worth while to do so, the rental value of the site of his factory would be reckoned among the expenses of production of his cloth; and rightly. But we have to go behind that fact. The general relations of demand and supply cause production to be carried up to a margin at which the expenses of production (nothing being entered for rent) are so high that people are willing to pay a high value for additional land in order to avoid the inconvenience and expense of crowding their work on to a narrow site. These causes govern site value; and site value is therefore not properly regarded as governing marginal costs.

Thus the industrial demand for land is in all respects parallel to the agricultural. The expenses of production of oats are increased by the fact that land, which could yield good crops of oats, is in great demand for growing other crops that enable it to yield a higher rent: and in the same way the printing-presses, which may be seen at work in London some sixty feet above the ground, could afford to do their work a little cheaper if the demand for ground for other uses did not push the margin of building up so high. Again a hop-grower may find that on account of the high rent which he pays for his land, the price of his hops will not cover their expenses of production where he is, and he may abandon hop-growing, or seek other land for it; while the land that he leaves may perhaps be let to a market-gardener. After a while the demand for land in the neighbourhood may again become so great that the aggregate price which the market-gardener obtains for his produce will not pay its expenses of production, including rent; and so he in his turn makes room for, say, a building company.

In each case the rising demand for land alters the margin to which it is profitable to carry the intensive use of land: the costs at this margin indicate the action of those fundamental causes which govern the value of the land. And at the same time they are themselves those costs to which the general conditions of demand and supply compel value to conform:

and therefore it is right for our purpose to go straight to
them; though any such inquiry would be irrelevant to the
purposes of a private balance sheet.

§ **6.** The demand for exceptionally valuable urban land The
comes from traders of various kinds, wholesale and retail, rents of
more than from manufacturers; and it may be worth while relation
to say something here as to the very interesting features of prices.
demand that are peculiar to their case.

If two factories in the same branch of trade have equal
outputs they are sure to have nearly equal floor space. But
there is no close relation between the size of trading
establishments and their turn-overs. Plenty of space is for
them a matter of convenience and a source of extra profit.
It is not physically indispensable; but the larger their space,
the greater the stock which they can keep on hand, and the
greater the advantage to which they can display specimens
of it; and especially is this the case in trades that are
subject to changes of taste and fashion. In such trades the
dealers exert themselves to collect within a comparatively
small space representatives of all the best ideas that are in
vogue, and still more of those that are likely soon to be so;
and the higher the rental values of their sites the more
prompt they must be in getting rid, even at a loss, of such
things as are a little behind the time and do not improve
the general character of their stocks. If the locality is one
in which customers are more likely to be tempted by a well-
chosen stock than by low prices, the traders will charge
prices that give a high rate of profit on a comparatively
small turn-over: but, if not, they will charge low prices and
try to force a large business in proportion to their capital
and the size of their premises; just as in some neighbourhoods
the market-gardener finds it best to gather his peas young
when they are full of flavour, and in others to let them grow
till they weigh heavily in the scales. Whichever plan the
traders follow, there will be some conveniences which they
are in doubt whether it is worth while to offer to the public;
since they calculate that the extra sales gained by such
conveniences are only just remunerative, and do not contribute any surplus towards rent. The goods which they sell

in consequence of these conveniences, are goods into whose expenses of marketing rent does not enter any more than it does into those of the peas which the market-gardener only just finds it worth his while to produce.

Prices are low in some very highly-rented shops, because their doors are passed by great numbers of people who cannot afford to pay high prices for the gratification of their fancy; and the shopkeeper knows that he must sell cheaply, or not sell at all. He has to be content with a low rate of profit each time he turns over his capital. But, as the wants of his customers are simple, he need not keep a large stock of goods; and he can turn over his capital many times a year. So his annual net profits are very great, and he is willing to pay a very high rent for the situation in which they can be earned. On the other hand, prices are very high in some of the quiet streets in the fashionable parts of London and in many villages; because in the one case customers must be attracted by a very choice stock, which can only be sold slowly; and in the other the aggregate turn-over is very small indeed. In neither place can the trader make profits that will enable him to pay as high a rent as those of some cheap but bustling shops in the East end of London.

A rise of ground values may be an indication of a scarcity of space that will tend to raise traders' prices.

It is however true that, if without any increase in traffic such as brings extra custom, a situation becomes more valuable for purposes other than shopkeeping; then only those shopkeepers will be able to pay their way who can manage to secure a large custom relatively to the prices which they charge and the class of business which they do. There will therefore be a smaller supply of shopkeepers in all trades for which the demand has not increased: and those who remain, will be able to charge a higher price than before, without offering any greater conveniences and attractions to their customers. The rise of ground values in the district will thus be an indication of a scarcity of space which, other things being equal, will raise the prices of retail goods; just in the same way as the rise of agricultural rents in any district will indicate a scarcity of land which will raise the marginal expenses of production, and therefore the price of any particular crop.

§ 7. The rent of a house (or other building) is a composite rent, of which one part belongs to the site and the other to the buildings themselves. The relations between these two are rather intricate. . . . A few words may however be said here as to composite rents in general. At starting there may appear to be some contradiction in the statement that a thing is yielding at the same time two rents: for its rent is in some sense a residual income after deducting the expenses of working it; and there cannot be two residues in regard to the same process of working and the same resulting revenue. But when the thing is composite each of its parts may be capable of being so worked as to yield a surplus of revenue over the expenses of working it. The corresponding rents can always be distinguished analytically, and sometimes they can be separated commercially[1].

For instance, the rent of a flour-mill worked by water includes the rent of the site on which it is built, and the rent of the water power which it uses. Suppose that it is contemplated to build a mill in a place where there is a limited water power which could be applied equally well on any one of many sites; then the rent of the water power together with the site selected for it is the sum of two rents; which are respectively the equivalent of the differential advantages which possession of the site gives for production of any kind, and which the ownership of the water power gives for working a mill on any of the sites. And these two rents, whether they happen to be owned by the same person or not, can be clearly distinguished and separately estimated both in theory and in practice.

But this cannot be done if there are no other sites on which a mill can be built: and in that case, should the water power and the site belong to different persons, there is nothing but "higgling and bargaining" to settle how much of the excess of the value of the two together over that which the site has for other purposes shall go to the owner of the latter.

[1] It will be borne in mind that if a house is not appropriate to its site, its aggregate rent will not exceed its site rent by the full building rent which the house would command on an appropriate site. Similar limitations apply to most composite rents.

And even if there were other sites at which the water power could be applied, but not with equal efficiency, there would still be no means of deciding how the owners of the site and the water power should share the excess of the producer's surplus which they got by acting together, over the sum of that which the site would yield for some other purpose, and of that which the water power would yield if applied elsewhere. The mill would probably not be put up till an agreement had been made for the supply of water power for a term of years: but at the end of that term similar difficulties would arise as to the division of the aggregate producer's surplus afforded by the water power and the site with the mill on it.

Difficulties of this kind are continually arising with regard to attempts by partial monopolists, such as railway, gas, water and electrical companies, to raise their charges on the consumer who has adapted his business arrangements to make use of their services, and perhaps laid down at his own expense a costly plant for the purpose. For instance, at Pittsburgh when manufacturers had just put up furnaces to be worked by natural gas instead of coal, the price of the gas was suddenly doubled. And the history of mines affords many instances of difficulties of this kind with neighbouring landowners as to rights of way, etc., and with the owners of neighbouring cottages, railways and docks[1].

[1] The relations between the interests of different classes of workers in the same business and in the same trade, have some affinity to the subject of composite rents.

CHAPTER XII.

EQUILIBRIUM OF NORMAL DEMAND AND SUPPLY, CONTINUED, WITH REFERENCE TO THE LAW OF INCREASING RETURN.

§ 1. WE may now continue the study begun in chapters V, XII, 1. III. and V.; and examine some difficulties connected with the relations of demand and supply as regards commodities the production of which tends to increasing return.

We have noted that this tendency seldom shows itself The tendency to increasing return does not act quickly. immediately on an increase of demand. To take an example, the first effect of a sudden fashion for watch-shaped aneroids would be a temporary rise of price, in spite of the fact that they contain no material of which there is but a scanty stock. For highly paid labour, that had no special training for the work, would have to be drawn in from other trades; a good deal of effort would be wasted, and for a time the real and the money cost of production would be increased.

But yet, if the fashion lasted a considerable time, then even independently of any new invention, the cost of making aneroids would fall gradually. For specialized skill in abundance would be trained, and properly graduated to the various work to be done. With a large use of the method of interchangeable parts, specialized machinery would do better and more cheaply much of the work that is now done by hand; and thus a continued increase in the annual output of watch-shaped aneroids would lower their price very much.

Here there is to be noted an important difference between Differences between demand and supply demand and supply. A fall in the price, at which a commodity is offered, acts on demand always in one direction. The

amount of the commodity demanded may increase much or
little according as the demand is elastic or inelastic: and
a long or short time may be required for developing the new
and extended uses of the commodity, which are rendered
possible by the fall in price[1]. But—at all events if exceptional
cases in which a thing is driven out of fashion by a fall in its
price be neglected—the influence of price on demand is
similar in character for all commodities: and, further, those
demands which show high elasticity in the long run, show
a high elasticity almost at once; so that, subject to a few
exceptions, we may speak of the demand for a commodity
as being of high or low elasticity without specifying how
far we are looking ahead.

But there are no such simple rules with regard to supply.
An increase in the price offered by purchasers does indeed
always increase supply: and thus it is true that, if we have
regard to short periods only, and especially to the transactions
of a dealer's market, there is an "elasticity of supply" which
corresponds closely to elasticity of demand. That is to say, a
given rise in price will cause a great or a small increase in the
offers which sellers accept, according as they have large or
small reserves in the background, and as they have formed
low or high estimates of the level of prices at the next market:
and this rule applies nearly in the same way to things which in
the long run have a tendency to diminishing return as to those
which have a tendency to increasing return. In fact if the
large plant needed in a branch of manufacture is fully
occupied, and cannot be rapidly increased, an increase in the
price offered for its products may have no perceptible effect
in increasing the output for some considerable time: while
a similar increase in the demand for a hand-made commodity
might call forth quickly a great increase in supply, though in
the long run its supply conformed to that of constant return
or even of diminishing return.

In the more fundamental questions which relate to long
periods, the matter is even more complex. For the ultimate
output corresponding to an unconditional demand at even

---

[1] See above III. iv. 5.

current prices would be theoretically infinite; and therefore V, XII, 2.
the elasticity of supply of a commodity which conforms to
the law of Increasing Return, or even to that of Constant
Return, is theoretically infinite for long periods[1].

§ 2. The next point to be observed is that this tendency We must
to a fall in the price of a commodity as a result of a gradual distinguish the econo-
development of the industry by which it is made, is quite a mies of a
different thing from the tendency to the rapid introduction whole in-
of new economies by an individual firm that is increasing dustry and of an indi-
its business. vidual firm.

We have seen how every step in the advance of an able
and enterprising manufacturer makes the succeeding step
easier and more rapid; so that his progress upwards is
likely to continue so long as he has fairly good fortune, and
retains his full energy and elasticity and his liking for hard
work. But these cannot last for ever: and as soon as they
decay, his business is likely to be destroyed through the
action of some of those very causes which enabled it to
rise; unless indeed he can pass it over into hands as strong
as his used to be. Thus the rise and fall of individual firms
may be frequent, while a great industry is going through
one long oscillation, or even moving steadily forwards; as
the leaves of a tree (to repeat an earlier illustration) grow
to maturity, reach equilibrium, and decay many times,
while the tree is steadily growing upwards year by year.

The causes which govern the facilities for production at Facilities
the command of a single firm, thus conform to quite dif- for increased
ferent laws from those which control the whole output of an production
industry. And the contrast is perhaps heightened, when we often opposed by
take the difficulties of marketing into account. For instance, difficulties
manufactures, which are adapted to special tastes, are likely of marketing.

---

[1] Strictly speaking, the amount produced and the price at which it can be sold,
are functions one of another, account being taken of the length of time allowed for
the evolution of appropriate plant and organization for production on a large scale.
But in real life, the cost of production per unit is deduced from the amount expected
to be produced, and not *vice versâ*. Economists commonly follow this practice; and
they follow also the practice of business life in inverting this order with regard to
demand. That is, they consider the increase of sales that will follow from a given
reduction of price, more frequently than the diminution of price which will be
required to effect a given increase of sales.

V, xii, 2. to be on a small scale; and they are generally of such a character that the machinery and modes of organization already developed in other trades, could be easily adapted to them; so that a great increase in their scale of production would be sure to introduce vast economies at once. But these are the very industries in which each firm is likely to be confirmed more or less to its own particular market; and, if it is so confined, any hasty increase in its production is likely to lower the demand price in that market out of all proportion to the increased economies that it will gain; even though its production is but small relatively to the broad market for which in a more general sense it may be said to produce.

In fact, when trade is slack, a producer will often try to sell some of his surplus goods outside of his own particular market at prices that do little more than cover their prime costs: while within that market he still tries to sell at prices that nearly cover supplementary costs; and a great part of these are the returns expected on capital invested in building up the external organization of his business[1].

Again supplementary costs are, as a rule, larger relatively to prime costs for things that obey the law of increasing return than for other things[2]; because their production needs the investment of a large capital in material appliances and in building up trade connections. This increases the intensity of those fears of spoiling his own peculiar market, or

---

[1] This may be expressed by saying that when we are considering an individual producer, we must couple his supply curve—not with the general demand curve for his commodity in a wide market, but—with the particular demand curve of his own special market. And this particular demand curve will generally be very steep; perhaps as steep as his own supply curve is likely to be, even when an increased output will give him an important increase of internal economies.

[2] Of course this rule is not universal. It may be noted, for instance, that the net loss of an omnibus, that is short of passengers throughout its trip, and loses a fourpenny fare, is nearer fourpence than threepence, though the omnibus trade conforms perhaps to the law of constant return. Again, if it were not for the fear of spoiling his market, the Regent Street shoemaker, whose goods are made by hand, but whose expenses of marketing are very heavy, would be tempted to go further below his normal price in order to avoid losing a special order, than a shoe manufacturer who uses much expensive machinery and avails himself generally of the economies of production on a large scale. There are other difficulties connected with the supplementary costs of joint products, e.g. the practice of selling some goods at near prime cost, for the purpose of advertisement (see above V. vii. 2). But these need not be specially considered here.

incurring odium from other producers for spoiling the common market; which we have already learnt to regard as controlling the short-period supply price of goods, when the appliances of production are not fully employed. We cannot then regard the conditions of supply by an individual producer as typical of those which govern the general supply in a market. We must take account of the fact that very few firms have a long-continued life of active progress, and of the fact that the relations between the individual producer and his special market differ in important respects from those between the whole body of producers and the general market[1].

§ 3. Thus the history of the individual firm cannot be made into the history of an industry any more than the history of an individual man can be made into the history of mankind. And yet the history of mankind is the outcome of the history of individuals; and the aggregate production for a general market is the outcome of the motives which induce individual producers to expand or contract their production. It is just here that our device of a representative firm comes to our aid. We imagine to ourselves at any

The solution of the difficulty is in the action of a representative firm.

Abstract reasonings as to the effects of the economies in production, which an individual firm gets from an increase of its output are apt to be misleading, not only in detail, but even in their general effect. This is nearly the same as saying that in such case the conditions governing supply should be represented in their totality. They are often vitiated by difficulties which lie rather below the surface and are especially troublesome in attempts to express the equilibrium conditions of trade by mathematical formulæ. Some, among whom Cournot himself is to be counted, have before them what is in effect the supply schedule of an individual firm; representing that an increase in its output gives it command over so great internal economies as much to diminish its expenses of production; and they follow their mathematics boldly, but apparently without noticing that their premises lead inevitably to the conclusion that, whatever firm first gets a good start will obtain a monopoly of the whole business of its trade in its district. While others avoiding this horn of the dilemma, maintain that there is no equilibrium at all for commodities which obey the law of increasing return; and some again have called in question the validity of any supply schedule which represents prices diminishing as the amount produced increases. . . .

The remedy for such difficulties as these is to be sought in treating each important concrete case very much as an independent problem, under the guidance of staple general reasonings. Attempts so to enlarge the *direct* applications of general propositions as to enable them to supply adequate solutions of all difficulties, would make them so cumbrous as to be of little service for their main work. The "principles" of economics must aim at affording guidance to an entry on problems of life, without making claim to be a substitute for independent study and thought.

time a firm that has its fair share of those internal and external economies, which appertain to the aggregate scale of production in the industry to which it belongs. We recognize that the size of such a firm, while partly dependent on changes in technique and in the costs of transport, is governed, other things being equal, by the general expansion of the industry. We regard the manager of it as reckoning up whether it would be worth his while to add a certain new line to his undertakings; whether he should introduce a certain new machine and so on. We regard him as treating the output which would result from that change more or less as a unit, and weighing in his mind the cost against the gain[1].

We thus get at the true long-period marginal cost, falling with a gradual increase of demand.

This then is the marginal cost on which we fix our eyes. We do not expect it to fall immediately in consequence of a sudden increase of demand. On the contrary we expect the short-period supply price to increase with increasing output. But we also expect a gradual increase in demand to increase gradually the size and the efficiency of this representative firm; and to increase the economies both internal and external which are at its disposal.

That is to say, when making lists of supply prices (supply schedules) for long periods in these industries, we set down a diminished supply price against an increased amount of the flow of the goods; meaning thereby that a flow of that increased amount will in the course of time be supplied profitably at that lower price, to meet a fairly steady corresponding demand. We exclude from view any economies that may result from substantive new inventions; but we include those which may be expected to arise naturally out of adaptations of existing ideas; and we look towards a position of balance or equilibrium between the forces of progress and decay, which would be attained if the conditions under view were supposed to act uniformly for a long time. But such notions must be taken broadly. The attempt to make them precise over-reaches our strength. If we include in our account nearly all the conditions of real life, the problem is too heavy to be handled; if we select a few, then

[1] See above V. v. 6.

long-drawn-out and subtle reasonings with regard to them become scientific toys rather than engines for practical work.

The theory of stable equilibrium of normal demand and supply helps indeed to give definiteness to our ideas; and in its elementary stages it does not diverge from the actual facts of life, so far as to prevent its giving a fairly trustworthy picture of the chief methods of action of the strongest and most persistent group of economic forces. But when pushed to its more remote and intricate logical consequences, it slips away from the conditions of real life. In fact we are here verging on the high theme of economic progress; and here therefore it is especially needful to remember that economic problems are imperfectly presented when they are treated as problems of statical equilibrium, and not of organic growth. For though the statical treatment alone can give us definiteness and precision of thought, and is therefore a necessary introduction to a more philosophic treatment of society as an organism; it is yet only an introduction.

The Statical theory of equilibrium is only an introduction to economic studies; and it is barely even an introduction to the study of the progress and development of industries which show a tendency to increasing return. Its limitations are so constantly overlooked, especially by those who approach it from an abstract point of view, that there is a danger in throwing it into definite form at all. But, with this caution, the risk may be taken. . . .

V, XII, 3.

The pure theory in its earlier stages diverges but little from actual facts; but if pushed far its practical value rapidly diminishes.

CHAPTER XIII.

THEORY OF CHANGES OF NORMAL DEMAND AND SUPPLY IN RELATION TO THE DOCTRINE OF MAXIMUM SATISFACTION.

§ 1. In earlier chapters of this Book, and especially in chapter XII., we have considered gradual changes in the adjustment of demand and supply. But any great and lasting change in fashion; any substantive new invention; any diminution of population by war or pestilence; or the development or dwindling away of a source of supply of the commodity in question, or of a raw material used in it, or of another commodity which is a rival and possible substitute for it:—such a change as any of these may cause the prices set against any given annual (or daily) consumption and production of the commodity to cease to be its normal demand and supply prices for that volume of consumption and production; or, in other words, they may render it necessary to make out a new demand schedule or a new supply schedule, or both of them. We proceed to study the problems thus suggested.

An increase of normal demand for a commodity involves an increase in the price at which each several amount can find purchasers; or, which is the same thing, an increase of the quantity which can find purchasers at any price. This increase of demand may be caused by the commodity's coming more into fashion, by the opening out of a new use for it or of new markets for it, by the permanent falling off in the supply of some commodity for which it can be used as a substitute, by a permanent increase in the wealth and general purchasing power of the community, and so on.

Changes in the opposite direction will cause a falling off in demand and a sinking of the demand prices. Similarly an increase of normal supply means an increase of the amounts that can be supplied at each several price, and a diminution of the price at which each separate amount can be supplied[1]. This change may be caused by the opening up of a new source of supply, whether by improved means of transport or in any other way, by an advance in the arts of production, such as the invention of a new process or of new machinery, or again, by the granting of a bounty on production. Conversely, a diminution of normal supply (or a raising of the supply schedule) may be caused by the closing up of a new source of supply or by the imposition of a tax.

§ 2. We have, then, to regard the effects of an increase of normal demand from three points of view, according as the commodity in question obeys the law of constant or of diminishing or of increasing return: that is, its supply price is practically constant for all amounts, or increases or diminishes with an increase in the amount produced.

Effects of an increase of normal demand.

In the first case an increase of demand simply increases the amount produced without altering its price; for the normal price of a commodity which obeys the law of constant return is determined absolutely by its expenses of production: demand has no influence in the matter beyond this, that the thing will not be produced at all unless there is some demand for it at this fixed price.

If the commodity obeys the law of diminishing return an increase of demand for it raises its price and causes more

[1] A rise or fall of the demand or supply prices involves of course a rise or fall of the demand or supply curve.

If the change is gradual, the supply curve will assume in succession a series of positions, each of which is a little below the preceding one; and in this way we might have represented the effects of that gradual improvement of industrial organization which arises from an increase in the scale of production, and which we have represented by assigning to it an influence upon the supply price for long-period curves. In an ingenious paper privately printed by Sir H. Cunynghame, a suggestion is made, which seems to come in effect to proposing that a long-period supply curve should be regarded as in some manner representing a series of short-period curves; each of these curves would assume throughout its whole length that development of industrial organization which properly belongs to the scale of production represented by the distance from Oy of the point in which that curve cuts the long-period supply curve . . . and similarly with regard to demand.

v, xiii, 2. of it to be produced; but not so much more as if it obeyed the law of constant return.

On the other hand, if the commodity obeys the law of increasing return, an increase of demand causes much more of it to be produced,—more than if the commodity obeyed the law of constant return,—and at the same time lowers its price. If, for instance, a thousand things of a certain kind have been produced and sold weekly at a price of 10s., while the supply price for two thousand weekly would be only 9s., a small rate of increase in normal demand may gradually cause this to become the normal price; since we are considering periods long enough for the full normal action of the causes that determine supply to work itself out. The converse holds in each case should normal demand fall off instead of increasing[1].

The argument of this section has been thought by some

---

[1] Diagrams are of especial aid in enabling us to comprehend clearly the problems of this chapter.

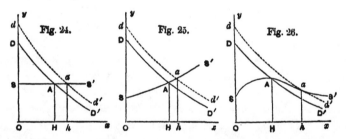

The three figures 24, 25, 26 represent the three cases of constant, diminishing and increasing return respectively. The return in the last case is a diminishing one in the earlier stages of the increase of production, but an increasing one in those subsequent to the attainment of the original position of equilibrium, *i.e.* for amounts of the commodity greater than *OH*. In each case *SS'* is the supply curve, *DD'* the old position of the demand curve, and *dd'* its position after there has been increase of normal demand. In each case *A* and *a* are the old and new positions of equilibrium respectively, *AH* and *ah* are the old and new normal or equilibrium prices, and *OH* and *Oh* the old and new equilibrium amounts. *Oh* is in every case greater than *OH*, but in fig. 25 it is only a little greater, while in fig. 26 it is much greater. (This analysis may be carried further on the plan adopted later on in discussing the similar but more important problem of the effects of changes in the conditions of normal supply.) In fig. 24 *ah* is equal to *AH*, in fig. 25 it is greater, in fig. 26 it is less.

The effect of a falling-off of normal demand can be traced with the same diagrams, *dd'* being now regarded as the old and *DD'* as the new position of this demand curve; *ah* being the old equilibrium price, and *AH* the new one.

writers to lend support to the claim that a Protective duty on
manufactured imports in general increases the home market
for those imports; and, by calling into play the Law of
Increasing Return, *ultimately* lowers their price to the home
consumer. Such a result may indeed ultimately be reached
by a wisely chosen system of "Protection to nascent industries" in a new country; where manufactures, like
young children, have a power of rapid growth. But even
there the policy is apt to be wrenched from its proper uses,
to the enrichment of particular interests: for those industries
which can send the greatest number of votes to the poll, are
those which are already on so large a scale, that a further
increase would bring very few new economies. And of course
the industries in a country so long familiar with machinery
as England is, have generally passed the stage at which they
can derive much real help from such Protection: while
Protection to any one industry nearly always tends to narrow
the markets, especially the foreign markets, for other industries. These few remarks show that the question is complex:
they do not pretend to reach further than that.

§ 3. We have seen that an increase in normal demand,
while leading in every case to an increased production, will
in some cases raise and in others lower prices. But now we
are to see that increased facilities for supply (causing the
supply schedule to be lowered) will always lower the normal
price at the same time that it leads to an increase in the
amount produced. For so long as the normal demand
remains unchanged an increased supply can be sold only at
a diminished price; but the fall of price consequent on a
given increase of supply will be much greater in some
cases than in others. It will be small if the commodity
obeys the law of diminishing return; because then the
difficulties attendant on an increased production will tend to
counteract the new facilities of supply. On the other hand,
if the commodity obeys the law of increasing return, the
increased production will bring with it increased facilities,
which will co-operate with those arising from the change in
the general conditions of supply; and the two together will
enable a great increase in production and consequent fall in

V, XIII, 3.

Protection
to nascent
industries.

Effects of
increased
facilities of
supply.

V, xiii, 8. price to be attained before the fall of the supply price is overtaken by the fall of the demand price. If it happens that the demand is very elastic, then a small increase in the facilities of normal supply, such as a new invention, a new application of machinery, the opening up of new and cheaper sources of supply, the taking off a tax or granting a bounty, may cause an enormous increase of production and fall of price[1].

[1] All this can be most clearly seen by the aid of diagrams, and indeed there are some parts of the problem which cannot be satisfactorily treated without their aid. The three figures 27, 28, 29 represent the three cases of constant and diminishing and increasing returns, respectively. In each case *DD'* is the demand curve, *SS'* the old position, and *ss'* the new position of the supply curve. *A* is the old, and *a* the new position of stable equilibrium. *Oh* is greater than *OH*, and *ah* is less than *AH* in every case: but the changes are small in fig. 28 and great in fig. 29. Of course the demand curve must lie below the old supply curve to the right of *A*, otherwise *A* would be a point not of stable, but of unstable equilibrium.

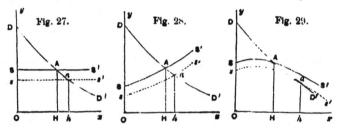

Fig. 27.　　　Fig. 28.　　　Fig. 29.

But subject to this condition the more elastic the demand is, that is, the more nearly horizontal the demand curve is at *A* the further off will *a* be from *A*, and the greater therefore will be the increase of production and the fall of price.

The whole result is rather complex. But it may be stated thus. Firstly, given the elasticity of demand at *A*, the increase in the quantity produced and the fall in price will both be the greater, the greater be the return got from additional capital and labour applied to the production. That is, they will be the greater, the more nearly horizontal the supply curve is at *A* in fig. 28, and the more steeply inclined it is in fig. 29 (subject to the condition mentioned above, that it does not lie below the demand curve to the right of *A*, and thus turn *A* into a position of unstable equilibrium). Secondly, given the position of the supply curve at *A*, the greater the elasticity of demand the greater will be the increase of production in every case; but the smaller will be the fall of price in fig. 28, and the greater the fall of price in fig. 29. Fig. 27 may be regarded as a limiting case of either fig. 28 or 29.

All this reasoning assumes that the commodity either obeys the law of diminishing return or obeys the law of increasing return throughout. If it obeys first one, and then the other, so that the supply curve is at one part inclined positively and at another negatively, no general rule can be laid down as to the effect on price of increased facilities of supply, though in every case this must lead to an increased volume of production. A great variety of curious results may be got by giving the supply curve different shapes, and in particular such as cut the demand curve more than once.

This method of inquiry is not applicable to a tax on wheat in so far as it is consumed by a labouring class which spends a great part of its income on bread;

If we take account of the circumstances of composite and V, XIII, 4.
joint supply and demand discussed in chapter VI., we have
suggested to us an almost endless variety of problems which
can be worked out by the methods adopted in these two
chapters.

§ 4. We may now consider the effects which a change Changes
in the conditions of supply may exert on consumers' surplus that raise
or rent. For brevity of language a tax may be taken as the supply
representative of those changes which may cause a general may be re-
increase, and a bounty as representative of those which may by a tax
cause a general diminution in the normal supply price for or bounty.
each several amount of the commodity.

Firstly, if the commodity is one, the production of which The case
obeys the law of constant return, so that the supply price return.
is the same for all amounts of the commodity, consumers'
surplus will be diminished by more than the increased payments to the producer; and therefore, in the special case of
a tax, by more than the gross receipts of the State. For on
that part of the consumption of the commodity, which is
maintained, the consumer loses what the State receives:
and on that part of the consumption which is destroyed by
the rise in price, the consumers' surplus is destroyed; and
of course there is no payment for it to the producer or to the
State[1]. Conversely, the gain of consumers' surplus caused

and it is not applicable to a general tax on all commodities: for in neither of
these cases can it be assumed that the marginal value of money to the individual
remains approximately the same after the tax has been levied as it was before.

[1] This is most clearly seen by aid of a diagram. SS', the old constant return
supply curve, cuts DD' the demand curve in A:
DSA is the consumers' surplus. Afterwards a
tax Ss being imposed the new equilibrium is found
at a, and consumers' surplus is Dsa. The gross
tax is only the rectangle $sSKa$, that is, a tax at
the rate of Ss on an amount sa of the commodity.
And this falls short of the loss of consumers' surplus by the area aKA. The net loss aKA is small
or great, other things being equal, as aA is or is
not inclined steeply. Thus it is smallest for those
commodities the demand for which is most inelastic, that is, for necessaries. If therefore a
given aggregate taxation has to be levied ruthlessly
from any class it will cause less loss of consumers'

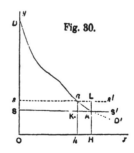

Fig. 80.

surplus if levied on necessaries than if levied on comforts; though of course the
consumption of luxuries and in a less degree of comforts indicates ability to
bear taxation.

V, XIII, 4. by a bounty on a commodity that obeys the law of constant return, is less than the bounty itself. For on that part of the consumption which existed before the bounty, consumers' surplus is increased by just the amount of the bounty; while on the new consumption that is caused by the bounty, the gain of the consumers' surplus is less than the bounty[1].

The case of diminishing return. If however the commodity obeys the law of diminishing return; a tax by raising its price, and diminishing its consumption, will lower its expenses of production other than the tax: and the result will be to raise the supply price by something less than the full amount of the tax. In this case the gross receipts from the tax *may* be greater than the resulting loss of consumers' surplus, and they *will* be greater if the law of diminishing return acts so sharply that a small diminution of consumption causes a great falling-off in the expenses of production other than the tax[2].

On the other hand, a bounty on a commodity which obeys the law of diminishing return will lead to increased production, and will extend the margin of cultivation to places and conditions in which the expenses of production, exclusive of the bounty, are greater than before. Thus it will lower the price to the consumer and increase consumers'

---

[1] If we now regard ss' as the old supply curve which is lowered to the position SS' by the granting of a bounty, we find the gain of consumers' surplus to be $sSAa$. But the bounty paid is Ss on an amount SA, which is represented by the rectangle $sSAL$: and this exceeds the gain of consumers' surplus by the area aLA.

[2] Let the old supply curve be SS' fig. 31, and let the imposition of a tax raise it to ss'; let A and a be the old and new positions of equilibrium, and let straight lines be drawn through them parallel to Ox and Oy, as in the figure. Then the tax being levied, as shown by the figure, at the rate of aE on each unit; and Oh, that is, CK units, being produced in the new position of equilibrium, the gross receipts of the tax will be $cFEa$, and the loss of consumers' surplus will be $cCAa$; that is, the gross receipts from the tax will be greater or less than the loss of consumers' surplus as $CFEK$ is greater or less than aKA; and in the figure as it stands it is much greater. If SS' had been so drawn as to indicate only very slight action of the law of diminishing return, that is, if it had been nearly horizontal in the neighbourhood of A, then EK would have been very small; and $CFEK$ would have become less than aKA.

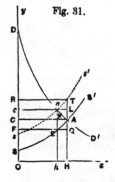

Fig. 31.

surplus less than if it were given for the production of a V, XIII, 4. commodity which obeyed the law of constant return. In that case the increase of consumers' surplus was seen to be less than the direct cost of the bounty to the State; and therefore in this case it is much less[1].

By similar reasoning it may be shown that a tax on a com- The case of modity which obeys the law of increasing return is more inju- increasing return. rious to the consumer than if levied on one which obeys the law of constant return. For it lessens the demand and therefore the output. It thus probably increases the expenses of manu- facture somewhat: sends up the price by more than the amount of the tax; and finally diminishes consumers' surplus by much more than the total payments which it brings in to the exche- quer[2]. On the other hand, a bounty on such a commodity causes so great a fall in its price to the consumer, that the consequent increase of consumers' surplus may exceed the total payments made by the State to the producers; and certainly will do so in case the law of increasing return acts at all sharply[3].

[1] To illustrate this case we may take ss' in fig. 31 to be the position of the supply curve before the granting of the bounty, and SS' to be its position afterwards. Thus a was the old equilibrium point, and A is the point to which the equilibrium moves when the bounty is awarded. The increase of consumers' surplus is only $cCAa$, while the payments made by the State under the bounty are, as shown by the figure, at the rate of AT on each unit of the commodity; and as in the new position of equilibrium there are produced OH, that is, CA units, they amount altogether to $RCAT$ which includes and is necessarily greater than the increase of consumers' surplus.

[2] Thus taking SS' in fig. 32 to be the old position of the supply curve, and ss' its posi- tion after the tax, A to be the old and a the new posi- tions of equilibrium, we have, as in the case of fig. 31, the total tax represented by $cFEa$, and the loss of con- sumers' surplus by $cCAa$; the former being always less than the latter. The statement in the text is put broadly and in simple outline. If it were applied to practical problems account would need to be taken of several considerations which have been ignored. An industry which yields an increasing return, is nearly sure to be growing, and therefore to be acquiring new economies of production on a large scale. If the tax is a small one, it may merely retard this growth and not cause a posi- tive shrinking. Even if the tax is heavy and the industry shrinks, many of the economies gained will be in part at least preserved. . . . In consequence ss' ought properly not to have the same shape as SS', and the distance aE ought to be less than AT.

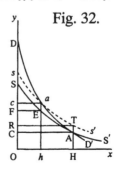

Fig. 32.

[3] To illustrate this case we may take ss' in fig. 32 to be the position of the

These
results
throw light
on the
doctrine of
*maximum
satisfac-
tion.*

    These results are suggestive of some principles of taxa-
tion which require careful attention in any study of financial
policy; when it will be necessary to take account of the
expenses of collecting a tax and of administering a bounty,
and of the many indirect effects, some economic and some
moral, which a tax or a bounty is likely to produce. But
these partial results are well adapted for our immediate
purpose of examining a little more closely than we have done
hitherto the general doctrine that a position of (stable)
equilibrium of demand and supply is a position also of
maximum satisfaction: and there is one abstract and
trenchant form of that doctrine which has had much vogue,
especially since the time of Bastiat's *Economic Harmonics*,
and which falls within the narrow range of the present
discussion.

There is
a limited
sense in
which the
doctrine is
generally
true.

    § 5. There is indeed one interpretation of the doctrine
according to which every position of equilibrium of demand
and supply may fairly be regarded as a position of maximum
satisfaction[1]. For it is true that so long as the demand price
is in excess of the supply price, exchanges can be effected at
prices which give a surplus of satisfaction to buyer or to
seller or to both. The marginal utility of what he receives
is greater than that of what he gives up, to at least one
of the two parties; while the other, if he does not gain by
the exchange, yet does not lose by it. So far then every
step in the exchange increases the aggregate satisfaction
of the two parties. But when equilibrium has been
reached, demand price being now equal to supply price, there
is no room for any such surplus: the marginal utility of
what each receives no longer exceeds that of what he gives
up in exchange: and when the production increases beyond

---

supply curve before the granting of the bounty, and *SS'* to be its position afterwards. Then, as in the case of fig. 31, the increase of consumers' surplus is
represented by *cCAa*, while the direct payments made by the State under the
bounty are represented by *RCAT*. As the figure is drawn, the former is much
larger than the latter. But it is true that if we had drawn *ss'* so as to indicate
a very slight action of the law of increasing return, that is, if it had been very
nearly horizontal in the neighbourhood of *a*, the bounty would have increased
relatively to the gain of consumers' surplus; and the case would have differed but
little from that of a bounty on a commodity which obeys the law of constant
return, represented in fig. 30.

[1] Compare V. i. 1. Unstable equilibrium may now be left out of account.

the equilibrium amount, the demand price being now less V, xiii, 5. than the supply price, no terms can be arranged which will be acceptable to the buyer, and will not involve a loss to the seller.

It is true then that a position of equilibrium of demand and supply is a position of maximum satisfaction in this limited sense, that the aggregate satisfaction of the two parties concerned increases until that position is reached; and that any production beyond the equilibrium amount could not be permanently maintained so long as buyers and sellers acted freely as individuals, each in his own interest.

But occasionally it is stated, and very often it is implied, But when that a position of equilibrium of demand and supply is one not taken
in this of maximum aggregate satisfaction in the full sense of the limited
sense, the term: that is, that an increase of production beyond the doctrine equilibrium level would directly (*i.e.* independently of the is open
to great difficulties of arranging for it, and of any indirect evils it exceptions. might cause) diminish the aggregate satisfaction of both parties. The doctrine so interpreted is not universally true.

In the first place it assumes that all differences in wealth It assumes between the different parties concerned may be neglected, that equal
sums of and that the satisfaction which is rated at a shilling by any money
measure one of them, may be taken as equal to one that is rated at equal
utilities a shilling by any other. Now it is obvious that, if the to all
concerned; producers were as a class very much poorer than the consumers, the aggregate satisfaction might be increased by a stinting of supply when it would cause a great rise in demand price (*i.e.* when the demand is inelastic); and that if the consumers were as a class much poorer than the producers, the aggregate satisfaction might be increased by extending the production beyond the equilibrium amount and selling the commodity at a loss[1].

This point however may well be left for future consideration. It is in fact only a special case of the broad proposition that the aggregate satisfaction can *primâ facie* be increased by the distribution, whether voluntarily or compulsorily, of

---

[1] In this illustration one of the two things exchanged is general purchasing power; but of course the argument would hold if a poor population of pearl divers were dependent for food on a rich population who took pearls in exchange.

V, xiii, 6. some of the property of the rich among the poor; and it is reasonable that the bearings of this proposition should be set aside during the first stages of an inquiry into existing economic conditions. This assumption therefore may be properly made, provided only it is not allowed to slip out of sight.

and it ignores the fact that a fall in price due to improvements benefits consumers without injuring producers.

But in the second place the doctrine of maximum satisfaction assumes that every fall in the price which producers receive for the commodity, involves a corresponding loss to them; and this is not true of a fall in price which results from improvements in industrial organization. When a commodity obeys the law of increasing return, an increase in its production beyond equilibrium point may cause the supply price to fall much; and though the demand price for the increased amount may be reduced even more, so that the production would result in some loss to the producers, yet this loss may be very much less than that money value of the gain to purchasers which is represented by the increase of consumers' surplus.

Aggregate satisfaction can therefore prima facie be increased beyond the level attained by the free play of demand and supply.

In the case then of commodities with regard to which the law of increasing return acts at all sharply, or in other words, for which the normal supply price diminishes rapidly as the amount produced increases, the direct expense of a bounty sufficient to call forth a greatly increased supply at a much lower price, would be much less than the consequent increase of consumers' surplus. And if a general agreement could be obtained among consumers, terms might be arranged which would make such action amply remunerative to the producers, at the same time that they left a large balance of advantage to the consumers[1].

We are not here concerned with the

§ 6. One simple plan would be the levying of a tax by the community on their own incomes, or on the production of goods which obey the law of diminishing return, and

[1] Though not of great practical importance, the case of multiple positions of (stable) equilibrium offers a good illustration of the error involved in the doctrine of maximum satisfaction when stated as a universal truth. For the position in which a small amount is produced and is sold at a high price would be the first to be reached, and when reached would be regarded according to that doctrine as that which gave the absolute maximum of aggregate satisfaction. But another position of equilibrium corresponding to a larger production and a lower price would be equally satisfactory to the producers, and would be much more satisfactory to the consumers; the excess of consumers' surplus in the second case over the first would represent the increase in aggregate satisfaction.

devoting the tax to a bounty on the production of those V, XIII, 6 goods with regard to which the law of increasing return indirect acts sharply. But before deciding on such a course they evils of would have to take account of considerations, which are artificial not within the scope of the general theory now before us, ments for but are yet of great practical importance. They would have this pur- to reckon up the direct and indirect costs of collecting a tax pose. and administering a bounty; the difficulty of securing that the burdens of the tax and the benefits of the bounty were equitably distributed; the openings for fraud and corruption; and the danger that in the trade which had got a bounty and in other trades which hoped to get one, people would divert their energies from managing their own businesses to managing those persons who control the bounties.

Besides these semi-ethical questions there will arise others of a strictly economic nature, relating to the effects which any particular tax or bounty may exert on the interests of landlords, urban or agricultural, who own land adapted for the production of the commodity in question. These are questions which must not be overlooked; but they differ so much in their detail that they cannot fully be discussed here[1].

---

[1] The incidence of a tax on agricultural produce will be discussed later on by the aid of diagrams similar to those used to represent the fertility of land. . . . Landlords' rent absorbs a share of the aggregate selling price of almost all commodities: but it is most prominent in the can of those which obey the law of diminishing return; and an assumption of no extreme violence will enable fig. 33 (a reproduction of 31) to represent roughly the leading features of the problem.

. . . [W]e are not properly at liberty to assume that the expenses of raising the produce from the richer lands and under the more favourable circumstances are independent of the extent to which the production is carried; since an increased production is likely to lead to an improved organization, if not of farming industries themselves, yet of those subsidiary to them, and especially of the carrying trade. We may however permit ourselves to make this assumption provisionally, so as to get a clear view of the broad outlines of the problem; though we must not forget that in any applications of the general reasonings based on it account must be taken of the facts which we here ignore. On this assumption then SS' being the supply curve before the imposition of a tax, landlords' rent is

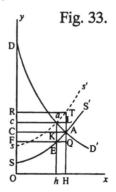

Fig. 33.

represented by CSA. After the tax has been imposed and the supply curve raised to ss' the landlords' rent becomes the amount by which cOha, the total price got for Oh

§ 7. Enough has been said to indicate the character of the second great limitation which has to be introduced into the doctrine that the maximum satisfaction is *generally* to be attained by encouraging each individual to spend his own resources in that way which suits him best. It is clear that if he spends his income in such a way as to increase the demand for the services of the poor and to increase their incomes, he adds something more to the total happiness than if he adds an equal amount to the incomes of the rich, because the happiness which an additional shilling brings to a poor man is much greater than that which it brings to a rich one; and that he does good by buying things the production of which raises, in preference to things the production of which lowers the character of those who make them[1]. But further, even if we assume that a shilling's worth of happiness is of equal importance to whomsoever it comes, and that every shilling's worth of consumers' surplus is of equal importance from whatever commodity it is derived, we have to admit that the manner in which a person spends his income is a matter of direct economic concern to the community. For in so far as he spends it on things which obey the law of diminishing return, he makes those things more difficult to be obtained by his neighbours, and thus lowers the real purchasing power of their incomes; while in so far

produce sold at the rate *ha*, exceeds the total tax *cFEa*, together with *OhES* the total expenses of production, exclusive of rent, for *Oh* produce: that is, it becomes *FSE*. (In the figure the curve *ss'* has the same shape as *SS'*, thereby implying that the tax is *specific*; that is, is a uniform charge on each unit of the commodity whatever be its value. The argument so far does not depend on this assumption, but if it is made we can by a shorter route get the new landlords' rent at *csa*, which then is equal to *FSE*.) Thus the loss of landlords' rent is *CFEA*; and this added to *cCAa* the loss of consumers' surplus, makes up *cFEAa*, which exceeds the gross tax by *aAE*.

On the other hand, the direct payment. under a bounty would exceed the increase of consumers' surplus, and of landlords' surplus calculated on the above assumptions. For taking *ss'* to be the original position of the supply curve, and *SS'* to be its position after the bounty, the new landlords' surplus on these assumptions is *CSA*, or which is the same thing *RsT*; and this exceeds the old landlords' rent *csa* by *RcaT*. The increase of consumers' surplus is *cCAa*; and therefore the total bounty, which is *RCAT*, exceeds the gain of consumers' surplus and landlords' rent together by *TaA*.

... [T]he assumption on which this reasoning proceeds is inapplicable to cases in which the supply curve is inclined negatively.

[1] Compare III. vi.

as he spends it on things which obey the law of increasing
return, he makes those things more easy of attainment to
others, and thus increases the real purchasing power of their
incomes.

Again, it is commonly argued that an equal *ad valorem*
tax levied on all economic commodities (material and immaterial), or which is the same thing a tax on expenditure,
is *primâ facie* the best tax; because it does not divert the
expenditure of individuals out of its natural channels: we
have now seen that this argument is invalid. But ignoring
for the time the fact that the direct economic effect of a tax
or a bounty never constitutes the whole, and very often not
even the chief part of the considerations which have to be
weighed before deciding to adopt it, we have found:—firstly,
that a tax on expenditure generally causes a greater destruction of consumers' surplus than one levied exclusively on commodities as to which there is but little room for the economies
of production on a large scale, and which obey the law of
diminishing return; and secondly, that it might even be
for the advantage of the community that the government
should levy taxes on commodities which obey the law of
diminishing return, and devote part of the proceeds to
bounties on commodities which obey the law of increasing
return.

These conclusions, it will be observed, do not by themselves afford a valid ground for government interference.
But they show that much remains to be done, by a careful
collection of the statistics of demand and supply, and a
scientific interpretation of their results, in order to discover
what are the limits of the work that society can with advantage do towards turning the economic actions of individuals
into those channels in which they will add the most to the
sum total of happiness[1].

[1] It is remarkable that Malthus, *Political Economy*, ch. III. § 9, argued that,
though the difficulties thrown in the way of importing foreign corn during the
great war turned capital from the more profitable employment of manufacture to
the less profitable employment of agriculture, yet if we take account of the consequent increase of agricultural rent, we may conclude that the new channel may
have been one of "higher national, though not higher individual profits." In
this no doubt he was right; but he overlooked the far more important injury
inflicted on the public by the consequent rise in the price of corn, and the

V, xiii, 7. consequent destruction of consumers' surplus. Senior takes account of the interests of the consumer in his study of the different effects of increased demand on the one hand and of taxation on the other in the case of agricultural and manufactured produce (*Political Economy*, pp. 118–123). Advocates of Protection in countries which export raw produce have made use of arguments tending in the same direction as those given in this Chapter; and similar arguments are now used, especially in America (as for instance by Mr H. C. Adams), in support of the active participation of the State in industries which conform to the law of increasing return. The graphic method has been applied, in a manner somewhat similar to that adopted in the present Chapter, by Dupuit in 1844; and, independently, by Fleeming Jenkin (*Edinburgh Philosophical Transactions*) in 1871.

CHAPTER XIV.

THE THEORY OF MONOPOLIES.

§ 1. It has never been supposed that the monopolist in seeking his own advantage is naturally guided in that course which is most conducive to the wellbeing of society regarded as a whole, he himself being reckoned as of no more importance than any other member of it. The doctrine of Maximum Satisfaction has never been applied to the demand for and supply of monopolized commodities. But there is much to be learnt from a study of the relations in which the interests of the monopolist stand to those of the rest of society, and of the general conditions under which it might be possible to make arrangements more beneficial to society as a whole than those which he would adopt if he consulted only his own interests: and with this end in view we are now to seek for a scheme for comparing the relative quantities of the benefits which may accrue to the public and to the monopolist from the adoption of different courses of action by him.

In a later volume a study will be made of the Protean shapes of modern trade combinations and monopolies, some of the most important of which, as for example "Trusts," are of very recent growth. At present we consider only those general causes determining monopoly values, that can be traced with more or less distinctness in every case in which a single person or association of persons has the power of fixing either the amount of a commodity that is offered for sale or the price at which it is offered.

§ 2. The *primâ facie* interest of the owner of a monopoly is clearly to adjust the supply to the demand, not in such a way that the price at which he can sell his commodity shall just cover its expenses of production, but in such a way as to afford him the greatest possible total net revenue.

But here we meet with a difficulty as to the meaning of the term Net revenue. For the supply price of a freely-produced commodity includes normal profits; the whole of which, or at all events what remains of them after deducting interest on the capital employed and insurance against loss, is often classed indiscriminately as net revenue. And when a man manages his own business, he often does not distinguish carefully that portion of his profits, which really is his own earnings of management, from any exceptional gains arising from the fact that the business is to some extent of the nature of a monopoly.

This difficulty however is in a great measure avoided in the case of a public company; where all, or nearly all, the expenses of management are entered in the ledger as definite sums, and are subtracted from the total receipts of the company before its net income is declared.

The net income divided among the shareholders includes interest on the capital invested and insurance against risk of failure, but little or no earnings of management; so that the amount by which the dividends are in excess of what may fairly be allowed as interest and insurance, is the *Monopoly Revenue* which we are seeking.

Since then it is much easier to specify exactly the amount of this net revenue when a monopoly is owned by a public company than when it is owned by an individual or private firm, let us take as a typical instance the case of a gas company that has the monopoly of the supply of gas to a town. For the sake of simplicity the company may be supposed to have already invested the whole of its own capital in fixed plant, and to borrow any more capital, that it may want to extend its business, on debentures at a fixed rate of interest.

The demand schedule is as usual; § 3. The demand schedule for gas remains the same as it would be if gas were a freely-produced commodity; it specifies the price per thousand feet at which consumers

in the town will among them use any given number of V, xiv, 8.
feet. But the supply schedule must represent the normal but the
expenses of production of each several amount supplied; and supply
these include interest on all its capital, whether belonging must be
to its shareholders or borrowed on debentures, at a fixed a special
normal rate; they include also the salaries of its directors, plan.
and permanent officials, adjusted (more or less accurately) to
the work required of them, and therefore increasing with an
increase in the output of gas. A *monopoly revenue schedule* The
may then be constructed thus:—Having set against each *Monopoly revenue*
several amount of the commodity its demand price, and its *schedule.*
supply price estimated on the plan just described, subtract
each supply price from the corresponding demand price and
set the residue in the monopoly revenue column against
the corresponding amount of the commodity.

Thus for instance if a thousand million feet could be sold
annually at a price of 3s. per thousand feet, and the supply
price for this amount were 2s. 9d. per thousand feet, the
monopoly revenue schedule would show 3d. against this
amount; indicating an aggregate net revenue when this
amount was sold, of three million pence, or £12,500. The
aim of the company, having regard only to their own immediate dividends, will be to fix the price of their gas at such
a level as to make this aggregate net revenue the largest
possible[1].

[1] Thus DD' being the demand curve, and SS' the curve corresponding to the
supply schedule described in the text, let MP_2P_1 be drawn vertically from any
point M in Ox, cutting SS' in P_2 and DD' in P_1; and from it cut off $MP_3=P_2P_1$,
then the locus of P_3 will be our third curve, QQ', which we may call the
monopoly revenue curve. The supply price for a small quantity of gas will of
course be very high; and in the neighbourhood of Oy the supply curve will be
above the demand curve, and therefore the net revenue curve will be below Ox.
It will cut Ox in K and again in H, points which are vertically under B and
A, the two points of intersection of the demand and supply curves. The maximum monopoly revenue will then be obtained by finding a point q_3 on QQ'
such that Lq_3 being drawn perpendicular to Ox, $OL \times Lq_3$ is a maximum.
Lq_3 being produced to cut SS' in q_2 and DD' in q_1, the company, if desiring to
obtain the greatest immediate monopoly revenue, will fix the price per thousand
feet at Lq_1, and consequently will sell OL thousand feet; the expenses of production will be Lq_2 per thousand feet, and the aggregate net revenue will be
$OL \times q_2q_1$, or which is the same thing $OL \times Lq_3$.

The dotted lines in the diagram are known to mathematicians as rectangular
hyperbolas; but we may call them *constant revenue curves*: for they are such
that if from a point on any one of them lines be drawn perpendicular to Ox

A tax,
fixed in
total
amount,
on a mo-
nopoly

§ 4. Now suppose that a change takes place in the conditions of supply; some new expense has to be incurred, or
some old expense can be avoided; or perhaps a new tax is
imposed on the undertaking or a bounty is awarded to it.

First let this increase or diminution of the expenses be a
fixed sum, bearing on the undertaking as one undivided
whole and not varying with the amount of the commodity
produced. Then, whatever be the price charged and the

and Oy respectively (the one representing revenue per thousand feet and the other
representing the number of thousand feet sold), then the product of these

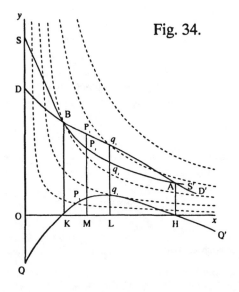

Fig. 34.

will be a constant quantity for every point on one and the same curve. This product
is of course a smaller quantity for the inner curves, these nearer Ox and Oy than it is
for the outer curves. And consequently since P_3 is on a smaller constant revenue
curve than q_3 is, $OM \times MP_3$ is less than $OL \times Lq_3$. It will be noticed that that q_3 is the
point in which QQ' touches one of these curves. That is, q_3 is on a larger constant
revenue curve than is any other point on QQ'; and therefore $OL \times Lq_3$ is greater than
$OM \times MP_y$ not only in the position given to M in the figure, but also in any position
that M can take along Ox. That is to say, q_3 has been correctly determined as the
point on QQ' corresponding to the maximum total monopoly revenue. And thus we
get the rule:—if through that point in which QQ' touches one of a series of constant
revenue curves, a line be drawn vertically to cut the demand curve, then the distance
of that point of intersection from Ox will be the price at which the commodity should
be offered for sale in order that it may afford the maximum monopoly revenue. . . .

amount of the commodity sold, the monopoly revenue will V, xiv, 4.
be increased or diminished, as the case may be, by this sum; will not
and therefore that selling price which afforded the maximum diminish
monopoly revenue before the change will afford it after- produc-
wards; the change therefore will not offer to the monopolist tion;
any inducement to alter his course of action. Suppose for
instance that the maximum monopoly revenue is got when
twelve hundred million cubic feet are sold annually; and
that this is done when the price is fixed at 30d. per thousand
feet: suppose that the expenses of production for this amount
are at the rate of 26d., leaving a monopoly revenue at the
rate of four pence per thousand feet, that is £20,000 in all.
This is its maximum value: if the company fixed the price
higher at, say, 31d. and sold only eleven hundred million feet,
they would perhaps get a monopoly revenue at the rate of
4·2 pence per thousand feet, that is £19,250 in all; while in
order to sell thirteen hundred millions they would have to
lower their price to, say, 28d. and would get a monopoly
revenue at the rate of perhaps 3·6d. per thousand feet, that
is £19,500 in all. Thus by fixing the price at 30d. they
get £750 more than by fixing it at 31d., and £500 more
than by fixing it at 28d. Now let a tax of £10,000 a year
be levied on the gas company as a fixed sum independent
of the amount they sell. Their monopoly revenue will
become £10,000 if they charge 30d., £9,250 if they charge
31d., and £9,500 if they charge 28d. They will therefore
continue to charge 30d.

The same is true of a tax or a bounty proportioned not nor will
to the gross receipts of the undertaking, but to its monopoly one propor-
tioned to
revenue. For suppose next that a tax is levied, not of one monopoly
fixed sum, but a certain percentage, say 50 per cent. of the revenue,
monopoly revenue. The company will then retain a monopoly revenue of £10,000 if they charge 30d., of £9,625 if
they charge 31d., and of £9,750 if they charge 28d. They
will therefore still charge 30d.[1]

---

[1] If to the expenses of working a monopoly there be added (by a tax or
otherwise) a lump sum independent of the amount produced, the result will
be to cause every point on the monopoly revenue curve to move downwards
to a point on a constant revenue curve representing a constant revenue smaller
by a *fixed amount* than that on which it lies. Therefore the maximum revenue

but it will
have that
effect if it
is propor-
tional to
the quan-
tity pro-
duced.

On the other hand a tax proportional to the amount produced gives an inducement to the monopolist to lessen his
output and raise his price. For by so doing he diminishes his
expenses. And the excess of total receipts over total outlay
may therefore be now increased by a diminution of output;
though before the imposition of the tax it would have been
lessened. Further, if before the imposition of the tax the net
revenue was only a little greater than that which would have
been afforded by much smaller sales, then the monopolist
would gain by reducing his production very greatly; and
hence in such cases as this, the change is likely to cause a
very great diminution of production and rise of price. The
opposite effects will be caused by a change which diminishes the expense of working the monopoly by a sum that
varies directly with the amount produced under it.

In the last example, for instance, a tax of 2d. on each
thousand feet sold would have reduced the monopoly revenue to £10,083 if the company charged 31d. per thousand
feet and therefore sold eleven hundred millions; to £10,000
if they charged 30d. and therefore sold twelve hundred millions, and to £8,666 if they charged 28d. and therefore sold
thirteen hundred million feet. Therefore the tax would
induce the company to raise the price to something higher
than 30d.; they would perhaps go to 31d., perhaps somewhat higher; for the figures before us do not show exactly
how far it would be their interest to go.

On the other hand, if there were a bounty of 2d. on the
sale of each thousand feet, the monopoly revenue would
rise to £28,416 if they charged 31d., to £30,000 if they
charged 30d., and to £30,333 if they charged 28d.: it would
therefore cause them to lower the price. And of course the

point on the new monopoly revenue curve lies vertically below that on the old: that
is, the selling price and the amount produced remain unchanged, and conversely with
regard to a fixed bounty or other fixed diminution of aggregate working
expenses. . . .

It should however be noticed that if a tax or other now additional expense
exceeds the maximum monopoly revenue, it will prevent the monopoly from being
worked at all; it will convert the price which had afforded the maximum monopoly
revenue into the price which would reduce to a minimum the loss that would result
from continuing to work the monopoly.

same result would follow from an improvement in the method of making gas, which lowered its cost of production to the monopolist company by 2*d*. per 1000 feet[1].

> [1] In the text it is supposed that the tax or bounty is directly proportional to the sales: but the argument, when closely examined, will be found to involve no further assumption than that the aggregate tax or bounty increases with every increase in that amount: the argument does not really require that it should increase in exact proportion to that amount.

Much instruction is to be got by drawing diagrams to represent various conditions of demand and of (monopoly) supply, with the resultant shapes of the monopoly revenue curve. A careful study of the shapes thus obtained will give more assistance than any elaborate course of reasoning in the endeavour to realize the multiform action of economic forces in relation to monopolies. A tracing may be made on thin paper of the constant revenue curves in one of the diagrams; and this, when laid over a monopoly revenue curve, will indicate at once the point, or points, of maximum revenue. For it will be found, not only when the demand and supply curves cut one another more than once, but also when

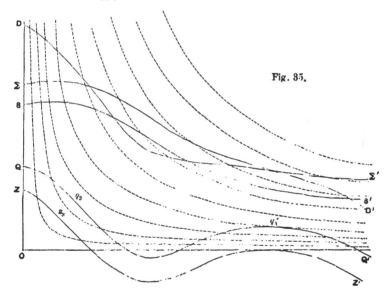

Fig. 35.

they do not, there will often be, as in fig. 35, several points on a monopoly revenue curve at which it touches a constant revenue curve. Each of these points will show a true maximum monopoly revenue; but one of them will generally stand out pre-eminently as being on a larger constant revenue curve than any of the others and therefore indicating a larger monopoly revenue than they.

If it happens, as in fig. 35, that this chief maximum q'_3 lies a long way to the right of a smaller maximum q_3, then the imposition of a tax on the commodity, or any other change that raised its supply curve throughout, would lower by an equal amount the monopoly revenue curve. Let the supply curve be raised from SS' to the position $\Sigma\Sigma'$; and in consequence let the monopoly

V, xiv, 5.

In comparing price with competition price,

§ 5. The monopolist would lose all his monopoly revenue if he produced for sale an amount so great that its supply price, as here defined, was equal to its demand price: the amount which gives the maximum monopoly revenue is always considerably less than that. It may therefore appear as though the amount produced under a monopoly is always less and its price to the consumer always higher than if there were no monopoly. But this is not the case.

it must be remembered that a monopoly can generally be worked economically.

For when the production is all in the hands of one person or company, the total expenses involved are generally less than would have to be incurred if the same aggregate production were distributed among a multitude of comparatively small rival producers. They would have to struggle with one another for the attention of consumers, and would necessarily spend in the aggregate a great deal more on advertising in all its various forms than a single firm would; and they would be less able to avail themselves of the many various economies which result from production on a large scale. In particular they could not afford to spend as much on improving methods of production and the machinery used in it, as a single large firm which knew that it was certain itself to reap the whole benefit of any advance it made.

This argument does indeed assume the single firm to be managed with ability and enterprise, and to have an unlimited command of capital—an assumption which cannot always be fairly made. But where it can be made, we may generally conclude that the supply schedule for the commodity, if not monopolized, would show higher supply prices

revenue curve fall from its old position QQ' to ZZ'; then the chief point of maximum revenue will move from q'_2 to z_2, representing a great diminution of production, a great rise of price and a great injury to the consumers. The converse effects of any change, such as a bounty on the commodity, which lowers its supply price throughout and raises the monopoly revenue curve, may be seen by regarding ZZ' as the old and QQ' as the new position of that curve. It will be obvious on a little consideration (but the fact may with advantage be illustrated by drawing suitable diagrams), that the more nearly the monopoly revenue curve approximates to the shape of a constant revenue curve, the greater will be the change in the position of the maximum revenue point which results from any given alteration in the expenses of production of the commodity generally. This change is great in fig. 35 not because DD' and SS' intersect more than once, but because two parts of QQ', one a long way to the right of the other, lie in the neighbourhood of the same constant revenue curve.

than those of our monopoly supply schedule; and therefore
the equilibrium amount of the commodity produced under
free competition would be less than that for which the demand price is equal to the monopoly supply price[1].

One of the most interesting and difficult applications of
the theory of monopolies is to the question whether the public
interest is best served by the allotment of a distinct basin to
each great railway, and excluding competition there. For the
proposal it is urged that a railway can afford to carry two million passengers, or tons of goods, cheaper than one million:
and that a division of the public demand between two lines
will prevent either of them from offering a cheap service. It
must be admitted that, other things being equal, the "monopoly revenue price" fixed by a railway will be lowered by
every increase in the demand for its services, and *vice versâ*.
But, human nature being what it is, experience has shown that
the breaking of a monopoly by the opening out of a competing
line accelerates, rather than retards the discovery by the older
line that it can afford to carry traffic at lower rates. There still
remains the suggestion that after a while the railways will
combine and charge the public with the expense wasted on
duplicating the services. But this again only opens out new
matters of controversy. The theory of monopolies starts rather
than solves practical issues such as these: and we must defer
their study[2].

But this raises questions which are incapable of general solution.

---

[1] In other words, though *L* lies necessarily a good deal to the left of *H*, according
to the notation in fig. 34; yet the supply curve for the commodity, if there were no
monopoly, might lie so much above the present position of *SS'* that its point of intersection with *DD'* would lie much to the left of *A* in the figure, and might not improb-
ably lie to the left of *L*. Something has already been said (. . . V. XI.) as to the advantages which a single powerful firm has over its smaller rivals in those industries in
which the law of increasing return acts strongly; and as to the chance which it might
have of obtaining a practical monopoly of its own branch of production, if it were
managed for many generations together by people whose genius, enterprise and
energy equalled those of the original founders of the business.

[2] The full theoretical treatment of questions relating to the influence exerted on
monopoly price by an increase of demand requires the use of mathematics for which the
reader is referred to an article on monopolies by Professor Edgeworth in the *Giornale degli
Economisti* for Oct. 1897. But an inspection of fig. 34 will show that a uniform raising of
DD' will push *L* much to the right; and that the resulting position of q_1 will probably be lower
than before. If, however, a new class of residents come into the district, who are so well to
do, that their willingness to travel is very little affected by the railway charges, then

V, xiv, 6.

The
monopolist
may lower
his price
with a
view to
the future
develop-
ment of his
business,

§ **6.** So far we have supposed the owner of a monopoly to fix the price of his commodity with exclusive reference to the immediate net revenue which he can derive from it. But, in fact, even if he does not concern himself with the interests of the consumers, he is likely to reflect that the demand for a thing depends in a great measure on people's familiarity with it; and that if he can increase his sales by taking a price a little below that which would afford him the maximum net revenue, the increased use of his commodity will before long recoup him for his present loss. The lower the price of gas, the more likely people are to have it laid on to their houses; and when once it is there, they are likely to go on making some use of it, even though a rival, such as electricity or mineral oil, may be competing closely with it. The case is stronger when a railway company has a practical monopoly of the transport of persons and goods to a sea-port, or to a suburban district which is as yet but partly built over; the railway company may then find it worth while, as a matter of business, to levy charges much below those which would afford the maximum net revenue, in order to get merchants into the habit of using the port, to encourage the inhabitants of the port to develop their docks and warehouses; or to assist speculative builders in the new suburb to build houses cheaply and to fill them quickly with tenants, thus giving to the suburb an air of early prosperity which goes far towards insuring its permanent success. This sacrifice by a monopolist of part of his present gains in order to develop future business differs in extent rather than kind from the sacrifices which a young firm commonly makes in order to establish a connection.

In such cases as these a railway company though not pretending to any philanthropic motives, yet finds its own interests so closely connected with those of the purchasers of its services, that it gains by making some temporary sacrifice of net revenue with the purpose of increasing consumers' surplus. And an even closer connection between the interests of the producers and the consumers is found when the land-

the shape of *DD'* will be altered; its left side will be raised more in proportion than its right; and the new position of q_1 may be higher than the old.

owners of any district combine to make a branch railway V, xiv, 7.
through it, without much hope that the traffic will afford
the current rate of interest on the capital which they
invest—that is, without much hope that the monopoly
revenue of the railway, as we have defined it, will be other
than a negative quantity—but expecting that the railway
will add so much to the value of their property as to make
their venture on the whole a profitable one. And when or from
a municipality undertakes the supply of gas or water, or interest
facilities for transport by improved roads, by new bridges, welfare of
or by tramways, the question always arises whether the scale consumers.
of charges should be high, so as to afford a good net revenue
and relieve the pressure on the rates; or should be low, so as
to increase consumers' surplus.

§ 7. It is clear then that some study is wanted of
calculations by which a monopolist should govern his actions,
on the supposition that he regards an increase of consumers'
surplus as equally desirable to him, if not with an equal
increase of his own monopoly revenue, yet with an increase,
say, one-half or one-quarter as great.

If the consumers' surplus which arises from the sale of the The total
commodity at any price, is added to the monopoly revenue monopoly
derived from it, the sum of the two is the money measure of of the
the net benefits accruing from the sale of the commodity to monopoly
producers and consumers together, or as we may say the and con-
total benefit of its sale. And if the monopolist regards a gain to surplus.
the consumers as of equal importance with an equal gain to
himself, his aim will be to produce just that amount of the
commodity which will make this total benefit a maximum[1].

[1] In fig. 36 DD', SS', and QQ' represent the demand, supply, and monopoly
revenue curves drawn on the same plan as in fig. 34. From P_1 draw P_1F
perpendicular to Oy; then DFP_1 is the consumers' surplus derived from the sale
of OM thousand feet of gas at the price MP_1. In MP_1 take a point P_4 such that
$OM \times MP_4$=the area DFP_1: then as M moves from O along Ox, P_4 will trace
out our fourth curve, OR, which we may call the consumers' surplus curve. (Of
course it passes through O, because when the sale of the commodity is reduced to
nothing, the consumers' surplus also vanishes.)

Next from P_3P_1 cut off P_3P_5 equal to MP_4, so that $MP_5=MP_3+MP$
Then $OM \times MP_5=OM \times MP_3+OM \times MP_4$: but $OM \times MP_3$ is the total monopoly
revenue when an amount OM is being sold at a price MP_1, and $OM \times MP_4$ is the
corresponding consumers' surplus. Therefore $OM \times MP_5$ is the sum of the monopoly revenue and the consumers' surplus, that is the (money measure of the) total
benefit which the community will derive from the commodity when an amount

V, xiv, 7.   But it will seldom happen that the monopolist can and

But if the will treat £1 of consumers' surplus as equally desirable with
consumers'
surplus be £1 of monopoly revenue. Even a government which con-
counted
at only a siders its own interests coincident with those of the people
fraction of has to take account of the fact that, if it abandons one source
its actual
value, the of revenue, it must in general fall back on others which have
sum of the
two may their own disadvantages. For they will necessarily involve
be called
compromise friction and expense in collection, together with some injury
benefit. to the public, of the kind which we have described as a loss
of consumers' surplus: and they can never be adjusted with
perfect fairness, especially when account is taken of the
unequal shares that different members of the community
will get of the benefits for the sake of which it is proposed
that the government should forego some of its revenue.

OM is produced. The locus of P_5 is our fifth curve, *QT*, which we may call the
total benefit curve. It touches one of the constant revenue curves at t_5, and this

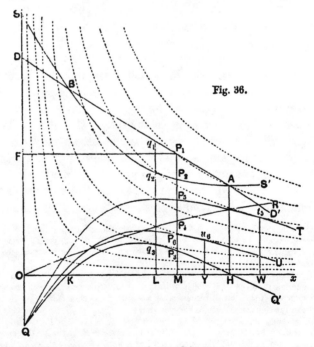

Fig. 36.

shows that the (money measure of the) total benefit is a maximum when the
amount offered for sale is *OW*; or, which is the same thing, when the price of
sale is fixed at the demand price for *OW*.

Suppose then that the monopolist makes a compromise, V, XIV, 8.
and reckons £1 of consumers' surplus as equivalent to say
10s. of monopoly revenue. Let him calculate the monopoly
revenue to be got from selling his commodity at any given
price, and to it let him add one half the corresponding consumers' surplus: the sum of the two may be called the *compromise benefit*; and his aim will be to fix on that price which
will make the compromise benefit as large as possible[1].

The following general results are capable of exact proof; General
but on a little consideration they will appear so manifestly results.
true as hardly to require proof. Firstly, the amount which the
monopolist will offer for sale will be greater (and the price at
which he will sell it will be less) if he is to any extent desirous
to promote the interests of consumers than if his sole aim is to
obtain the greatest possible monopoly revenue; and secondly,
the amount produced will be greater (and the selling price will
be less) the greater be the desire of the monopolist to promote
the interests of consumers; *i.e.* the larger be the percentage of
its actual value at which he counts in consumers' surplus with
his own revenue[2].

§ 8. Not many years ago it was commonly argued that: The impor-
"An English ruler, who looks upon himself as the minister tance of the
interests of
of the race he rules, is bound to take care that he impresses consumers
their energies in no work that is not worth the labour that has been
is spent upon it, or—to translate the sentiment into plainer underestimated,
language—that he engages in nothing that will not produce
an income sufficient to defray the interest on its cost[3]."

---

[1] If he compromises on the basis that £1 of consumers' surplus is equally desirable
with £n of monopoly revenue, n being a proper fraction, let us take a point P_6 in P_3P_5 such
that $P_3P_6 = n.P_3P_5$, or, which is the same thing, nMP_4. Then $OM \times MP_6 = OM \times MP_3$, +
$nOM \times MP_4$; that is, it is equal to the monopoly revenue derived from selling an amount
OM of the commodity at the price MP_1, + n times the consumers' surplus derived from
this sale: and is therefore the compromise benefit derived from that sale. The locus of P_6
is our sixth curve, QU, which we may call the *compromise benefit curve*. It touches one
of the constant revenue curves in u_6; which shows that the compromise benefit attains it.
maximum when amount OY is sold; or which is the same thing, when the selling price is
fixed at the demand price for the amount OY.

[2] That is to say, firstly, OY fig. 36 is always greater than OL; and secondly, the
greater n is, the greater OY is. . . .

[3] The words are quoted from a leading article in *The Times* for July 30, 1874:
they fairly represent a great body of public opinion.

V, XIV, 8. Such phrases as this may sometimes have meant little more than that a benefit which consumers were not willing to purchase at a high price and on a large scale, was likely to exist for the greater part only in the specious counsels of those who had some personal interest in the proposed undertakings; but probably they more often indicated a tendency to under-estimate the magnitude of that interest which consumers have in a low price, and which we call consumers' surplus[1].

[1] Fig. 37 may be taken to represent the case of a proposed Government undertaking in India. The supply curve is above the demand curve during

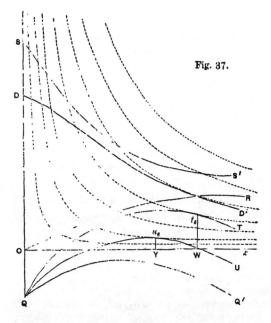

Fig. 37.

its whole length, showing that the enterprise to which it refers is unremunerative, in the sense that whatever price the producers fix, they will lose money; their monopoly revenue will be a negative quantity. But QT the total benefit curve rises above Ox; and touches a constant revenue curve in t_5. If then they offer for sale an amount OW (or, which is the same thing, fix the price at the demand price for OW), the resultant consumers' surplus, if taken at its full value, will outweigh the loss on working by an amount represented by $OW \times Wt_5$. But suppose that, in order to make up the deficiency, Government must levy taxes, and that taking account of all indirect expenses and other evils, these cost the public twice what they bring in to the Government, it will then be necessary to count two rupees of the consumers' surplus as

One of the chief elements of success in private business is the faculty of weighing the advantages and disadvantages of any proposed course, and of assigning to them their true relative importance. He who by practice and genius has acquired the power of attributing to each factor its right quantity, is already well on the way to fortune; and the increase in the efficiency of our productive forces is in a great measure due to the large number of able minds who are devoting themselves ceaselessly to acquiring these business instincts. But unfortunately the advantages thus weighed against one another are nearly all regarded from one point of view, that of the producer; and there are not many who concern themselves to weigh against one another the relative quantities of the interests which the consumers and the producers have in different courses of action. For indeed the requisite facts come within the direct experience of only a very few persons, and even in the case of those few, only to a very limited extent and in a very imperfect way. Moreover when a great administrator has acquired those instincts with regard to public interests which able business men have with regard to their own affairs, he is not very likely to be able to carry his plans with a free hand. At all events in a democratic country no great public undertaking is secure of being sustained on consistent lines of policy, unless its advantages can be made clear, not only to the few who have direct experience of high public affairs, but also to the many who have no such experience and have to form their judgment on the materials set before them by others.

Judgments of this kind must always be inferior to those which an able business man forms, by the aid of instincts based on long experience with regard to his own business. But they may be made much more trustworthy than they

V, XIV, 8.

——

because direct personal experience is seldom helps much towards forming correct estimates of them,

and our public statistics are not yet properly organized.

compensating for a Government outlay of only one rupee; and in order to represent the net gain of the undertaking on this supposition, we must draw the compromise benefit curve QU as in fig. 36, but putting $n = \frac{1}{2}$. Thus $MP_6 = MP_8 + MP_4$. (Another way of putting the same thing is to say that QU is drawn midway between the monopoly revenue (negative) curve QQ' and the total benefit curve QT.) QU so drawn in fig. 37 touches a constant revenue curve in u_6, showing that if the amount OY is offered for sale, or, which is the same thing, if the price is fixed at the demand price for OY, there will result a net gain to India represented by $OY \times Yu_6$.

are at present, if they can be based on statistical measures of the relative quantities of the benefits and the injuries which different courses of public action are likely to cause to the several classes of the community. Much of the failure and much of the injustice, in which the economic policies of governments have resulted, have been due to the want of statistical measurement. A few people who have been strongly interested on one side have raised their voices loudly, persistently and all together; while little has been heard from the great mass of people whose interests have lain in the opposite direction; for, even if their attention has been fairly called to the matter, few have cared to exert themselves much for a cause in which no one of them has more than a small stake. The few therefore get their way, although if statistical measures of the interests involved were available, it might prove that the aggregate of the interests of the few was only a tenth or a hundredth part of the aggregate of the interests of the silent many.

Statistical arguments are often misleading at first; but free discussion clears away statistical fallacies. No doubt statistics can be easily misinterpreted; and are often very misleading when first applied to new problems. But many of the worst fallacies involved in the misapplications of statistics are definite and can be definitely exposed, till at last no one ventures to repeat them even when addressing an uninstructed audience: and on the whole arguments which can be reduced to statistical forms, though still in a backward condition, are making more sure and more rapid advances than any others towards obtaining the general acceptance of all who have studied the subjects to which they refer. The rapid growth of collective interests, and the increasing tendency towards collective action in economic affairs, make it every day more important that we should know what quantitative measures of public interests are most needed and what statistics are required for them, and that we should set ourselves to obtain these statistics.

Hopes for the future from the statistical study of demand and consumers' surplus. It is perhaps not unreasonable to hope that as time goes on, the statistics of consumption will be so organized as to afford demand schedules sufficiently trustworthy, to show in diagrams that will appeal to the eye, the quantities of consumers' surplus that will result from different courses of

public and private action.   By the study of these pictures V, xiv, 9.
the mind may be gradually trained to get juster notions of
the relative magnitudes of the interests which the community
has in various schemes of public and private enterprise; and
sounder doctrines may replace those traditions of an earlier
generation, which had perhaps a wholesome influence in
their time, but which damped social enthusiasm by throwing
suspicion on all projects for undertakings by the public on
its own behalf which would not show a balance of direct
pecuniary profit.

The practical bearings of many of the abstract reasonings
in which we have recently been engaged will not be fully
apparent till we approach the end of this treatise.   But
there seemed to be advantages in introducing them thus
early, partly because of their close connection with the main
theory of equilibrium of demand and supply, and partly
because they throw side lights on the character and the
purposes of that investigation of the causes which determine
distribution on which we are about to enter.

§ 9.   So far it has been assumed that the monopolist can The problem of two monopolies dependent on each other's aid is incapable of a universal solution.
buy and sell freely.   But in fact monopolistic combinations
in one branch of industry foster the growth of monopolistic
combinations in those which have occasion to buy from or
sell to it: and the conflicts and alliances between such associations play a rôle of ever increasing importance in modern
economics.   Abstract reasoning of a general character has
little to say on the subject.   If two absolute monopolies
are complementary, so that neither can turn its products
to any good account, without the other's aid, there is no
means of determining where the price of the ultimate product will be fixed.   Thus if we supposed, following Cournot's
lead, that copper and zinc were each of them useless except
when combined to make brass: and if we supposed that one
man, A, owned all the available sources of supply of copper;
while another, B, owned all those of zinc; there would then
be no means of determining beforehand what amount of
brass would be produced, nor therefore the price at which it
could be sold.   Each would try to get the better of the
other in bargaining; and though the issue of the contest

V, xiv, 9. would greatly affect the purchasers, they would not be able
to influence it[1].

There
are *primâ
facie*
reasons for
thinking
that the
public
interest
calls for
their
fusion,

Under the conditions supposed, A could not count on
reaping the whole, nor even any share at all of the benefit,
from increased sales, that would be got by lowering the
price of copper in a market in which the price of zinc
was fixed by natural causes rather than strategical higgling
and bargaining. For, if he reduced his price, B might take
the action as a sign of commercial weakness, and raise the
price of zinc; thus causing A to lose both on price and
on amount sold. Each would therefore be tempted to bluff
the other; and consumers might find that less brass was put
on the market, and that therefore a higher price could be
exacted for it, than if a single monopolist owned the whole
supplies both of copper and of zinc: for he might see his way
to gaining in the long run by a low price which stimulated
consumption. But neither A nor B could reckon on the
effects of his own action, unless the two came together and
agreed on a common policy: that is unless they made a
partial, and perhaps temporary fusion of their monopolies.
On this ground, and because monopolies are likely to disturb allied industries it may reasonably be urged that the
public interest generally requires that complementary monopolies should be held in a single hand.

but such
a fusion
would in
many cases
introduce
greater
and more
lasting
discords
than it
removed.

But there are other considerations of perhaps greater
importance on the other side. For in real life there are
scarcely any monopolies as absolute and permanent as that
just discussed. On the contrary there is in the modern
world an ever increasing tendency towards the substitution
of new things and new methods for old, which are not being
developed progressively in the interests of consumers; and

---

[1] Thus there is a slight analogy between this case and that of composite rent
óf water power, and the only site on which it could be turned to account (see
above V. xi. 7), so far as the indeterminateness of the division of the producer's
surplus is concerned. But in this case there is no means of knowing what the
producer's surplus will be. Cournot's fundamental equations appear to be based
on inconsistent assumptions, see *Recherches sur les principes mathématiques des
Richesses*, Ch. ix. p. 113. Here, as elsewhere, he opened up new ground, but
overlooked some of its most obvious features. Prof. H. L. Moore (*Quarterly
Journal of Economics*, Feb. 1906), basing himself partly on the work of Bertrand
and Prof. Edgeworth, lays down clearly the assumptions which are appropriate to
monopoly problems.

the direct or indirect competition thus brought to bear is V, xiv, 9.
likely to weaken the position of one of the complementary
monopolies more than the other. For instance if there be
only one factory for spinning and only one for weaving in
a small isolated country, it may be for the time to the public
interest that the two should be in the same hands. But the
monopoly so established will be much harder to shake than
would either half of it separately. For a new venturer
might push his way into the spinning business and compete
with the old spinning mill for the custom of the old weaving
sheds.

Consider again a through route, partly by rail and partly
by sea, between two great centres of industry. If competition on either half of the route were permanently impossible,
it would probably be to the public interest that the ships and
the railway line should be in the same hands. But as things
are, no such general statement can be made. Under some
conditions it is more to the public interest that they should
be in one hand; under others, and those perhaps the conditions that occur the more frequently, it is in the long run
to the public interest that they should remain in different
hands.

Similarly the *primâ facie* arguments in favour of the
fusion of monopolistic cartels, or other associations, in complementary branches of industry, though often plausible and
even strong, will generally be found on closer examination
to be treacherous. They point to the removal of prominent
social and industrial discords; but at the probable expense
of larger and more enduring discords in the future[1].

---

[1] Book III. of *Industry and Trade* is occupied with a study of problems akin to
those which have been sketched in this chapter.

CHAPTER XV.

SUMMARY OF THE GENERAL THEORY OF EQUILIBRIUM OF DEMAND AND SUPPLY.

§ 1. THE present chapter contains no new matter: it is a mere summary of the results of Book V. The second half of it may be of service to anyone who has omitted the later chapters: for it may indicate, though it cannot explain, their general drift.

In Book V. we have studied the theory of the mutual relations of demand and supply in their most general form; taking as little account as possible of the special incidents of particular applications of the theory, and leaving over for the following Book the study of the bearings of the general theory on the special features of the several agents of production, Labour, Capital, and Land.

The difficulties of the problem depend chiefly on variations in the area of space, and the period of time over which the market in question extends; the influence of time being more fundamental than that of space.

Even in a market of very short period, such as that of a provincial corn-exchange on market-day, the "higgling and bargaining" might probably oscillate about a mean position, which would have some sort of a right to be called the equilibrium price: but the action of dealers in offering one price or refusing another would depend little, if at all, on calculations with regard to cost of production. They would look chiefly at present demand on the one hand, and on the other at the stocks of the commodity already available. It is true that they would pay some attention to such movements

of production in the near future as might throw their _{V, xv, 1.}
shadow before; but in the case of perishable goods they would
look only a very little way beyond the immediate present.
Cost of production has for instance no perceptible influence
on the day's bargaining in a fish-market.

In a rigidly stationary state in which supply could be _{Chs. III.}
_{IV. V.}
perfectly adjusted to demand in every particular, the normal _{Equili-}
expenses of production, the marginal expenses, and the _{brium of}
_{normal}
average expenses (rent being counted in) would be one and _{demand}
_{and}
the same thing, for long periods and for short. But, as it is, _{supply.}
the language both of professed writers on economics and of _{The}
_{element}
men of business shows much elasticity in the use of the _{of time.}
term Normal when applied to the causes that determine
value. And one fairly well marked division needs study.

On the one side of this division are long periods, in which _{Long}
_{period}
the normal action of economic forces has time to work itself _{or true}
out more fully; in which therefore a temporary scarcity of _{normal}
_{price.}
skilled labour, or of any other of the agents of production,
can be remedied; and in which those economies that normally
result from an increase in the scale of production—normally,
that is without the aid of any substantive new invention—
have time to develop themselves. The expenses of a representative firm, managed with normal ability and having
normal access to the internal and external economies of
production on a large scale, may be taken as a standard for
estimating normal expenses of production: and when the
period under survey is long enough to enable the investment
of capital in building up a new business to complete itself
and to bear full fruits; then the marginal supply price is
that, the expectation of which in the long run just suffices
to induce capitalists to invest their material capital, and
workers of all grades to invest their personal capital in the
trade.

On the other side of the line of division are periods of _{Short-}
_{period}
time long enough to enable producers to adapt their produc- _{normal}
tion to changes in demand, in so far as that can be done with _{price or}
_{sub-normal}
the existing provision of specialized skill, specialized capital, _{price.}
and industrial organization; but not long enough to enable
them to make any important changes in the supplies of these

V, XV, 2. factors of production. For such periods the stock of material and personal appliances of production has to be taken in a great measure for granted; and the marginal increment of supply is determined by estimates of producers as to the amount of production it is worth their while to get out of those appliances. If trade is brisk all energies are strained to their utmost, overtime is worked, and then the limit to production is given by want of power rather than by want of will to go further or faster. But if trade is slack every producer has to make up his mind how near to prime cost it is worth his while to take fresh orders. And here there is no definite law, the chief operative force is the fear of spoiling the market; and that acts in different ways and with different strengths on different individuals and different industrial groups. For the chief motive of all open combinations and of all informal silent and "customary" understandings whether among employers or employed is the need for preventing individuals from spoiling the common market by action that may bring them immediate gains, but at the cost of a greater aggregate loss to the trade.

Ch. VI.
Joint and
composite
demand
and
supply.

§ 2. We next turned aside to consider the relations of demand and supply with reference to things that need to be combined together for the purposes of satisfying a joint demand; of which the most important instance is that of the specialized material capital, and the specialized personal skill that must work together in any trade. For there is no direct demand on the part of consumers for either alone, but only for the two conjointly; the demand for either separately is a derived demand, which rises, other things being equal, with every increase in the demand for the common products, and with every diminution in the supply price of the joint factors of production. In like manner commodities of which there is a joint supply, such as gas and coke, or beef and hides, can each of them have only a derived supply price, governed by the expenses of the whole process of production on the one hand, and on the other by the demand for the remaining joint products.

The composite demand for a thing, resulting from its being used for several different purposes, and the composite supply

of a thing, that has several sources of production, present no V, xv, 3.
great difficulty; for the several amounts demanded for the
different purposes, or supplied from different sources, can
be added together, on the same plan as was adopted in
Book III., for combining the demands of the rich, the middle
classes and the poor for the same commodity.

Next we made some study of the division of the supple- Ch. VII.
mentary costs of a business,—and especially those connected Distribu-
with building up a trade connection, with marketing, and supple-
with insurance—among the various products of that business. costs.

§ 3.   Returning to those central difficulties of the equi- Chs. VIII.
librium of normal demand and supply which are connected The value
with the element of time, we investigated more fully the of an
relation between the value of an appliance for production for pro-
and that of the things produced by it.   duction in
                                                              relation to
When different producers have different advantages for that of the
producing a thing, its price must be sufficient to cover produced
the expenses of production of those producers who have by it.
no special and exceptional facilities; for if not they will
withhold or diminish their production, and the scarcity of
the amount supplied, relatively to the demand, will raise the
price.   When the market is in equilibrium, and the thing
is being sold at a price which covers these expenses, there
remains a surplus beyond their expenses for those who
have the assistance of any exceptional advantages. If these
advantages arise from the command over free gifts of nature,
the surplus is called a producer's surplus or producer's rent:
there is a surplus in any case, and if the owner of a free gift
of nature lends it out to another, he can generally get for its
use a money income equivalent to this surplus.

The price of the produce is equal to the cost of production
of that part of it, which is raised on the margin, that is
under such unfavourable conditions as to yield no rent. The
cost of this part can be reckoned up without reasoning in
a circle; and the cost of other parts cannot.

If land which had been used for growing hops, is found
capable of yielding a higher rent as market-garden land, the
area under hops will undoubtedly be diminished; and this
will raise their marginal cost of production and therefore

v, xv, 4. their price. The rent which land will yield for one kind of
produce, calls attention to the fact that a demand for the
land for that kind of produce increases the difficulties of
supply of other kinds; though it does not directly enter into
those expenses. And similar arguments apply to the relation
between the site values of urban land and the costs of things
made on it.

Thus when we are taking a broad view of normal value,
when we are investigating the causes which determine normal
value "in the long run," when we are tracing the "ultimate"
effects of economic causes; then the income that is derived
from capital in these forms enters into the payments by
which the expenses of production of the commodity in
question have to be covered; and estimates as to the
probable amount of that income directly control the action
of the producers, who are on the margin of doubt as to
whether to increase the means of production or not. But,
on the other hand, when we are considering the causes which
determine normal prices for a period which is short relatively
to that required for largely increasing the supply of those
appliances for production; then their influence on value is
chiefly indirect and more or less similar to that exerted by
the free gifts of nature. The shorter the period which we
are considering, and the slower the process of production of
those appliances, the less part will variations in the income
derived from them play in checking or increasing the supply
of the commodity produced by them, and in raising or
lowering its supply price.

Ch. XII.
The in-
fluence of
the law of
increasing
return on
supply
price does
not show
its true
character
in short
periods.

§ 4. This leads to the consideration of some difficulties
of a technical character connected with the marginal expenses
of production of a commodity that obeys the law of increasing return. The difficulties arise from the temptation to
represent supply price as dependent on the amount produced,
without allowing for the length of time that is necessarily
occupied by each individual business in extending its internal,
and still more its external organization; and in consequence
they have been most conspicuous in mathematical and semi-
mathematical discussions of the theory of value. For when
changes of supply price and amount produced are regarded

as dependent exclusively on one another without any refer- V, xv, 4.
ence to gradual growth, it appears reasonable to argue that
the marginal supply price for each individual producer is the
addition to his aggregate expenses of production made by
producing his last element; that this marginal price is likely
in many cases to be diminished by an increase in his output
much more than the demand price in the general market
would be by the same cause.

The statical theory of equilibrium is therefore not Short-
wholly applicable to commodities which obey the law of of the
increasing return. It should however be noted that in many Method.
industries each producer has a special market in which he is
well known, and which he cannot extend quickly; and that
therefore, though it might be physically possible. for him to
increase his output rapidly, he would run the risk of forcing
down very much the demand price in his special market, or
else of being driven to sell his surplus production outside on
less favourable terms. And though there are industries in
which each producer has access to the whole of a large market,
yet in these there remain but few internal economies to be got
by an increase of output, when the existing plant is already
well occupied. No doubt there are industries as to which
neither of these statements is true: they are in a transitional
state, and it must be conceded that the statical theory of
equilibrium of normal demand and supply cannot be profitably applied to them. But such cases are not numerous;
and with regard to the great bulk of manufacturing industries, the connection between supply price and amount
shows a fundamentally different character for short periods
and for long.

For short periods, the difficulties of adjusting the internal
and external organization of a business to rapid changes in
output are so great that the supply price must generally be
taken to rise with an increase, and to fall with a diminution
in the amount produced.

But in long periods both the internal and the external Its
economies of production on a large scale have time to develop in long
themselves. The marginal supply price is not the expenses periods.
of production of any particular bale of goods: but it is the

V, xv, 5. whole expenses (including insurance, and gross earnings of
management) of a marginal increment in the aggregate process of production and marketing.

Ch. XIII.   § 5. Some study of the effects of a tax, regarded as
Changes
in normal   a special case of a change in the general conditions of
demand
and   demand and supply suggests that, when proper allowance is
supply,
with some   made for the interests of consumers, there is on abstract
reference   grounds rather less *primâ facie* cause than the earlier
to the
doctrine of economists supposed, for the general doctrine of so-called
Maximum
Satisfac-   "Maximum Satisfaction"; *i.e.* for the doctrine that the free
tion.   pursuit by each individual of his own immediate interest,
will lead producers to turn their capital and labour, and
consumers to turn their expenditure into such courses as
are most conducive to the general interests. We have
nothing to do at this stage of our inquiry, limited as it
is to analysis of the most general character, with the important question how far, human nature being constituted as
it is at present, collective action is likely to be inferior to
individualistic action in energy and elasticity, in inventiveness
and directness of purpose; and whether it is not therefore
likely to waste through practical inefficiency more than it
could save by taking account of all the interests affected by
any course of action. But even without taking account of
the evils arising from the unequal distribution of wealth,
there is *primâ facie* reason for believing that the aggregate
satisfaction, so far from being already a maximum, could be
much increased by collective action in promoting the production and consumption of things in regard to which the
law of increasing return acts with especial force.

Ch. XIV.   This position is confirmed by the study of the theory of
Theory
of mono-   monopolies. It is the immediate interest of the monopolist
polies.   so to adjust the production and sale of his wares as to
obtain for himself the maximum net revenue, and the course
which he thus adopts is unlikely to be that which affords the
aggregate maximum satisfaction. The divergence between
individual and collective interests is *primâ facie* less important with regard to those things which obey the law of
diminishing return, than with regard to those which obey the
law of increasing return: but, in the case of the latter, there

is strong *primâ facie* reason for believing that it might often be to the interest of the community directly or indirectly to intervene, because a largely increased production would add much more to consumers' surplus than to the aggregate expenses of production of the goods. More exact notions on the relations of demand and supply, particularly when expressed in the form of diagrams, may help us to see what statistics should be collected, and how they should be applied in the attempt to estimate the relative magnitudes of various conflicting economic interests, public and private. V, xv, 5.

Ricardo's theory of cost of production in relation to value occupies so important a place in the history of economics that any misunderstanding as to its real character must necessarily be very mischievous; and unfortunately it is so expressed as almost to invite misunderstanding. In consequence there is a widely spread belief that it has needed to be reconstructed by the present generation of economists. . . . Ricardo's theory of value.

GREAT MINDS PAPERBACK SERIES

ART

☐ Leonardo da Vinci—
  A Treatise on Painting

ECONOMICS

☐ Charlotte Perkins Gilman—
  Women and Economics:
  A Study of the Economic Relation
  between Women and Men
☐ John Maynard Keynes—
  The End of Laissez-Faire and
  The Economic Consequences
  of the Peace
☐ John Maynard Keynes—
  The General Theory of
  Employment, Interest, and Money
☐ John Maynard Keynes—
  A Tract on Monetary Reform
☐ Thomas R. Malthus—An Essay on
  the Principle of Population
☐ Alfred Marshall—
  Money, Credit, and Commerce
☐ Alfred Marshall—
  Principles of Economics
☐ Karl Marx—
  Theories of Surplus Value
☐ John Stuart Mill—Principles of
  Political Economy
☐ David Ricardo—Principles of
  Political Economy and Taxation
☐ Adam Smith—Wealth of Nations
☐ Thorstein Veblen—
  The Theory of the Leisure Class

HISTORY

☐ J. B. Bury—Freedom of Thought
☐ Edward Gibbon—On Christianity
☐ Alexander Hamilton, John Jay,
  and James Madison—
  The Federalist
☐ Herodotus—The History
☐ Charles Mackay—
  Extraordinary Popular Delusions
  and the Madness of Crowds
☐ Thomas Paine—The Crisis
☐ Thucydides—History of the
  Peloponnesian War

LAW

☐ John Austin—The Province of
  Jurisprudence Determined

LITERATURE

☐ Jonathan Swift—A Modest
  Proposal and Other Satires
☐ H. G. Wells—
  The Conquest of Time

POLITICS

☐ Walter Lippmann—
  A Preface to Politics

PSYCHOLOGY

☐ Sigmund Freud—Totem and Taboo

RELIGION/FREETHOUGHT

☐ Desiderius Erasmus—
  The Praise of Folly
☐ Thomas Henry Huxley—
  Agnosticism and Christianity and
  Other Essays
☐ Ernest Renan—The Life of Jesus
☐ Upton Sinclair—
  The Profits of Religion
☐ Elizabeth Cady Stanton—
  The Woman's Bible
☐ Voltaire—A Treatise on Toleration
  and Other Essays
☐ Andrew D. White—A History of
  the Warfare of Science with
  Theology in Christendom

SCIENCE

☐ Jacob Bronowski—
  The Identity of Man
☐ Nicolaus Copernicus—On the
  Revolutions of Heavenly Spheres
☐ Francis Crick—
  Of Molecules and Men
☐ Marie Curie—
  Radioactive Substances
☐ Charles Darwin—
  The Autobiography
  of Charles Darwin

- Charles Darwin—
  The Descent of Man
- Charles Darwin—
  The Origin of Species
- Charles Darwin—
  The Voyage of the Beagle
- René Descartes—*Treatise of Man*
- Albert Einstein—*Relativity*
- Michael Faraday—
  The Forces of Matter
- Galileo Galilei—*Dialogues
  Concerning Two New Sciences*
- Francis Galton—*Finger Prints*
- Francis Galton—
  Hereditary Genius
- Ernst Haeckel—
  The Riddle of the Universe
- William Harvey—*On the Motion
  of the Heart and Blood in Animals*
- Fred Hoyle—*Of Men and Galaxies*
- Julian Huxley—
  Evolutionary Humanism
- Thomas H. Huxley—
  Evolution and Ethics and
  Science and Morals
- Edward Jenner—
  Vaccination against Smallpox

- Johannes Kepler—*Epitome of
  Copernican Astronomy
  and Harmonies of the World*
- James Clerk Maxwell—
  Matter and Motion
- Isaac Newton—*Opticks, Or
  Treatise of the Reflections,
  Inflections, and Colours of Light*
- Isaac Newton—*The Principia*
- Louis Pasteur and Joseph Lister—
  *Germ Theory and Its Applications
  to Medicine* and *On the Antiseptic
  Principle of the Practice of Surgery*
- Moritz Schlick—*Space and Time
  in Contemporary Physics*
- William Thomson (Lord Kelvin)
  and Peter Guthrie Tait—
  *The Elements of Natural
  Philosophy*
- Alfred Russel Wallace—
  Island Life

SOCIOLOGY

- Emile Durkheim—*Ethics and the
  Sociology of Morals*

GREAT BOOKS IN PHILOSOPHY PAPERBACK SERIES

ESTHETICS

- Aristotle—*The Poetics*
- Aristotle—*Treatise on Rhetoric*

ETHICS

- Aristotle—
  The Nicomachean Ethics
- Marcus Aurelius—*Meditations*
- Jeremy Bentham—*The Principles
  of Morals and Legislation*
- John Dewey—
  Human Nature and Conduct
- John Dewey—*The Moral Writings
  of John Dewey, Revised Edition*
- Epictetus—*Enchiridion*
- David Hume—*An Enquiry
  Concerning the Principles
  of Morals*
- Immanuel Kant—
  *Fundamental Principles of the
  Metaphysic of Morals*

- John Stuart Mill—*Utilitarianism*
- George Edward Moore—
  Principia Ethica
- Friedrich Nietzsche—
  Beyond Good and Evil
- Plato—*Protagoras, Philebus,* and
  Gorgias
- Bertrand Russell—*Bertrand Russell
  On Ethics, Sex, and Marriage*
- Arthur Schopenhauer—
  The Wisdom of Life and *Counsels
  and Maxims*
- Adam Smith—
  The Theory of Moral Sentiments
- Benedict de Spinoza—
  Ethics including
  *The Improvement of the
  Understanding*
- Alfred North Whitehead—
  The Concept of Nature

LOGIC

❑ George Boole—
The Laws of Thought

METAPHYSICS/EPISTEMOLOGY

❑ Aristotle—De Anima
❑ Aristotle—The Metaphysics
❑ Francis Bacon—Essays
❑ George Berkeley—Three Dialogues
Between Hylas and Philonous
❑ W. K. Clifford—The Ethics of
Belief and Other Essays
❑ René Descartes—Discourse on
Method and The Meditations
❑ John Dewey—How We Think
❑ John Dewey—
The Influence of Darwin on
Philosophy and Other Essays
❑ Epicurus—The Essential Epicurus:
Letters, Principal Doctrines,
Vatican Sayings, and Fragments
❑ Sidney Hook—
The Quest for Being
❑ David Hume—
An Enquiry Concerning Human
Understanding
❑ David Hume—
A Treatise on Human Nature
❑ William James—
The Meaning of Truth
❑ William James—Pragmatism
❑ Immanuel Kant—
The Critique of Judgment
❑ Immanuel Kant—
Critique of Practical Reason
❑ Immanuel Kant—
Critique of Pure Reason
❑ Gottfried Wilhelm Leibniz—
Discourse on Metaphysics
and the Monadology
❑ John Locke—An Essay
Concerning Human
Understanding
❑ George Herbert Mead—
The Philosophy of the Present
❑ Michel de Montaigne—Essays
❑ Charles S. Peirce—
The Essential Writings
❑ Plato—The Euthyphro, Apology,
Crito, and Phaedo

❑ Plato—Lysis, Phaedrus, and
Symposium
❑ Bertrand Russell—
The Problems of Philosophy
❑ George Santayana—
The Life of Reason
❑ Arthur Schopenhauer—On the
Principle of Sufficient Reason
❑ Sextus Empiricus—
Outlines of Pyrrhonism
❑ Ludwig Wittgenstein—
Wittgenstein's Lectures:
Cambridge, 1932–1935

PHILOSOPHY OF RELIGION

❑ Jeremy Bentham—The Influence
of Natural Religion on the
Temporal Happiness of Mankind
❑ Marcus Tullius Cicero—
The Nature of the Gods and
On Divination
❑ Ludwig Feuerbach—
The Essence of Christianity
❑ Ludwig Feuerbach—
The Essence of Religion
❑ Paul Henri Thiry, Baron
d'Holbach—Good Sense
❑ David Hume—Dialogues
Concerning Natural Religion
❑ William James—The Varieties of
Religious Experience
❑ John Locke—
A Letter Concerning Toleration
❑ Lucretius—
On the Nature of Things
❑ John Stuart Mill—
Three Essays on Religion
❑ Friedrich Nietzsche—
The Antichrist
❑ Thomas Paine—
The Age of Reason
❑ Bertrand Russell—Bertrand Russell
On God and Religion

SOCIAL AND POLITICAL
PHILOSOPHY

❑ Aristotle—The Politics
❑ Mikhail Bakunin—The Basic
Bakunin: Writings, 1869–1871
❑ Jeremy Bentham—The Rationale
of Punishment

- Edmund Burke—*Reflections on the Revolution in France*
- John Dewey—*Freedom and Culture*
- John Dewey—*Individualism Old and New*
- John Dewey—*Liberalism and Social Action*
- G. W. F. Hegel—*The Philosophy of History*
- G. W. F. Hegel—*Philosophy of Right*
- Thomas Hobbes—*The Leviathan*
- Sidney Hook—*Paradoxes of Freedom*
- Sidney Hook—*Reason, Social Myths, and Democracy*
- John Locke—*The Second Treatise on Civil Government*
- Niccolo Machiavelli—*The Prince*
- Karl Marx (with Friedrich Engels)—*The German Ideology*, including *Theses on Feuerbach* and *Introduction to the Critique of Political Economy*
- Karl Marx—*The Poverty of Philosophy*
- Karl Marx/Friedrich Engels—*The Economic and Philosophic Manuscripts of 1844* and *The Communist Manifesto*

- John Stuart Mill—*Considerations on Representative Government*
- John Stuart Mill—*On Liberty*
- John Stuart Mill—*On Socialism*
- John Stuart Mill—*The Subjection of Women*
- Montesquieu, Charles de Secondat—*The Spirit of Laws*
- Friedrich Nietzsche—*Thus Spake Zarathustra*
- Thomas Paine—*Common Sense*
- Thomas Paine—*Rights of Man*
- Plato—*Laws*
- Plato—*The Republic*
- Jean-Jacques Rousseau—*Émile*
- Jean-Jacques Rousseau—*The Social Contract*
- Bertrand Russell—*Political Ideals*
- Mary Wollstonecraft—*A Vindication of the Rights of Men*
- Mary Wollstonecraft—*A Vindication of the Rights of Women*